The Other Side of Western Civilization

Readings in Everyday Life

Third Edition

Volume II

The Sixteenth Century
to the Present

The Other Side of Western Civilization

Readings in Everyday Life

Third Edition

Volume II

The Sixteenth Century
to the Present

Edited by
Peter N. Stearns

Carnegie-Mellon University

HARCOURT BRACE JOVANOVICH, PUBLISHERS
San Diego   New York   Chicago   Atlanta   Washington, D.C.
London   Sydney   Toronto

Library of Congress Catalog Card Number: 83-81926
ISBN: 0-15-567652-0
Printed in the United States of America

Picture Credits:

p. 14: Courtesy of The Detroit Institute of the Arts, City of Detroit purchase; p. 96: Culver Pictures; p. 174: Prints Division, The New York Public Library, Astor, Lenox and Tilden Foundations; p. 276: Picture Collection, The Branch Libraries, The New York Public Library; p. 280: The Bettmann Archive; p. 350: Photo S.N.C.F. Publicité Documentation Française Phototheque.

Copyrights and acknowledgments appear on pages 401–402, which constitute a continuation of the copyright page.

For Cordelia Raymond

Preface

The Third Edition of *The Other Side of Western Civilization*, Volume II, focuses on the involvement of the common people of Europe in some of the massive social changes that have occurred over the past three hundred years as Western society became more urban and industrial. In addition, the book provides an opportunity to measure the considerable progress made by historians in getting to the roots of the modern social process. Unlike most surveys, this volume's major concern is not with the leaders of society, the prominent people whose names and deeds are well known and whose importance is obvious. Instead, it treats the masses of ordinary people, the "inarticulate," whose impact on history is not well documented. The intent is to provide some insight into the impact of change on the daily lives of these people, and through this insight to promote a better understanding of the nature and evolution of modern society.

This last point is crucial. We have long been attuned to some understanding of the power of history in affecting political behavior. People are most likely to vote as their parents did; each nation has something of a historically determined political character that shines through even in our day, distinguishing the behavior of, say, the British Labour Party from French communists from American liberal democrats. We are now coming to understand that other activities have a similar historical baggage. What we believe about making love and to an extent even how we do it are partly determined by historical trends that go back at least two centuries. What we think about hospitals is powerfully affected by changes in the position of doctors that began in the later eighteenth century, and changes in hospitals themselves that are only slightly more recent. The history of ordinary people and their daily concerns carries a living freight that helps us understand why we ourselves behave and think as we do.

To make valid judgments about how liberating or oppressive modernization has been, we must first analyze and evaluate the nature of premodern society. In addition, we must ascertain the origins of social change: Was change imposed on the masses by forces beyond their control, or did the people actively participate in the construction of modern society? The opening selections represent a number of different interpretations of these issues so that students may assess for themselves the impact of change, the adjustments it promoted, and the resistance it provoked.

Although this collection focuses on only some of the many facets of modern European history, the bibliographies provide numerous suggestions of additional material for further reading.

Some topics in this volume are relatively familiar: the meaning of political involvement in the modern world, the nature of industrial work, and the plight of the industrial worker. Other subjects are less common: the evolution of the family, the impact of modernization on women, innovation and continuity in health practices, new attitudes toward madness and deviant social behavior, and the changing nature of sexual relationships. The essays included here were chosen with an eye to recent research presented in a stimulating manner and with an awareness of the major conceptual problems involved. Collectively, they suggest important debates over the nature of modern life. Topics that would hardly have been mentioned ten years ago, such as the history of love, are now supported by a diverse literature. Today the history of women and youth receives more sophisticated treatment as historians reach directly into the lives of women and young people in the past. The history of leisure roles is receiving new attention, perhaps a sign that we are trying to come to terms with the meaning of leisure in our own lives. Work on the limitations of modern attitudes toward death has direct bearing on current reassessments of hospital practices.

Undergirding the treatment of novel topics, developments in the study of the common people in Western society show a concern for the popular mentality and for the ideas, values, and impulses that motivated measurable behavior. Although the actions and values of most people were undoubtedly affected by the politics set forth by society's leaders (and a number of essays in the book discuss this connection), the masses of people shaped society through their own actions. Ultimately, the effort to reach back to the minds of our forebears—to their attitudes toward health, children, death, and the possible unities in an approach to life — represents an exciting chance to place ourselves in context: to understand how, to what extent, and in what directions we are really changing beneath the obviously new trappings of an advanced industrial society.

A number of people provided vital assistance in the preparation of this book. I am grateful to those who read and commented on the original plan for this work: J. Kim Munholland, University of Minnesota; James T. Sheehan, Northwestern University; Mack Walker, Johns Hopkins University; Edward Shorter, University of Toronto; Donald Sutton, Carnegie-Mellon University; John Gillis, Rutgers University; Louise Tilly, University of Michigan; and William Weber, California State University, Long Beach. The editorial and production staffs at Harcourt Brace Jovanovich were of great aid. For suggesting readings and for other assistance, I also thank Andrew Barnes, Carnegie-Mellon University, and my wife, Carol. I am, finally, grateful to the many students, both graduate and undergraduate, at Rutgers University and Carnegie-Mellon University, who have helped me apply some of the key problems of modernization to the study and teaching of European social history.

Peter N. Stearns

Contents

Topical Table of Contents

The Other Side of Western Civilization

Readings in Everyday Life

Third Edition

Volume II

The Sixteenth Century
to the Present

Introduction

Most of the people who lived in the past rarely appear in historical studies. Instead, histories of European civilization concentrate on rather small groups of people—the thinkers, the artists, the political leaders. Of course, the importance of these elites is undeniable. They have left unusually clear records, so that historians can study them without too much difficulty. But their acts and ideas form only a part of human history. This book focuses on the other, and possibly the more important, part. It deals with groups of people who are rarely heard from in surveys of Western civilization—women and workers, criminals and the insane, soldiers and peasants. They are a diverse lot, but they have in common the fact that contemporary social elites and later historians usually regarded them as inarticulate. Periodically, popular revolutions brought them into the scheme of history, but in normal times they were largely ignored.

The result of such disregard is incomplete history. More to the point, it is the kind of history that lacks relevance. We do not judge our present on the basis of the doings of the elite and their formal institutions alone, although of course these are vital. When we take our social temperature we think of the stability of families, the condition of women, the fate of the work ethic, the problems of commercialized leisure—in other words, activities whose evaluation depends on knowledge of what various kinds of people, and large numbers of people, are doing. These activities, and the folk who engage in them, have histories. These histories in turn can be as important as, and possibly more interesting than, the narrow accounts of the politics of the past. They can help us to understand ourselves.

Most elites in the past, and most historians more recently, have tended to place ordinary people and their activities in rather simple categories. This does not necessarily mean that they were insensitive to them, but it does suggest that they knew rather little about them. Until the nineteenth century most ordinary people in Europe were peasants, a word that immediately suggests a formless, stolid mass, in terms of the little that most conventional historical surveys say about peasants. According to the simplest definition, peasants normally valued tradition and stability; when they rebelled, as they did occasionally, they did so against change and in the name of the past. But did peasants have a real history, or were they a mindless constant beneath the surface of great events? In fact, from time to time, their economic habits and values, their definitions of crime and morality changed. Peasant families rose and fell in social standing, often with great rapidity. Many of them were geographically mobile, many welcomed new ideas and methods, and some even produced them, despite the peasant tendency to resist novelty. We should not be content with merely occasional references to the millions of people who were peasants in Europe as Western civilization developed. Although we cannot know the details of their individual lives and ideas, we must seek to fill in broader generalizations. Simply knowing that a peasantry existed is meaningless unless we also know what trends operated in each major period and area. In some periods peasants regularly practiced infanticide because they could not support their children; in others they were eager to have many children, and not just because of special economic opportunities. Much of modern civilization sprang from the variety and evolution of peasant culture in western Europe.

In the last two centuries, the masses of people have received more attention, if only because they have impinged more often on the political process. Still, many aspects of their lives are ignored, while others are subjected to judgments by people who are remote from their ordinary existence. Working-class families have decayed, say conservatives who deplore modern times. Many socialists, seeking to condemn the disruptive effects of capitalism, agree. Until recently few scholars even tried to look at the actual evolution of family patterns. With rare exceptions, historians have directed their attention to the masses only when the masses rocked the boat, annoying conservatives and giving heart to radicals. But protest, although important, can prove too difficult for people whose lives are so demanding even in the best of times. Consequently, most of the history of people long went unrecorded.

A great deal of historical research is now being devoted to the history of "inarticulate" people. It is now clear that historians have regarded these people as mute in part because they themselves have not tried to listen. To be sure, it is much more difficult to know what "the workers" thought than it is to outline the philosophy of Descartes. Some speculation, some historical intuition is essential if we are to get at popular ideas, which means that there is considerable room for disagreement. The history of the inarticulate remains a rather new field of study. It is rife with debate (and it is exciting for this very reason), but already some points are reasonably well established. Aspects of popular behavior can be measured with some precision, even if the outlook that prompted the behavior is more difficult to determine. The common people had ideas, and they left their own kinds of records. In protest, in crime, in family behavior, and in religious practices we can discern the mentality of the masses, even those who lived centuries ago. We can know how many people were born and died, how they structured their families, how often they rioted, perhaps even how they felt about their husbands or children.

Now that historians are looking for them, sources of information about the inarticulate are proving abundant, even overwhelming. These kinds of sources differ from those historians have been accustomed to. Many reveal information only about large groups of people rather than about individuals. But there are individual records as well, which can rescue this new kind of history from impersonality. Criminals, workers, and many others have left statements of what their lives were like and what they thought about.

So we can learn about the common people. But why should we want to? E. P. Thompson has argued eloquently that the common people must be rescued from "the enormous condescension of posterity." He means, among other things, that history, even when written by radical historians, has usually been colored by an upper-class bias that regarded the mass of humanity as a silent lump to be shaped or abused by the elites. This is a valid point, which does not mean that we must appreciate the history of the inarticulate only if we wish to demonstrate democratic or socialist purity.

Because it adds a vast new dimension to what we can learn about people, the history of the inarticulate fascinates many students of the past—but not all. Many historians and students of history continue to be most interested in great men and great ideas. Some people, however, who could never get terribly excited about the "greats" can now find a new meaning in history through studying the masses; others who began with a conventional interest in history may decide that the real meaning of history lies in this new approach and the issues it raises.

Reactions of this sort are personal, of course. But whether or not one is really enthusiastic about studying the history of the inarticulate, there are three reasons why students should know something about it. First, the history of the common people provides one measure of the nature and quality of civilization. Did peasants and artisans gain a new outlook during the Italian Renaissance? Did their lives change, and, if so, did the changes follow the same direction as those that took place in the lives of the political and intellectual elites? Many Enlightenment thinkers believed in humanitarianism and in progress. When and to what extent did such beliefs enter the popular mentality? When the ideas of the Enlightenment were applied to child-rearing or the treatment of the insane, did they bring the benefits that "humanitarianism" implies? We cannot fully determine the historical importance of great men and great ideas unless we know what impact they had on the bulk of society. Often the process of disseminating the effects of "greatness" is more important than the initial cause.

Furthermore, although perhaps they have reacted to outside forces more than they have acted spontaneously, we must dispel the notion that the masses of people have not themselves been active agents in history. In many of the readings in this volume, this point is implicitly debated. Did the common people adopt more modern attitudes toward work and sex because they were prodded and compelled to do so by forces from above, or did they have, to some extent at least, their own reasons for changing their outlook? There is no question that the common people had an important voice in determining exactly how they adapted to change. They often resisted change as well, and their resistance was an important historical force in its own right. When masses of people changed their views about their sexual goals or about the number of children they wanted, they played a direct role in altering the course of history.

These arguments apply to the history of the common people at any place and time. There is a final, more specific reason for studying the common people in modern times. The simple fact is that most of us, as ordinary citizens, judge modern society by criteria different from those most historians have used in judging the past. Many of us think of our own time more in terms of divorce rates and crime rates than in terms of, say, artistic achievements. We think in terms of the quality and nature of life of *most people*, and this means that we need histories of precisely these areas. Is the suicide rate rising or falling in modern societies? Has child abuse increased or decreased as families have grown smaller and attitudes toward child-rearing changed? Perhaps some day students of modern history will have as much information on patterns of this sort, and as satisfactory explanations for major changes in these patterns, as they now have about formal political theory and the development of new forms of government.

We return here to the fact that historians long ignored many significant kinds of activities in the past. What has been studied in most Western

Civilization survey courses is vitally important, but it is incomplete. We are left without genuine historical knowledge of many of the features of our own society that are closest to us. Consequently, in a real sense, we cannot asssess the direction our society is taking. For example, until recently historians have virtually ignored the history of crime, while piling study upon study of the details of diplomatic interchanges. Historians are empiricists. They learn from observation and therefore need sources; sources from diplomats are more abundant than sources from criminals. So historians tend to study diplomats, although it might be argued that criminals are at least as important in shaping society. (Some might even argue that the different labels exaggerate the differences between the two groups.) But the fact that historians honor diplomats more than criminals leads us to assume that diplomats' historical importance is greater, until we consider our own times and realize that most of us devote a great deal of attention to crime and its significance for us personally and for our society.

This is not to say that every current opinion reflects an important historical reality. Some historians who demand that history be "relevant" really mean only that it should reinforce their own views of what should happen in the future. But history is relevant. We can't understand crime today if we don't know about crime in the past, for we will have no sense of direction or means of comparison. We will have no way of knowing if crime is rising, falling, changing in nature, or staying the same. Yet contemporary comments on crime often assume a historical knowledge. Newspaper accounts, for example, talk about a rising crime rate as an inescapable aspect of modern urban society. This is a historical judgment. But in view of how little is generally known about the history of crime, it is an invalid historical judgment. Modern urbanization has not necessarily produced more crime; the situation is more complex.

The readings in this book stress topics that are not generally considered in historical surveys, such as popular health attitudes and the dynamics of large groups, such as youth, factory workers, and thieves. However it is important to realize that these are not separate strands of history, but parts of a larger social process. Increasingly, social historians, who claim a special interest in the inarticulate and in mundane social activities, are realizing their kinship with students of culture and politics. Topics like crime or the social contributions of housewives should be juxtaposed to more familiar historical phenomena. The modern criminal mentality, for example, may have developed in relationship to Enlightenment ideas about material well-being and individualism. The altered behavior of women in the nineteenth century changed the character of religion; as men left religious activities increasingly to their wives, religion became gentler—less riveted, for example, on condemnation of evil—and certainly more inclined to equate womanhood with purity.

This collection is not, then, merely a sample of interesting insights into the history of contemporary concerns, much less a hymn to unfairly neglected groups in European history. The readings have been selected and organized to relate to a large, unifying theme in the history of the last four centuries, the transition from a traditional to a modern society, the process broadly termed *modernization*. The hypothesis here is that in recent centuries Western society has developed through a sometimes complex pattern that links various groups, so that some common developments can be seen among paupers and the rich. This pattern also links the various facets of human activity, so that changes in sexuality bear some relationship to changes in attitudes toward health, and in turn to developments in the world of formal ideas and politics. It gives coherence to our recent past and relates our present to it integrally; it might even cast some light on our probable future.

However, modernization—the model used to asssess the less familiar side of Western civilization since 1550—is a sticky term and concept. The word itself invites confusion; we are by definition modern in the sense of existing right now, so what is special about seeing modernization as a process? The term has been variously described in social science and historical literature as "too big and slippery for deft manipulation," "historically crude," "better than no model at all," "elusive," and "inadequate . . . for comprehending the diversity of the human experience during several centuries of social transformation." In one sense, the present collection of essays is an effort to have our cake and eat it, too: It invokes modernization while raising questions about not only its definition, but also its existence as a process at all. It will be perfectly possible to emerge from the following readings with a firm belief that social changes over the last four centuries have no coherent direction, much less a "modern" one; certainly any two readers may disagree vigorously over what modernization has been and where it is heading. Because many historians reject the concept of modernization, the concept must be debated and discussed wherever it is used. And the best method to launch discussion is by way of introduction.

Modernization relates to concepts about the direction of historical change first devised by the German sociologist-historian Max Weber. As a term, however, modernization was first used in the 1950s by social scientists, particularly by Americans eager to predict where nonwestern societies were heading and where they should head. See what we in the West have done? Surely Japan or Turkey or Nigeria must/should/will do the same. Many of the criticisms of modernization result from ethnocentrism. But we are concerned here with Western society. We must first discover whether or not a coherent process of modernization has occurred in the West and what the conditions for it were. We may then wish to determine whether or not the process suggests patterns for understanding what is happening elsewhere in the world now. There may in fact be interconnections such that societies which industrialize, for example, also develop Western practices about women. This, certainly, would be an important reason to grasp the Western model. But modernization is also useful simply because it puts our own present in context, suggesting ongoing trends in the West itself. This effort at self-understanding is the focus of the varied views that follow.

Modernization raises a number of objections or questions when it is directly applied to Western civilization. When did it begin? Many people equate the process with clear structural change. We know that in the late eighteenth and early nineteenth centuries, western European countries began to industrialize (a relatively definable phenomenon), to urbanize, and so on. Some would date modernization using these phenomena. But, increasingly, some historians are claiming that before this, indeed as a precondition for structural change, values were altered; people, or at least some people in key positions, began to think in new ways, to innovate—for example, in the way they raised children. These historians push modernization back to the early eighteenth century or even the seventeenth century. But can one talk of a coherent process that has spanned such a long and diverse period, that began with changes so difficult to pin down and measure? Here is one source of the claim that modernization is too fuzzy and all-inclusive, that it gives a false sense of pattern to the very diverse realities of human life in the past.

Modernization encounters geographical objections as well, even within Western society. How different was English modernization from French or German modernization? How does one fit specific national phenomena—German Nazism, or the English public school experience—into a single package? (And if the United States were added, as is the case in a few of the essays that follow, what additional complexity: How do specifically American patterns of crime, divorce, or race relations fit any broader model?) The essays in this collection deal with single countries or regions, or with a number of areas, in a variety of ways. In combination, they do suggest that some basic changes still override national boundaries. But it is certainly legitimate to argue, as many conventional historians would, that a region or nation is the key unit for analysis because it puts its own vital stamp on general phenomena such as new cities, factory industries, or the concept of adolescence. The trees may well be far more important than the woods.

Periodization is a problem as well. Is modernization a straight-line phenomenon, starting in the seventeenth or eighteenth century and moving ever upward (or downward, or in some clear direction)? Are there definite stages of modernization? The idea of stages of industrialization has some support: A period of early technological experimentation and limited introduction of factories is followed by the fuller application of relevant technology, with appropriate levels of urbanization, business organization, and so on. But modernization, because it is so much more amorphous in including basic behavior patterns and values, may not lend itself to this kind of approach. How, for example, does the twentieth century fit after the nineteenth? Are we witnessing further gains of modernization, a souring of the process, or a reversion to older, premodern patterns? The essays in this book offer support for all of these views. Twentieth-century woman may be seen as entering the modern world in new ways, and gaining a more clearly modern mentality in the process. Phenomena such as Nazism and, one selection argues, basic trends within the contemporary family suggest a sharp deterioration from nineteenth-century patterns. Modernization, if applicable at all, would here be seen not as a straight-line development, but a series of curves, differentiating the nature and quality of life in one period from those in another. Or, as another judgment holds, the contemporary family, after considerable innovation and disruption in the nineteenth century, is returning to something like a premodern structure, notably when both husband and wife participate in economic production as they did in the seventeenth century but did not in the nineteenth. Modernization would seem scarcely applicable in this view, because the quality of family behavior proves more cyclical than directional.

But the overriding issue surrounding modernization relates to its capacity to integrate developments in diverse areas of human activity. Are all trends in a modernizing society linked, moving in some definable direction (whether for better or worse)? Or are some phenomena simply immune to modernization? Leisure is a case in point. Some observers see leisure as a distinctly modern activity, different from traditional recreation, notably in being open to freer choice. Others point to vast continuities, with contemporary leisure expressing a traditional social need to give outlets to youth, to male violence, to courtship. But if modernization is not a whole package, if older values persist along with the development of new ones, where do we draw the lines that define modernization?

One approach to this problem suggests a distinction between structural and behavioral modernization—that is, between changes in the human environment (urbanization, industrialization) and changes in the way people act, particularly in private areas over which they have most control, and the values they apply to their acts and to their environment. There is no question that the framework of life has greatly changed since the eighteenth century, and that many of the changes are interlinked. Western society has industrialized, moved to the cities, developed greater wealth, more bureaucratic apparatus, higher literacy and smaller families. Most observers would also admit that modern societies try to induce certain kinds of thought in their citizens through education, advertising and other means. "Modern" public opinion therefore tends to express national loyalty, some belief in social mobility, some desire for material progess—in contrast to officially-approved attitudes in premodern societies. Broadly speaking, each aspect of this structural and opinion-molding modernization seems to involve the others, although the precise mix may vary from one society to the next. The essays in this book do not deal primarily with structural modernization, but with the more complex issue of how, or whether, behavior and attitudes have changed. Here, modernization theory normally holds that, as part of structural modernization, people become more rationalistic, individualized, and acquisitive. But how do values of this sort apply to groups such as workers or youth, to activities such as leisure? Does the structure of modern society compel a particular kind of behavior on the part of women? The basic questions are these: Does modernization describe a process by which new normal personalities have been produced over the last few centuries? Is there some coherence to the interaction of various groups in modern society, in their various activities, relating one to another and to modern structures? We cannot expect simplicity. Modernization of outlook and behavior may reach some groups before others (the periodization problem again), and may take different, precise forms from one segment of society to another. Will modernized men and women turn out to share the same viewpoint and, with due qualifications for a bit of biology, behavior forms? Or should we expect distinct gender patterns in modernization? And again, some activities, possibly some definable groups, may not modernize at all, but can best be seen in a different kind of interaction with modern structures, moving in a cyclical fashion, or not changing at all.

With all this undeniable complexity, why not just give up on modernization? Some scholars clearly have done so. They talk of specific changes, not a grand pattern. They warn of the danger in seeing direction in history instead of the hodgepodge that the past really is. (How, for example, can we speak in the same breath of modernization as the expansion of bureaucracy and modernization as greater individualization?) Western civilization, even before modern times, has undeniably tended to see a direction in history, moving toward a final coming of Christ, a better society, new knowledge, improved medicine—the goals vary greatly, but the desire for a goal is deep within us. Perhaps, if we were honest, we could admit that the past gives us no direction, no real interconnectedness among our various activities. But the desire to see some sense, some pattern, runs deep. And just possibly, in a sophisticated concept of modernization, a pattern really has been there. A careful reading of the essays in this collection will, it is hoped, give some basis for judgment.

But if modernization exists, if there has been some coherent movement in the thoughts and behavior of people in the modern centuries, the problems are not over. What caused modernization and its specific manifestations both in structures and mentalities? Indeed, which came first: Did structures change, forcing or encouraging people to think differently, or did some tentative changes in ideas prompt developments such as industrialization? Modernization is not a clear statement of causation; rather, it describes and summarizes major changes. Yet several of the selections in this book go beyond summary to an assessment of cause, which includes careful attention to those elements of premodern society that could permit change.

Even more pervasive is the issue of the quality of modernization. Critics of the concept properly note its teleological implications: History has a purpose. But while most formal advocates of modernization theory have been optimists (modern society is not just different from, but better than, traditional society), many other analysts, implicitly agreeing that modernization has distinguished contemporary society from past society in coherent and definable ways, are profoundly pessimistic. We have changed, but we have lost in basic human values.

Consequently, a study of the impact of modernization on the common people—of Europe or elsewhere—invites some value judgments. The term modernization may be loaded, suggesting a kind of blanket approval of change, because many people have been conditioned to believe that anything modern is good. This is profoundly different from the traditional outlook, which tended to look to the past for standards. We know that formal Christianity saw a golden age in the past (although, significantly, it looked forward to a brighter future as well). Before the onset of modernization, peasants tended to believe that rural society had been better in past ages; artisans looked back to the ideals of the early guilds. Indeed the common people had little historical sense and tended to merge past with present. Since the advent of modernization, however, we have become acutely, perhaps exaggeratedly, conscious of how different we are, and often how much better we are than our predecessors. So when we talk of something becoming more modern, we may be too quick to praise or at least to find the development entirely natural and easily understandable. For example, one important aspect of modernization is the development of a belief in the possibility and desirability of material progress, for oneself as well as for society as a whole. Most Americans probably find this a good change, at least when contrasted with the resignation and stagnancy of a more traditional view. A minority—those concerned about the ecological damage that material progress can cause, for instance—would find this aspect of modernization dangerous. But almost everyone would find it natural. It's hard for us to believe that people might think anything else. Economic thought from the early nineteenth century onward has assumed that the goal of "economic man" is to maximize his wealth. Yet, applied to most people even in the nineteenth century, this is not a proper historical view. Interest in material improvement constituted a profound change in the popular mentality. It came slowly and, in fact, has not yet been completed.

"Modernization" is probably not a sufficiently neutral word to describe what it must describe, but we have not yet found a better one.

Our focus on the common people may appeal to a different set of values, leading to a condemnation of trends within modern society itself. Debates over the effects of industrialization and urban growth on the lower classes, for example, began a century and a half ago, and they continue today. Historians still debate whether or not material conditions improved during the first stage of British industrialization—and the topic is significant in the history of any area undergoing the initial stages of an industrial revolution. This is an important question, because conditions in such a formative stage of working-class life may have influenced worker outlook to such an extent that attitudes and behavior persisted even after the material setting changed. But our concern is broader; we are trying to assess general outlook and style of life, not just of workers but of other groups. Still, some of the problems of interpretation are similar. If one dislikes contemporary society, it is easy to emphasize how much people have suffered since its inception; or, if one finds current conditions improving, it is tempting to assume a constant process once traditional society began to break down. In the debates over the British standard of living, historians who favor capitalism and are convinced of the essential soundness of the modern world generally try to show that conditions were improving even during early industrialization. Leftist historians, who dislike capitalism and commiserate with the workers, invariably look for signs of deterioration. Note that the connection between political judgment and historical judgment is not entirely logical. One could well argue that capitalism has proved a good thing in the long run and that modern life is lovely, even for the workers, while admitting that in the first stage of industrialization conditions deteriorated. Or one could urge the need for fundamental reforms in modern life while admitting that conditions have improved somewhat compared with preindustrial times. Obviously, ideological commitments can predetermine an approach—and most of us have an ideology, even if it is not neatly labeled. Changes in mood can also change our historical perspective. After a decade of political uncertainties and economic malaise, what American of the 1980s can blithely assume that the United States is superior to Europe? Yet twenty-five years ago it was normal for intelligent historians to focus on Europe's instability, bellicosity, and economic inferiority. Once historians viewed medical change as a clear story of progress; now, many pick at doctors' exaggerated claims as a new source of enslavement to authority. Perspectives change quickly, as do historical trends, which means that it may be impossible to offer a simple characterization of any development affecting the common people during the modernization process. A sense of debate over key issues is vital to an intelligent study of modernization.

The readings that follow present a variety of approaches, some commending the liberating aspects of modernization, others stressing the deterioration. Few historians who deal with these vital topics content themselves with simply saying that things have changed, which might be the most objective view. They generally try to assess the quality of that change. Try to study the modern history of women, for example, without asking whether their status has improved or worsened. Many now argue that with modernization and the decline in the family as a productive unit, woman's inferior status became more pronounced, because her economic utility was less obvious and her dependence on her husband greater.

Others point to better education and the declining birth rate as indications of improvements in woman's lot.

Students of history must make up their own minds about trends. Several preliminary points should be kept in mind. First, most historians drawn to the study of the common people have been sympathetic. They have tended to dwell on the hardships of their subjects, who they see as having been victimized by some outside force—workers by capitalists, women by men, and so on. But we must study the ways in which the common people adjusted to their situations and the values they used and changed in doing so. Moreover, we must view the common people as an active force, not just in protest—though this is a significant aspect of their lives—but also in shaping family structure, recreational patterns, and so on. This view is quite consistent with an emphasis on the hardships of life, but it goes beyond a dreary catalogue of exploitation. Finally, any judgment of trends must use some basis of comparison. Too often this basis is not clearly spelled out. A historian who argues that the horizons of middle-class women in Victorian England were becoming more limited must describe an antecedent situation in which they were less so. Overall, most large evaluations of modernization involve an implicit or explicit comparison with premodern life. We must know where we came from to know where we are going.

In fact, whether or not one is a historian, it is impossible to study modernity without asking "where from?"—which is of course a historical question. Any journalist or politician who claims that values or behavior patterns are changing, that violence is rising or falling, or that a situation is unprecedented is making a historical judgment. Such a judgment should be made intelligently. Some of the judgments are short-term, of course. It is possible and useful to compare crime rates and patterns of the 1960s with those of the 1920s. But the larger evaluations—those, for example, which concern the nature of industrial life or of urban man—should involve a knowledge of the premodern world. We have no other way to assess the direction of change, and we are far from agreeing on the direction, because our knowledge of facts is limited. So is our ability to cut through biases and slogans. We hear of the loosening of family ties. We therefore assume that premodern families were closeknit and jolly—but has the subject really been studied by those who claim a new "modern" collapse? Only a historical view can reveal the extent to which present problems are recent and human-caused, as opposed to being durable reflections of human nature or at least the nature of Western man. Divorce, for example, is a rather new institution, but does it signify a really new problem in family life or does it represent a new answer to a persistent tension? We must look at the past to find out. We might avoid a lot of nonsense from advocates of the brand new as well as from critics of the present if we required every statement of "never before" or "a sign of these troubled times"—unquestionably judgments of the present in terms of the past—to be backed by solid historical evidence. This book stems from the need to approach key trends in modern life in the only way such trends can really be understood.

The book obviously does not cover all the major topics in the history of the common people during the centuries of modernization. It largely avoids the study of modern states and institutional structures, vital topics in their own right, in favor of activities normally closer to the common people. Even many of the topics dealt with in this book have only been outlined. There is insufficient information on some of them; there is a great disagreement on others. We are not in total ignorance, however, and the whole issue of modernization is so essential that we cannot constantly beg off on grounds of insufficient data. If we are to understand ourselves and our society, we must attempt to establish a genuine historical view of the evolution of family emotions, the situation of youth, and other such topics. Confusing signals and outright disagreement add spice to our effort to know.

The readings are arranged more or less chronologically, but they can also be grouped into topics that cover essential aspects of the formation of a modern outlook in the general population. Readings on rural society discuss the nature of preindustrial life and allow an assessment of the changes in the countryside in recent times. A section on modern attitudes presents varying interpretations of our current status. Two large groupings of the inarticulate, women and workers, receive extensive treatment. Children and youth are considered as well. The family is elaborately studied, for, although its nature has changed in a number of aspects, it remains a basic institution in the lives of most people. The family must also be understood if we are to comprehend what values children bring into adulthood: If modernization has produced a new personality type, or as some would argue a succession of new types, then new child-raising practices must be involved. Readings on education and popular culture deal both with the formal values taught to the lower classes and with new and old types of recreation that played a growing role in life outside of work. Health and death practices, a new and exciting area of social history, receive explicit attention. Discussions of crime and insanity consider changes in forms of individual protest and maladjustment and how modern society defines deviance. Readings on protest concern the evolution of the forms and goals of collective action.

The focus is for the most part on western Europe, where the process of modernization began, and where it has gone farthest. The history of modernization in other regions is equally interesting and important, but many of the major issues and trends can be suggested within the more familiar context of Britain, France, and Germany. Even this zone is by no means homogeneous; and this involves the problem of the geographic coherence of modernization. If modernization is a process involving important general features, national and regional differences are nevertheless important in any detailed study. Although not explicitly comparative, the readings allow some asssessment of the differences in rates and patterns of change from one country to the next. They also invite comparisons between European and North American modernizations. But the main focus is on developments of wide applicability, even where regional variations would modify the basic generalizations to some extent.

Because historians are just beginning to sketch the history of the common people, we cannot easily pinpoint when decisive time breaks occurred. Conventional periodization (1715–63, 1870–1914, and so on) has little relevance, because most people's lives were not always decisively shaped by the doings of diplomats and politicians. Indeed, we must seek a decade or more in which some measurable change occurred—when rapid population growth began or waned, for example—rather than a single year. The chronological organization of this book is meant to be loose and suggestive, but it does provide a necessary framework. The first section, 1550–1750, allows an understanding of the society and the traditions that were to change. But during the period itself there were important developments that set a partial basis for modernization. Between 1750 and 1850 the confrontation betwen tradition and change was extremely intense. Industrialization began but was not yet dominant, while the attitudes of ordinary people began to take more modern form. Between 1850 and 1914 the nature of industrial society became clearer. Problems of adaptation remained, but they were more subtle. To many Europeans, at least in retrospect, this period seemed a golden age. However, those who lived through it, outside of the upper classes, may have judged it differently. The period from 1918 to the present opened with the intense dislocation caused by the First World War. The confused nature of European society between the two world wars is important in its contribution to more enduring social trends. But the overriding theme of the twentieth century is the extent to which a new society is taking shape and what kind of society it it is. Many observers talk of a postmodern or postindustrial age; we must discover what this means in human terms. There is a strong temptation to see our own age as one of unprecedented change—for modern people are attuned to look for change; but a good historical understanding of modernization allows us to place these claims in context, for more basic changes may well have occurred earlier. And of course the whole issue of the coherence of modernization, from one major period to the next, should be considered. Given a sense of the direction of modernization, we might even forecast future trends. What, for example, is the probable fate of the family as modernization progresses? But some analysts, accepting modernization as a pattern for the recent past, would disclaim the ability to forecast.

In many ways, the history of the common people is a new kind of history, but it is not a total departure. It involves testing many conventional historical themes to see how major ideas and political forms affected the masses. Therefore, although the readings do consider some unusual subjects, they can and should be linked to the more obvious developments in modern European history. Rural society was clearly affected by religious doctrine and organization. The spread of popular education involved a deliberate attempt to inculcate in the peasant attitudes such as nationalism, liberalism, and a belief in science and progress. New forms of protest related to changes in political ideology, most obviously the rise of socialism. The world that workers lived in was conditioned by the actions of the state and of employers. These effects can in turn be assessed in terms of liberalism and other political doctrines. Connections of this sort are seldom simple. One cannot assume that liberal ideas about the treatment of workers fully represent the actual ideas of employers, even employers who claimed to be liberal. But the connections are there, and they clearly relate the history of the common people to history in general. Other links can be found as well. We will see how the rise of rationalism changed the definition of madness and, therefore, the attitudes toward the treatment of insanity. Changes in the family or in sexual behavior cannot be understood solely in terms of formal ideas or political activities, but they are not entirely independent either. By the late eighteenth century, people in Europe seemed to have gained a new interest in romantic and sexual love. Surely this must have helped cause the rise of romanticism, or at least that aspect which stressed human emotions. Historians deepen their understanding of the common themes in political and intellectual history by studying the relationship of these themes with the world of the common people.

Modernization, if it works at all as a concept, may allow us to interpret the familiar and the unfamiliar in our past, and, as a result provide some basis for assessing what we are now, and how the various facets of our society relate to each other. Conversely, a sophisticated assessment of modernization may suggest that contemporary society is painfully unintegrated, with groups and activities pulling in different, perhaps contradictory, directions. Students of the basic process of modern society are trying to fathom what we have become, and why. The quest is one of the most exciting developments in historical study.

BIBLIOGRAPHY

A bibliography follows the introduction to each section, to provide further reading on each of the topics covered. No general survey of the period from 1600 to the present satisfactorily treats all the subjects included in this volume. For the first part of the period, Fernand Braudel, *The Mediterranean and the Mediterranean World in the Age of Philip II* (2 vols., New York, 1972), constitutes a major study; see also Braudel's *Capitalism and Material Life* (New York, 1974). Henry Kamen, *The Iron Century: Social Change in Europe 1550–1660* (New York, 1971), stresses developments among the lower classes. New work on economic change prior to the industrial revolution introduces the vital concept of "protoindustrialization," which has an important bearing on the early stages of modernization: Peter Kriedte, Hans Medick and J. Schlumbohm, *Industrialization Before Industrialization* (Cambridge, Eng., 1981). Another approach, related to economic modernization though with different political implications, is Immanuel Wallerstein's world-systems theory: *The Modern World System: Capitalist Agriculture and the Origins of the European World Economy in the 16th Century* (New York, 1974) and *The Capitalist World Economy* (Cambridge, Eng., 1979). See also Daniel Chirot, *Social Change in a Peripheral Society: The Creation of a Balkan Colony* (New York, 1976).

Important works on industrialization include David Landes, *The Unbound Prometheus: Technological Change and Industrial Development in Western Europe from 1750 to the Present* (New York, 1969), and Alexander Gerschenkron, *Economic Backwardness in Historical Perspective* (Cambridge, Mass., 1962). W. W. Rostow, *The Stages of Economic Growth* (New York, 1960), is a controversial work that suggests an economic periodization possibly related to major stages in the broader modernization process. Cyril Black, *The Dynamics of Modernization: A Study in Comparative History* (New York, 1966), offers a historical sketch of the general process. A major interpretation of basic types of modernization is Barrington Moore, *Social Origins of Dictatorship and Democracy* (Boston, 1966). A more general survey is Peter N. Stearns, *European Society in Upheaval,* 2nd ed. (New York, 1975).

On modernization, see Richard D. Brown, *Modernization: The Transformation of American Life* (New York, 1976); Samuel N. Eisenstadt, *Tradition, Change, and Modernity* (New York, 1973); Daniel Lerner, *The Passing of Traditional Society* (Glencoe, Ill., 1958); Edward B. Harvey, ed., *Perspectives on Modernization* (Toronto, 1972); and Myron Weiner, *Modernization: The Dynamics of Growth* (New York, 1966). A trenchant criticism is Dean C. Tipps, "Modernization Theory and the Comparative Study of Societies: A Critical Perspective," *Comparative Studies in Society and History* (1973), pp. 199–227.

PART 1

Premodern People
1550–1750

Detail from "The Wedding Dance," Pieter Bruegel the Elder, 1566.

Premodern People

Young as it is compared to the span of human history, the modern world has broken decisively with the past. Yet to understand modernity we must begin with the past.

One key assumption of modernization theory posits the existence of a definable traditional society to be changed. In many views, traditional society seems a virtual antithesis of modernity: static, wedded to the past, superstitious, and of course, in terms of structure, poor, agricultural, and politically aristocratic and/or monarchical. Can premodern society be characterized so neatly? Many historians, arguing that it cannot, point to great regional variations, even within western Europe, as well as great periodic fluctuations in the status of individuals and groups. They would find the label traditionalist a vast oversimplifier.

If a traditional society did exist and can be defined, then other questions follow: Was preindustrial society a pleasant or unpleasant place? Did preindustrial society have characteristics so valuable, perhaps even so natural to the human species, that we should look for attempts to preserve them amid the later structural changes of modernization? In other words, we might look to our preindustrial past not simply as a contrast to our own day, but as the source of much that remains viable in areas such as family life.

The impulse to see preindustrial society as static—not capable of fundamental change—obviously raises the issue of how and when modernization began. Some historians are now pushing the quest for modernization back into the seventeenth century (to older traditions in intellectual history, which stressed the importance of the new science). But if these historians' view is valid, does modernization gain or lose as a model of change? Some contend that if modernization originated so early, the process has been so gradual that it is meaningless. Others are attracted to the idea of a new mentality as the first assignable source of change because it deepens the concept of modernization beyond questions of economic and political structure.

Causation itself, like chronology, is a complex problem. If modern and preindustrial societies differ so greatly, then what external force compelled a break, and to whom did it apply? Was there some aspect of traditional Western society, particularly in Great Britain, that allowed the only spontaneous, nonimitative modernization that the world will ever know? Might change in fact have occurred within? Both questions turn us squarely to European society prior to 1750, before clear structural changes, such as the early factories, were evident. Causes of fundamental change were certainly visible in the seventeenth and early eighteenth centuries. Premodern society was never static; many new trends developed in Europe between 1550 and 1750. Since the end of the Middle Ages, Europe had witnessed important shifts in population levels, social structure, and popular culture. By the sixteenth and seventeenth centuries, some of the changes began to point toward the formation of modern society. Under absolutism, governments became more centralized and efficient. Most of these governments encouraged economic change, if only in the interest of augmenting the tax base for the royal coffers. By the early eighteenth century, several governments were promoting the cultivation of new crops, such as the potato, and establishing new factories, which encouraged the utilization of new machinery.

During the seventeenth and eighteenth centuries, the tone of intellectual life was dramatically altered. Leading intellectuals, vaunting man's power to reason and the possibility of progress, urged further scientific and technological advances. The new world of the intellectuals was aggressively secular. God and religion receded in importance; in some cases, they were directly attacked. The scientific revolution merged into the new general Enlightenment.

Somewhat apart from both government and intellectuals, a variety of businessmen and landowners, primarily in Great Britain and Holland, were experimenting with new farming and manufacturing techniques as well as new forms of economic organization. New crops, drainage methods, and farming equipment began to increase agricultural production. Many landowners—and not just those who directed great estates—began to produce primarily for sales to distant markets. In business, the most spectacular innovators were the merchants who organized great trading companies for worldwide commerce. New systems of investing and accounting developed. Manufacturing changed more slowly, but by the eighteenth century, manufacturers were rapidly extending the systems of rural production, drawing hundreds of thousands of peasants into a new market system. The manufacturers provided raw materials and sold the finished products. Rural workers set up looms or spindles in their homes and produced what they were told to produce. Never before had so many people been involved in a capitalistic production system.

Historians still debate the relative importance and interconnections of governments, intellectuals, and entrepreneurs as obvious and significant sources of change. Many new entrepreneurs, for example, knew little about scientific discoveries or the growing belief in progress. They increased industrial production by applying new techniques, but most of the techniques were devised by artisans. It is more likely that the success of the new technology led industrialists to believe in science and progress rather than the other way around. The essays that follow, however, deal with groups that were remote from the most obvious sources of change. The majority of Europe's preindustrial people were rural; the peasantry, the archetypical preindustrial group, was wedded to a belief in a stable society. The rural population was diverse, including landowning peasants, near-landless cottagers, and artisans. But, like most of their counterparts, the common people of the countryside shared a set of values that was fundamentally opposed to change.

Even a brief glimpse at Europe's preindustrial people returns us to two vital and related issues. First, in order to assess the impact of modernization, we must make a judgment about the nature of preindustrial life. If rural life was in fact comfortable and secure, the advent of industrialization and urban life must have been profoundly disruptive. If, on the other hand, rural life was marked by persistent tension and frustration, perhaps change was welcome. (We need not, of course, regard the preindustrial lower classes as homogeneous. Certain areas, personality types, or even age groups may have been particularly restless.)

Second, we must deal with the extent to which the common people of western Europe actively contributed to modernization. We might assume that the common people were forced into new political and economic roles by the State, the new philosophers, the pioneering businessmen. This approach is presumably most compatible with a belief that modernization imposed profound dislocation on most people. But perhaps some change was spontaneous, stemming from the values of the common people themselves. During the eighteenth century, for example, the spread of domestic manufacturing, although sponsored in part by urban capitalists, found a quick response in the countryside. Rural workers learned new consumption habits. They adopted more urban styles of dress and bought processed food products such as tea and sugar. This was the first step in a new esteem for material acquisitions that would ultimately prove vital to the industrialization process. Family patterns also changed; many rural workers married at an earlier age.

In other words, the lower classes in preindustrial western Europe may have been ripe for change. Although no one can deny that disruption was involved—bringing not only material hardship, but intense psychic stress—the common people may have been more than passive victims in the modernization process. Indeed, some of the key innovators stemmed from their ranks. The ancestors of many dynamic factory owners of the early nineteenth century were peasants and artisans. Their rise was unusual, but it may have drawn on a more widely shared openness to change that served to cushion the shock of modernization for those who remained in the lower classes.

So we are trying to determine both the distance ordinary Europeans had to travel to become "modern" and the extent to which they launched the process themselves in the seventeenth and eighteenth centuries. Obviously, any discussion of the values of the "common" people is chancy, even for the present day. For the premodern period, historians must use very fragmentary records. In a few cases there is good statistical evidence on behavior patterns—size of families, for example—but the motives and values that gave rise to the patterns are open to speculation.

Consequently, the historian's own preconceptions assume added importance. There has been a constant tendency to idealize the past. As far back as the beginning of the nineteenth century, many people turned to the preindustrial past as a solace from the evils of the present. Even late into the nineteenth century, workers retained a nostalgia for the countryside, although they seldom acted on it. In the United States, as in Europe, "back to the land" impulses continue to appear, based at least in part on a belief in the purity and simplicity of preindustrial life. Not surprisingly, many historians who try to assess this existence have similar yearnings, in contrast to most modernization theorists who point to the drawbacks of traditional conditions and ideas. Because the peasants and artisans left few direct records of their thoughts, it is impossible to be certain how they viewed their own life—and it is all too easy for nostalgic historians or modernization enthusiasts to fill in the gaps with their own projections of what preindustrial life must have been like.

In America and Europe, the study of preindustrial society is being actively pursued on a number of fronts. Our knowledge is increasing. We can already make some tentative conclusions about why modernization began on the shores of the Atlantic, in western Europe and North America, and what impact it had on the people.

BIBLIOGRAPHY

Studies of preindustrial rural society are varied. For France, see Emmanuel Le Roy Ladurie, *The Peasants of Languedoc* (Urbana, 1974); Marc Bloch, *French Rural History* (Berkeley, 1970); and Pierre Goubert, *Louis XIV and Twenty Million Frenchmen* (New York, 1969). On England, Alan MacFarlane, *The Origins of English Individualism* (New York, 1979) argues for a distinctive English rural history; see also Margaret Spufford, *Contrasting Communities: English Villagers in the 16th and 17th Centuries* (Cambridge, Eng., 1974). B. H. Slicher von Bath, *The Agrarian History of Western Europe, A.D. 500-1850* (New York, 1963) deals with the traditional rural economy. Traian Stoianovich, *A Study in Balkan Civilization* (New York, 1967), outlines a society unique in some respects, but one perhaps more genuinely "premodern" than the society of western Europe. Early changes in English rural life are discussed in Joan Thirsk, ed., *The Agrarian History of England 1500-1640* (Cambridge, Eng., 1967); Charles Wilson, *England's Apprenticeship* (New York, 1965); and G. R. Mingay, *English Landed Society in the Eighteenth Century* (Toronto, 1963). John Lough, *An Introduction to Seventeenth Century France*, 2nd ed. (New York, 1969), is a valuable survey of French society and politics. For one aspect of material culture, see Olwen Hufton, *The Poor of Eighteenth Century France* (New York, 1975). Although it deals with the end of the eighteenth century, Charles Tilly, *The Vendée* (New York, 1967), shows the impact of economic change on peasants and the readiness of some to come to grips with it in contrast to the bitter resistance of others—a division that depended on an earlier exposure to a market economy. Finally, for an effort at at general statement on the nature of the peasantry, see Eric Wolf, *Peasants* (Englewood Cliffs, N.J., 1966).

On preindustrial population behavior, see E. A. Wrigley, *Population and History* (New York, 1969); Carlo Cipolla, *Economic History of World Population* (Baltimore, 1962); E. A. Wrigley and R. H. Schofield, *The Population History of England 1541-1871* (Cambridge, Mass., 1982); and O. J. Willigan and Katherine Lynch, *Sources and Methods of Historical Demography* (New York, 1982).

For an understanding of premodern attitudes, including popular religion and superstition, see Christopher Hill, *The World Turned Upside Down: Radical Ideas During the English Revolution* (New York, 1972); Alan MacFarlane, *The Family Life of Ralph Josselin* (New York, 1970), and *Witchcraft in Tudor and Stuart England* (New York, 1978); and Natalie Davis, *Society and Culture in Early Modern France* (Stanford, 1975). An interesting effort to connect new ideas with early industrial technology is A. E. Musson and Eric Robinson, *Science and Technology in the Industrial Revolution* (Toronto, 1969).

The position of the elderly and of women in preindustrial society, involved in the witchcraft craze, can be pursued in Peter N. Stearns, ed., *Old Age in*

Preindustrial Society (New York, 1983) and R. Bridenthal and Claudia Koonz, eds., *Becoming Visible: Women in European History* (New York, 1977). See also Roger Thomson, *Women in Stuart England and America* (London, 1974) and Carolyn Lougee, *Le Paradis des Femmes: Women, Salons and Social Stratification in 17th-Century France* (Princeton, 1976). On witchcraft itself there are many excellent studies, including E. William Monter, ed., *European Witchcraft* (New York, 1969); Erik Midelfort, *Witch Hunting in Southwest Germany* (Stanford, 1972); and E. William Monter, *Witchcraft in France and Switzerland* (Ithaca, N.Y., 1976).

The preindustrial family is beginning to receive considerable attention. A pioneering work, with an important general thesis about the development of the modern family, is Philippe Ariès, *Centuries of Childhood: A Social History of Family Life* (New York, 1962). A good summary is Michael Anderson, *Approaches to the West European Family, 1500-1914* (London, 1980). On family structure, see Peter Laslett and R. Wall, *Household and Family in Past Time* (New York, 1972). Two histories of French villages provide important information on family structure: Thomas Sheppard, *Lourmarin in the Eighteenth Century: a Study of a French Village* (Baltimore, 1971), and Patrice Higonnet, *Pont-de-Montvert: Social Structure and Politics in a French Village, 1700-1914* (Cambridge, Mass., 1971). Another major work on the period, though with an American focus, is Philip J. Greven, Jr., *Four Generations: Population, Land, and Family in Colonial Andover, Massachusetts* (Ithaca, N.Y., 1970).

On the nature of work, leisure, and of changes in both with early modernization, E. P. Thompson, *The Making of the English Working Class* (New York, 1964); W. G. Hoskins, *The Midland Peasant: The Economic and Social History of a Leicestershire Village* (New York, 1957); and three classic studies by J. L. and Barbara Hammond: *The Village Labourer, 1760-1832* (New York, 1970 [reprint of 1911 edition]), *The Town Labourer, 1760-1832* (New York, 1968 [reprint of 1917 edition]), and *The Skilled Labourer, 1760-1832* (New York, 1970 [reprint of 1919 edition]). The decline of traditional leisure in the nineteenth century is traced in Robert Storch, ed., *Popular Leisure in the 19th Century* (London, 1982).

The Peasantry: Material Life and Rational Controls

KEITH WRIGHTSON and DAVID LEVINE

The peasantry was the key ingredient of preindustrial society in terms of its numbers and its value systems. Yet it proves an elusive entity when examined with any precision. The peasant world differed greatly from one region to the next—and it changed significantly over time. Even its basic wealth could alter. Too easily we imagine uniform material conditions for the peasantry; in fact, significant gradations occurred within a single region. In western Europe, the peasant economy usually maintained some contact with the market, even though many peasants produced only enough for their own needs, with any surplus going to cover tax obligations and landlord exactions. There were peasant owners, peasant employers, as well as peasants who hired themselves out as laborers or sharecroppers. The peasant economy as a whole is often termed a subsistence operation, producing only basic human needs. Yet periodically there was a surplus beyond that necessary to support a small upper class. On this basis, population could occasionally grow.

The following selection deals with peasants in the English village of Terling, Essex, in the late sixteenth and early seventeenth centuries. It stresses the diversity of economic conditions among peasants, a diversity that increased with economic changes and population growth in the sixteenth century. By modern standards, even wealthy peasants were poor, of course, but they had significant items of personal property in addition to their land. Terling is, of course, a single village—many recent peasant studies are local, which provides important detail but can hamper generalizations. Almost surely, English peasants at this point were wealthier than West European peasants in general.

Aside from wealth levels, some features of peasant material life and values were shared by most West European peasants. In the village of Terling, the importance of wills as arrangements to pass on the holdings within the family demonstrates the peasant fixation on property—a characteristic interest in Western Europe since the Middle Ages. This concern for transmitting property could lead to a desire to conserve, rather than to risk.

The peasant interest in protecting property also shows in the highly rational arrangements for birth control, which were beefed up in reaction to population growth in the sixteenth century. The revelation of such careful planning should modify any impression of traditional peasants as superstitious creatures at the mercy of forces beyond their control. Peasant demography was in some ways more rational than its modern counterpart; peasants arranged marriage age and sexual restraint so that, on the whole, poor people had fewer children than wealthier couples.

However, peasant rationalism was not directed toward promoting change, but toward retarding it. Of course their poverty might lead some agricultural workers to welcome a different economic system; the peasant society was not so uniformly pleasant and protective as more favorable images of preindustrial life may imply. But the most deprived peasants were hardly in a position to initiate change, and their more substantial employers were above all concerned with maintaining existing standards. Consequently, sixteenth-century population pressure led, not to a new economic system, but to new population controls. This locked-in quality of traditional society most clearly contrasts with later modernization. Peasant society witnessed change, diversity, and some effective rational planning; but it did not welcome innovation. What, then, were the causes of later modernization? What kind of peasants could accept, much less produce, fundamental change?

Exactly how the expanded numbers of the laboring poor supported themselves is a difficult question. They must have found work as and when they could in Terling and the surrounding parishes, and we must assume that local employment opportunities had grown. Perhaps a more intensive cultivation was being practiced on the larger farms of the parish. Perhaps the rising prosperity of the farmers provided more employment for petty craftsmen. Perhaps again the servants in husbandry, living with the farmers, were giving way to laborers dwelling in their own cottages. All of these factors may have played some part. What is equally evident is that many laborers were unable to maintain themselves fully, as we shall see when we turn to the analysis of the position of the poor in the later seventeenth century. But before engaging in what will be an analysis of the economics of mere survival, something more can be said of the experience of more fortunate villagers for whom the period saw not impoverishment but a real, if modest, prosperity.

It is by now generally agreed among historians that the later sixteenth and early seventeenth centuries witnessed significant improvements in the living standards of the middling sort of English countrymen. In a justly famous passage written in the middle years of the reign of Elizabeth, William Harrison, parson of the Essex parish of Radwinter, described how in his time, despite the inflation of the period, farmers and artificers "doo yet find the means to obtein and atchive such furniture as heretofore hathe beene unpossible." The greybeards of Harrison's own village "noted three things to be marvellouslie altred in England within their sound remembrance": first, "the multitude of chimnies latelie erect-

From Keith Wrightson and David Levine, *Poverty and Piety in an English Village* (New York: Academic Press, 1979), pp. 36–42, 65–71.

ed''; second, "the great (although not generall) amendment of lodging" (i.e., bedding); third, "the exchange of vessell" (i.e., tableware) from wood to pewter and even silver. The study of both inventories and physical evidence by historians has abundantly confirmed Harrison's testimony concerning the improvement of both housing and furniture among the yeomanry of the period.

Only two inventories survive for Terling in this period. The wills of the villagers, however, are sufficiently specific about personal possessions and refer commonly enough to the rooms of their houses for us to form an impression of living standards that broadly confirms the improvements discovered elsewhere. This evidence, however, relates only to the middling ranks of village society, Terling testators being overwhelmingly drawn from . . . yeomen, husbandmen, and the more substantial craftsmen. This qualification accepted, the evidence speaks clearly.

Housing standards certainly seem to have improved around the turn of the century. The map of 1597 shows the houses of the village as being for the most part single-story dwellings, though some have an upper story built at one end. Many have chimneys, a significant contribution to domestic comfort. Where internal arrangements are referred to in wills of the later sixteenth century, the rooms mentioned are usually the hall and the chamber (an upper room), though there are infrequent references to "the parlor." The yeomen and husbandmen of the period would seem to have lived in dwellings already improved beyond the standards of the medieval hall house but not yet up to the standards that became established in the seventeenth century. By 1650, references to hall, chamber *and* parlor were commonplace, while by 1700 a wide variety of rooms might be mentioned. John Humphrey's will of 1655, for example, contains references to hall, parlor, parlor chamber, and the chamber above the buttery, and is not atypical. Confirmation of the impression of improving standards given by the wills of villagers comes from the report made on the village in 1921 by the Royal Commission on Historical Monuments. Several late-medieval houses are listed that had seen the division of the hall to provide two stories and the addition of chimneys in the late sixteenth and early seventeenth centuries. Even more prominent are the many fine houses of the earlier seventeenth century. These buildings provide living evidence of the prosperity of the upper levels of village society in this period.

If the wills offer us only a glimpse of the progress of the "great rebuilding" of rural England in which Terling shared, they allow us to chart the improvement of furnishings more exactly. Bedding was sufficiently valuable to be frequently listed in detail by testators. From the 1550s through the 1580s, flockbeds and even featherbeds, together with sheets and bolsters, are commonly mentioned, but there is only a single reference to an actual bedstead below the level of the gentry. Between

1590 and 1610, "joyned" bedsteads begin to appear, usually standing in the parlor an commonly containing the testator himself while the will was dictated! From the 1610s onward, bedsteads with all their "furniture" become commonplace, while the wealthier villagers might even possess two or more and distribute them among their heirs. In the 1660s and 1670s "high beds" complete with curtains appear among the wealthier, while the latter decade saw the first appearance of a further element of sophistication—the warming pan.

Improvements in other furnishings followed a similar chronology. Cupboards and "hutches" seem to have been widely owned since at least 1550, but "joyned" tables and chairs appear regularly only after 1600. Earlier references are to trestle or "foylding" tables accompanied by stools and forms. The only joined table found before 1600 was [mentioned] in the will of a carpenter who died in 1592. Pewter tableware is occasionally mentioned even before 1550, but became commonplace in the later sixteenth century, as did brass cooking pots. Before 1600 there were occasional yeomen who left a silver spoon or two but in the early seventeenth century the possession of such treasured items became fairly common amongst yeomen. Brass candlesticks also appeared in these years to grace the tables of the prosperous. In the later seventeenth century, testators gave much less detail of such possessions, perhaps an indication that they were now sufficiently normal to be simply taken for granted and lumped together with other goods and chattels.

Finally, a word can be said about clothing. Clothes were valuable enough to be passed on from generation to generation. In 1566, for example, Agnes Biggen left her daughter "my kyrtell that I had of Mother Lerner"; she herself had been left the garment ten years before: It had been Margery Learner's best gown too. This practice was assisted by the fact that there appears to have been little change of fashion in the main items of clothing between 1550 and 1650. Throughout the period, women's costume seems to have consisted of underlinen, smock and petticoat (very often red, sometimes green or blue), gown, "crosse cloths," apron, neckerchief, and coat. Men had their doublets, hose or (later) breeches and stockings, jerkins, and coats. One yeoman, for example, left in 1551 "a coot, a doublett of fustian, a pere hose . . . and a gyrken," and another husbandman in 1622 left his best suit of apparel "that is, my dublett, britches and Jerken." The contents of the wardrobe had changed little by 1660, but one has the impression that more clothes were possessed—some testators were leaving several sets of clothing.

The matters are not trivial. These various goods were their owners' pride, lovingly detailed in will after will. The fine table laid with pewter and brass, the great bedstead in the parlor with its featherbed, pillows, and coverlet, even the best "stuffe dublet lines with bayes" were the outward and very visible signs of success among those best placed to take advantage of the opportunities of the age. The prestige that they conferred was perhaps the more important because these comforts were new and because they were not usually available to the mass of the villagers. The century of improving standards for the middling sort of the village, 1550–1650, was a century of impoverishment for the laboring poor.

These inventories present one vivid picture of the living conditions of the laboring poor in the 1620s. Another comes from the confession of Robert Whitehead, who stole and ate a sheep in the winter of 1623/4, "beinge a verie poore man and haveinge a wiefe and seaven smale children and being very hungery." Direct evidence of this kind is rare, but something can be done to fill out the picture of the lives of those families that by the mid-seventeenth century made up half the population of the village.

Constructing a "typical" budget for a poor family is fraught with difficulties, but is perhaps less difficult for Terling than for some other villages. For the last six years of the seventeenth century very detailed overseers of the poor accounts survive that enable us to gain some insight into the costs of maintaining a pauper at the end of our period. Adult paupers received varying sums for their relief, but a fairly typical regular payment was 2s. per fortnight (£2 12s. per annum). A pauper child would appear to have cost £1 10s per annum. These payments can be taken to represent the costs of food and drink only, since additional sums were also granted to those receiving regular relief for clothing, fuel, and rent. Clothing an adult man with coat, shirt, breeches, shoes, and stockings cost about 18s. A woman's linen, gown, shoes, and stockings cost 15s. A child's shirt or shift, breeches or undercoat, and shoes cost around 5s. Some of these items were the subject of annual expenditure, others were needed more rarely. Nevertheless a man, wife and three children might well need £2 a year for clothing as well as £9 14s. for food. In addition, the overseers spent about £1 a year on wood for each pauper and paid rents for them of £1 to £1 10s. a year. Whether these rents were typical one cannot easily tell. The housing stock of the village must have been expanded in the later sixteenth and earlier seventeenth centuries in order to meet population expansion, and many of the one-hearth cottages on which the poor were assessed in 1671 must have been erected in this period. Some were possibly tied cottages with negligible rents. However, an allowance of £1 a year can be made for rent. The following expenditure might be typical for a poor family of five in the 1690s:

Food	£9 14s.
Clothing	2
Fuel	1
Rent	1
Total	£13 14s.

Other expenses may also have been incurred, of course, but this hypothetical budget is intended only to give an idea of the minimum costs of keeping a family at the level that the parish overseers considered appropriate for paupers.

Our next question must be to ask what the typical laborer earned. According to official wage assessments, an Essex laborer in 1599 should receive 8d. or 10d. a day, without food and drink, depending on the season. In the 1610s the official rate, without food and drink, varied from 8d. to 16d. a day, depending on the task, with higher payments for harvest work. For comparison, tailors and collarmakers were assessed at 10d. to 14d. a day, carpenters at 12d. to 16d. In 1661 laborers were to have 12d. to 14d. a day for normal work, tailors the same, collarmakers, sawyers, and coopers 14d. to 16d., and carpenters 16d. to 20d. Details of *actual* payments for a day's labor from the Terling churchwardens' accounts show that common laborers in the last two decades of the seventeenth century received a usual payment of 1s. a day, though sums paid could be higher on occasion. Let us assume that our hypothetical laborer worked six days a week every week, giving a total of 312 days a year. This is, of course, an unwarranted assumption since the underemployment of labor in this period was notorious. However, this assumption may make some allowance for extra earnings in harvest time and for the occasional earnings of wives and children. On this assumption, laborers and craftsmen working for wages may have had the following maximum incomes at different points in the course of the seventeenth century:

Years	Employment	Wages per diem	Income per annum
1599	Laborer	9d.	£11 14s.
1610s	Laborer	12	15 12
	Tailor or collarmaker	12	15 12
	Carpenter	13	16 18
1661	Laborer	13	16 18
	Tailor	13	16 18
	Collarmaker, sawyer, or cooper	15	19 10
	Carpenter	18	23 8
1680-1700	Terling laborer	12	15 12
1688	Gregory King's estimate of total income of a laboring family		15 00

On these estimates, then, (which are, if anything, likely to be too high), a Terling laborer in the 1690s (or, for that matter, some of the petty craftsmen who largely shared his position) would be able to maintain his family at a level slightly above that at which the overseers of the poor maintained the village paupers. These estimates, of course, assume that laboring families were entirely dependent on wages for their subsistence. Certainly the laborers of Terling had no common pasture on which to keep animals. Yet we might consider that some would have the produce of at least garden plots to ease their burdens, while others may have been partly paid in kind or allowed to buy foodstuffs at cheap rates from their employers. Of these matters we have no evidence. What is certain is that the laborer's lot was hard enough at the best of times. Any additional expense over and above mere subsistence needs, any period of bad luck in finding work, any and period of illness, would threaten to push him (and his family) under. Above all, any severe rise in the price of foodstuffs would have disastrous results. The family expenditure calculated above is based upon the overseer's accounts of the year 1697/8, which tell us that barley—the principal breadcorn of the poor in seventeenth-century England—was priced at 2s. 6d. a bushel. Earlier in the century, occasional references reveal that barley had stood at about 3s. 4d. in some normal years and even higher in years of bad harvest such as the later 1590s, 1631, and 1647–1650. In 1599, for example, in the aftermath of the terrible dearth years of the later 1590s, an Essex jury presented to the justices of the county "that the rate [of wages] for laborers in husbandrie be to smale" and suggested that they be raised. In 1604/5 a much less drastic enhancement of the price of corn led the authorities to predict that the laboring poor were "like to suffer great want and penury." In 1631 the poor of Witham Hundred, unable to afford their normal breadcorns, "were constreyned to by Branke and Teares which was brought by shipping . . . to serve their necessities for bread." Eighteen years later barley cost 5s. a bushel in north Essex, other grains still more, and one clergyman described his people as "pincht with want of food." In the later decades of the seventeenth century it is likely that the laboring poor of Terling were experiencing their first rise in real wages after a century and a half of steady inflation in which wages had lagged behind food prices. Their existence remained marginal enough but had probably actually improved since 1650.

There were elements of real stability in the economic and social history of Terling between 1520 and 1700 but there were also major elements of change. The villagers of 1700 knew both a greater prosperity and a more widespread, more abject poverty and dependence than had those of 1524. The former can be seen in the uses to which the yeomen and more substantial husbandmen and craftsmen put their greater wealth. The latter is less directly visible in historical documents. Yet it forms the essential background against which the petty dramas of village life were acted out...

It is clear that the most important brake on Terling's population growth was exerted by the decline in marital fertility, which was itself the product of a somewhat later age at marriage acting in concert with a pronounced fall in age-specific fertility for women over thirty-five. In contrast to the direct action taken through the "prudential" check, the role of rising mortality was small. Indeed, the decline in the level of illegitimacy can be seen to have been of more importance than rising mortality. This simulation is suggestive in that it goes no little way toward undermining belief in the efficacy of the Four Horsemen—war, famine, pestilence, and fire—during the *ancien régime*. In a community like Terling there was only one serious epidemic, in 1625. Otherwise, . . . there were few other spectacular swathes made by the grim reapers. Rather, like a kind of background noise, the presence of death was always there. Family reconstitution studies—such as the Terling example being discussed here—are making it clear that mortality was not a major agent in furthering population control. In almost all studies it is being discovered that variations in age at marriage and marital fertility were basic methods to which a population had recourse when it was trying to limit its numbers.

As far as we can determine, Terling's population size remained stable for almost 150 years after 1625. In the annual totals of baptisms and burials, this stability gains an added resonance. . . . There was a reduction in the net rate of replacement but not a total one. Even after 1625 the villagers continued to produce sons and daughters over and above the numbers needed for simple replacement. What became of these children and young adults? Instead of viewing the seventeenth-century stabilization in simple demographic terms, it is necessary to add to it another potent factor: migration from and immigration to the village community. A great deal of recent work in historical demography has been devoted to this subject and it is becoming quite apparent that the immobile swain of days gone by has been relegated to the dustbin of history. A consensus is now developing that stresses, on the one hand, extraordinary age-specific mobility among youths and, on the other, a solid core of stable, usually substantial families. By readjusting our focus it becomes possible to bring both aspects of reality into a single field of vision. Bygone historians and antiquarians were not simply wrong when they asserted the immutability of the village community. Rather, they were dyslexic. To be sure, the village notable and local worthies of the "better sort" were tied to a community by the bands of property. The proletarianized day-laborer's experience was quite different.

Popular Religion in Preindustrial Society

NATALIE ZEMON DAVIS

The importance of religion in European society before the nineteenth century is familiar enough. Indeed, some portrayals of medieval Europe have focused so heavily on religion that the strong economic and family motives of ordinary people—of the sort discussed in the previous selection—have been forgotten. Nevertheless there can be no question that religion was a vital part of the lives of almost all people, affecting health care, recreation, and community solidarity as well as in spiritual life per se. The Reformation and subsequent Catholic revival of the sixteenth century revealed the strong currents of popular faith.

The following selection deals with popular religion in the growing city of Lyons, at the confluence of the Saône and Rhône rivers in east-central France. Lyons had 65,000 residents in 1560, making it second only to Paris in size and economic importance. The city had been strongly affected by the Reformation, although at least two-thirds of its inhabitants remained Catholic. Relying heavily on concepts drawn from anthropology—an important trend as social historians try to get at popular beliefs—Natalie Davis interprets the symbols of Catholic practice to show how the religion fit intimately into urban life. Religion answered both practical problems—the need for help in sickness, concern about the dangerous river Rhône—and more generalized concerns about the unknown. It was not a separate category of life.

This portrayal raises one obvious question about the future: What could replace religion in ordinary life in a more secular age? Modernization in Europe has meant a decline of religion, though not its complete disappearance. The quarrels of the Reformation period helped launch growing skepticism. By 1800, religion in a city like Lyons was much less pervasive than it had been two and a half centuries before. What values and symbols would replace religion in explaining adversity and providing common bonds among people in a complex society?

Where is the sacred in the sixteenth-century French city? We think readily of church towers and spires, which in the old engravings give the town its characteristic profile. We hear the bells ring for terce and nones and other hours of the priest's day, which mark the sacrifice of the mass, which announce the feast's arrival, the neighbour's death and the funeral's passage. We visualize the penitential processions winding through the streets with their relics, statues and great crosses, to appease God's wrath at time of famine or an act of sacrilege. We see the confraternities' processions, more joyous perhaps, banners flying, drums beating, blessed bread held high, all to the devotion of their patron saint. We see the city's poor, in queues or clumps, waiting for their alms of bread in courtyards, at doors and gates. We see Protestant worshippers, dressed in sober clothes, singing the Psalms of David as they move through the town to their preachers; Protestant crowds, breaking idols in the cathedral, mocking the host and threatening the priests; Catholic crowds, throwing themselves on those who have dared affront the body of Jesus Christ and insult his holy mother.

Such scenes are familiar ones, and historians have used them for a variety of purposes: to ascertain whether religious behaviour is or is not bringing people spiritual security and tranquillity, is or is not living up to standards of Erasmian or Lutheran piety. They have been used to describe the conflict between clergy and laity—an important perspective —and to characterize the religious style of different social groups, such as the merchants. But despite a growing documentation on urban piety in the sixteenth century, on urban charitable institutions, on the events of the Protestant and Catholic Reformations in individual cities, and on urban witchcraft and possession, we have come to few conclusions on the ways in which religion formed and gave expression to urban values and mentality in that period. . . .

The space of the Catholic city was not at all homogeneous or symmetrical. The nine parishes, established for centuries and with well-known boundaries, bore no relationship to the distribution of population. The huge parish of St. Nizier, in the heart of the artisanal quarter, had 22,000 communicants at Easter, so it was said in 1534, while the parish of St. Pierre-le-Vieux and St. Romain embraced only a little circle of families. Catholic space was full of special places and sacred spots. The presence of relics—the jaw of St. John the Baptist at the cathedral, the body of St. Irénée (the second bishop of Lyon) at the church on the hill of Fourvière, of St. Bonaventure at the Franciscan church, of St. Ennemond (a seventh-century bishop of the city) at St. Nizier, of one St. Reine, "who did miracles for the health," at the cloister of the Carmelites,

From Natalie Zemon Davis, "The Sacred and the Body Social in Sixteenth-Century Lyon," *Past and Present* No. 90 (February, 1981), pp. 40–41, 52–57, 60–61, 64, 67–68.

among many others—intensified the sanctity of certain locations. Catholic devotion to this sense of space was, if anything, strengthened by the Calvinist iconoclasm of 1562–3; they hastened to purify buildings and to locate and verify relics (such as St. Irénée's head, miraculously preserved among the ruins for ten years) and put them on display.

Catholic ceremonial was also very sensitive to the natural features of the urban environment—the hill of Fourvière, which dominated the city, and the rivers. Processions of the clergy climbed up at least twice a year to the little chapel of Our Lady of Fourvière, and for most of the sixteenth century a "Kingdom" of the newly-wed made a pilgrimage there on Assumption Day. The choir-boys of the cathedral, dressed up as adult canon-counts, went up the hill after Christmas to the heights of St. Just, received a blessing from their boy-bishop and paid their respects to the bones of one of the Innocents slaughtered by Herod. The hill was viewed as a source of protection and help for the city. Often yielding ruins from its Roman past, discovered by gardeners and treasured by wealthy townsmen and humanists, it also contained the blood and bones of the early Christian founders and martyrs.

The slow-moving feminine Saône—the characterization is theirs— was the place for joyous festivals, sacred and popular. In the fourteenth century, in the days before the fairs when the Saône was the central artery of the city, a Feast of Marvels had been celebrated on the river in June, in honour of St. Pothin, first bishop of Lyon, and his comrades. The entire clergy of the city was afloat, praying and singing on the Saône, accompanied by officers, notable citizens and artisans; enormous boats performed a complicated ritual, which started at a rock at the north of the city, centred on the Saône bridge, and moved down to the point where the Saône flowed into the Rhône. This festival had ended in the late fourteenth century, but there still existed on Ascension Day a colourful pilgrimage by boat of laity and clergy up to Our Lady of Île-Barbe, north of the city. In addition to mass at the ancient abbey, which was near the border between France and Savoy, the master of the ports at Lyon and his aides took down the escutcheon of the duke of Savoy and replaced it with the arms of France. On Sundays and feast-days during the summer the boatmen of the parishes of St. George and St. Vincent on either side of the Saône marked their common boundary by jousting on the river. On the eve of the major feast of St. John the Baptist, it was from the Saône bridge that the consulate set off the fireworks.

The Rhône, by contrast, was a powerful, masculine (again their characterization) and dangerous river. As sixteenth-century people still remembered, the building of the bridge over it had initially been commanded by the Lord himself in a miraculous message to a shepherd boy in the mid-thirteenth century. Its difficult construction had had to be preached like a crusade, and financed by the many indulgences that penitents could purchase through visiting the chapel of the Holy Ghost at the Lyon end of the bridge. It was finally completed only at the beginning of the sixteenth century, and people still feared it would collapse—and with reason, for the strong currents often swept away some of the stanchions. As for the Rhône itself, there was constant worry not only that it would be too high or too low for the navigation essential to the fairs, but also that it would overflow. The flood of 1570 was so furious that Catholics claimed that "the water had wished to purge the filth . . . scattered about by the Calvinians," while the Protestants claimed it as a judgement of God against the Catholics for their persecution of his church. In any case, now that the Rhône was so important to Lyon life, Catholic ceremonial took increased note of it and many processions passed by the little chapel on the bridge, especially at Pentecost, the festival of the Holy Ghost. As with the Saône, there were associated popular festivals: at Pentecost young men dressed themselves as horses (more precisely as *chevaux fous*, or horse-fools) and danced through the streets from the end of the peninsula, where the Rhône and Saône "embraced," up to the Rhône bridge. This custom, which exists elsewhere in France and which has been interpreted variously as a fertility cult and a male initiation rite, was thought by some sixteenth-century Lyonnais to signify escape and uncontrollability. In this case, wild horses might well dance and jump towards a barely tamed river.

Catholic processions did not serve only to visit the border points of Lyon, such as the Rhône bridge and the Île-Barbe, but also to unite the two parts of the city cut by the Saône—the Church of Lyon, the king's men at the Palais de Roanne, and the bankers on the side of the hill of Fourvière (Côte de Fourvière) with the town hall, the merchants and the artisans of the St. Nizier side (Côte de St. Nizier). For example, a general procession of the parishes for Corpus Christi Day or a procession of the Confraternity of the Holy Cross for its feast on 3rd May assembled at the cathedral of St. Jean with their monstrances for the holy wafer, their crosses, banners, bells, candles and torches; went north to St. Paul; crossed the Saône bridge to St. Nizier, over to the Franciscans along the Rhône at St. Bonaventure; down to the Rhône bridge hospital, across to the Dominicans at Nôtre Dame du Confort in the midst of the printing quarter; and then, taking the rue Mercière (the main commercial route in the city), returned to St. Jean.

Can we conceive of this fashion of moving through and marking urban space as significant for, as functional in, the economic and social life of Lyon? For the most part, yes. These processions could dramatize the city's identity and give protection to the body of the town, and this effect could last in fair-time and outside fair-time (*en foire et hors foire*). And note that these were not rites to give a sense of closure to Lyon (as did rural processions, when among other activities the parish bounds were beaten and sprinkled with holy water); these processions . . . did *not* go around the enlarged town fortifications constructed in the 1520s. Rather, one visited the Rhône bridge to keep it open.

Furthermore, with the exception of a newly established house of mendicants on the hill of Fourvière, who protested the bellowing of animals at the cattle market across the road, the church objected rather little in the sixteenth century to the proximity of commerce to sacred things. Vintners and candle-makers hawked their wares outside the cathedral door to supply the needs of pilgrims on the feast-day of St. John the Baptist. People selling food came there at other times as well, and the canon-counts made only half-hearted efforts to stop them. Especially illustrative is the quarrel that broke out over the mercers and petty traders who surrounded the church of St. Nizier. The canons had no desire to expel them, so long as they left enough room in front of the doors and four feet between their stalls and the church (canon law prescribed thirty feet, but who cared?). The quarrel of 1559 was between the canons and the city council: who was going to collect the rent for those stalls? The church won, and the tradespeople remained (in fact, they are there to this day)...

Catholic ceremonial time was complex, bunched and irregular. Any parish or neighbourhood might have special rhythms of its own; in the area around the cathedral, for instance, from May to mid-August, at least six local feasts were held—for young law clerks, or for the furriers, or in honour of St. Christopher and St. Roch—and this quite apart from the major holidays that fell within those weeks. But the festive calendar for the city as a whole was not homogeneous either. It expanded and contracted, like the diets of the devout, who moved from eating to fasting; like the spirits of the penitent, who moved from carnival to Lent. Putting together the events of the church's liturgical calendar with those initiated by the city council (a procession and mass on Trinity Sunday up to the municipal College of the Trinity; a procession and mass on the Sunday after Easter, of all the poor receiving aid from the municipal charity, and the like) and with those events initiated by parishioners (such as street-dancing at Pentecost), we have periods of high activity in late December and early January; carnival and early Lent; Easter; May and June, a time of intense ceremonial life; and August. Autumn and Advent were the relatively quiet times.

The Catholic city breathed in and out as did the commercial and manufacturing city. How did the rhythms relate? The peak of May and June was not matched by a peak of economic busyness; but apart from that, the festive calendar clustered around three of the four fairs: the Fair of Kings, the Easter Fair and the August Fair. Only the Hallowmas Fair in November, following fast on the sombre Day of the Dead, had rather little liturgical build-up or follow-up. . . .

Having protected the exterior of the body social, Catholic preachers, such as the Jesuit Emond Auger, insisted strongly on the communion and sacred alliance within. Through the mass and the sacrament of the Eucharist, where Christ is really present and ingested, we are joined tightly to our brothers. The fruits of the mass and the prayers accompanying it are numerous, even if the Christian cannot understand the words: one can help the dead, one can help children, one can help those who are absent, the governors of the city and the kingdom, and many others. Auricular confession and the sacrament of Penitence also had social advantages. "How many evil projects," said Auger, "how many domestic conspiracies have been halted by this sacrament! How many enemies have been reconciled!"

The liturgical event which gave the best expression to this Catholic image of community was the rite of conjuration and exorcism. The one that took place in 1582 at the Fransiscan convent can serve as our example. The victim was Pernette Pinay, a fifty-seven-year-old widow from a village near Lyon. Through the evil-doing of a witch in her village, she had been possessed by seven devils. Six of them she had forced out of herself by a pilgrimage and by prayers to Mary; now there was left a single devil named Frappan. Pernette had a holy soul and she had struggled with Frappan, so that he had been able to take over only her body. The exorcism, led by the preacher and theologian Jean Benedicti, lasted several days before a large audience. Frappan shouted a great deal, insulted people, and stammered over the name of Jesus Christ. Everyone in the gathering purified herself or himself by prayers, fasts, confession and communion. Everyone prayed for Pernette and vowed to make a pilgrimage to Our Lady at Île-Barbe. Twice during the rite a fountain appeared, distilled from the tears of all the spectators. Finally, Frappan departed during the mass. At that very instant a citizen on the Rhône bridge saw a great flash of fire above the Franciscan church. Thus were refuted the lies of the Calvinists about the mass; thus were demonstrated the power of the priest, the virtue of widows and the direct aid that Christian can give to Christian. Indeed, one could nourish another person spiritually, as the liver and heart nourished the body with blood, natural spirits and vital spirits. . . .

With the Catholics I have pointed to their deep regional roots; their connection with a wide range of occupations, from banking to baking; and their location in traditional collective organization as the elements of experience which, interacting with Catholic doctrine and ritual, perpetuated a distinctive sense of place, rhythm and community in the city...

Sixteenth-century Catholicism could adapt its magic and ceremony readily to the varying character and risks of commercial and banking life in Lyon and could tolerate business practice up to its very walls. . . .

Catholicism had some resources to assist the integration of the different quarters and social groups in Lyon. . . . It could add sanctity to some of the familiar features of the environment, and try to pacify the dangerous ones. For a city with walls, which housed a population that ran from nobles to day-labourers, and an advanced economy as well as traditional economies—for such a city, perhaps this body social, with its changing physical states, its particular organs, its hierarchical order, its arteries, veins and umbilical cords of aid, made some sense.

Witchcraft and Social Tensions in Europe

EDWARD BEVER

The witchcraft scare that consumed portions of Western Europe as well as New England into the seventeenth century—beginning in the sixteenth century in Europe—has drawn a variety of explanations from historians. The scare, in which hundreds of thousands of people were arrested and scores of thousands executed, seems to relate in part to the religious turmoil of the Reformation; in most deeply-affected regions the rivalry between Protestants and Catholics was intense. The scare may also relate to uncertainties stemming from new ideas about science and medicine, new ways of viewing the world. Ultimately, these new ideas would sufficiently assure the public that belief in witches abated; but in their early period they may have provoked heightened anxieties. Another explanation focuses on a growing distaste for the poor, a desire to avoid traditional forms of charity in a period when population growth and economic change increased the number and visibility of those needing society's aid. Witchcraft accusations allowed solid citizens to conceal their guilt by attacking some of society's most vulnerable members, through accusation and trial. Historians have not agreed on what combination of causes best explains the extraordinary witchcraft phenomenon. They do agree, however, that some basic social and cultural changes must have been involved, because although witchcraft belief dates back to the Middle Ages and before, the widespread trials and persecutions that arose in Britain, Southwestern Germany, Switzerland and parts of France had not been part of medieval patterns.

Historians also look at the witchcraft trials because what was brought out in this time of popular crisis, reveals much about society's attitudes toward certain groups. Witchcraft accusations focused disproportionately not only on the poor, but also on women and the elderly. Did new fears bring out long-cherished prejudices about these groups, or were changes in the position of the groups themselves causing the witchcraft reaction? Protestantism, for example, gave women new religious rights, and ultimately encouraged new attention to the importance of women in the family. Were witchcraft accusations an early popular response to these shifts, before they would be more constructively integrated into normal social behavior?

The following selection focuses on the reasons why witchcraft accusations increasingly singled out not just women, but older women. This had not been the medieval emphasis; but, in witchcraft trials during the craze period, between half and three quarters of all accused witches were over fifty. Edward Bever attributes the timing of the witchcraft craze to a new need to use scapegoats to promote religious conformity. But he attributes the isolation of elderly women as scapegoats to actual behaviors of many of these people in response to their lack of security and authority in rural society. In turn, he speculates that the witchcraft craze may have contributed to altering both the image and behavior of many women in European society.

W itchcraft cases typically involved a long period of suspicion before an accusation could be made and accepted. "Suspicions gradually built up in a village," and except during mass panics, an accusation was unlikely to be accepted in court unless it was supported by a history of suspect incidents. No one has yet calculated the average time lag involved, but evidence supporting an accusation often extended back well beyond a decade. Agatha Stosser, an elderly woman from Sulz in Württemberg, for example, was first accused by an incarcerated suspect in 1630. She was arrested and investigated for bewitching animals in 1645, but let off because "no matter how much one repeated the accusations against her, she stuck firmly to her conviction" that she was innocent. Fourteen years later, though, she was convicted of a long list of charges accumulated over the intervening period. First accused at forty-four, she was finally burned at seventy-three.

Why did women like Agatha continue to provoke suspicion for so long? The answer lies both in the pressures on early modern elderly women and in their response to them. Women, especially elderly, lower-class women, were during this period in a double bind: if they were in a position of relative security, they possessed little authority, while if they had independent responsibility, they were unlikely to have much security. This is a dilemma perhaps inherent to life, but for these women the contrasts were especially stark. Elderly women in early modern villages had many reasons to act like witches.

Most women lived as dependents in households headed by men. Daughters were normally subordinate to their fathers, servants to their employers, spinsters to their brothers, wives to their husbands, and widows to their sons. Some women, especially widows, escaped this predicament, but they, as we shall see, had formidable problems of their own. For the most part, by the sixteenth century "the patriarchal family . . . was paramount." Among their Germanic and Latin ancestors, women had been subordinate to their men, but this subordination was tempered by some property rights and the protection of extended kinship ties. "The feudal system . . . gradually curtailed the property rights of women," and "lowered their status." By the early modern period, "the power of the

From Edward Bever, "Old Age and Witchcraft in Early Modern Europe," Peter N. Stearns, ed., *Old Age in Preindustrial Society* (New York: Holmes and Meier, 1983), pp. 173–180.

husband to enforce obedience to his will by threats, blows, and confinement . . . was rarely questioned." Women were reduced to "complete . . . subordination."

The gradual reduction of women's status was not only legal and social, but cultural and psychological as well. Many men and women shared a "belief in the biological inferiority of women," considering them, "the weaker vessell, of a frail heart, inconstant, and with a word soon stirred to wrath." Women in the sixteenth and seventeenth centuries were exhorted to be "docile and submissive . . . silent . . . and at all times submissive to men." This ideal has found favor among many men throughout history, but the contemporaneous legal and social developments in early modern Europe lent it particular force.

The later years of life were especially stressful for women because of the widespread system of contractual retirement. During the Middle Ages, many lords insisted that their peasants set an age at which men would hand over control of their farms to their sons in exchange for a promise of support. The system continued, via individual family arrangements, into the early modern period, as aging peasants often found it difficult to maintain their lands. The retired parents lived within the household or in a special outbuilding, but in either case, one contemporary observed, "they were often not treated the way they should be." There was "an underlying hostility towards" them, "and a reluctance to devote much of society's limited resources to them." But even if the younger generation fulfilled its material obligations, elderly women still lost their place at the center of domestic activity. While older men might continue to exercise public functions, older women had virtually no role other than informal advisor and critic, "wise woman" and witch.

The intent of the European retirement system was to increase production within the male sphere of farm activity, but it had at least as much impact on women's lives since they tended to marry younger, live longer, and, as widows, retire as soon as a son came of age. Traditionally, a propertied widow might strike a favorable bargain in a remarriage; in the sixteenth and seventeenth centuries this avenue was blocked as a new marriage pattern arose in response to overpopulation. Age-at-marriage rose, and remarriage, especially for women, was discouraged, sometimes violently. A young woman lucky enough to marry a well-off widower could easily find herself a ward of her stepson for her last decades. The other point of view in this relationship has been preserved in fairy tales about children's fear of their stepmother, who was often explicitly identified as a witch. But the relationship could be just as hard on the woman, at least in its later phases when roles were reversed. As a contemporary observer noted, "no prison can be more irksome to a parent than a son's or daughter's house."

Most independent women were widows with minor children or without children due to infertility, death, or migration. Many women lost their husbands at a relatively young age, and enjoyed control of a household at least temporarily. But for this independence and responsibility they paid a heavy price. A woman could earn only a fraction of a man's wage, and "the jobs available to these [widowed] women . . . were notoriously poorly paid." Hence, they could not live on their earnings alone. Widows' names "predominate" on charity rolls, and "they often sent their children off to charitable institutions, or to fend for themselves.". . . Whether they lived from charity and poor relief or struggled to keep alive a farmstead or shop, women who exercised independence and commanded authority generally did so in the face of numerous and formidable obstacles.

In addition to these problems related to dependence and insecurity, elderly women in both positions suffered from some common complaints. First of all was sexual frustration. By the seventeenth century opportunities for remarriage were rare. Sexual urges in the postmenopausal were "condemned as both disgusting and unhealthy" by "universal agreement." While people in the upper strata of society enjoyed some latitude, in general, "the aged were to refrain from sexual competition . . . Lust in the elderly was an infallible occasion for ridicule and censure." These legal and cultural barriers definitely hindered sexual activity, but they could not eliminate the desire for it. According to modern studies of sexuality, menopause tends to heighten rather than depress women's sexuality. "There is no time limit drawn by the advancing years to female sexuality," and, freed from the psychic burden of fertility, women "frequently manifest increased levels of sexual activity." Strong sexuality in women obsessed many of the proponents of witch-hunting. . . . Barred from remarriage and discouraged from promiscuity, elderly women were frustrated at exactly the point in life when sex lost its responsibility. Cultural norms inhibited recognition of these bodily desires and hindered their fulfillment, but elementary psychology suggests that they could not eliminate them. The net result was probably similar to the predicament of modern elderly women who, "deprived of normal sexual outlets . . . exhaust themselves . . . in conscious or unconscious effort to dissipate their accumulated . . . sexual tensions.". . .

All of these negative developments were exacerbated by the demographic and economic trends of the sixteenth and seventeenth centuries. During the second half of the sixteenth century, when the trials became widespread, real wages were falling, the land was filling up, and food prices were soaring. The trials peaked in the first half of the next century, when the European economy stagnated and in many places declined. In the second half of the seventeenth century and into the eighteenth, the economy recovered and the prosecutions of elderly women for witchcraft tapered off.

Early modern elderly women clearly felt a variety of pressures which made increased levels of irritability, hostility and aggression understandable. Most were completely subordinate to males, and many had lost even their limited authority within the domestic sphere to younger women. Those who enjoyed independence lost as much as they gained, for its price was generally economic insecurity, legal weakness, and social marginality. And for most elderly women, limitations on remarriage and sanctions against sex frustrated their normal sexuality, while the subordination of local communities to centralized bureaucracies undermined the social value of their memories and judgment.

But we cannot understand the roots of witchlike behavior simply by listing the pressures on elderly women. Elderly women today suffer from many similar problems—limited opportunities for sex, lack of a challenging social role, and economic insecurity—but the most widely-noted problem among them is depression, not aggression. We need also to understand the attractions of witchcraft; why some early modern elderly women accepted and even cultivated socially disapproved attitudes and behavior patterns.

The basic attraction of witchlike behaviors was that they worked. While its intellectual foundations may have been faulty and some of its practices ineffectual, witchcraft could endow an elderly woman (or anyone) with considerable power in a village setting. A witch's armory contained numerous natural weapons whose effectiveness has never been in doubt, although their significance has generally been slighted. Poison, arson, and the aphrodisiac and anti-aphrodisiac qualities of tastes and smells could obviously be used to inflict harm or influence behavior. Furthermore, because belief in curses was so widely shared, "the formal imprecation could be a power weapon . . . it could strike terror into the hearts of the credulous and the guilty." This terror was not inconsequential, for the fear and anxiety curses and other magical attacks caused could, in fact, create or contribute to real maladies. "Many observers have noticed how the inhabitants of modern primitive societies can afflict their enemies with aches and pains, vomiting and insomnia, by sheer suggestion; and the dramatic even fatal, effect of the voodoo curse . . . is well authenticated." Such ailments did not just threaten "the credulous and the guilty," for all people are vulnerable to the connection between the psychic and somatic dimensions of health. According to "most investigators and clinicians . . . psychosocial factors influence the onset and course of all illnesses." Psychosomatic problems not only make people think they are sick, they make them sick, sometimes alone and often in combination with other agents. A poor elderly woman in a closely knit peasant community had good reason to manifest behaviors and attitudes geared to intimidate and punish through interpersonal pressure. A reputation as a witch no doubt added to resentment of her already burdensome existence, but in many cases it was the only alternative to passive acceptance of a miserable fate.

For elderly people to actively enforce respect and obedience was hardly unusual. In primitive societies "their security has been more often an achievement than an endowment," an achievement gained less through "the manipulation of things" than "the adjustment to and manipulation of people." Anthropologists have long been aware that "in virtually all preliterate societies aged persons . . . especially women . . . derive considerable advantage from the practice of magic." Recent historical studies of the early modern period have shown that "if . . . the elderly retained authority, it was because of the material resources at their disposal," and the present study suggests that these material "levers of power" could be supplemented or replaced by magical ones. Beset by numerous socioeconomic problems and hampered by equally numerous sociocultural restrictions, many elderly women had to rely heavily on their traditional source of influence: "force of personality and knowledge of human nature." If they found it necessary to prolong and even intensify the unpleasant attributes we associate with the menopause and climacteric, this was the price they had to pay for the increased respect and obedience they could command. Considering the pressures of their situation, it was a reasonable bargain. At least, until the magistrates arrived.

Our Disney image of the witch as an old woman reflects historical reality. It continues a tradition found among many primitive peoples, and in European culture as well, that particularly associates old women and witchcraft. Independent of the demonologists' theories, early modern Europeans suspected and tried older women more often than any other comparable group in society. The demonologists' opponents, convinced that the fears were distorted and exaggerated, emphasized age as well as sex and class to belittle the beliefs behind the persecutions. Long unheeded, their arguments eventually won the day, transformed diabolism into *dementia*, a moral problem into a medical one, and the trials came to an end. . . .

In an atmosphere pervaded by hardship and fear, people were all too ready to find scapegoats onto whom they could project their anger and hostility. Some old women, burdensome and vulnerable, defiantly or compliantly adopted the very attitudes and behaviors for which they were vilified, and hallucinated the fantastic experiences concocted by their enemies. Through repetition and torture, suspicions and accusations proliferated until the stereotype of the eccentric old woman broke down, accusations against magistrates and their relatives became frequent, and the elite came to its senses and abandoned the witch ideology.

Consideration of the psychology of old age as well as the sociocultural situation of elderly women in early modern Europe suggests that the rationalist tradition, while it has added much to our knowledge of the witchcraft persecutions, has neglected the role of the suspected witches in witch beliefs. The elite's fear of a diabolic conspiracy does seem to have combined misunderstandings of group magic, drug experiences, schizophrenic delusions, and its own metaphorical conception of sin and guilt. But fears of *maleficium*, the heart of village suspicions, reflected the real patterns of behavior which expressed real needs and could have real results. Some women really acted like witches, really hurt other people, and really came to accept that in so doing they were performing the Devil's work. Either totally subordinate to men or precariously independent, women, especially as they reached old age, found themselves beset by socioeconomic problems and frustrated by sociocultural restrictions. At an age when irritable and other socially disruptive behaviors are likely to emerge anyway, some elderly women accepted and even cultivated them in order to enforce respect and obedience.

The demonologists, of course, blew the problem posed by these women all out of proportion, for their work was part of an ambitious program to systemize Christian morality and impose it on society. . . . The witch trials, like the Stalinist purges, were an attempt at sociodemographic engineering. The middle-aged and elderly male elites were determined to eradicate the truly wicked people and educate the rest, to remold human nature in the image of God's word and according to His desires. Many villagers and townspeople were willing to collaborate in order to rid themselves of their burdensome and threatening neighbors. Elderly women naturally bore the brunt of this effort, for they depended most on "'neighborly' highly integrated and mutually interdependent village society," and were therefore its most aggressive defenders.

One final point deserves consideration before we close, one which has only recently begun to receive the attention it deserves. What were the effects of the witch hunts, particularly on their principal victims, elderly women? Most older accounts ended on a note of relieved discontinuity, implying that for all their horror and violence, the main result of the trials was to discredit magical beliefs by taking them to their extreme. More recent historians have linked the witch trials to the sociocultural transition to the modern world; by permitting communal obligations to be repudiated, accusations resolved "fundamental questions as to the nature and structure of the social order . . . on the side of individual freedom." Individualism, especially individual accumulation of wealth, was insured, and care of the poor and elderly had to be restructured to reflect this new irresponsibility.

These were certainly important effects of the trials, but were they the only ones? What of the hundreds of thousands of elderly women who were suspected, accused, investigated, tortured, and burned? Were the ones who survived changed? We cannot answer this question with any certainty, but we can suggest a hypothesis. . . . The trials were not simply a means of control, an attempt to "contain" diabolism. Instead, they represented an attempt to restructure European social demography and transform popular culture, to "roll back" the Devil's dominion. Every student of subsequent European history knows that they failed to eradicate the truly wicked people and reform the rest, but short of that goal, they may well have had an important impact. During the late Middle Ages, women were characterized as bawdy, aggressive, and domineering. In extreme form, these were the attributes ascribed to witches. By the nineteenth century, the stereotype of women had changed completely. They were expected to be asexual, passive, and submissive. How accurately these images reflected social and psychological reality is not known, but they suggest a dramatic shift in attitudes and behavior. Certainly there were many forces during the intervening centuries contributing to the changing status of women in Western society, but the witch hunts, protracted, brutal, and pervasive, would seem to have been a primary cause.

Religion and the Decline of Magic

KEITH THOMAS

The first clear signs of society's changing mentality are found in the seventeenth century, and they antedate clear structural change such as the new technology involved in the industrial revolution. The scientific revolution, along with the political and economic attitudes that accompanied it, has long been seen as a key development in intellectual history. Keith Thomas here argues that it decisively changed the framework for popular outlook as well. The following excerpt briefly outlines the nature and function of traditional superstition, indicates the means by which it began to be superseded, and raises the important question of why the massive change in culture occurred.

The selection also suggests two other issues. The new mentality developed at the top of society, among intellectuals and their immediate audience. How far did it penetrate? It is not possible to go too simply from the new science to new business forms or agricultural techniques, for the people responsible for the latter were not directly exposed to the cutting edge of science. Modernization has long been seen as splitting society, leaving many people with a traditional set of beliefs and others, the more powerful, with a new, activist outlook. How many people remained traditionalists, and why? And what happened to them as structural modernization (economic and political change, most obviously) took hold? This leads to the second issue: How thoroughly has modernization altered traditional belief even today? Is society still divided between modern and unmodern people? Do we all harbor a magical approach to nature and society that is now usually clad in the guise of science?

England was the first society to industrialize. Thomas suggests a basic cause was a prior modernization of belief systems. Countries able to copy England's industrialization might not have the same popular mentality with which to work. In other words, questions on the extent of modernization of attitudes, difficult to answer for England, are even more difficult to answer for other European countries. Even for England, Thomas suggests, the key problem is one of assessing the extent of change, particularly since there was such a long period in which a new mentality was not accompanied by a new control of the environment. What could impel human beings to put themselves through this transition? In the final analysis, perhaps traditional kinds of faith were applied to new objects; and perhaps we have, or need, some of this faith still.

What the scientific revolution did was to supersede the traditional type of reasoning and to buttress up the old rationalist attitude with a more stable intellectual foundation, based on the mechanical philosophy. It did not matter that the majority of the population of eighteenth-century England had possibly never heard of Boyle or Newton and certainly could not have explained the nature of their discoveries. At all times most men accept their basic assumptions on the authority of others. New techniques and attitudes are always more readily diffused than their underlying scientific rationale. "The average man of today," wrote the psychoanalyst, Ernest Jones, "does not hesitate to reject the same evidence of witchcraft that was so convincing to the man of three centuries ago, though he usually knows no more about the true explanation than the latter did." Most of those millions of persons who today would laugh at the idea of magic or miracles would have difficulty in explaining why. They are victims of society's constant pressure towards intellectual conformity. Under this pressure the magician has ceased to command respect, and intellectual prestige has shifted elsewhere.

It is thus possible to argue that these primitive beliefs declined because they had come to be seen as intellectually unsatisfactory. But it must be confessed that the full details of this process of disillusion are by no means clear. One cannot simply attribute the change to the scientific revolution. There were too many "rationalists" before, too many believers afterwards, for so simple an explanation to be plausible. Let us therefore examine the question from a different point of view. Instead of concentrating on the intellectual status of these beliefs let us consider them in their social context. . . .

The most important cause of man's recourse to magic is his lack of the necessay empirical or technical knowledge to deal with the problems which confront him. "Magic is dominant when control of the environment is weak." When the appropriate techniques become available, magic grows superfluous and withers away. Only in the case of those problems to which men still have no adequate solution does it retain its appeal. It is science and technology which make magic redundant; the stronger man's control of his environment, the less his recourse to magical remedies.

This explanation does not of course make clear why magical rituals should take one form rather than another, for it leaves aside the origin of the mental ingredients which go to make up individual magical fantasies and beliefs. But it does offer an explanation of why magic is invoked at one time rather than another. When applied to the facts of sixteenth- and seventeenth-century society, it makes a good deal of initial sense. The purposes for which most men had recourse to charms or cunning men were precisely those for which an adequate alternative technique was lack-

From Keith Thomas, *Religion and the Decline of Magic* (New York: Charles Scribner's Sons, 1971), pp. 646–68.

ing. Thus in agriculture the farmer normally relied upon his own skills; there are no magical charms extant for such automatic tasks as reaping corn or milking cows. But when he was dependent on circumstances outside his control—the fertility of the soil, the weather, the health of his animals—he was more likely to accompany his labours with some magical precaution. There were all the traditional fertility rites and seasonal observances: Plough Monday to ensure the growth of corn; wassailing to bless the apple trees; Rogation processions and Midsummer fires for the crops; corn dollies at harvest time. In Colchester in 1532 a smith's wife was said to practise magic "to make folks believe they should have a sely [lucky] plough." In the absence of weed-killers, there were charms to keep weeds out of the corn, and, in place of insecticide and rat-killers, magical formulae to keep away pests. There were also charms to increase the land's fertility.

Similar precautions surrounded other potentially uncertain operations. Care was taken to time such tasks as sowing corn or cutting trees to harmonise with the phases of the moon or some other propitious factor. There were divinatory systems for ascertaining the weather or the future price of corn. There were charms to make horses work harder, to protect cows from witchcraft, to procure healthy stock, and even to influence the sex of future calves. Bee-keeping and chicken-raising had their semi-magical precautions. So did the making of bread, beer, yeast and butter—spheres in which witchcraft was particularly feared. Ritual precautions surrounded other household operations: no menstruating woman, for example, could ever pickle beef or salt bacon. Similar prescriptions related to hunting and fishing, both speculative activities; in the fishing trade the fear of witchcraft lingered until the nineteenth century. There was also magic designed to counter human deficiencies, moral and physical: charms to prevent the crops being robbed, herbs to allay weariness at the plough, devices like spitting on one's hands to give renewed energy for work.

In many other occupations magical aids were also invoked when problems were too great to be solved by human skill. The dangers of seafaring made sailors notoriously superstitious and generated a large number of ritual precautions designed to secure favourable weather and the safety of the ship. The risks of military adventure encouraged the use of amulets and protective talismans of many kinds. The deficiencies of contemporary medicine drove the sick into the hands of the cunning men and wise women. The slowness of communications and the lack of a police force fostered dependence upon village wizards for the recovery of stolen goods and missing persons. Ignorance of the future encouraged men to grasp at omens or to practise divination as a basis for making decisions. All such devices can be seen as attempts to counter human helplessness in the face of the physical and social environment.

Correspondingly, the decline of magic coincided with a marked improvement in the extent to which this environment became amenable to control. In several important respects the material conditions of life took a turn for the better during the later seventeenth century. The pressure of population, which had caused much hardship during the previous hundred years, now slackened off. Agricultural improvement brought an increase in food production; in the later seventeenth century the country became virtually self-sufficient in corn, while increased imports were used to keep down prices at times of dearth. The growth of overseas trade and the rise of new industries created a more diversified economic environment. There was no major plague epidemic after 1665 and in the 1670s the disease disappeared from England altogether. By 1700 Englishmen enjoyed a higher level of material welfare than the inhabitants of any other country in the world, save Holland. General circumstances of this kind must have done something to increase human self-confidence. Moreover several further developments may have borne a particular responsibility for the declining appeal of the magical solution.

The first of these was a general improvement in communications. Printed news-sheets began in the early seventeenth century, proliferated during the Interregnum and, though checked until 1695 by the licensing laws, had become an indispensable feature of London life by the end of the century. Thereafter they spread to the provinces. Between 1701 and 1760 a hundred and thirty provincial newspapers had made at least a temporary appearance, and they emanated from no fewer than fifty-five different towns. A penny post was introduced in London in 1680 and the letter-carrying service greatly improved thereafter. These developments were accompanied by an increase in popular literacy which may have reached a peak in the third quarter of the seventeenth century, when nearly forty per cent of the adult male population may have been able to read. Changes in the mobility of the population are harder to measure, but it is clear that even in Tudor England the village population was never constant. In the later seventeenth century mobility may have increased with the growth of new industries and the constant movement in and out of London. The general effect of all these trends was to keep the provinces more closely in touch with the metropolis, to break down local isolation and to disseminate sophisticated opinion.

Also important were the advertisements which the newspapers had begun to carry. Notices about lost property and missing persons were a feature of the Commonwealth news-sheets and continued thereafter. Lost dogs, stolen horses, runaway apprentices, suspected thieves—all could now be notified to a wider public than the village wizard or town crier had ever been able to command. In 1657 a projector announced the foundation of an Office of Public Advice with eight branches in the London area to deal with inquiries about lost goods and a weekly bulletin of runaway servants and apprentices. From May to September of that year the sixteen-page *Publick Adviser* was devoted to weekly advertisements of this kind; and it had a rival in *The Weekly Information from the Office of Intelligence*, which appeared in July and was also made up of advertisements. There were many later attempts at developing such advertising agencies. For the urban middle classes the coffee-house or newspaper office had become the obvious place to which to refer problems about lost goods. The need for the cunning man was accordingly reduced.

Meanwhile certain devices were introduced to lessen the incidence of human misfortune. Greater security for men of property was provided by the rise of deposit banking, but nothing yields greater testimony to the new spirit of self-help than the growth of insurance at the end of the seventeenth century. Of course, schemes designed to cushion sufferers from theft, fire, sickness or other disasters were not without precedent. Many of the gilds of medieval England had operated as friendly societies, taking common responsibility for the cost of burying their members or recompensing their losses by fire. Manorial customs of inheritance often provided for the maintenance of the elderly. But the gilds had disappeared and manorial customs were being eroded. For most inhabitants of late Tudor and Stuart England fire, flood, or the sudden death of a close relative could mean total disaster.

Steps to provide artificial security against such hazards were first taken by merchants and shipowners. Marine insurance developed in fourteenth-century Italy and had taken root in England by the mid-sixteenth century. In 1574 indeed the notaries were claiming to have registered policies "time out of mind." But for a long time the system remained rudimentary. Underwriting was done by individuals rather than companies and most traders only thought about insuring their goods when the ship was already overdue. The insurance of ships as well as the goods they carried did not become common until the reign of William III. The law relating to the arbitration of insurance disputes also remained unsatisfactory. In such circumstances many merchants preferred to lighten their risks by dividing ownership of the ship and its goods between a number of different individuals. All these uncertainties were reflected in the numerous insurance problems which were brought to astrologers like William Lilly. But in the early eighteenth century the situation changed, with the development of Lloyds coffee-house as a regular meeting-place for underwriters and the foundation in 1720 of two substantial joint-stock companies devoted to marine insurance, the London Assurance and the Royal Exchange. . . .

Contemporaries thus gradually grew less vulnerable to certain kinds of disaster. They also developed new kinds of knowledge to supersede mystical explanations of misfortune in terms of witches, ghosts or divine providence. Here the social sciences were as important as the natural ones. Embryonic economics and sociology had developed considerably during the period. By the end of the seventeenth century, it was commonplace for intellectuals to reveal their awareness of the extent to which economic and social hardships could be attributed to impersonal causes, and of the way in which education and social institutions could explain the differences between different peoples and different social classes. This was to be one of the main themes of the Enlightenment. The explanatory aspirations of astrological inquiry were taken over by these new disciplines. They rejected the notion that social phenomena were purely random; every event, they held, had a cause, even if it was still hidden. This was why Bacon listed Fortune as a non-existent entity. It was to be replaced by new historical laws. "No government is of so accidental or arbitrary an institution as people are wont to imagine," thought James Harrington, "there being in societies natural causes producing their necessary effects as well as in the earth or the air." The immediacy of the doctrine of divine providence was inevitably much reduced by this assumption that God had bound himself to work through sociological causes as well as physical ones. Witch-beliefs, by contrast, were less affected at first, for they were concerned to explain individual misfortunes, whereas the aim of the social sciences was to account for social developments as a whole. But in the long run psychology and sociology were to supersede the idea of witchcraft by providing a new way in which the victim could blame others for his fate. Instead of accusing witches, he could attribute his misfortunes to the way in which his parents had brought him up, or to the social system into which he had been born.

A further development undermining more primitive explanations of misfortune was the growing awareness, particularly among mathematicians, of the way in which even chance and misfortune were subject to statistical laws and thus capable, up to a point, of being rationally predicted. The formulation of theories of probability was the work of a long series of European mathematicians—Cardan, Fermat, Huygens, Pascal, the Bernouillis and de Moivre. But Englishmen made a distinctive contribution through the empirical study of mortality tables by Graunt, Petty and Halley; and the Royal Society showed considerable interest in the subject. In the last decade of the seventeenth century probability theory was widely discussed in English scientific circles. It was also in the later seventeenth century that the word "coincidence," in the sense of the juxtaposition of causally unrelated events, first appeared. In 1692 John Arbuthnot made the new theories available to a wider public in a translation of Huygens's treatise on gaming odds. A chance event, he declared in the preface, was merely one whose causes were not known; but it was possible to calculate the probability of its taking one form rather than another, even when human beings were involved. For what was politics, but "a kind of analysis of the quantity of probability in casual events"? There were, thought Arbuthnot, very few topics incapable of being reduced to mathematical reckoning.

It was this nascent statistical sense, or awareness of patterns in apparently random behaviour, which was to supersede much previous speculation about the causes of good or bad fortune. Today it is even possible to predict the likely number of fatal accidents or crimes of violence in the coming year. We take steps to hedge ourselves against misfortunes, but if they happen to us we do not feel the need to seek mystical causes for their occurrence. No doubt few of us today are capable of stoical acceptance of the random caprices of misfortune, but it is the awareness that they are indeed random which distinguishes us from our ancestors.

The decline of magic was thus accompanied by the growth of the natural and social sciences, which helped men to understand their environment, and of a variety of technical aids—from insurance to fire-fighting—by which they were able to increase their control of it. Yet the more closely Malinowski's picture of magic giving way before technology is examined, the less convincing does it appear. For the correspondence between magic and social needs had never been more than approximate. It is true that magic was seldom invoked when a technical solution was available. But the corollary was not true: the absence of a technical remedy was not of itself sufficient to generate a magical one. For magic was conservative in subject-matter, as well as in its techniques. The village wizards of our period had little in their repertoire to distinguish them from their medieval or possibly even their Anglo-Saxon predecessors. Their remedies were traditional and so were the problems for which they catered. The astrologers similarly offered answers to questions which had originally been drawn up by Arabs, living in a different social environment. English magic, in other words, did not automatically expand to fill all new technological gaps, in the way Malinowski suggested. Society's magical resources were the result of its cultural inheritance, as much as of its current problems. Magic has always had to come from somewhere. In Tudor and Stuart England it came from the medieval and classical past, and it was slow to adapt itself to new situations.

This brings us to the essential problem. Why was it that magic did not keep pace with changing social circumstances? Why did its sphere become more limited, even as the English economy was expanding into new domains? For the paradox is that in England magic lost its appeal before the appropriate technical solutions had been devised to take its place. It was the abandonment of magic which made possible the upsurge of technology, not the other way round. Indeed, as Max Weber stressed, magic was potentially "one of the most serious obstructions to the rationalisation of economic life." The technological primacy of Western civilisation, it can be argued, owes a sizable debt to the fact that in Europe recourse to magic was to prove less ineradicable than in other parts of the world. For this, intellectual and religious factors have been held primarily responsible. The rationalist tradition of classical antiquity blended with the Christian doctrine of a single all-directing Providence to produce what Weber called "the disenchantment of the world"—the conception of an orderly and rational universe, in which effect follows cause in predictable manner. A religious belief in order was a necessary prior assumption upon which the subsequent work of the natural scientists was to be founded. It was a favourable mental environment which made possible the triumph of technology.

There is inevitably a chicken-and-the-egg character to any debate as to whether economic growth produces its appropriate mental character or is produced by it. Most sociologically-minded historians are naturally biased in favour of the view that changes in beliefs are preceded by changes in social and economic structure. But so far as magic and technology are concerned, it seems indisputable that in England the former was on the wane before the latter was ready to take its place. The fourteenth-century Lollards who renounced the Church's supernatural protection against disease and infertility had no effective alternative to put in its place. Their doctrines gave them spiritual security, but no new means of material aid. Neither did the Reformation coincide with any technological revolution: the men of the sixteenth century were more or less as vulnerable in face of epidemics, bad harvests, illness, fire, and all the other environmental hazards as their medieval predecessors. Yet many were able to discard the apparatus of the Church without devising a new magic in its place.

In the later seventeenth century the more general rejection of magic was still unaccompanied by the discovery of new remedies to fill the gap. It is often said that witch-beliefs are a consequence of inadequate medical technique. But in England such beliefs declined before medical therapy had made much of an advance. It is true that the seventeenth century witnessed notable contributions to the study of physiology, anatomy and botany. No history of medicine can omit mention of the work of Harvey on the circulation of the blood, of Glisson on rickets, Willis on the nervous system, and Sydenham on epidemics. The invention of the microscope enabled Robert Hooke to pioneer the study of the cell and paved the way for the eventual discovery of bacteria and the formulation of the germ theory of disease. Robert Boyle's chemical inquiries destroyed the whole basis of old humoral physiology.

But so far as actual therapy was concerned, progress was negligible. Harvey's great discovery had no immediate practical consequences. "It seemed to illustrate the theory of medicine," declared a contemporary, "yet it made no improvement in the practice thereof." The sad truth, wrote another, was that although physicians had laboured mightily in chemistry and anatomy, they had added almost nothing to the diagnosis of disease (and, we might add, even less to its cure). "It was necessary to obtain clear concepts of the action of the body in health," explains a modern historian of medicine, "before venturing into discussion of its action in disease." Indeed it has recently been argued that, with the exception of smallpox inoculation, introduced in the eighteenth century, medical innovatons did little to increase the expectation of life until at least the nineteenth century, and made no substantial contribution, sanitary reform apart, until the second quarter of the twentieth. This may be unduly pessimistic. But it seems clear that the expectation of life at birth was *lower* in the late seventeenth century than it had been in the reign of Elizabeth I; it did not regain its mid-Tudor level until the late eighteenth century.

The difference between the eighteenth and sixteenth centuries lies not in achievement but in aspiration. For the intervening period had seen the beginning of positive efforts to improve the level of medical therapy. The Paracelsians introduced new mineral remedies. Bacon wanted a systematic drive to raise the expectation of life and improve therapeutic medicine. Sydenham pioneered epidemiology, looking forward to the time "when the world, valuing learning for that only therein which is necessary for the good of human life, shall think as well of him that taught to cure diseases as those that taught to discourse learnedly about them." Growing overseas trade with the East made possible a new pharmacology; the volume of drugs imported by the end of the seventeenth century was at least twenty-five times what it had been at the beginning. Only a few of these, such as quinine for malaria and guiacum for syphilis, were to gain a permanent place in the medical pharmacopoeia, but their introduction reflected a significant urge to experiment. The eighteenth century saw the founding of nearly fifty new hospitals. Whether these institutions did more to spread disease than to cure it is debatable. But, whatever their merits, they helped to displace the amateur, the empiric and the wise woman. They also reflected a new practical, optimistic attitude. . . .

We are, therefore, forced to the conclusion that men emancipated themselves from these magical beliefs without necessarily having devised any effective technology with which to replace them. In the seventeenth century they were able to take this step because magic was ceasing to be intellectually acceptable, and because their religion taught them to try self-help before invoking supernatural aid. But the ultimate origins of this faith in unaided human capacity remain mysterious. We do not know how the Lollards were able to find the self-reliance necessary to make the break with the Church magic of the past. The most plausible explanation seems to be that their spirit of sturdy self-help reflected that of their occupations. Few of these early heretics were simple agriculturists dependent on the uncontrollable forces of nature. In the fifteenth century most of them were artisans—carpenters, blacksmiths, cobblers, and, above all, textile-workers. They spoke of religion in practical terms, rejecting the miracle of the Mass, because "God made man and not man God, as the carpenter doth make the house, and not the house the carpenter"; or asserting that "Ball the carpenter or Pike the mason could make as good images as those which were worshipped." Their trades made them aware that success or failure depended upon their unaided efforts, and they despised the substitute consolations of magic. . . .

It is therefore possible to connect the decline of the old magical beliefs with the growth of urban living, the rise of science, and the spread of an ideology of self-help. But the connection is only approximate and a more precise sociological genealogy cannot at present be constructed. Too many of the participants in the story remain hidden from view and the representative status of those who are visible is too uncertain. The only identifiable social group which was consistently in the van of the campaign against certain types of magic is the clergy, but their attitude to supernatural claims in general was highly ambivalent. It does not seem possible to say whether the growing "rationalism" of natural theology was a spontaneous theological development or a mere response to the pressures of natural science. It would make sense, no doubt, if one could prove that it was the urban middle classes, the shopkeepers and artisans, who took the lead in abandoning the old beliefs, but at present there seems no way of doing so. An equally convincing claim could be made for the Arminian clergy of the early seventeenth century or the aristocratic sceptics of the Restoration period.

What can, however, be clearly seen is that by the mid-seventeenth century the new intellectual developments had greatly deepened the gulf between the educated class and the lower strata of the rural population. Of course, evidence of the disdain felt by intellectuals for popular "superstition" can be found from classical times. But in the seventeenth century the gulf was emphasised by the appearance of well-born collectors of popular folklore, like Sir Thomas Browne in his *Vulgar Errors* or John Aubrey in his *Remaines of Gentilisme and Judaisme*, for despite their tolerance towards the old ways such men were acutely conscious of belonging to a different mental world. Aubrey himself was convinced that it was during the Civil War period that old beliefs had lost their vitality. But there is plenty of evidence to suggest that in rural areas there was still much life left in these ways of thought. "Notwithstanding the great advances in learning and knowledge which have been made within the last two centuries," declared a preacher in 1795, "lamentable experience but too clearly proves how extremely deep these notions are still engraven upon the minds of thousands." Nineteenth-century students of popular folklore discovered everywhere that the inhabitants of rural England had not abandoned their faith in healing wells, divination, cunning folk, witch-craft, omens or ghosts. "Those who are not in daily intercourse with the peasantry," it was reported from Lincolnshire in 1856, "can hardly be made to believe or comprehend the hold that charms, witchcraft, wise men and other like relics of heathendom have upon the people."

Nor had popular religion necessarily changed either. The religion of the nineteenth century, said Jacob Burckhardt, was "rationalism for the few and magic for the many." The belief in "judgments" was frequently upheld by influential clergymen, while many persons who incurred misfor-tune continued to ask what they had done to "deserve" it. The convic-tion that religion "worked" and that prayer got results sustained innumer-able people in adversity. Every kind of religious enthusiasm—mystical healing, millenarian prophecy, messianic preaching—made its periodic return, and not only at a working-class level. Many of the nineteenth-century middle classes were interested in spiritualism and automatic writ-ing, astrology, haunted houses and all the paraphernalia of the occult. Even the fear of witchcraft, that is of occult damage as a result of another's malignity, was revived in Mary Baker Eddy's concept of "mali-cious animal magnetism." Today astrologers and fortune-tellers continue to be patronised by those for whom psychiatrists and psycho-analysts have not provided a satisfactory substitute. The presence of horoscopes in the newspapers and of lucky mascots in cars is consistent with a recent investigator's conclusion that "about a quarter of the population . . . holds a view of the universe which can most properly be designated as magical." This is a much smaller figure than any which could ever be produced for the seventeenth century, were such analysis possible, but it is not a trivial one.

Indeed the role of magic in modern society may be more extensive than we yet appreciate. There is a tautological character about Malinowski's argument that magic occupies the vacuum left by science, for what is not recognised by any particular observer as a true "science" is deemed "magic" and vice versa. If magical acts are ineffective rituals employed as an alternative to sheer helplessness in the face of events, then how are we to classify the status of "scientific" remedies, in which we place faith, but which are subsequently exposed as useless? This was the fate of Galenic medicine, which in the sixteenth century was the main rival to folk-healing. But it will also be that of much of the medicine of today. Sociologists have observed that contemporary doctors and surgeons engage in many ritual practices of a non-operative kind. Modern medicine shares an optimistic bias with the charmers and wise women and it has similar means of explaining away any failure. In many other spheres of modern life we also put our trust in activities designed to "work" (for example, in diplomatic conferences as a means of avoiding war), when all the evidence, if we wished to consider it, suggests that they do not.

Anthropologists today are unsympathetic to the view that magic is simply bad science. They stress its symbolic and expressive role rather than its practical one.

They would therefore maintain that the wizard's conjurations or the wise woman's charms were not really comparable with pseudo-science. In so far as the two activities had a different pedigree and a different intellectual status this is obviously true. But all the evidence of the sixteenth and seventeenth centuries suggests that the common people never formulated a distinction between magic and science, certainly not between magic and medicine. "We go to the physician for counsel," argued contemporaries, "we take his recipe, but we know not what it meaneth; yet we use it, and find benefit. If this be lawful, why may we not as well take benefit by the wise man, whose courses we be ignorant of?" The modern working-class woman who remarks that she doesn't "believe" in doctors is acknowledging the fact that the patient still brings with him an essentially uninformed allegiance. Usually he knows no more of the underlying rationale for his treatment than did the client of the cunning man. In such circumstances it is hard to say where "science" stops and "magic" begins.

What is certain about the various beliefs discussed in this book is that today they have either disappeared or at least greatly decayed in prestige. This is why they are easier to isolate and to analyse. But it does not mean that they are intrinsically less worthy of respect than some of those which we ourselves continue to hold. If magic is to be defined as the employment of ineffective techniques to allay anxiety when effective ones are not available, then we must recognise that no society will ever be free from it.

The World We Have Lost

PETER LASLETT

In the following selection the author seeks to define the essential characteristics of preindustrial society, which he regards as sharply differentiated from its
modern counterpart. He shows us a carefully controlled social environment,
dominated by small units of organization in which affectionate ties prevail. The
family is obviously crucial, and although the author notes the tensions that family
life can create, he is preoccupied with the family's success as an emotional as well
as economic unit. The essence of modernization, correspondingly, is a change in
the family, and presumably a weakening of ties. Factories have replaced families
as units of production. The author does not spell out the relationship, if any,
between the rise of factories and changes in family structure, but he has no doubt
that industrialization has severely altered what the family can offer modern people.

This is an intelligently nostalgic picture. The author admits the importance
of material limitations, even outright misery, and acknowledges such vital aspects
of preindustrial life as high mortality rates. But in terms of human relationships it
is clear that the author thinks the modern world has lost a great deal. The picture
of preindustrial life he paints is one of stability and close personal ties. There can
be little doubt, if this picture is accurate, that most people's lives were profoundly
disrupted as they entered modern society—or rather, as they were forced into it,
since there is no clear motive in this preindustrial society spontaneously to seek
change. Note that the author judges preindustrial society to be rather homogeneous in its basic values. Important class differences existed, but they did not inter-
fere with a common devotion to religion and a patriarchal family structure.

Laslett's views regarding the quality of preindustrial life and the causes and
impact of change should be compared with the previous selections on the peasantry, which among other things deal with the less stable decades of the late sixteenth century, in contrast to Laslett's late seventeenth-century focus. Laslett
insists on the integrity and adequacy of traditional values. What then would cause
change? And how could people tolerate the advent of modernity? It would be
easy to go from Laslett to a view that modern life is hopelessly disruptive, if the
strengths of premodern society were as great as this selection suggests.

In the year 1619 the bakers of London applied to the authorities for an increase in the price of bread. They sent in support of their claims a complete description of a bakery and an account of its weekly costs. There were thirteen or fourteen people in such an establishment: the baker and his wife, four paid employees who were called journeymen, two apprentices, two maid-servants and the three or four children of the master baker himself. Six pounds ten shillings a week was reckoned to be the outgoings of this establishment of which only eleven shillings and eight-pence went for wages: half a crown a week for each of the journeymen and tenpence for each of the maids. Far and away the greatest cost was for food: two pounds nine shillings out of the six pounds ten shillings, at five shillings a head for the baker and his wife, four shillings a head for their helpers and two shillings for their children. It cost much more in food to keep a journeyman than it cost in money; four times as much to keep a maid. Clothing was charged up too, not only for the man, wife and children, but for the apprentices as well. Even school fees were claimed as a justifiable charge on the price of bread for sale, and it cost sixpence a week for the teaching and clothing of a baker's child.

A London bakery was undoubtedly what we should call a commercial or even an industrial undertaking, turning out loaves by the thousand. Yet the business was carried on in the house of the baker himself. There was probably a *shop* as part of the house, *shop* as in work*shop* and not as meaning a retail establishment. Loaves were not ordinarily sold over the counter: they had to be carried to the open-air market and displayed on stalls. There was a garner behind the house, for which the baker paid two shillings a week in rent, and where he kept his wheat, his *sea-coal* for the fire and his store of salt. The house itself was one of those high, half-timbered overhanging structures on the narrow London street which we always think of when we remember the scene in which Shakespeare, Pepys or even Christopher Wren lived. Most of it was taken up with the living-quarters of the dozen people who worked there.

It is obvious that all these people ate in the house since the cost of their food helped to determine the production cost of the bread. Except for the journeymen they were all obliged to sleep in the house at night and live together as a family.

The only word used at that time to describe such a group of people was "family." The man at the head of the group, the entrepreneur, the employer, or the manager, was then known as the master or head of the family. He was father to some of its members and in place of father to the rest. There was no sharp distinction between his domestic and his

From Peter Laslett, *The World We Have Lost* (New York: Charles Scribner's Sons, 1965), pp. 1–5, 7–9, 11–13, 17–18, 21, 69–72.

economic functions. His wife was both his partner and his subordinate, a partner because she ran the family, took charge of the food and managed the women-servants, a subordinate because she was woman and wife, mother and in place of mother to the rest.

The paid servants of both sexes had their specified and familiar position in the family, as much part of it as the children but not quite in the same position. At that time the family was not one society only but three societies fused together: the society of man and wife, of parents and children and of master and servant. But when they were young, and servants were, for the most part, young, unmarried people, they were very close to children in their status and their function. Here is the agreement made between the parents of a boy about to become an apprentice and his future master. The boy covenants to dwell as an apprentice with his master for seven years, to keep his secrets and to obey his commandments.

> Taverns and alehouses he shall not haunt, dice, cards or any other unlawful games he shall not use, fornication with any woman he shall not commit, matrimony with any woman he shall not contract. He shall not absent himself by night or by day without his master's leave but be a true and faithful servant.

On his side, the master undertakes to teach his apprentice his "art, science or occupation with moderate correction."

> Finding and allowing unto his said servant meat, drink, apparel, washing, lodging and all other things during the said term of seven years, and to give unto his said apprentice at the end of the said term double apparel, to wit, one suit for holydays and one suit for worken days.

Apprentices, therefore, were workers who were also children, extra sons or extra daughters (for girls could be apprenticed too), clothed and educated as well as fed, obliged to obedience and forbidden to marry, unpaid and absolutely dependent until the age of twenty-one. If apprentices were workers in the position of sons and daughters, the sons and daughters of the house were workers too. John Locke laid it down in 1697 that the children of the poor must work for some part of the day when they reached the age of three. The sons and daughters of a London baker were not free to go to school for many years of their young lives, or even to play as they wished when they came back home. Soon they would find themselves doing what they could in *bolting*, that is sieving flour, or in helping the maidservant with her panniers of loaves on the way to the market stall, or in playing their small parts in preparing the never-ending succession of meals for the whole household.

We may see at once, therefore, that the world we have lost, as I have chosen to call it, was no paradise or golden age of equality, tolerance or loving kindness. It is so important that I should not be misunderstood on this point that I will say at once that the coming of industry cannot be shown to have brought economic oppression and exploitation along with it. It was there already. The patriarchal arrangements which we have begun to explore were not new in the England of Shakespeare and Elizabeth. They were as old as the Greeks, as old as European history, and not confined to Europe. And it may well be that they abused and enslaved people quite as remorselessly as the economic arrangements which had replaced them in the England of Blake and Victoria. When people could expect to live for only thirty years in all, how must a man have felt when he realized that so much of his adult life, perhaps all, must go in working for his keep and very little more in someone else's family?

But people do not recognize facts of this sort, and no one is content to expect to live as long as the majority in fact will live. Every servant in the old social world was probably quite confident that he or she would some day get married and be at the head of a new family, keeping others in subordination. If it is legitimate to use the words exploitation and oppression in thinking of the economic arrangements of the pre-industrial world, there were nevertheless differences in the manner of oppressing and exploiting. The ancient order of society was felt to be eternal and unchangeable by those who supported, enjoyed and endured it. There was no expectation of reform. How could there be when economic organization was domestic organization, and relationships were rigidly regulated by the social system, by the content of Christianity itself?

Here is a vivid contrast with social expectation in Victorian England, or in industrial countries everywhere today. Every relationship in our world which can be seen to affect our economic life is open to change, is expected indeed to change of itself, or if it does not, to *be* changed, made better, by an omnicompetent authority. This makes for a less stable social world, though it is only one of the features of our society which impels us all in that direction. All industrial societies, we may suppose, are far less stable than their predecessors. They lack the extraordinarily cohesive influence which familial relationships carry with them, that power of reconciling the frustrated and the discontented by emotional means. Social revolution, meaning an irreversible changing of the pattern of social relationships, never happened in traditional, patriarchal, pre-industrial human society. It was almost impossible to contemplate.

Almost, but not quite. Sir Thomas More, in the reign of Henry VIII, could follow Plato in imagining a life without privacy and money, even if he stopped short of imagining a life where children would not know their parents and where promiscuity could be a political institution. Sir William Petty, 150 years later, one of the very first of the political sociologists, could speculate about polygamy; and the England of the Tudors and the Stuarts already knew of social structures and sexual arrangements, existing in the newly discovered world, which were alarmingly different from their own. But it must have been an impossible effort of the imagination to suppose that they were anything like as satisfactory.

It will be noticed that the roles we have allotted to all the members of the capacious family of the master-baker of London in the year 1619 are, emotionally, all highly symbolic and highly satisfactory. We may feel that in a whole society organized like this, in spite of all the subordination, the exploitation and the obliteration of those who were young, or feminine, or in service, everyone belonged in a group, a family group. Everyone had his circle of affection: every relationship could be seen as a love-relationship.

Not so with us. Who could love the name of a limited company or of a government department as an apprentice could love his superbly satisfactory father-figure master, even if he were a bully and a beater, a usurer and a hypocrite? But if a family is a circle of affection, it can also be the scene of hatred. The worst tyrants among human beings, the murderers and the villains, are jealous husbands and resentful wives, possessive partners and deprived children. In the traditional, patriarchal society of Europe, where practically everyone lived out his whole life within the family, often within one family only, tension like this must have been incessant and unrelieved, incapable of release except in crisis. Men, women and children have to be very close together for a very long time to generate the emotional power which can give rise to a tragedy of Sophocles, or Shakespeare, or Racine. Conflict in such a society was between individual people, on the personal scale. Except when the Christians fought with the infidels, or Protestants fought with Catholics, clashes between masses of persons did not often arise. There could never be a situation such as that which makes our own time, as some men say, the scene of perpetual revolution.

All this is true to history only if the little knot of people making bread in Stuart London was indeed the typical social unit of the old world in its size, composition and scale. There are reasons why a baker's household might have been a little out of the ordinary, for baking was a highly traditional occupation in a society increasingly subject to economic change. We shall see, in due course, that a family of thirteen people, which was also a unit of production of thirteen, less the children quite incapable of work, was quite large for English society at that time. Only the families of the really important, the nobility and the gentry, the aldermen and the successful merchants, were ordinarily as large as this. In fact, we can take the bakery to represent the upper limit in size and scale of the group in which ordinary people lived and worked. Among the great mass of society which cultivated the land, and which will be the major preoccupation of this essay, the family group was smaller than a London craftsman's entourage. . . . One reason for feeling puzzled by our own industrial society is that the historian has never set out to tell us what society was like before industry came and seems to assume that everyone knows.

We shall have much more to say about the movement of servants from farmhouse to farmhouse in the old world, and shall return to the problem of understanding ourselves in time, in contrast with our ancestors. Let us emphasize again the scale of life in the working family of the London baker. Few persons in the old world ever found themselves in groups larger than family groups, and there were few families of more than a dozen members. The largest household so far known to us, apart from the royal court and the establishments of the nobility, lay and spiritual, is that of Sir Richard Newdigate, Baronet, in his house of Arbury, within his parish of Chilvers Coton in Warwickshire, in the year 1684. There were thirty-seven people in Sir Richard's family: himself; Lady Mary Newdigate his wife; seven daughters, all under the age of sixteen; and twenty-eight servants, seventeen men and boys and eleven women and girls. This was still a family, not an institution, a staff, an office or a firm.

Everything physical was on the human scale, for the commercial worker in London, and the miner who lived and toiled in Newdigate's village of Chilvers Coton. No object in England was larger than London Bridge or St. Paul's Cathedral, no structure in the Western World to stand comparison with the Colosseum in Rome. Everything temporal was tied to the human life-span too. The death of the master baker, head of the family, ordinarily meant the end of the bakery. Of course there might be a son to succeed, but the master's surviving children would be young if he himself had lived only as long as most men. Or an apprentice might fulfil the final function of apprenticehood, substitute sonship, that is to say, and marry his master's daughter, or even his widow. Surprisingly often, the widow, if she could, would herself carry on the trade. . . .

We may pause here to point out that our argument is not complete. There was an organization in the social structure of Europe before the coming of industry which enormously exceeded the family in size and endurance. This was the Christian Church. It is true to say that the ordinary person, especially the female, never went to a gathering larger than could assemble in an ordinary house except when going to church. When we look at the aristocracy and the church from the point of view of the scale of life and the impermanence of all man-made institutions, we can see that their functions were such as make very little sense in an industrial society like our own. Complicated arrangements then existed, and still exist in England now, which were intended to make it easier for the noble family to give the impression that it had indeed always persisted. Such, for example, were those intricate rules of succession which permitted a cousin, however distant, to succeed to the title and to the headship, provided only he was in the male line. Such was the final remedy in the power of the Crown, the fountain of honour, to declare that an anomalous succession should take place. Nobility was for ever.

But the symbolic provision of permanence is only the beginning of the social functions of the church. At a time when the ability to read with understanding and to write much more than a personal letter was confined for the most part to the ruling minority, in a society which was otherwise oral in its communications, the preaching parson was the great link between the illiterate mass and the political, technical and educated world. Sitting in the 10,000 parish churches of England every Sunday morning, in groups of 20, 50, 100 or 200, the illiterate mass of the people were not only taking part in the single group activity which they ordinarily shared with others outside their own families. They were informing themselves in the only way open to them of what went on in England, Europe, and the world as a whole. The priesthood was indispensable to the religious activity of the old world, at a time when religion was still of primary interest and importance. But the priesthood was also indispensable because of its functions in social communication. . . .

Not only did the scale of their work and the size of the group which was engaged make them exceptional, the constitution of the group did too. In the baking household we have chosen as our standard, sex and age were mingled together. Fortunate children might go out to school, but adults did not usually go out to work. There was nothing to correspond to the thousands of young men on the assembly line, the hundreds of young women in the offices, the lonely lives of housekeeping wives which we now know only too well. We shall see that those who survived to old age in the much less favourable conditions for survival which then were prevalent, were surprisingly often left to live and die alone, in their tiny cottages or sometimes in the almshouses which were being built so widely in the England of the Tudors and the Stuarts. Poor-law establishments, parochial in purpose and in size, had begun their melancholy chapter in the history of the English people. But institutional life was otherwise almost unknown. There were no hotels, hostels, or blocks of flats for single persons, very few hospitals and none of the kind we are familiar with, almost no young men and women living on their own. The family group where so great a majority lived was what we should undoubtedly call a "balanced" and "healthy" group.

When we turn from the hand-made city of London to the hand-moulded immensity of rural England, we may carry the same sentimental prejudice along with us. To every farm there was a family, which spread itself over its portion of the village lands as the family of the master-craftsman filled out his manufactory. When a holding was small, and most were small as are the tiny holdings of European peasants today, a man tilled it with the help of his wife and his children. No single man, we must remember, would usually take charge of the land, any more than a single man would often be found at the head of a workshop in the city. The master of a family was expected to be a householder, whether he was a butcher, a baker, a candlestick maker or simply a husbandman, which was the universal name for one whose skill was in working the land. Marriage we must insist, and it is one of the rules which gave its character to the society of our ancestors, was the entry to full membership, in the enfolding countryside, as well as in the scattered urban centres.

But there was a difference in scale and organization of work on the land and in the town. The necessities of rural life did require recurrent groupings of households for common economic purposes, occasionally something like a crowd of men, women and children working together for days on end. Where the ground was still being tilled as open fields, and each household had a number of strips scattered all over the whole open area and not a compact collection of enclosures, ploughing was co-operative, as were many other operations, above all harvesting, and this continued even after enclosure. We do not yet know how important this element of enforced common activity was in the life of the English rural community on the eve of industrialization, or how much difference enclosure made in this respect. But whatever the situation was, the economic transformation of the eighteenth and nineteenth centuries destroyed communality altogether in English rural life. The group of men from several farmsteads working the heavy plough in springtime, the bevy of harvesters from every house in the village wading into the high standing grass to begin the cutting of the hay, had no successors in large-scale economic activity. For the arrangement of these groups was entirely different in principle from the arrangement of a factory, or a firm, or even of a collective farm.

Both before and after enclosure, some peasants did well: their crops were heavier and they had more land to till. To provide the extra labour needed then, the farming householder, like the successful craftsman, would extend his working family by taking on young men and women as servants to live with him and work the fields. This he would have to do, even if the land which he was farming was not his own but rented from the great family in the manor house. Sometimes, we have found, he would prefer to send out his own children as servants and bring in other children and young men to do the work. This is one of the few glimpses we can get into the quality of the emotional life of the family at this time, for it shows that parents may have been unwilling to submit children of their own to the discipline of work at home. It meant, too, that servants were not simply the perquisites of wealth and position. A quarter, or a third, of all the families in the country contained servants in Stuart times, and this meant that very humble people had them as well as the titled and the wealthy. Most of the servants, moreover, male or female, in the great house and in the small, were engaged in working the land.

The boys and the men would do the ploughing, hedging, carting and the heavy, skilled work of the harvest. The women and the girls would keep the house, prepare the meals, make the butter and the cheese, the bread and the beer, and would also look after the cattle and take the fruit to market. At harvest-time, from June to October, every hand was occupied and every back was bent. These were the decisive months for the whole population in our damp northern climate, with its one harvest in a season and reliance on one or two standard crops. So critical was the winning of the grain for bread that the first rule of gentility (a gentleman never worked with his hands for his living) might be abrogated. . . .

The factory won its victory by outproducing the working family, taking away the market for the products of hand-labour and cutting prices to the point where the craftsman had either to starve or take a job under factory discipline himself. It was no sudden, complete and final triumph, for the seamstresses were working in the garrets right up to the twentieth century, and the horrors of sweated labour which so alarmed our grandfathers took place amongst the out-workers, not on the factory floor. It was not a transformation which affected only commerce, industry and the towns, for the hand-work of the cottages disappeared entirely, till, by the year 1920, rural England was an agrarian remnant, an almost lifeless shell. The process was not English alone, at any point in its development, and its effects on the Continent of Europe were in some ways more obviously devastating than ever they were amongst our people. But ours was the society which first ventured into the industrial era, and English men and women were the first who had to try to find a home for themselves in a world where family and household seemed to have no place.

But Marx and the historians who have followed him were surely wrong to call this process by the simple name of the triumph of capitalism, the rise and victory of the bourgeoisie. The presence of capital, we have seen, was the very circumstance which made it possible in earlier times for the working family to preserve its independence both on the land and in the cities, linking together the scattered households of the workers in such a way that no one had to make the daily double journey from home to workshop, from suburb to office and factory. Capitalism, however defined, did not begin at the time when the working household was endangered by the beginnings of the factory system, and economic inequality was not the product of the social transformation which so quickly followed after. Though the enormous, insolent wealth of the new commercial and industrial fortunes emphasized the iniquity of the division between rich and poor, it is doubtful whether Victorian England was any worse in this respect than the England of the Tudors and the Stuarts. It was not the fact of capitalism alone, not simply the concentration of the means of production in the hands of the few and the reduction of the rest to a position of dependence, which opened wide the social gulf, though the writers of the eighteenth and nineteenth centuries give us ample evidence that this was observed and was resented—by the dispossessed peasantry in England especially. More important, it is suggested, far more likely a source for the feeling that there is a world which once we all possessed, a world now passed away, is the fact of the transformation of the family life of everyone which industrialism brought with it.

In the vague and difficult verbiage of our own generation, we can say that the removal of the economic functions from the patriarchal family at the point of industrialization created a mass society. It turned the people who worked into a mass of undifferentiated equals, working in a factory or scattered between the factories and mines, bereft forever of the feeling that work, a family affair, carried with it. The Marxist historical sociology presents this as the growth of class consciousness amongst the proletariat, and this is an important historical truth. But because it belongs with the large-scale class model for all social change it can also be misleading, as we shall hope to show. Moreover it has tended to divert attention from the structural function of the family in the preindustrial world, and made impossible up till now a proper, informed contrast between our world and the lost world we have to analyse. . . .

European society is of the patriarchal type, and with some variations, of which the feudal went the furthest, it remained patriarchal in its institutions right up to the coming of the factories, the offices and the rest. European patriarchalism, we may notice, was of a rather surprising kind, for it was marked by the independence of the nuclear family, man, wife and children, not by the extended family of relatives living together in a group of several generations under the same patriarchal head. Yet society was patriarchal, nevertheless, right up to the time of industrial transformation: it can now no longer be said to be patriarchal at all, except vestigially and in its emotional predisposition. The time has now come to divide our European past in a simpler way with industrialization as the point of critical change.

The word alienation is part of the cant of the mid-twentieth century and it began as an attempt to describe the separation of the worker from his world of work. We need not accept all that this expression has come to convey in order to recognize that it does point to something vital to us all in relation to our past. Time was when the whole of life went forward in the family, in a circle of loved, familiar faces, known and fondled objects, all to human size. That time has gone for ever. It makes us very different from our ancestors. . . .

In every one of the village communities too, the families of craftsmen, labourers and paupers tended to be smaller than the families of yeomen, and those of the gentry to be largest. The traffic in children from the humbler to the more successful families shows up in the relative numbers in the various groups. Poverty, in our day, or, at least, in the very recent past, was associated with large numbers of children, but . . . in the seventeenth century exactly the reverse was true. The richer you were, the more children you had in your household. In [the village of Goodnestone] in 1676, the gentry with children had an average of 3.5 in their families, the yeomen 2.9, the tradesmen 2.3, the labourers 2.1 and the paupers 1.8.

These figures from Goodnestone are too good to be true and it is common enough to find humble families with many children at home, too many for the meagre resources of the wage-earner and a promise of destitution for his widow if he should die too soon. Nevertheless, the association of few children with modest position and resources is almost as marked a feature of social structure in the traditional world as the association of smaller families generally with the poor. It was not simply a matter of the poor offering up their children to the rich as servants; they probably also had fewer children born to them, and of those which were born, fewer survived. It is likely that works on the expectation of life and size of the biological family will confirm what early impressions seem to show, which is that poor men and their wives could not expect to live together long enough to have as many offspring as the rich. This loss of potential labour-power was a matter of consequence, for it always must be remembered that the actual work on most of the plots of land was done by the working family, the man, his wife and children.

At harvest-time, of course, there was a difference: the individual farming family could no longer cope with the work. From the making of the hay in June until the winning of the corn and pease in late September, every able-bodied person in the village community was at work on everyone's land. How much co-operation there was is difficult to say, but when the crisis of the agricultural year came round, right up to the time of mechanized farming, the village acted as a community. When all was in, there was harvest home.

> It is usual, in most places, after they get all the pease pulled or the last grain down, to invite all the workfolks and their wives (that helped them that harvest) to supper, and then they have puddings, bacon, or boiled beef, flesh or apple pies, and then cream brought in platters, and every one a spoon; then after all they have hot cakes and ale; for they bake cakes and send for ale against that time: some will cut their cake and put it into the cream, and this feast is called cream-pot, or cream-kit; for on the morning that they get all done the workfolks will ask their dames if they have good store of cream and say they must have the cream-kit anon.

This was the Yorkshire custom in the 1640's when it was necessary, at harvest-time, to go even beyond the carpenters, the wheelwrights and the millers, in order to bring in the sheaves off the fields. The richer men had to make a home in the barns during harvest for folk, pastoral in their ways, who came down from the wild moorland. Migration of labour at harvest was common enough in the eighteenth century, but eating and drinking together was a universal characteristic of rural life at all times. Whatever the churchwardens or the overseers of the poor did, when the church-bell was rung in celebration, or the churchyard mowed, there was an entry in the ill-written accounts for ale drunk on the occasion. . . . The meticulous, unpopular Rector of Clayworth in the last quarter of the seventeenth century, entertained the *husbandry* of the two settlements in his parish separately to dinner every year.

When the curate of Goodnestone returned the names of all his parishioners in April, 1676, "according to their families, according to their quality and according to their religion," he did as he was bid and told his lordship, the bishop, how many of them had been to holy communion that Eastertide. Apart from sixteen exceptions every person in the community known by their priest to be qualified for the sacrament had actually taken it at some during the festival, which fell in that year between March 19th and 26th: 128 people communicated that is to say, out of a population of 281. Even the defaulters had promised to make amends at Whitsuntide, all but the one family in the village which was nonconformist. But William Wanstall, senior, one of the absentees, was given no such grace; he had been "excluded the Holy Sacrament for his notorious drunkenness, but since hath promised reformation." Francis Nicholson, the priest-in-charge, was evidently a devoted pastor, for he could give an account of every one of the absentees. Mrs. Elizabeth Richards, the widowed head of one of the households of gentry, was excused as "melancholy," and Barbara Pain since she was "under a dismal calamity, the unnatural death of her husband," who had left her at the head of a yeoman family, three children and two servants.

This . . . draws attention to a feature of the village community and of the whole of the world we have now half-forgotten which has scarcely been mentioned so far. All our ancestors were literal Christian believers, all of the time. Not only zealous priests, such as Francis Nicholson, not only serious-minded laymen, but also the intellectuals and the publicly responsible looked on the Christian religion as the explanation of life, and on religious service as its proper end. Not everyone was equally devout, of course, and it would be simple-minded to suppose that none of these villagers ever had their doubts. Much of their devotion must have been formal, and some of it mere conformity. But their world was a Christian world and their religious activity was spontaneous, not forced on them from above. When Francis Nicholson refused the cup to William Wanstall, in March, 1676, the scores of other people in the church that morning no doubt approved of what he did, as no doubt Wanstall deserved this very public rebuke. When William Sampson, the formidable Rector of Clayworth, did exactly the same thing in April, 1679, to Ralph Meers and

Anne Fenton "upon a common fame that they lived and lodged together, not being married," he also had the community behind him. He knew what he was doing too, for Anne Fenton's first baby was christened two months later, only a week or two, presumably, after she had married Ralph Meers.

It has been shown only very recently how it came about that the mass of the English people lost their Christian belief, and how religion came to be a middle-class matter. When the arrival of industry created huge societies of persons in the towns with an entirely different outlook from these Stuart villagers, practically no one went to church, not if he was working class and was left untouched by religious emotion. Christianity was no longer in the social air which everyone breathed together, rich and poor, gentleman, husbandman, artificer, labourer and pauper. So much has been written about the abuses of the clergy in earlier times, so much about the controversies and doubts, about the revivals, especially the Wesleyan revival, that the religious attitude of common folk has been lost sight of. Perhaps the twelve labourers who lived at Goodnestone in 1676 did not know very clearly what Our Lord's Supper meant, and perhaps they felt that it would displease Squire Hales if they stayed away, but every single one of them took communion. Their descendants in the slums of London in the 1830's, '40's and '50's did not do so: they already looked on Christianity as belonging to the rural world which they had lost. It was something for their employers, something for the respectable, which, perhaps, they might go in for if ever they attained respectability and comfort. This was not true of the hard-working, needy, half-starved labourers of pre-industrial times.

Premodern Families

DAVID HUNT

Much of our image of premodern society depends on an evaluation of the family. A sense that family life is decaying goes back to the beginning of industrialization and continues to the present day, making it sometimes difficult to understand how anything remains to deteriorate further. The family as an economic unit has undoubtedly declined. The question is, what has happened to it as a unit of affection?

Peter Laslett stressed the bonds of love that united the family. More recent work, however, emphasizes the tensions that existed within the family. There is evidence of serious discord between young adults and their parents, as the young people generally could not marry or even enjoy adult status until their parents died or retired, leaving them with the land. Laslett himself suggests one possible result of this friction: the practice of putting children into the service of other families.

There is also serious question about the attitudes toward and the treatment of young children in the early modern family. The following selection relies for its evidence primarily on documents from the upper classes, particularly the account of the upbringing of Louis XIII when he was dauphin. But the author generalizes about French society as a whole, a dangerous practice but perhaps necessary in this murky area. He also applies some of the theories of modern psychology (notably those of Erik Erikson) to a decidedly unmodern family structure. This approach, too, can be criticized; it might be argued that premodern families produced a different set of psychological problems. (Hunt clearly suggests they produced a different personality, but he bases his views on modern notions of personality.) If we cannot apply psychological theories to the past, or develop them in relationship to the past, though, we clearly restrict our claims to a full knowledge of history and of personality alike; this is a serious issue in dealing with human behavior.

Hunt's picture, if correct, has a number of implications for the history of modernization. In contrast to Laslett's view, it suggests that in the seventeenth century the family as an affectionate unit was barely developed. In other words, the picture of preindustrial life as emotionally and psychologically satisfying must be seriously qualified—there may not have been as much for industrialization to disrupt as some authorities claim. And as a more affectionate family did develop, it may well have added important new dimensions to human experience, thus serving as some compensation for whatever new stresses modernization did produce.

At the same time, certain aspects of family life had to change before modernization was possible. In particular, there is evidence that the extremely authoritarian treatment of children, designed to break their will and to retard individual initiative and innovation, did begin to change in the eighteenth century. Swaddling (tightly wrapping an infant in strips of cloth), for example, was abandoned in France. It is also possible that the affection for young children increased. These changes, discussed in several selections in the "early industrial" section of this volume, have important implications. Why did they occur? Some historians have argued that in the late seventeenth century the upper classes began to develop new emotions about young children and that these new attitudes filtered down to the lower classes. David Hunt mentions that Enlightenment thinkers urged greater affection and specifically criticized practices such as swaddling. Declining child mortality rates in the eighteenth century may have encouraged parents to make a greater emotional investment in their children. The reasons are not fully clear, and we cannot at this point be sure that the lower-class outlook toward children did actually change significantly during the eighteenth century. We cannot be sure whether or not the common people began to revise their own attitudes before they were caught up in externally imposed change. In any event, the long-term changes in behavior toward children suggest the need to reinterpret the role of the family in modernization. Rather than family decline, which Laslett suggests, family intensification and redefinition may be a key to the modernization process, helping to cause it in Western Europe rather than simply reflecting the dislocations it brought.

One caution: Hunt portrays a very different approach to childrearing from that of our own time. It is important to remember that people's approaches to children probably have some common ingredients, stemming from basic human reactions over time; thus the differences may in fact be less great than Hunt implies. Further, it is important to seek *reasons* for the differences that do exist, so that premodern people do not seem mere museum pieces. Swaddling, for example, may best be seen as a way to protect young children when both parents are busy, rather than some horrible device to restrain young beasts. An interpretation such as Hunt's requires a real effort of empathy with the past if it is to make full sense.

For every new-born infant, whether he was from a rich family or a poor one, whether he was raised by a nurse, a governess, or by his parents, the major difficulty in the first months of life was getting enough to eat. Without bottles or good baby foods, adults were very hard pressed to nourish children fully and safely. Our effort to understand childhood in the seventeenth century ought to begin with a discussion of this fundamental issue.

The experience of Louis XIII, as recorded by Héroard, provides a good starting point. From the beginning, the dauphin had feeding problems. The difficulty was first attributed to the "fiber" (*filet*) under the infant's tongue. His surgeon, Jacques Guillemeau, cut this fiber in the hope of making it easier for the young prince to suck properly. In the days that followed, attention shifted to the nurse. She did not seem to have enough milk to satisfy the baby, who sucked in "such great gulps ... that he drew more in on one try than others did in three." The woman attempted to correct this deficiency by eating more than usual, a tactic which succeeded only in giving her an upset stomach. A supplementary nurse was brought in and then almost immediately dismissed because enemies at court managed to discredit her with the queen. When Louis was eleven weeks old, and obviously undernourished, a medical conference was summoned to consider further remedies. This situation gives occasion for some sober thought. With unlimited resources at their disposal, and with the child enjoying the best possible living conditions available at that time, the doctors nonetheless found themselves confronted with a case of virtual starvation: the muscles of the dauphin's chest were "completely wasted away," and his neck was so thin that the folds in the skin had disappeared. A third nurse arrived, but she lasted only a short time; people thought she was not "clean." The fourth and permanent nurse was not in place until the baby was sixteen weeks old.

This account is in no way extraordinary. For example, the operation on the dauphin's tongue was routinely performed. Almost all the medical authorities mentioned it, with Guillemeau giving the fullest explanation:

> In children that are newly borne there are commonly found two strings: the one comes from the bottome of the tongue, and reacheth to the very tip and end thereof. This string is very slender and soft and it hindreth the child from taking the nipple . . . so that he cannot sucke well. This string must be cut with a sizzer within a few daies after he is borne.

Paré agreed with this advice, adding that, if not cut, the "string" would later cause the child to stutter. These comments were not dictated by the

From David Hunt, *Parents and Children in History: The Psychology of Family Life in Early Modern France* (New York: Basic Books, 1970), pp. 113–17, 119–23, 124–30, 154–57.

surgeon's desire for an extra commission; Vallambert's remark that the cutting was well performed with one's thumbnail indicates that the doctors thought anyone could do the job. One folklorist has maintained that the custom of cutting the infant's *filet* persisted into the twentieth century in rural France.

The trouble with the nurses was also common, and in fact Louis' appetites were rather modest when compared to those of other children in the royal line. Michelet claimed that as an infant Henri IV went through eight nurses; Louis XIV may have had as many as nine. In the *livres de raison*, several families hired and discarded one nurse after another because no one among them was able to satisfy the demands of the infant she had been contracted to feed. These accounts give us another perspective on the use of the nurse. In a situation where breastfeeding was clearly the best and the safest way to nourish children, the financial ability to employ a nurse, or better yet a whole string of them, was a major advantage for a family anxious about the welfare of its offspring. If something happened to the mother nursing her own children, if she became ill or if another pregnancy interrupted the regime of breastfeeding (it was felt that carrying a child and feeding one at the same time was too taxing an undertaking for a woman to attempt), she could fall back on her family's economic reserves and bring in a nurse to help out. In a number of cases, the mother shared from the moment of birth feeding chores with a nurse, so that there were always two women available to her infant.

Since their families could not afford nurses, most children must have been forced to work even harder than the dauphin to get enough to eat. Mothers seem to have felt that, because of their many other duties, they were not in a position to devote a great deal of time even to very young children. The medical literature was almost unanimously in favor of feeding children on demand, but of all the pieces of advice offered by the experts this suggestion was among the most academic. The doctors indicate that the common practice was to limit feeding to particular times and places determined by the women rather than by their offspring. Even if the poor mother managed to stay with her child at all times, it was thought that she still would not have enough milk to satisfy him. As Vallambert observed: "Because of their continual labor and poor life, [these mothers] do not have a lot of milk, so that they would not be capable of feeding the child if he did not take other nourishment in addition to the milk from the breast."

This "other nourishment" was "gruel" (*bouillie*), a combination of cow's or goat's milk with wheat flour or the crumbs of white bread soaked in water. The mixture was to be baked until it thickened, then served to the infant on his mother's or nurse's finger. This staple appears to have been very widely used. Dionis commented: "There are no women who do not know how to make *bouillie.*" Yet the doctors were very suspicious of it. *Bouillie* was too "viscous and thick," causing "indigestion and constipation." Women made the mixture carelessly, not sifting the flour or neglecting the baking stage.

However, in a characteristic way, these experts would break their discussion in two parts. Recognizing the strength of the custom, and apparently deciding to make the best of a bad situation, they would add all sorts of recommendations on the use of *bouillie*, for example, that egg yolk or honey added to the mixture would serve as a purgative, counteracting the "obstruction" normally caused by the food. Several of them were content with very modest prohibitions against its use, forbidding *bouillie* in the first two weeks of a child's life. Mauriceau's belief that it should not be added to the infant's diet until the second or third month seems utopian by comparison.

Badly prepared *bouillie*, fed to the infant on the end of his mother's finger, must have created serious problems for untested digestive systems. However, the use of this staple was unavoidable:

> Long before the first teeth appear, even before the age of three months, . . . the women of the countryside, and the other poor women of the towns [give *bouillie* to their children] because if the latter took no other nourishment besides milk, they would not be able to go so long without sucking as they do, during the time when mothers are absent and held down by their work.

Even the dauphin was given *bouillie* only eighteen days after birth. Here, as elsewhere, the experience of the most precious child in the kingdom enables us to imagine the even more somber circumstances of his less fortunate peers. A squad of nurses barely managed to feed the dauphin, and his diet had to be filled out with *bouillie* before he was three weeks old. In spite of all the efforts of the household, Louis almost succumbed. We might well wonder how other children survived the precarious first months of life.

In fact, when the infant did not get enough milk at the breast and was unable to digest the *bouillie*, he starved. The willingness to have children suckled by farm animals (a practice condoned in the medical literature) indicates the gravity of the food problem. In this respect, the story of the feeding of children represents very well the insecurity of their situation as a whole. For whatever reason, a shocking number of children died. This mortality rate has been fairly conclusively documented. In one rural area during the seventeenth century, more than one-quarter of the children born at a given time did not reach the age of one, and almost a half died before the age of four. There are no equally reliable statistics for urban areas within France during this period, but from what we know of European cities in general, it seems safe to conclude that rates there would have been at least as high. The fact that infants were so vulnerable, that it was tremendously difficult to feed them properly and to protect them from disease and death, is the fundamental precondition which we of a more comfortable milieu must grasp if we are to understand what childhood was like in the seventeenth century. . . .

With these thoughts in mind, it is interesting to turn to actual descriptions of very small children in the seventeenth century. In fact, grownups had a highly developed awareness of the infant's tireless capacity for appropriation, of his tenacious parasitism. The picture Héroard sketched of a greedy Louis gulping in huge swallows of milk is not without a tinge of the sinister. It was commonly believed that birth was prompted by the hunger of the infant who, because he could no longer satisfy himself in the womb, tried "with great impetuousness to get out." Avarice was the child's principal trait: "All children are naturally very greedy and gluttonous." At the same time that they called for feeding on demand, the doctors cautioned mothers against overfeeding. While being indulgent, they could not let the unquenchable appetite of the infant hold full sway.

These opinions take on their full significance when we note that the experts thought the mother's milk was actually whitened blood. They do not seem to have understood the fact that secretion of milk in the mother's body is a self-sustaining process designed specifically to meet the special demands of the new-born infant. The nursing situation was not seen as a cooperative effort, but as a struggle in which the interests of the two parties were at least to some extent at odds. In fact, the infant prospered at the expense of his mother, from whose body he sucked the precious substance he needed for his own survival. These views explain why breastfeeding was seen as a debilitating experience for a woman, why she was counseled to hire a nurse after a difficult delivery, or if she again became pregnant. Only the healthy mother could afford to sacrifice a part of herself for the welfare of her children.

In a world where people believed that resources of all kinds were fixed and in short supply, the prosperity of one person or group was always linked to the bad luck of others. From this perspective, adults were naturally disturbed by the incessant demands of small children. For example, I think that such sentiments underlie the story recorded by Louise Bourgeois about a Strasbourg mother who fell asleep while nursing her child. A snake with poisonous fangs attached itself to her breast and began to suck. The woman and her husband could not remove the animal for fear that it would bite, and for ten months it continued to suck, growing to monstrous proportions on the strength of this nourishment. Bourgeois thought the incident showed "how much substance there is in woman's milk." The mother was forced to put her child out to nurse and to go everywhere with the unwelcome guest, carrying it in a basket. The child at the breast had been transformed into a serpent, symbol of evil.

At the end of the story, only the magic charms of a sorceress succeeded in tempting away this covetous intruder.

The fear of being bitten expressed in the story was manifested more generally by adults in a great deal of anxiety about teething. Parents reacted very specifically to this step in infantile development and regarded teething as a serious disease which might lead to all sorts of complications: diarrhea, fevers, epilepsy, spasms, and even death. Paré wrote:

> Monseigneur de Nemours sent to fetch me to anatomize his dead son, aged eight months or thereabouts, whose teeth had not erupted. Having diligently searched for the cause of his death, I could not find any, if not that his gums were very hard, thick and swollen; having cut through them, I found all his teeth ready to come out, if only someone had cut his gums. So it was decided by the doctors present and by me that the sole cause of his death was that nature had not been strong enough to pierce the gums and push the teeth out.

Remedies abounded for this "disease," and parents were advised to rub the sore gums with all sorts of magical panaceas. If this did not help, Guillemeau suggested: "Rub the legs, thighs, shoulders, backe and nape of the child's necke, drawing still downwards, thereby to alter and turne the course of humours which fall downe upon the gummes and passages of the throat." As a last resort, the surgeon was supposed to cut the gums so that the teeth might more easily emerge.

In these comments, doctors stress the fact that teeth are the infant's first aggressive tools, although they limit themselves to discussing the ways in which children themselves can be harmed by such sharp instruments. However, I think that the tone of the discussion, the awe with which doctors analyze the eruption of teeth, indicate an underlying fear of the child's biting impulses, the potentially dangerous use he can make of his mouth. In this respect, the interpretation of teething is consistent with the tendency to see children as gluttonous little animals and with the belief that they were sucking away the mother's blood. Collecting together these images, we have a picture of the small child as a predatory and frightening creature capable of harming the woman whose duty it was to care for him. Returning to [Erik] Erikson's hypothesis, we can say that in the eyes of his elders the seventeenth-century infant was an "oral sadist."

I have no doubt that similar themes appear in the childrearing literature of all cultures. In fact, they are built into the breastfeeding relationship: the infant does suck with striking intensity, because his life depends on it; women are to some extent tied down by the demands of their very small offspring; and breastfeeding is always complicated by the child's teething. At the same time, I believe that images of the child as a greedy little animal had a special power in the seventeenth century and that they exerted a relatively pronounced negative influence on efforts to feed the very young.

I picture a mother, who herself probably did not get enough to eat, and who was forced to work long and difficult hours, turning to the task of breastfeeding with mixed feelings. The child was a parasite; he did nothing and yet his appetites seemed to be endless. He was sucking a vital fluid out of her already depleted body. This situation must have been tremendously difficult for mothers to tolerate. In turn, children sensed the anxiety of their providers, perhaps in the tense way they were held, in the tentativeness of the breast being offered to them. Aware of the unreliability of this source of life, they redoubled their efforts to "get" as much as possible. These efforts impressed mothers as especially gluttonous and devouring, and in reaction they developed an image of children as greedy little animals, who were harmful to their guardians. These fantasies worked to undermine the resolution of mothers, whose gathering ambivalence would be communicated to children, who in turn would become all the more peremptory in their demands for more milk.

Some hypothesis along these lines is necessary to account for the frequent breakdown in efforts to feed little children. The poverty of the society, while it provided the necessary, and very powerful, initial impetus for the process by which mother and child became wary of each other, is not in itself a sufficient explanation for the problem. Mothers in equally poor societies manage to keep their children close by and to feed them on demand. Medically speaking, there is no reason why a woman, even if she is relatively undernourished, cannot adequately breastfeed a child. Further, we know that lactation does not weaken mothers who undertake it. This analysis is not intended as a critique of seventeenth-century mothers. Given their situation, it is entirely natural that they should have been ambivalent about children. My point is that economic or physiological arguments do not in themselves explain the great difficulty experienced in getting enough food into the child's belly. These difficulties make sense only if we picture the specifically economic factors overlaid with a set of disturbing fantasies about children at the breast. The problem was first of all in the seventeenth-century economy, but at the same time it was also in the minds and the deportment of parents.

This point is clearly illustrated in the royal court, and in the houses of the rich, where nurses, who almost certainly got enough to eat, were often unable to produce enough milk for the children they were supposed to breastfeed. Poor living conditions cannot explain these failures which the literature accepted as a matter of course. The situation of the nurse must have created conflicts of its own. Given their low status, and the constant critical scrutiny of people like Héroard, who were alert to any sign of their inadequacy as providers, these women may well have had trouble relaxing and devoting themselves wholeheartedly to the task of feeding the children of their superiors. On the other hand, I suspect that some part of the problem was independent of the woman's identity as a nurse, but instead grew out of her image of children, her sense of them as demanding and dangerous little animals, a sense she shared with all other mothers, of the time. . . . In his analysis of the first phase of childhood growth, Erik Erikson maintains that the incorporative mode of behavior is expressed most obviously through the mouth, but that it is also manifested in the activity of the infantile organism as a whole. The child must be seen as a personality, facing a total existential situation, and not simply as an oral creature who must be fed. By contrast, in the seventeenth century infantile experience was grasped by adults primarily in terms of feeding. The discussion of the doctors concentrated heavily on the problem of how best to nourish the child. In the same spirit, parents contracted with nurses to serve simply as suppliers of milk, rather than as maternal figures in a broader sense, because they believed that the infant's alimentary needs were the only ones worthy of serious attention. The fact that small children needed conversation, companionship, and play, as well as nourishment of a more tangible sort, was not well understood by adults of the period.

Of course parents were amused and diverted by infants and did take notice of them in situations other than those connected with feeding. On the other hand, I think it is significant that in the seventeenth century the notion of "playing" with children had an ambiguous ring. Some critics thought that in this play adults betrayed a careless, self-indulgent attitude. In casting about for the words to describe their impressions, these observers hit upon a comparison which we have already encountered in the discussion of feeding: parents treated children like pets, or little animals. Montaigne argued: "We have loved [infants] for our own amusement, like monkeys, not like human beings." And Fleury commented: "It is as if the poor children had been made only to amuse the adults, like little dogs or little monkeys."

This comparison of the child to an animal is something more than a useful device, a way of characterizing the infant at the breast. The image appears throughout seventeenth-century literature on children. In a total sense, the small child was an intermediate being, not really an animal (although he might often be compared to one), but on the other hand not really human either. This quasi-evolutionary model of the ages of life was so ingrained that adults often hardly noticed its presence in their own speech. Thus in describing the battle of Paris, Jean Burel wrote that the Parisians "were besieged by the King of Navarre so closely that they were forced to eat animals: dogs, horses, everything right up to, and almost including, little children." In the chain of being, a separate link—infancy —connected the animal and the human worlds without belonging completely to either one.

　　　I have already argued that, with respect to the specifically oral forms of this image of the child as little animal, in an area where infant survival was very much at stake, parents struggled with their negative feelings and managed to stay in touch with their offspring.　Once the child had been safely fed, however, it is possible that adults gave vent to their aversion and disgust and treated the infant with the callousness which his subhuman station deserved.　We must try to ascertain whether the feeding of infants was somehow special, or if, on the other hand, parental attitudes in that area carried over into the whole of relations with the child during the first year of life.

　　　I think the best way to approach this problem is through an examination of the practice of swaddling.　The eighteenth-century philosophes have already experimented with a similar tactic.　In turning their attention to childrearing, they found evidence of negligence on every side, but nowhere more obnoxiously manifested than in the practice of swaddling. In detailing the evils of the custom, these critics conjured up a whole gallery of cruel images: the infant was wrapped up tight and tossed "in a corner"; or the nurse hung a crying baby in swaddling clothes from a nail on the wall, so that the bands tightened, suffocating the child and choking off his cries; or the nurse placed the swaddled baby in his cradle and rocked him until he fell into a groggy sleep.　In all these instances, swaddling represented a general point of view toward children, a deficiency in that sympathy or generostiy which the philosophes thought a child had a right to expect from his elders.　While reserving judgment on the exact meaning of the practice, I follow the eighteenth-century critics by discussing swaddling in this symbolic sense, as a key to understanding what adults thought of the first stage of life.

　　　The swaddling of infants, which to us is one of the most exotic features of childrearing in the seventeenth century, was utterly taken for granted by the adults of that period.　Doctors, who showed such a lively interest in the various controversial issues of childrearing, barely took notice of swaddling and offered only a few scraps of advice on the subject; as Mauriceau put it, "There are no women who do not know all about something which is so common."　In describing Louis' birth, Héroard mentions that the infant was swaddled soon after being washed and fed, but he never refers to the clothes again.　In an account otherwise rich in detail, there is nothing on the regime of swaddling: how the wrapping was done, when during the day the clothes were removed, not even a hint as to when in the life of the dauphin the practice was terminated.　Although swaddling has almost completely disappeared in modern France, the custom was once so deeply rooted in everyday life that it was put into practice almost automatically.　This combination of factors makes it a particularly useful, as well as difficult, subject for the historian interested in the distinctive qualities of childrearing in the old regime.

The swaddling band (called the *maillot*) was a roll of cloth about two inches across. The infant was wrapped up with this length of cloth, arms straight at his sides and legs extended, with a few extra turns around the head to hold it steady, so that only a small circle of his face would be left exposed. Doctors advised that the pressure of the band should be equal on all parts of the body, to avoid crippling the infant, and that especial care should be taken in wrapping the chest and stomach so that breathing would not be impeded. The swaddling was left in place at all times during the first weeks of an infant's life except when it was necessary to clean and change him. Vallambert suggested that if an infant cried excessively, one could "unswaddle him, and massage and move his limbs, for that often causes the crying and the screaming to stop." At some time early in his life (according to doctors, between the first and fourth month), the infant's arms would be freed and the wrappings applied only to his legs and torso. Finally, when he was eight or nine months old, or at the latest around his first birthday, the infant would be left unswaddled for good.

Intuitively—and wrongly—we imagine that such a regime would leave infants deformed or retarded. Actual details on the physical development of babies in the seventeenth century are very scarce, but Héroard's *Journal* does suggest something of the dauphin's progress in this respect and helps to show that swaddling did not stunt the growth of children. At first, the doctor describes Louis performing acts compatible with a regime of swaddling: listening, staring, speaking, laughing. At four months, Louis was "playing" with the king and queen, and in one session Henri studied the feet of his son, which, he had been told, resembled his own. At five and a half months, "he dances gaily to the sound of a violin." Obviously this was not real dancing, but perhaps some rhythmic movement of the arms. A week later, he stretched out his hand for an object (a book) for the first time. Louis was throwing things at the age of six months and was also being put to bed with his arms free (it will be remembered that while he was teething Héroard sat up holding his hand). At eight months, the dauphin was fitted for his first pair of shoes, and six weeks later the "leading strings" (*lisières*), which would be used by adults to help him learn to walk, were attached to his clothes.

This circumstantial evidence seems to fit well enough the schedule suggested by the doctors. No later than five and a half months after his birth, Louis' arms were left unswaddled so that he was free to "dance," to grasp a book, to be held by the hand. In fact, he may have been completely unswaddled by this time since Henri IV was able to study his feet; but it is also possible that the dauphin was specially unwrapped for his parents' visit. In any case, the *maillot* was definitively discarded by eight or nine months when Louis was fitted for shoes and *lisières*.

Swaddling had little effect on subsequent motor development. Apparently children did not spend much time crawling. There are almost no pictorial representations of a stage between swaddling and walking, and, on the other hand, every effort seems to have been made to help children learn how to walk. Around his first birthday, the dauphin was indeed walking with "firmness, held under the arms." When Louis was nineteen months old, Héroard describes him running, and in going from place to place he was now led (*mené*) as often as carried (*porté*). The descriptions offered of his play corroborate the impression of the dauphin's rapidly growing dexterity, "fencing" with Héroard (ten months), playing the violin and the drum (about a year and a half), and striking a blow of fifty-five paces with his "bat" (*palemail*) when he was just over two.

Swaddling obviously did not cripple children. In fact the practice performed a number of positive functions. From the recent literature on the subject, we know that (like a high-walled cradle or play-pen) swaddling limits potentially dangerous motor activity; that (like a carriage) it makes children easier to carry; and that it provides a measure of security and reassurance by relieving the infant of responsibility for the control of his limbs in a period when he does not yet have sufficient physical mastery to handle the job completely on his own.

All of these reasons may have been considered in the seventeenth century, but they were not mentioned by experts in their terse discussions of the practice. Among the reasons which were given for swaddling, the first and most important seems to have been that it kept the baby warm:

> Nor then forget that wrappers be at hand,
> Soft flannels, linen, and the swaddling band,
> T'enwrap the babe, by many a circling fold,
> In equal lines, and thus defend from cold.

This function was very important; we are dealing with a world in which even the royal palaces were so poorly insulated that children had to be admonished to stay close to the fireplace on the coldest days. One doctor cautioned against freeing the child's arms during the winter. Even if he was past the age of three or four months, the baby was to remain fully swaddled "until he is older and it is not so cold."

Doctors also argued that swaddling was necessary to help the infant's limbs grow straight. Apparently this belief in the effectiveness of the wrapping is not unfounded, especially when one considers the prevalence of rickets among young children at that time. There was also some notion that swaddling prevented the child from hurting himself by striking a hard object or by falling. More generally, swaddling immobilized the child under reasonably beneficial circumstances and thus served as a substitute for the constant attention which the unhindered baby would have required from its elders. This substitution may often have been dictated by a lack of interest in children and could therefore by interpreted (in the tradition of the philosophes) as a sign of parental neglect. However, in this respect as in others, we must be careful to distinguish matters of choice from those of necessity. For many poor women, the *maillot*, no less than *bouillie*, was an essential device which enabled them to spend long periods of time at work and away from their infants. For any society which could not afford to be too child-centered, swaddling, or some other practice which relieved adults of the need for constant supervision of children, was inevitable and can hardly be construed as a sign of some special parental malice and neglect.

In fact, swaddling can be interpreted as an antidote to the more extreme forms of parental ambivalence. We have seen how much contempt adults were likely to feel for children and how they seemed to regard their offspring as little animals. Swaddling allowed parents to defend against the consequences of their own distaste. This distinctive custom helped to place infants. It defined with a more reassuring precision the limbo of childhood, leaving it distinct from the sphere of adult life, but also firmly marking it off from the animal kingdom. As Mauriceau observed, children were swaddled for fear they would otherwise never learn to stand erect, but would always crawl on all fours like little animals. Swaddling embodied the promise of a future humanity and saved infants from a descent to that animal world into which their own strangeness and frailty threatened to propel them.

In the same spirit, adults wanted children either in swaddling clothes or walking on two feet. Crawling was discouraged precisely because it made more ambiguous that distinction between infants and animals which adults knew in their hearts they had to maintain. We have already seen how a kind of collective repression protected parents from their fear of the predatory appetites of growing infants. With its numerous benefits, and as a means of defining the first stage of life, swaddling operated on an even more general plane as a way of caring for infants and at the same time of binding up the anxiety which adults experienced in dealing with the animality of small children. . . .

I would maintain that in the seventeenth century people felt strongly the contrast between the loyalties and duties incumbent upon them as a consequence of their station in society on the one hand, and their natural inclinations on the other. Institutional arrangements always implied a gradation of rank and were thus held to be incompatible with friendship, in which equality between the partners was so important. Far from accepting the fact that personal relations were almost always arranged according to hierarchical principles, individuals were made acutely uncomfortable by this situation. In personal letters, writers often distinguished sincere and spontaneous affection from the more perfunctory good will which went with the formal relationship to their correspondent. Thus Madame de

Sévigné, in sending good wishes to her daughter, stipulated that, "In this case, maternal love plays less of a part than inclination."

As the quote indicates, the family was caught up in this system. To be a brother, son, or wife was a status, with its special obligations, its place in a grid of rule and submission. Members of the family were supposed to love one another; paternal, maternal, fraternal love were all often cited as models of human fellow feeling. At the same time, even within the family, it was terribly hard to imagine a relationship of mutual affection which was not simultaneously one of ruler and ruled. Like the bond between master and servant, between seigneur and peasant, between king and subject, family ties, while steeped in a folklore of pious harmony, implied as well the power to dominate others, to claim rewards, or, on the contrary, the awareness of a helpless dependence.

This line of argument will help to explain further the distinction which, as we have seen, observers made with such clarity between marriages of love and those of interest. Marriages of love implied spontaneous affection between the two lovers, who were concerned primarily with their own happiness. Marriage of interest involved social and financial considerations to be arranged for the benefit of families. These observers understood very well that in a social system which attempted to subordinate the wishes of marriageable children to the ambitions of their parents, and in which the wife was regarded simply as the means of cementing alliances between families, marriage could not at the same time be expected to provide for the happiness and the emotional satisfaction of the partners.

Fraternal relations were compromised by similar pressures. As the dauphin was being forced to acknowledge himself as his father's valet, it was also being pointed out to him that his brothers, who were younger and hence subordinate, would serve him just as he served the king. Books of etiquette often struggled with the problem of fraternal affection and the rights of primogeniture. How do you reconcile "natural" ties with the principle which arranges brothers one above the other in a hierarchy of prerogatives? Corneille built the play *Rodogune* around this dilemma. The twins Seleucus and Antiochus are the model of fraternity. Since they do not know who is older (the oddity of the situation demonstrates how hard it was in the seventeenth century to conceive of real equality), they can be familiar and trusting in relations with one another. Their mother, however, decides to disclose the order of birth, and the two brothers are thrown into a panic. They know that if this information is revealed, one will become the arrogant master, the other, his resentful servant (full of "shame and envy"), and their accord will be ruined.

We can see that gradations of rank within the household were interpreted simply as a matter of power and of usage, and that people believed this situation discouraged close and mutually satisfying relationships among family members. Ideally, those of lower rank should have accepted the eminence of their superiors and been warmed by the benefits they received from an admittedly unequal partnership. In fact, inequality within the domestic unit filled people not with love and warmth, but with resentment and a feeling of "shame and envy."

Among the members of the family, the infant is the most prone to these feelings. His physical and intellectual inferiority is a basic fact of nature as is his subjection to the will of older, stronger adults. Precisely because it is so completely unearned by any merit, but instead is derived from an amoral biological fact, parental authority might legitimately be expected to embody whatever sense of justice adults profess to respect. The child has to obey; in what ways do grownups persuade him that he ought to obey?

It seems to me that no one could deny the paramount importance of force and intimidation in the upbringing of the dauphin. The beating Louis received at the hands of his father demonstrated the lengths to which adults were willing to carry the matter: an obstinate child was in physical danger. Grownups relied heavily on their ability to frighten the young prince. They rightly assumed that he remembered what had happened the last time he had been too defiant. Childish fears were exploited in a variety of petty ways. For example, when it was discovered that Louis was afraid of someone (a hunchbacked member of the guard, or a mason in the king's service), that person would be summoned whenever it was necessary to make Louis toe the line.

The whippings continued, gradually settling into a fixed ritual. Louis was beaten first thing in the morning the day after his infractions: "Scarcely were his eyes open when he was whipped." Often he would get up early and hide or block the door in order to avoid these sessions. When it became impossible for Madame de Montglat to handle the dauphin, his father instructed soldiers of the guard to hold him while the whippings were administered. Louis was beaten even after becoming king of France, and at the age of ten, he still had nightmares about being whipped. As late as January, 1614, adults continued to threaten Louis with the switch, but by this time his physical development was at last putting a stop to such means of punishment.

As I suggested earlier, formalized coercion was probably better for the infant than the erratic and unrestrained cruelty which no doubt characterized discipline in families where parents had to deal directly with their offspring. But even in the royal household, it is obvious that fear was one of the principal forces steering the child into that social role which adults required him to assume. Such fear was not incompatible with love. Louis always demonstrated an intense feeling for his father, and it would be foolish to pretend that their relationship was entirely negative. Yet this love (corresponding to the sentiment which many historians have thought tied together master and servant in the old regime) does not change the fact that terrorizing children was inhumane and wrong. At the core of its domestic life, I think we find a telling indictment of the old regime.

We now have a better idea of how life cycles "interlocked" in the seventeenth century. It is no accident that fathers whipped their sons for their own good, because they themselves were whipped as children. These fathers had been thwarted in their own infantile efforts to be autonomous. Punished for attempting to establish selfhood, and deprived of control over their bodies, they were left with a pervasive sense of shame and doubt. Such sentiments fit the adult life they could lead in a hierarchical society indifferent to the dignity of the individual and held together principally by coercive means. In turn, people formed along these lines were necessarily going to respond to their children's search for independence with rigid counterassertions and panicky violence. The inability of the king himself, the only man in the society who was without a master, to break out of this vicious circle attests to the power of the cycle of unfreedom.

Popular Recreations in English Society

ROBERT W. MALCOLMSON

What options have we lost in losing the traditional world of recreation? Historians are just beginning to turn to this question, as they grapple with the proper meaning and function of leisure in modern life. Yet laments for the lost gaiety of village festivals began with the rise of industrial society; the nineteenth century, with its stern work ethic and its middle-class fear of unruliness, unquestionably cut into a host of popular pastimes.

Traditional recreations are not without their modern critics. Historians dealing with the European continent, more than with England, have claimed that leisure in its truest sense is actually a modern phenomenon. They point out that before industrialization few people had much time for extensive nonwork activities. Free time, consisting principally of festival days, was rigorously controlled by community custom, allowing no individual choice of leisure forms. Also, it is valid to ask if the criticisms levied against modern leisure cannot also be directed against its preindustrial counterparts: undue violence, undue concentration on youth, manipulation by the upper classes to keep the masses in line, undue conformity (although to custom rather than to the media of our own day).

Preindustrial recreation was clearly not pure joy. Instead, it had a variety of social functions. Are these functions—outlets for youth, community feeling, acceptable hostility against the ruling class, acceptance of death—as necessary in modern society, and if so, are they as well served by modern leisure? Again, the question is: how much have we lost?

Perhaps, we have lost little after a period of adjustment to urban and industrial life in the nineteenth century. Leisure may be a phenomenon that does not modernize, serving basic human needs that have not greatly changed. For, without question, we have preserved or revived many of the games and pastimes of preindustrial England, including the sacred football game—and, quite possibly, for many of the same purposes. But the importance of leisure in preindustrial society at least suggests that the modern passion for leisure is not as great a gain over the past as we sometimes like to imagine.

Many recreations arose directly out of the fabric of common interests and common sentiments among the working people themselves. The fundamental social basis for several of the calendar festivities was the relatively small, tightly-knit rural community, and it was in this kind of community that a large number of labouring men spent most of their time and developed their basic sense of social identity. It was a world of face-to-face contacts, deriving its unifying forces from the common experiences of daily (and yearly) routine and a shared oral culture. The people's social relationships stemmed mostly from the ties of family, the ties of neighbourhood (a village, a hamlet, one end of town), and the ties which were formed in the course of their work. The range of their social encounters was normally fairly limited; in most rural areas, aside from the market towns, they would have had relatively infrequent contact with complete strangers. Some of their recreations reflected the personal character of their day-to-day experiences. During the Christmas season friends from the parish, and perhaps relatives from nearby, were in the habit of gathering together at a public house or in each others' cottages. It was said that on Christmas Day "at Danby Wisk in ye North-Riding of Yorkshire, it is the custom for ye Parishioners after receiving ye Sacrament, to goe from Church directly to the Ale House and there drink together as a testimony of Charity and friendship." A morris dance in the market place or through the village streets would have attracted an audience from the bulk of the inhabitants, many of whom would have known one another personally. There was a communal basis for the ritual. The community's sense of solidarity might also have been expressed in some athletic competition—the village hero contending in a wrestling match, a football game against a neighbouring parish. Some festive occasions arose out of a consciousness of mutual interests among people of the same trade. St Crispin's feast, the 25th of October, was regularly celebrated by the shoemakers in Knaresborough; Plough Monday was an occupational holiday for the ploughmen, St Andrew's Day (November 30th) for the lacemakers; February 3rd was widely observed by the woolcombers with parades and merry-makings, in honour of their patron saint, Bishop Blaze.

The ties of kinship, friendship, and neighbourliness among the common people were especially important as supports for the annual wake, probably the principal occasion for individuals to come together in order to reaffirm their social relationships. Henry Bourne remarked that at the time of a wake the people "deck themselves in their gaudiest Clothes, and have open Doors and splendid Entertainments, for the Reception and Treating of their Relations and Friends, who visit them on that Occasion,

From Robert W. Malcolmson, *Popular Recreation in English Society, 1700–1850* (New York: Cambridge University Press, 1973), pp. 52–56, 67–80, 84–85.

from each neighbouring Town''; and in September 1738 a contributor to the *Gentleman's Magazine* declared that "I hear of one [parish feast] every Sunday kept in some Village or other of the Neighbourhood, and see great Numbers of both Sexes in their Holiday Cloaths, constantly flocking thither, to partake of the Entertainment of their Friends and Relations, or to divert themselves with the rural Games and athletick Exercises." John Clare also wrote of the social connections which underlay the wake:

> The woodman and the thresher now are found
> Mixing and making merry with their friends
> Children and kin from neighbouring towns around
> Each at the humble banquet pleas'd attends
> For though no costliness the feast pretends
> Yet something more than common they provide
> And the good dame her small plum pudding sends
> To sons and daughters fast in service tied
> With many a cordial gift of good advice beside

The feast was pre-eminently a time of hospitality and generous provision. It was said in 1759 that in Fallow, a hamlet of the parish of Sparsholt in Berkshire, "the feast day at the old chapel at Fallow, now demolished, had been on the Sunday following the feast of St James, which day the neighbourhood of Fallow keep in the way of having better cheer and open hospitality." At the wakes in Stamford, "An abundance of good cheer, which every individual in the parish provides, whose circumstances will permit him to obtain it, supplies his table nearly the whole of the week, to which a host of ready cousins, friends, and neighbours, are welcome: and on the Saturday night, the round of festivity is commonly concluded with ass races and dancings." Similarly, Samuel Bamford recalled that on the Sunday of the wake "the very best dinner which could be provided was set out . . . and the guests were helped with a profusion of whatever the host could command. It was a duty at the wakes to be hospitable, and he who at that time was not liberal according to his means, was set down as a very mean person."

On many festive occasions the most active participants, as one might expect, were men and women in their teens and early twenties. John Aubrey reported that the Michaelmas fair at Kington St Michael, Wiltshire was "much resorted unto by the young people," a feature which was noticed of many other fairs. "Here met the village youths on pleasure bent," wrote James Withers of the annual petty fair in his Cambridgeshire village. Since almost all servants were single, young people were especially prominent at hiring fairs. Guy Fawkes Day seems to have been particularly associated with the revelries of younger men; Shrove Tuesday was traditionally the special holiday of apprentices, and May Day was primarily for the benefit of young men and women.

The most important reason for the prominent involvement of young people in recreational events was the fact that they served as occasions for courtship and sexual encounters. This was most noticeably the case at fairs and feasts. On 29 October 1781 Sylas Neville referred in his diary to the "country Beauties and their sweethearts enjoying themselves at the fruit stalls and mountebank's stage" at a fair in Burton-upon-Trent; and at Norwich on 8 April 1784 he wrote of a "fair on Tombland for toys etc., full of Beaux and Belles before dinner." An observer of the hiring fair at Studley, Warwickshire, noticed that "towards evening each lad seeks his lass, and they hurry off to spend the night at the public houses." It was said that at the fairs and statutes in Cumberland "it is customary for all the young people in the neighbourhood to assemble and dance at the inns and alehouses"; after a hiring, with "fiddlers tuning their fiddles in public houses, the girls begin to file off, and gently pace the streets, with a view of gaining admirers; while the young men . . . follow after, and having eyed the lasses, pick up each a sweetheart, whom they conduct to a dancing room, and treat with punch and cake." The feast at Pudsy was reported to be a major occasion for match-making. Dancing was always a standard attraction at wakes and pleasure fairs and it provided a focal point for courting and flirtation. John Clare, for instance, wrote of the dancing at a village feast:

> Where the fond swain delighteth in the chance
> To meet the sun tann'd lass he dearly loves
> And as he leads her down the giddy dance
> With many a token his fond passion proves
> Squeezing her hands or catching at her gloves
> And stealing kisses as chance prompts the while

It would have been strange if many holiday gatherings had not catered to the special interests of unmarried men and women. Festive assemblies offered them some of the best opportunities for establishing new contacts and for pursuing acquaintances already made; they widened the range of choice, and because of their free and easy and relatively uninhibited textures, they encouraged the kinds of gallantries and personal displays which were not usually possible in everyday life. Eustace Budgell must have had this sort of setting in mind when, in his portrayal of a foot-

ball game at a country wake, he noted that one "Tom Short behaved himself so well, that most People seemed to agree it was impossible that he
should remain a Batchelour till the next Wake." Sir Thomas Parkyns was
assuming a similar set of circumstances when he was publicizing the satisfactions which were to be gained from his favourite sport:

> For the most Part our Country Rings for Wrestlings, at Wakes and other
> Festivals, consist of a small Party of young Women, who come not thither
> to choose a Coward, but the Daring, Healthy, and Robust Persons, fit to
> raise an Offspring from: I dare say, they sufficiently recommend themselves
> to their Sweet-hearts, when they demonstrate that they are of hail Constitu-
> tions, and enjoy a perfect state of Health, and like the Fatigue of that Day...

In the same vein, John Gay's *The Shepherd's Week* had the maid Marian
speak warmly of how

> Young *Colin Clout*, a Lad of peerless Meed,
> Full well could dance, and deftly tune the Reed;
> In ev'ry Wood his Carrols sweet were known,
> In ev'ry Wake his nimble Feats were shown.
> When in the Ring the Rustic routs he threw,
> The Damsels Pleasures with his Conquests grew;
> Or when aslant the Cudgel threats his Head,
> His Danger smites the Breast of ev'y Maid. . . .

However, although the young may have been particularly active on
many holidays and even dominant on a few, they seldom monopolized the
pleasures of a festive gathering. On most occasions there would have
been ample room for the participation, in some form or other, of the
middle-aged and the elderly. On 9 July 1715 Nicholas Blundell reported
that at Little Crosby "the Little Boyes and Girles of this Town diverted
themselves with Rearing a May-pole in the West-Lane, they had Morrys
dansing and a great many came to it both old and young." Similarly, John
Denson of Waterbeach claimed that "both old and young participated" in
the afternoon diversions of May day—the rites of the morning were
exclusively for the young people—"and those whom age and infirmity
prevented, appeared to enjoy our sports as they sat at their cottage doors."
On those occasions when youth enjoyed the limelight there was nothing to
prevent the older people from looking on. At the annual harvest feast in

Warton, Lancashire, during the early eighteenth century "the Old People after Supper smoak their Pipes, and with great Pleasure and Delight behold the younger spending the Evening in Singing, Dancing, etc." On Midsummer Eve, according to Henry Bourne,

> it is usual in the most of Country Places, and also here and there in Towns and Cities, for both Old and Young to meet together, and be Merry over a large Fire, which is made in the open Street. Over this they frequently leap and play at various Games, such as Running, Wrestling, Dancing, etc. But this is generally the Exercise of the younger Sort; for the old Ones, for the most Part, sit by as Spectators, and enjoy themselves and their Bottle.

Matrons would watch the games and dancing at a wake and older men would be keen observers at a match of football, wrestling, or cudgelling. "Aged men also, hardly able to walk, were to be seen moving towards this scene of riot," complained a clergyman of the bull-running at Stamford, "anxious to witness a repetition of such exploits as they, when young, had often performed."

Even when the young were the most vigorous participants, then, it is clear that a good many older people attended a festive event as spectators—often to gossip, to pronounce judgements, and to display the wisdom of experience. James Withers wrote of how at a village fair, "The old folks talked of times when they were young, / And the same songs, year after year, were sung." Indeed, the crowds at many fairs and most feasts were drawn from all age groups of the population. Moreover, there were a number of holidays and diversions which placed no special premium on youth. The celebrations of the Christmas season, for instance, were appropriate for people of all ages. Several of the principal pastimes favoured no particular age group: bull-baiting and cock-fighting retained an appeal for many older men, and bell-ringing could be enjoyed and practised by people of almost any age. Sex, in fact, was probably a social determinant of greater weight than age, for while many of the major holidays involved women almost as much as men, most of the sporting events assumed that women would attend only as spectators, or not at all. . . .

During much of the eighteenth century the dominant attitude of the gentry towards the recreations of the people seems to have been one of acquiescence and tolerance. To a certain extent gentlemen shared some of the same recreational interests as the common people, and there was only limited room for conflict when their tastes were often so similar. The common denominator was particularly noticeable in the practice of animal sports. Although there were murmurings of disapproval before the middle of the century, there is no indication that any substantial number of gentlemen had as yet become seriously opposed to them; in fact, they were more likely to be keen spectators, and sometimes even participants. "My Black-Bull was Baited at Mrs Ann Rothwells," wrote Nicholas Blundell on 8 September 1712, "there played but three right Doggs and two of them were ill hurt." On 20 October 1714 the physician Claver Morris gave 1s. 6d. for the bull-baiting at a public house; and on 5 September 1759 James Woodforde wrote that "I went to the Bear-baiting in Ansford" (his father was rector of the parish). During the festivities on the day of the mayor's election in Liverpool it was said that "every house and window in the vicinity of the spot where the bear was baited, was adorned by the appearance of the most elegant ladies and gentlemen in the town"; and an observer of the Stamford bull-running probably had men of substance in mind when he claimed in 1785 that "I have heard some of the natives, who have lived in the metropolis, aver that they never saw any diversion there comparable to it, and if they were to pay a visit to their friends, have construed to come down a little before this day in order to become actors in it." Cock-fighting drew its followers from genteel as much as from plebeian sportsmen; and the informal field sports, especially fishing and coursing, sometimes brought together a diversity of social ranks.

The point to bear in mind is that, during the first half of the eighteenth century in particular, many gentlemen were not entirely disengaged from the culture of the common people. They frequently occupied something of a half-way house between the robust, unpolished culture of provincial England and the cosmopolitan, sophisticated culture which was based in London. Most of the country houses were not yet principally seasonal extensions of a polite and increasingly self-conscious urban culture, and many of their occupants remained relatively uncitified. They still retained some of the characteristics of rusticity, traits which they shared with the common people. The fact that the drama of the late seventeenth and earlier eighteenth centuries was full of booby-squires (boobies from London's point of view) is an indication, not that the characterization was necessarily accurate, but that there actually were a large number of gentlemen whose modes of thought and behaviour were deeply imbedded in the experiences of rural life. There were points at which genteel and plebeian experiences overlapped, and many a gentleman must have been prepared to accept the traditional customs of that community on which he himself depended for some of his satisfactions—not only economic, but psychic and social as well. He too was often a traditionalist, a cultural as well as a political conservative. Moreover, as one student of the period has justly observed, "to an English landowner popularity was of real importance," and the less social insulation was possible, the more was popularity valued. Nicholas Blundell cannot be regarded as a typical squire of the early eighteenth century—he was a Catholic and he lived in a relatively remote part of the country—but his diary is certainly an instructive testimony of the extent to which one gentleman was involved in those traditional activities which were also shared by the common people of the community. An intimate involvement in rural culture imposed certain common experiences on lord and labourer alike.

The paternalism and tolerance which did exist was not, of course, entirely disinterested. Sometimes it was very much in a gentleman's own interest to accommodate himself to the customary expectations of the common people. Despite the reservations which he may have held, it would often have been inexpedient to fly in the face of popular tradition. It was just this kind of self-interest which one observer had in mind when he wrote in 1759 of the custom of providing harvest feasts:

> These rural entertainments and usages . . . are commonly insisted upon by the reapers as customary things, and a part of their due for the toils of harvest, and complied with by their masters perhaps more through regards of interest, than inclination. For should they refuse them the pleasures of this much expected time, this festal night, the youth especially, of both sexes, would decline serving them for the future, and employ their labours for others, who would promise them the rustic joys of the harvest supper, mirth, and music, dance, and song.

There was, in other words, the need to accept a certain amount of give and take. It is often difficult, however, to determine how much of the gentry's behaviour was motivated by an awareness of their own self-interest and how much resulted from their uncritical acceptance of traditional practice. At times certainly there must have been a tension between the conflicting pulls of two inclinations, the one traditional and the other "progressive." Sir Joseph Banks seems to have felt this sort of tension when he wrote from Revesby, Lincolnshire, on 20 October 1783 that "This is the day of our fair when according to immemorial custom I am to feed and make drunk everyone who chooses to come, which will cost me in beef and ale near 20 pounds." His conformity to the customary obligations was probably prompted largely by the desire to maintain his reputation. Certainly some popular traditions must have been ambivalently regarded by the gentry: although many customs served to keep the people contented and sympathetically attached to their social superiors, they also assumed the expenditure of time and money. The crucial distinction, it seems, was between those who accepted the traditional practices, more or less willingly and without much consideration (probably the more common disposition), and those who regarded them as impediments to their freedom of action, as unacceptable and anachronistic popular impositions. The latter view . . . was to become increasingly powerful as the century advanced. . . .

Festive gatherings could also serve as a medium for the direct expression of hostility against the prevailing structures of authority. In these instances an active defiance was displayed against norms and constraints which were imposed from above; recreations became opportunities for irreverence, occasions for challenging conventional proprieties. This was one of the objections which was advanced against popular festivities by a writer in the mid-seventeenth century. Recreational events sometimes included incidents of aggression specifically intended to embarrass and irritate men of higher rank. The Swiss visitor César de Saussure complained in the 1720s of the populace "throwing dead dogs and cats and mud at passers-by on certain festival days." This sort of aggressiveness was commonly observed at the time of Derby's Shrovetide football match, for it was customary for unpopular or just well-dressed persons among the spectators to be "dusted" with bags of soot or powder. The ritual celebrations of November the 5th were sometimes employed to castigate some prominent individual in the community, usually by substituting the person's effigy for that of Guy Fawkes. On 5 November 1831, for example, the effigies of several bishops were paraded and burnt in a number of towns, a popular protest against their opposition to the Reform Bill.

Popular assemblies were potential threats to the gentry's tranquility, and occasionally a disturbance materialized. "I went to drink Tea at Mr Knapp's at Shenley," reported William Cole on Sunday, 30 August 1767, "where was the Feast and great Rioting, fighting and quarreling: some of the People affronted Mr Knapp [the rector] as he returned from Church." On many holidays the common people were animated by a confidence which stemmed in part from numbers (plebeian crowds, they knew, had to be treated more respectfully than plebeian individuals), and as a result they were able to neglect for the moment the habit of deference; they could more easily insult established authorities and mollify, or even reverse, the perquisites of social rank. . . .

As well as functioning as outlets for hostile feelings, popular recreations also served to foster social cohesiveness and group unity. Competitive team sports, for instance, often reinforced the sense of solidarity of the communities from which the opposing players were drawn. One observer said of the traditional sports of the people, no doubt with some exaggeration, that "the victory obtained by their parish or hundred, served them for the next half-year, till another holiday brought another trial of strength." At times when a community's aggressiveness was externally directed, its feeling of unity was likely to be enhanced. Moreover, when internal conflicts were well modulated, there was often a binding force in the competition itself, if only because the attention of many individuals was concentrated on one widely-embracing social event. It was said of the Derby football match that

> No public amusement is calculated to call forth so high a degree of public excitement. Horse races and white apron fairs must not be named in comparison with it. The aged and the young are drawn from their homes to witness the strife in which the robust and vigorous population of the town and immediate neighbourhood engage with all the energy of eager but amicable competition.

The rituals which were observed on certain holidays—club day feasts, Plough Monday processions, weavers' parades, Bishop Blaze festivities —were affirmations of common interests and common sentiments, and always helped to consolidate group pride. Parish feasts, as we have noticed, encouraged social cohesiveness through their emphasis on fellowship, hospitality, and good cheer. Indeed, most festive occasions which were rooted in the small community served to articulate a vision of the social harmony for which its members wished; festivities celebrated those ideals which transcended self, they reinforced the individual's sense of his social identity. "Games and amusements," a French social historian has concluded, "extended far beyond the furtive moments we allow them: they formed one of the principal means employed by a society to draw its collective bonds closer, to feel united."

Another function of popular recreations was that they provided realistic opportunities for the common people to acquire prestige and self-respect. Through them the people were able to create, as one writer has aptly put it, "small-scale success systems of their own." Even a critical observer of Derby's Shrovetide football match could reveal some of this rationale for the game's popularity: "I have seen this coarse sport carried to the barbarous height of an election contest; nay, I have known a football hero chaired through the streets like a successful member, although his utmost elevation of character was no more than that of a butcher's apprentice." A clergyman complained in 1830 of the Stamford bull-running that "he who is the most daring, in facing the enraged animal, gains a sort of enviable notoriety among his fellows, which urges him on to fresh feats of adventure." It was said that during games of camping "the spirit of emulation prevails, not only between the adverse sides, but [also] among the individuals on the same side, who shall excel his fellows." John Clare had a similar competitive mood in mind when he wrote of the wrestling at a village wake:

For ploughmen would not wish for higher fame
Than be the champion all the rest to throw
And thus to add such honours to his name
He kicks and tugs and bleeds to win the glorious game

Football, cricket, boxing, running, wrestling, cudgelling: all these sports provided channels for gaining personal recognition. In fact, they were among the few kinds of opportunities which labouring men had to perform publicly for the esteem of their peers.

PART 2

Early Industrialization
1750-1850

Detail from "Interior of the Great Industrial Exhibition," London, 1851.

Early Industrialization

The rate of social change in western Europe greatly increased after 1750. The industrial revolution began in England in the late eighteenth century and spread to France and other nearby countries after 1820. Its central feature was the application of power machinery to manufacturing, but it involved much more than this. The introduction of machines and factories necessarily imposed new systems of work. Rapidly rising production required new forms of consumption. Industrialization led to urbanization; many cities grew phenomenally. People were on the move. In the cities they found themselves surrounded by strangers, other new arrivals, and an unfamiliar environment. Urban life had always been different from rural. Now more people than ever before would experience these differences, ranging from greater sexual activity to greater literacy.

The industrial revolution was in part the product of other developments affecting the common people. Most important, the population began to increase rapidly in the eighteenth century. This forced people to seek new ways of making a living. Parents at all levels of society had to figure out what to do with and for children who in the past would not have survived. These same children, as they reached adulthood, often had to seek out new livelihoods, for there were not enough traditional jobs to go around. Here was a powerful disruptive force, challenging every social group and institution.

Partly because of population pressure, many economic activities became increasingly commercialized. Domestic manufacturing spread as one means of supporting excess rural labor. More and more peasants became involved with production for the market. By specializing in cash crops, they could hope to maintain growing families. In the cities, many artisan masters altered their business methods, treating their journeymen as paid employees rather than as fellow craftsmen. Journeymen found it harder to become masters because established masters reserved their places for their own children. This general commercialization of the economy affected far more people than did the early stages of the industrial revolution and very likely was profoundly disturbing to people accustomed to traditional economic relationships. Even the necessity of dealing with strangers, which commercialization required of peasants engaged in market agriculture or domestic manufacturing, may have been upsetting.

The period of early industrialization witnessed a host of developments in popular life and outlook, of which the industrial revolution proper, which began between 1780 and 1830 in most of Western Europe, was only part.

Obviously, then, the leading question for this period of European history concerns the impact of change. Was change simply imposed on the common people? Many peasants entered cities and factories only with the greatest reluctance—population pressure and other economic factors left them no other means of earning a living. A large number of these people endured a massive deterioration in their conditions before making a move. But other peasants may have been more eager for a change. Tensions with their parents (most migrants to the city were in their late teens or early twenties, an age at which disputes in a peasant household were particularly likely) or an active desire for a better life may have drawn them away from the countryside. Without question, some of the forces of change were beyond the control of the common people, but there may have been positive attractions as well. There are signs, too, that rural values themselves were changing, leaving some people better able to cope with a new life style. New forms of family life were an important part of Western Europe's history after 1700, and although some of the changes may first have affected the upper classes, other alterations in family functions spread widely across class lines.

Indeed, many of the most striking studies of social change in the decades around the beginnings of the industrial revolution have focused not on industrialization itself, but on other shifts in outlook and behavior beneath the level of formal intellectual or political life. Some of these shifts—for example, in aspects of family or sexual behavior—were genuinely popular; others—like some new attitudes toward physical and mental health—affected middle-class groups more than the population at large. In combination, the shifts suggest a broad pattern of change—of modernization—that soon included the industrial revolution. Factory industry and growing cities would produce changes and dislocations of their own, but they would also build on some of the new uses of the family or new kinds of sexual behavior.

Furthermore, although the industrial revolution caused a huge and rapid transformation, it did not occur overnight. We must not imagine there were modern factory conditions even by 1850. Early factories were small and sometimes rather informal. Many had no more than twenty workers and therefore were not necessarily impersonal or rigidly organized. Actually, most people were not working in factories at all, but rather in agriculture or in the crafts. Life for peasants and artisans was changing, but traditions yielded slowly. The common people themselves found ways to modify the shock of new conditions. Most people who moved to cities in this early period did so gradually: One generation moved to a village closer to a big city, the next to the city outskirts, and so on. Factory workers found ways to take time off so that they would not have to surrender completely their own notions of work and leisure. Even the middle class, more persuaded of the desirability of progress, harbored many traditional values.

So, along with the shock and disturbance of change, we must consider successful resistance and positive adaptation. Which reaction predominated depended on the particular circumstances—specific economic conditions, for example—and personality types. Few people could adapt to the new life without regret; but probably most people were not completely confused by it either. Even in their outright protests, the common people began to show signs of accepting the industrial system; protest gradually moved away from traditional goals toward demands for greater rewards within the new social order.

The century after 1750 saw the most dramatic structural changes associated with modernization, although usually still in incomplete form. Industrial technology and organization were accompanied by significant political change, including more representative parliaments, wider suffrage, and government involvement in areas such as education. In addition, the rapid increase in population was a new phenomenon to Europe, and although temporary, it produced great dislocation and an upsurge in the number of young people. The key questions of the period, in terms of human life, relate to the interaction between values and the new structures. What caused change? Impersonal forces and a few social groups such as factory owners and doctors, who had developed new or newly vigorous values, may have imposed changes on the bulk of the population. But some advantages in this first wave of modernization probably gave even ordinary people a motivation to change. How extensive and how damaging was the dislocation? The thread of persistence must be assessed here. Many groups, although deeply affected by new structures, may not have changed their outlook or their basic hopes and expectations much at all. Their efforts would show in protest, perhaps, but also in an uneven pattern of change. This pattern was so uneven that many observers would prefer not to use a blanket term like modernization, as opposed to labels for separate processes such as urbanization, to cover the diversity of situations compatible with the new industrial and urban framework. Not only peasants and artisans—still a majority of the population in 1850—but many big-city residents might differ little in their views on health, for example, from their preindustrial ancestors. Against this, others would argue that immense changes, associated particularly with demography and the family, can be seen, suggesting that in the popular mind, the preindustrial world was already lost.

BIBLIOGRAPHY

On population growth, E. A. Wrigley, *Population and History* (New York, 1969) is an excellent general introduction. See also Thomas McKeown, *The Modern Rise of Population* (New York, 1976). Several explanations of population growth are presented in Michael Drake, ed., *Population in Industrialization* (New York, 1969). Another convenient survey is Carlo Cipolla, *Economic History of World Population* (Baltimore, 1962). These demographic studies, in discussing rising fertility rates in the eighteenth century, bear some relation also to the history of sex, which is only now acquiring a bibliography of its own.

Changes in family life are stressed in Lawrence Stone, *Family, Sex and Marriage in England, 1500-1800* (New York, 1977) and Randolph Trumbach, *The Rise of the Egalitarian Family* (New York, 1978); see also the *Journal of Social History*, special issue, vol. 15, no.3 (1982). On sexuality specifically, Peter Laslett, *Family Life and Illicit Love in Earlier Generations* (New York, 1977) and Paul Robinson, *The Modernization of Sex* (New York, 1981). On children, see Ivy Pinchbeck and Margaret Hewitt, *Children in English Society* (London, 1973) and Lloyd De Mause, ed., *The History of Childhood* (New York, 1974).

Despite the currency of generalizations about the middle class, there have been surprisingly few real studies of this group. Charles Morazé, *The Triumph of the Middle Classes* (New York, 1968), interprets modern history in the light of middle-class ascendancy. See also W. J. Reader, *Professional Men* (London, 1966) and R. S. Neale, *Class and Ideology in the 19th Century* (London, 1972). Social mobility studies bear heavily on the middle class; see Hartmut Kaeble, *Historical*

Research on Social Mobility (New York, 1981). An excellent overview on middle-class development is E. J. Hobsbawm, *The Age of Capital 1848-1875* (New York, 1975). The key issue of contacts between middle-class values and those of the lower classes is taken up in Reinhard Bendix, *Work and Authority in Industry: Ideologies of Management in the Course of Industrial Labor* (New York, 1956); Sidney Pollard, *The Genesis of Modern Management* (Cambridge, Mass., 1965); and Peter N. Stearns, *Paths to Authority* (Urbana, Ill., 1978). The question of what the middle class was needs further exploration; outlines of a debate can be followed in Lenore O'Boyle, "The Middle Class in Western Europe," *American Historical Review* (1966), pp. 826-45, and Alfred Cobban, "The 'Middle Class' in France, 1816-1848," *French Historical Studies* (1967), pp. 42-51.

The topic of popular health and medicine is just beginning to receive attention. See the *Journal of Social History* (June 1977) for a variety of approaches to the topic in Europe and the United States. See also M. J. Peterson, *The Medical Profession in Mid-Victorian London* (Berkeley, 1978). Two useful books are John S. Haller and Robin M. Haller, *The Physician and Sexuality in Victorian America* (New York, 1977) and Paul Starr, *The Rise of Modern Medicine* (in the U.S.) (New York, 1982).

A rich literature is developing on preindustrial and early industrial protest. A good general statement is George F. Rudé, *The Crowd in History, 1730-1848* (New York, 1964). See also Eric J. Hobsbawm, *Primitive Rebels* (New York, 1965). Specific studies include Malcolm I. Thomis, *The Luddites: Machine-Breaking in Regency England* (Hamden, Conn., 1970); Eric Hobsbawm and George Rudé, *Captain Swing* (New York, 1968); and Robert Bezucha, *The Lyon Uprising of 1834* (Cambridge, Mass., 1974), all of which allow discussion of the persistence of traditional values. Important studies on the transition to new protest goals include John Merriman, ed., *Consciousness and Class Experience in 19th Century Europe* (New York, 1979) and Ted Margadant, *French Peasants in Revolt: The Insurrection of 1850* (Princeton, 1979). Peter N. Stearns, *1848: The Tide of Revolution in Europe* (New York, 1974) surveys a key period. Two important general assessments are Edward Shorter and Charles Tilly, *Strikes in France 1830-1968* (Cambridge, Eng., 1974) and James Cronin, *Industrial Conflict in Modern Britain* (Totowa, N.J., 1979). For a provocative overview of protest and its limitations, see Barrington Moore, Jr., *Injustice: The Social Bases of Obedience and Revolt* (New York, 1979).

On changing views of insanity and the treatment of the insane, see: Michel Foucault, *Madness and Civilization,* trans. Richard Howard (New York, 1965); Andrew Scull, *Museums of Madness: The Social Organization of Insanity in 19th-Century England* (New York, 1979); George Rosen, *Madness in Society* (New York, 1968); and Klaus Doerner, *Madmen and the Bourgeoisie* (Oxford, 1981). The topic has also been debated in American history; see David Rothman, *The Discovery of the Asylum* (Boston, 1971) and Gerald N. Grob, *The State and the Mentally Ill* (Chapel Hill, 1966).

A New Definition of Home Sweet Home

CAROLE SHAMMAS

One of the most striking findings by social historians in recent years has centered around the development of new functions and definitions in the Western European (and North American) family, that began as early as the seventeenth century. Elements of family life that we tend to take for granted, at least as ideals, turn out to have been rather recent historical inventions that contrast notably with family patterns before modern times. These inventions may, furthermore, have been basic parts of the initial transformation of Western people—even quite ordinary people—away from traditional patterns, toward more modern ones. New family styles reflected new values, and they also may have promoted new kinds of people—the products of growing up in the new family environment.

Carole Shammas stresses the gradual nature of the changing definition of home life—how it picked up steam in the eighteenth century, crossed social lines, and continued into more recent times. Her account raises important questions: Why did this change come about? Obviously more elaborate home life reflected growing prosperity among ordinary people, but it was not the only possible use of greater resources. Was the home beginning to be seen as a refuge from a somewhat confusing outside world, and so made as comfortable as possible? Issues also arise concerning the roles of family members in the new household arrangements. Women gained new kinds of power as they administered a more complex household. Was this a consolation prize for failure to gain power in the wider world? And were men made uncomfortable by the new household routines?

Shammas mentions one final twist to this particular strand of modern family history. Are we now witnessing the end of this long modern trend—and if so why, and with what consequences? If the modern household stressed elaborate home rituals, is the contemporary household entering a postmodern phase in which household functions will shrink once again in favor of non-family ties? This aspect of the analysis need not be taken for granted—in some ways (as regard leisure time) the importance of home seems to be increasing still—but it is worth consideration.

Currently in the United States we are emerging from a long period of intensive investment in domesticity. By domesticity, I mean making home the center for most non-market social interaction. The creation of this environment, where family members relax together and entertain select members of the outside world, has invariably fallen to the woman, the "homemaker." The widespread re-entry of married females into the labor force, the drop in fertility, the rising number of divorces, and other demographic phenomena are now resulting, however, in a decline in the quantity and quality of goods and labor devoted to the home. Vinyl upholstery, double-knits, and fast food restaurants all herald the dawn of the new age.

The change in attitude toward domesticity in the last few years has also been pronounced. From *Diary of a Mad Housewife* to *Interiors*, the message clearly reads that too refined a sensibility in regard to such things as turkey dressing or furniture placement can lead to familial strife and mental instability. In her recent novel, *Happy all the Time*, Laurie Colwin has valiantly attempted to rehabilitate the image of the household aesthete by making her heroine, Holly, a strong character who cogently argues the case for the "domestic sensualist." How persuasive such arguments can be, though, when the real life exponents of the ideal have become dress manufacturers and book editors, is doubtful. In fact, it should be noted that those who express themselves most vehemently on the importance of domesticity, the Total Woman crowd, concentrate on new ways to serve up sex, not tuna.

The passing or at least alteration of an institution always sparks interest in its origins, because people want some reassurance that what they are abandoning is not one of life's constants without which civilization will collapse. It is not surprising, therefore, that there is a growing literature on the rise of domesticity in Western society. Although domesticity is usually associated with the Victorian middle class during industrialization, historians of the family have detected signs of it developing as far back as the sixteenth century. At that time, according to one interpretation, the aristocratic households of Western Europe began a retreat into privacy. While the medieval nobility had eaten, slept, and lived "publicly" with a large number of retainers, kin, and servants in constant attendance, by the early modern period the concept of hospitality and display had declined and the desire to withdraw into the nuclear family manifested itself. A century or so later, the bourgeoisie began constructing their cozy nests.

Let us begin with the sixteenth century household. It was common for books giving advice in husbandry during the Tudor period to include a section toward the end, after plowing, harvesting, and animal diseases had

From Carole Shammas, "The Domestic Environment in Early Modern England and America," *Journal of Social History*, Vol. 14 No. 1 (Fall, 1980), pp. 3, 5–6, 11, 17–19.

been thoroughly discussed, that related to the obligations of the "hus-wife." One of the earliest of the genre was Fitzherbert's *The Book of Husbandry*, published in 1534. The list of housewifely duties he reeled off is rather awe inspiring and has been quoted many times, but what he left out or gave short shrift is also significant. Fitzherbert counselled the wife,

> First in a morning when thou art waked, and proposeth to rise, lift up thy hand, and bless thee, and make a sign of the holy cross . . . in the name of the father, the son and the holy ghost. And if thou say a Pater noster, an Ave, and a Creed, and remember thy maker, thou shalt speed much the better. And when thou art up and ready, then first sweep thy house, dress up thy dishboard, and set all things in good order within thy house, milk the cows, suckle thy calves, sye up thy milk, take up thy children and array them, and provide for thy husbands breakfast, dinner, supper and for thy childrens and servants, and take thy part with them.

That was all he had to say about family dining, childcare, house-cleaning, and decoration. The rest of the schedule concerned food, drink, and cloth production for the household: taking grain to the mill, checking the miller did not cheat you, baking, brewing, processing butter and cheese, feeding the pigs, caring for the poultry, planting the herb and vegetable garden, sowing flax and hemp, and making linen and wool cloth. If the farm had no sheep then Fitzherbert directed the housewife to "take wool to spin of clothmakers and by that means . . . have a convenient liv-ing." In time of need she should help her mate "fill the dung cart, drive the plough, load hay, corn, and such other." She might also go to the local market to buy and sell commodities. Here Fitzherbert cautioned both her and her husband to be honest with one another and not try to cheat by lying to their spouse about the prices paid and received.

What about after supper when all the tasks had been accomplished? The author quite clearly instructed the head of the household to go to bed unless some work activity was going on.

> One thing I will advise thee to remember, and specially in wintertime, when thou sittest by the fire, and hast supped, to consider in thy mind, whether the works that thou, thy wife, & thy servants shall do, be more advantage to thee than the fire, and candlelight, meat and drink that they shall spend, if it be more advantage, then sit still: and if not, then go to thy bed and sleep.

Now obviously few housewives performed all the tasks Fitzherbert out-lined, and not every peasant couple promptly retired after supper in order to rise early the next morning and repeat the whole regimen over again. What is amazing, however, was Fitzherbert's assumptions about the proper conduct of the peasant family, particularly the low value he attached to sociability and human interaction within the household. His peasant home resembled a workplace. It was unclear if the husband and the rest of the family ate together, whether the mother's childcare duties involved more than dressing and feeding her offspring, and how families relaxed with each other at home. Not only did husbands and wives have to be on their guard constantly to prevent people from cheating them, but they could not even trust one another. This is the kind of document that has prompted historians of the family to conclude that the emotional ambiance in the preindustrial home differed markedly from that found in *Little Women*. Fitzherbert's people exhibited their respect and concern for one another by getting their work done rather than by attending to each other's personal development.

Of course many working people, even those who had their own cottages, did not regularly dine at home but received victuals at the table of their employer or in the alehouse. Unlike the Victorian establishment who considered the working class pub an unmitigated evil, the Tudor-Stuart authorities actually granted alehouses some legitimacy. The statutes passed condemning the drunkenness and illegal activities that sometimes occurred in these places also recognized the need for each parish to have one "for such supply of the wants of those people who are not able by greater quantities to make their provision of victuals." The alehouse might be little more than a widow's shack, but it provided a place where poor people and laborers, lacking the time or means to prepare meals at home, could resort. They also became the spots where neighbors congregated to drink, hear the news, and play games. By going to an alehouse rather than relaxing at home, one saved the expense of firewood and candles. The government, however, did not approve of *this* use of alehouses and tried to limit the amount of time that could be spent in them and restrict the clientele on Sunday to travelers.

The primary times set aside for leisurely enjoyment of food, drink, and one's fellow human beings came on feast days. Rather than sociability being mixed in with everyday life in the home, people of this period seemed to go more for orgies of it on special occasions. This mentality comes out in the housewifery literature where the woman is told not to "keep companie" with her neighbors "except when she may doe them good, or helpe them," *or* "when she maketh some marriage or assemblies of great companie." Major feasts in England included harvest dinner, the churchales, and Wake or Saint's day, and the celebration of most of them occurred elsewhere than inside the average home. They took place in the hall of the local great man, the church house, a mill, a large barn or in the village square. Lasting often all day and into the night, many feasts involved such an array of dishes that the requisite supplies, labor, and space exceeded the resources of the individual husbandman and his wife, so the community pooled its provisions and dishes for the special day.

Most of the recipe books of this period seem primarily directed towards these feasts and banquets. After going through menus for such elaborate events, one early seventeenth century writer then turned to what he called a "humble feast" of two courses with sixteen dishes each day that *any* housewife could prepare herself with little or no help. Needless to say, even the "humble feast" was not the kind of meal you served to a few friends who happened to drop by for dinner.

By the eighteenth century, the investment patterns found in the inventories [of household goods] imply some [major] changes in the household environment had occurred. Bedding, linen, and brass/pewter assets only took up a third of consumer goods investment in pre-Revolutionary Massachusetts as opposed to one half in sixteenth century Oxfordshire, and a whole group of commodities that promoted domesticity began to surface in ordinary households.

What really marked the mid-eighteenth century off from previous periods, then, was the diffusion of eating and drinking goods into the ordinary household. As one student of eighteenth century domesticity has suggested, dinner was probably the most popular form of entertainment. Knives and forks, glassware, and tea equipment appeared in a majority of inventories of decedents in the average wealth category. Small craftsmen, husbandmen, and even some laborers fell into this classification, and not only did the majority of them have these goods but nearly a third owned some pieces of china and a fifth possessed coffee equipment. Research on Maryland and on France indicates an increase in tableware around the same time or even a few decades earlier.

Perhaps the eighteenth century artifacts that reveal the most about changes in the domestic environment are those associated with tea drinking. Early in the century, the use of this beverage was the preserve of the upper classes. When the *Spectator*, the gossipy London journal, first began publication in 1711, one of the editors recommended the paper "to all well regulated families, that set apart an Hour in every Morning for Tea and Bread and Butter." Make it "a Part of the Tea Equipage," he joked... However, the practice of drinking tea spread beyond the *Spectator* readership and those with mahogany tea tables and silver spoons. Tea became the drink of the people probably because, in adulterated form, it could be drunk at home without the expense of preparation entailed with beer or even cider, and eighteenth century households did seem to show a preference for goods that could be consumed *en famille*. The breakfast at home with tea replaced the morning draft gulped down at the alehouse or at the abode of an employer.

What the tea equipment, the knives and forks, crockery, glassware and such seem to indicate is that, during the course of the eighteenth century, the family meal began to take shape along with more entertainment of small groups of outsiders in the home. Besides the shift in breakfast that I just discussed, the evidence from domestic economy books reinforces the impression given by the artifacts found in the inventories that other everyday meals, dinner and supper, became more sociable occasions. For one thing, cookery books dealt more with problems encountered in daily food preparation—giving advice on marketing, recipes for Lenten meals, menus for farm servants and sick people—while feasts received less and less emphasis. In 1708, the *Ladies' Diary*, an almanac popular in England and the colonies, contained in its calendar the fixed and moveable feast days, biblical passages to be read on those days, the times during the year marriages were allowed, and fillers at the bottom of the page giving further information on holiday activities. By 1771, all that material, except for the name of the saints days, had been excluded. The passing of the housewife as server also was an important benchmark. By mid-century she less often stood and served throughout the meal, carving and attending to the needs of those at the table, but more frequently sat down with the rest and ate with them.

In addition, literary evidence indicates some increased attention to washing and cleaning although I do not have sufficient quantitative materials to show when this evolved and who was affected.

The change in relations between household members identified by historians of the early modern family was accompanied by alterations of a material nature that implied a change in the allocation of household labor and involved the purchase of consumer goods. Domesticity cannot be described solely in terms of feelings, for the conversion of homes into centers of sociability required a shift in female work patterns. The change might be described as one of specialization: women's labor in behalf of home consumption gradually ceased being spread thinly over primary, intermediary, and final processes and became concentrated on the last stage. This alteration eventually took place not only in the production of food but clothing, furnishings and even children. Cooking, sewing, decorating, cleaning, and childrearing are final processes, and the special attention devoted to these activities is what domesticity was all about. While female participation in primary and intermediary processes hardly disappeared, more and more it occurred within the context of market production.

The inventories reveal that more than just the elite experienced a change in living habits, for laboring class households readily purchased the less expensive tools of domesticity, teapots, knives and forks, cheap crockery, and so forth. The concept of two stages between the sixteenth century and 1800 seems a sound one. The changes in the domestic environment that began occurring during the sixteenth century made the house a more comfortable place to live for many people as improvements once enjoyed by only the privileged members of society started cropping up in the inventories of husbandmen. The evidence does not suggest, however, the acquisition of new commodities or additional expenditures of female time to promote sociability in the home. Only the increased presence of Bibles indicates a new domestic function and it was a religious one supervised by the male household head. So what one finds in the first period is a type of patriarchal domesticity.

By the mid-eighteenth century, though, all levels of society showed some traces of new, secular, domestic activities, particularly in relation to eating and drinking. Yeomen and husbandmen households moved slowest into the domestic revolution, but they did move. My samples, of course, are limited in area, and what happened in Germany or France or other areas of the West I cannot tell. Still, it would be a mistake, I think, to assume New England or London were completely different from all other communities and that no changes in domesticity among average households occurred elsewhere until industrialization. Wherever researchers investigate the subject of early modern material culture, whether in the Dutch countryside, on Maryland plantations, or French villages many of the same patterns discussed here can be found.

Increased affluence was undoubtedly necessary for these changes. Bedding, tableware, and furnishings cost money. Plus no one would have wanted to invest in these things and retreat into the home unless the house itself had not grown sturdier, warmer, and lighter—improvements that also require investment. Something else, though, happened. Over the three century period, the same wealth groups progressively invested a higher proportion of their wealth in consumer goods. This trend, I suspect, resulted from the substitution of market for home produced commodities. If you did not manufacture certain goods at home you did not have to invest in the goods needed to produce them. In the long run, it probably raised the family's standard of living because household production of a wide variety of items was inefficient and beyond the economic reach of the laboring class. Non-farm households, both rich and poor, most quickly made this transformation as can be seen in the tea equipment probabilities. These households of course were also growing in number among the general population over time.

It was probably no coincidence that increased investment in domesticity occurred at a time when according to some sources, new "opportunities" for female employment opened up. The availability of wage labor for women and children during the eighteenth century allowed families to purchase more on the market and more of what they bought reflected feminine interests.

In many ways women had the most to gain, considering the constraints placed on their conduct, by added investments in homemaking. They, traditionally, had been in charge "within doors," the house and surrounding yard comprised their workspace. The nature of their work and their childbearing-childcare responsibilities meant they were more tied to the house than men and probably could take less advantage of community gathering places. The evolution of the house into a home made social interaction more accessible to women and put it more under their control. And, then, much of the work connected with the home production of cloth and food could only be described as physically gruelling. Women might have to engage in such activities for wages, but release from some of these tasks—such as bleaching linen or making malt—must have been a welcome relief. Moreover, the improvements they promoted in the domestic environment are those that modern society identifies with a higher standard of living.

Certainly in the historical record one finds much less ambivalence about domesticity among women than men. Males complained about housecleaning upsetting their routine, about the expense of substituting crockery for trenchers and adding parlors, about more elaborate cookery, and so forth. The pub evolved into an anti-domesticity hangout for men, something, for all its rowdiness, the alehouse had never been because there was no need for it. It is difficult not to see a contest of wills in all this. The oppressive interiors and constricting social conventions that stifled the middle-class Victorian female and the technologically complex home whose labor-saving devices drove the twentieth century housewife up the wall may in their origins have been a source of power and influence for the physically vulnerable and legally unequal woman of the early modern period.

The Rise of Romantic Love

JEAN-LOUIS FLANDRIN

The way Western European family members related to each other began
to change during the eighteenth century. Relationships that had been based on
economic functions began to include new emotional functions as well. The relationship between husband and wife, as well as that between parent and child,
become less authoritarian and increasingly affectionate. A corresponding shift in
the range of emotions mentioned in family advice literature—mostly authored by
religious writers at this point—took place as a result. Anger and hostility, which
apparently had been extremely visible in earlier families, were played down in
favor of a more positive view of love. An early phase of modernization thus
included a major redefinition of the family and of acceptable emotions. Without
much question, love matches had been discouraged in earlier periods, because
they might endanger economically sound matchmaking. Undoubtedly, people fell
in love sometimes, both before and after marriage. Accounts of romantic expectations in seventeenth-century England are numerous. Because romantic love was
not regarded favorably by parents or church officials, however, it is almost certain
that the emotion was experienced or sought less often than we find normal today.
In the following selection, Jean-Pierre Flandrin takes a rather strong position concerning the absence of love in premodern times. He also stresses that the conversion to more affectionate criteria was not complete by the eighteenth century, at
least not in France, but that a major shift was clearly underway.

The idea that emotions have a history, and thus change over time, is a start-
ling discovery. The causes of the early modern transformation from a relationship
based on authority and convenience to one founded on affection remain somewhat obscure. There was certainly some influence from the new Puritan
emphasis, which downplayed friendships outside the family and so stressed a wife
as a friend and a loving partner; but the trend spread in Catholic countries like
France as well. Some authors have suggested that the growth of domestic
manufacturing and the growth of market relationships in the pre-industrial economy fostered a new image of non-family members as rivals and competitors,
which thereby shifted emotional expectations to the family.

The idea of a major change in emotional life has encountered some important criticism. Flandrin and other authorities stress that the redefinition first took
place among people in the aristocracy and middle class, and only gradually trickled
down to the lower class. But critics contend that the lower classes may have had
just as rich an emotional life as their "betters." Flandrin relies heavily on literary
sources—that is, materials written about what the family should be like. Is this
good evidence concerning the *actual* family environment? Flandrin does adduce
examples from real life behavior, but inevitably they are impressionistic; there is

no easy way to measure the incidence of romantic expectations. Some critics argue that although Flandrin proves that marriages were once handled differently from our own day, he only asserts that actual emotional life has changed with modern times. Was love in fact so novel? The concept, certainly, was not new; literature had long dealt with love. Beneath the surface of arranged marriages and economic functions, love may have been a frequent emotion in family life even in premodern times.

Nevertheless, the idea of a shift in family emotions is intriguing. Even critics grant a shift in emotional balance, with new emphasis on love. Did this shift have a wider impact? For example, during the eighteenth century, the population increased dramatically. In large part, this resulted from the discovery of new crops like the potato. But might it in part have followed from greater family affection, which heightened the importance (and frequency) of sexual activity and made children the objects of new emotions? In the nineteenth century, the family was a refuge from the outside world; surely this was possible in part because of the redefinition of family emotions. And Flandrin directly links the changes he describes as beginning in the eighteenth century to similar characteristics in the twentieth century—he considers the twentieth century the completion of this "modernization" of the family as an emotional unit. Many authorities indeed see even some of the characteristic problems of the contemporary family, such as high divorce rates, as the result of the rising expectations of love. Changes in emotion, then, may be a key part of the Western modernization process. Do these trends, unlike the elaboration of household routines discussed in the previous selection, continue in our own day?

In drawing attention to the respect and obedience which the wife, the children and the servants owed to the head of the family, and to the duties of protection, supervision and chastisement of the latter, it is not certain that we have characterized domestic relationships with sufficient precision, since most of the other social relationships were similarly based on the principle of authority, and on the duties of protection, supervision and chastisement which were incumbent on the superiors. Did one not also expect the members of a family to feel for one another those specific sentiments of family relationships which we term conjugal love, maternal love, paternal love and brotherly affection, and which, rightly or wrongly, we distinguish from what Christianity understands by 'love of one's neighbour'? To what extent did the morality of family relationships refer to these specific sentiments and to others, and how did it characterize them?

For the purposes of such a study, let us examine closely the terminology employed by a particular moralist [of the early eighteenth century],

From Jean-Louis Flandrin, *Families in Former Times* (Cambridge: Cambridge University Press, 1977), pp. 145, 148, 149–50, 151, 152–3, 155, 164–5, 166–7, 171–3.

Antoine Blanchard; . . . an innovator, in comparison with the confessors of the late sixteenth and early seventeenth centuries.

In the first category we have grouped the sentiments connected with the hierarchical character of domestic relationships. *Respect* and *deference* are what the writer expects from inferiors, that is, in this context, the children and servants. He asks the children: 'Have you not been lacking in respect toward your father and your mother?' and the servants: 'Have you shown to [your masters] all the deference due to them?' *Contempt* was another, and negative, way of referring to the respect due to one's superiors. It could happen that children felt contempt for their parents 'on account of their poverty or of some natural defect'; as for the servants suspected of having 'had contempt' for their masters, they are asked in the same article: 'Have you not spoken ill of them?' The wife also, as an inferior, is capable of having 'contempt for the counsels of her husband' and for his 'remonstrances' to her. On the other hand, parents are not asked if they have felt contempt for their children, nor masters if they have felt it for their servants, because they did not owe them any respect. This being the case, it is worth observing that, when examining the sins of the husband towards his wife, Blanchard asks: 'Have you not treated her too harshly and with contempt? . . . Have you not rendered her contemptible to your children and your servants by the contempt that you have shown for her. . . . Have you not allowed that creature [meaning the husband's mistress] to insult her and speak to her with contempt?' The reason for this is that the wife, in spite of being subordinate to her husband, is his equal, as Fernandes de Moure had emphasized a century earlier; and she was, within the house, superior to the children and the servants, and most certainly to that despicable creature, her husband's mistress.

On their side, however, those subject to his governance are guilty when they arouse the master's anger. 'Have you not given them reason to become angry with you and to use abusive words to you?' Blanchard enquires, when examining the sins of servants against their master. Examining those of children against their parents, he asks: 'Have you not given them reason to be angry with you on account of your disobedience and your bad behaviour?' He asks the wife: 'Have you not given him reason to be angry and have fits of rage on account of your arrogance and your obstinacy? . . . Have you not refused him his conjugal rights without legitimate cause? Has your refusal not been the motive for some fit of rage or some other disturbance?' And she is urged to show *patience, obligingness* and *charity*. 'Have you maintained a close union with your husband, suffering his shortcomings with patience and charity? . . . Have you not been insufficiently obliging towards him?' The reason for this is that fits of rage and anger are the normal reactions of the head of the family to the clumsiness or impertinence of his servants, the disobedience of his children, the obstinacy of his wife or, worse still, the refusal of her body. In this, he is doing no more than follow the example of Yahweh, whose anger was so often aroused by the insubordination of the Jews. Anger formed part of the manifestations of authority. One could reproach the master of the house only for indulging in it to excess.

It was to evil sentiments, even more than to sorrowful sentiments, that Antoine Blanchard alluded with great frequency: *envy, jealousy, dislike, hatred, desire for someone's death.* These evil sentiments are the most numerous (seven different notions), the most frequently mentioned (nineteen times), and the most evenly shared, since they could be felt by the husband towards his wife and by the wife towards her husband, by the children towards their parents, by the parents towards their children, and by the children towards one another. Only the servants, apparently, were incapable of feeling or provoking such sentiments.

It is true that the confessor was concerned about the *hatred* that the wife might harbour towards her husband. However, he was worried less by the gravity of this sentiment or the acts to which it might induce the woman than by his fear that this hatred might give the husband 'reason to attach himself to some strange woman', and that 'some debauchery' might ensue as a result. It is only on the part of the other members of the family that hatred appears dangerous.

The husband is first asked some innocuous questions: 'Have you not had hatred for your wife?' or 'Have you not uttered abusive reproaches to your wife out of the hatred that you had for her?' Then he goes on to enquire about desire for her death and attempts to murder her:

> Have you not desired her death, in order to be able to marry another? . . . By the ill-treatment and the vexation that you have given your wife, have you not made her sick? Have you not refused her needs and the necessary assistance in that condition? During the course of her illness, have you not tried to make it even worse, with the object of procuring her death, heaping imprecations and curses on her?

It is true that in none of these three articles is hatred specifically referred to: it may simply be that the husband loves another woman. . . . The Frenchmen of pre-Revolutionary times, too, were suspected of practising 'divorce Italian style.'

Children were suspected of somewhat heinous intentions towards their parents: 'Have you not desired their death? Was it out of hatred or with the object of acquiring the inheritance earlier? Have you not continued to harbour hatred towards them? For how long did it last? Have you given them external signs of it which they were able to perceive?' If one is to believe Freud, of course, this desire for one's parents' death is present in all ages and in all countries. However, the confessors of past times were not dealing with the unconscious, and all of them, from

Gerson to Blanchard, asked the same question. The reason is that, in a society in which one lived, to a far greater extent than nowadays, on an ancestral patrimony, the child was really—and not just unconsciously—dependent until his father's death. The ownership of the patrimony, as much as laws and morality, gave the father the power to impose on his children an occupation or a spouse, and to correct his 'depraved' tendencies—that is, to oppose what the child wanted to be. This dependence, in relation to the parents and the patrimony, lent further strength to the hatred of unloved children for an unjustly favoured child.

More surprising, at first sight, is the hatred that parents might harbour for certain of their children. This sentiment was envisaged as being entertained by fathers who favoured one of their children at the expense of the others 'out of the indifference or hatred' which they felt for them. Should one assume that, in this context, the term 'hatred' is incorrect, or that it had at that time a less strong connotation than today, which its association with the term 'indifference' in this article and in others in fact suggests? The following articles provide evidence of the possible force of this hatred: 'Have you not beaten any of your children, excessively and without cause, out of bad-temper and because you did not love him? Have you not refused him his needs? Have you not desired his death?' There is no doubt about the fact that this hatred could be carried to great lengths. Why? How were children, so defenceless legally and economically in relation to their parents, capable of inspiring their hatred—and not merely their dislike?

The only proof that Blanchard demands of affection between spouses on the one hand, and between parents and children on the other, is that he condemns the *indifference* of the woman towards her husband or of parents towards their children, and the *coldness* of children towards their parents. Furthermore, it must be noted that when the wife is asked if she has not had 'indifference or hatred' for her husband, the juxtaposition of these two notions does not suggest a very emphatic demand for affection; and that, besides, this indifference or even this hatred were feared less for themselves than because they could 'give reason' to the husband 'to transfer his affection elsewhere'. As for the husband, affection is not demanded of him in either positive or negative terms, doubtless because his indifference was not considered liable to impel the wife to adultery.

Similarly, the indifference that parents were reproached for showing to certain of their children was associated with hatred; and they were reproached for these sentiments in so far as they aroused envy and jealousy between the children. The only question in which a lack of affection is in itself denounced is this one, addressed to children: 'Have you not shown coldness or callousness towards [your parents] because they were a burden to you?' Even so, the terms 'coldness' and 'callousness' appear to refer to external conduct rather than to the absence of good sentiments which it manifests.

This image of marital relationships was not, perhaps, that of the common run of the faithful, but it certainly permeated the mental attitudes of the pious and also circulated in other, entirely different, sectors. One may read once again, for example, what Montaigne wrote about conjugal relationships.

> These shameless caresses which our first excitement suggests to us in this game [of love] are not only indecent but also injurious when indulged in with our wives. *Let them learn shamelessness, at least, from another hand.* They are always aroused enough for our needs. I have used only natural and simple instruction. Marriage is a religious and devout tie: that is why the pleasure that one derives from it should be a pleasure circumspect, serious and mingled with a certain severity; it should be a voluptuousness in some ways prudent and conscientious. And, since its principal end is procreation, there are some who cast doubts as to whether, when we are without the hope of that fruit—as when the women are beyond childbearing age, or pregnant—it is permissible to seek their embraces.

Going further, he uttered a warning against an excess of conjugal affection.

> The affection which we have for our wives is quite legitimate: nevertheless, theology does not neglect to curb and restrain it. I think I have read in the past in the works of Saint Thomas, in a passage in which he condemns marriages between kinsfolk within the prohibited degrees, this reason among others: that there is a danger that the affection that one has for such a woman may be immoderate; for if marital affection exists there entire and perfect, as it should do, and one overburdens this further with the affection that one owes to one's kinsfolk, there is no doubt that this addition will transport such a husband beyond the bounds of reason.

This passage supports the idea recently expressed by an ethnologist, that all societies—with the exception of our own, in which the intermediary structures have disappeared, leaving the State and the conjugal nucleus face to face—have distrusted the excessive love of married couples for one another because it risks making them forget their other social obligations.

It was different in the case of the English Puritans: 'unlesse there be a ioyning of harts, and knitting of affections together, it is not Mariage indeed, but in shew & name', wrote Henrie Smith, as early as the second half of the sixteenth century. The love of which these Puritans spoke resembled, in many respects, that which Catholic couples should have for one another: it consisted of desiring the true good of the other person, which implied for the husband not only providently ensuring the material well-being of his wife, honouring her in every way, not humiliating her or exasperating her by his idleness, his prodigality, his keeping bad company or feeling an unjustified jealousy, but also reproving her with patience and gentleness when she committed a fault, instilling good manners into her and educating her as a co-heiress of the Kingdom of God.

Nevertheless, the Puritans were already more insistent than the Catholics on married love as a duty. 'For the first', wrote William Whately, 'a man must love his wife above all the creatures in the world besides . . . no neighbour, no kinsman, no friend, no parent, no child should be so near and dear.' Also, more than being a duty, love is a grace that permits, and alone permits, the fulfilment of conjugal obligations. In the view of Robert Pricke, this 'is not only the fountain and cause, but also the director and life of all duties. For where it is wanting, either no duties will be performed, or untowardly and from the teeth outward, or not continually.' And Robert Bolton added: 'Without this mutual complacency, that I may so speak, and loving contentment in each other, I doubt whether I should encourage any to proceed.' This 'lovingness which is drawing into action' is also 'a sweet, loving and tender-hearted pouring out of their hearts, with much affectionate dearness, into each other's bosom; in all passages, carriages and behaviour, one towards another'.

There is also, however, an honourable sexual dimension in this love. One does not have to repudiate it and purge oneself of it, as Catholic morality of former times proposed; on the contrary, the sexual instinct exists, according to a recent analyst of Puritan thought, to bring the man and the woman together and to permit them, in marriage, to express, sustain and fortify their love. This already foreshadowed present-day Catholic teaching.

This love of the married couple for one another comes from God and cannot be made to exist by human fiat. 'As Faith', wrote Thomas Gataker, 'so love cannot be constrained.' And he went on to explain: 'the Woman that thou wouldest be suitor to is God's Daughter. . . .It is God who disposes of her heart. . . .Parents who have the power to grant her in marriage cannot command affections, but God is able to incline them.' He inclines them, the Catholics might have said, by the grace of the sacrament of marriage. The Puritans, however, did not believe that marriage was a sacrament, but they did believe in predestination: it was, therefore, from all eternity that God inclined the future spouses to that love, in order to lead them to marriage. Love is mysterious, observes Daniel Rogers; the pagans attribute it to the stars, but it is God who has made it particularly strong between certain men and certain women for the purpose of marriage. It was in this respect that the Puritan teaching differed most markedly from the earlier Catholic doctrine of marriage, and it is in this respect, above all, that it seems to constitute the origin of our present-day 'marriage of love'. . . .

Love had existed for centuries. Among the social élites, and particularly, perhaps, for the women, it constituted an essential value, one of the principal motives for living. However, one could only speak about it in profane literature—since the twelfth century, this had been almost exclusively devoted to the topic—and one could only live it outside marriage or at the risk of upsetting the social order. Yet illicit love-affairs had been severely harassed both by the public authorities and by the Church. After the twelfth century the latter slightly liberalized its doctrine of marriage—and the same could be said of the Protestants—but only to put an end to adultery, concubinage and prostitution. More or less convinced of the immorality of this type of love, the élites of society, in the second half of the eighteenth century, refused to repress any longer their feelings and their desires. They claimed the right to satisfy them openly, legitimately, within marriage. This was a first revolt against the traditional morality, before that of the twentieth century, which is beginning to cast doubts on the virtues of the marriage of love and to wonder whether it is not a new form—the Puritan form—of repression.

Behind the overt gestures of defiance, the underlying developments were slow and unobserved. The series of catechisms and of manuals for confessors have indicated some of these. Others can be revealed by an examination of the legal proceedings involved in the breaking-off of engagements. In 1527 a certain Gabriel Songis complained to the officiality of Troyes that his fiancée refused to celebrate their wedding. The girl, an orphan, retorted that she had been forced into this 'so-called marriage' by her guardians, and that she was unable to contract a valid marriage, being only 'ten or twelve years old'. The plaintiffs contested this defence by alleging that she was thirteen or fourteen. In a judgment delivered on 18 January 1528, the accused girl was 'adjudged to Gabriel Songis as his future wife' and condemned to pay costs.

To break a promise of marriage, at that time, one had to have more serious grounds. In the second half of the seventeenth century, this was no longer the case. In 1665 Jeanne Pluot declared that she had never intended to fulfil the promises made to a certain Lasnier 'against her will and out of the respect that she bore to her father and mother who had browbeaten her'; that she 'has never loved and still does not love the said Lasnier, and would choose death rather than marry him'. The court released her from her promises.

Others obtained the same liberation without adopting this tragic tone: in 1666, Elizabeth Bernard said simply that she 'has never had, any more than at present, any affection for the said Grosos', her fiancé. Odart Courtois, a painter and glazier who had become engaged to a comparatively rich widow at the instigation of his parents, said that he had not been given 'time to know her' and that, now that he did know her, he did not have 'any affection' for her; in 1673 Nicole Mussot wished to break off the engagement because her fiancé 'has not fulfilled the duties that a fiancé owes to his fiancée, which has chilled the affection that she had for him'. In short, all those who refused to get married despite their promises won their cases. It is true that between the beginning of the sixteenth century and the middle of the seventeenth, there was an essential change of attitude of the Church, not towards love but towards the sacredness of 'promises for the future'. Whatever the reason, however, the effect is evident: young men and girls could now be freed from their promises of marriage, giving as the sole reason the fact that they do not love or no longer love their proposed future spouse.

Both a progressive development, and a failure to complete the process, can be observed. In 1785, the author of the *Catéchisme de Bruxelles* still does not carry his discussion of the marriage of love to its logical conclusion. 'It is, nevertheless, just', he writes,

> that a child who is not capable of discernment should not be free to bind himself, without the authority of his parents, by an indissoluble knot. This would be, on the part of the latter, an act of outrageous inhumanity, to abandon him to thoughtlessness and temerity, which are only too common at his age; when it is a question of deciding, by a marriage, the happiness or misfortune of his life. His natural guardians may, without his being able to complain about it, prevent his committing himself, or defer his commitment, if they consider it unworthy of him or precipitate. Of course, they should consent to it when the match appears *eligible.*

Whereas in the preceding passage the author based marriage on love and love on virtue, it is no longer to the absence of virtue that the word 'eligible' refers: it is to disparity of social standing. Fundamentally, the author has contented himself with clothing in a fresh argument—based on the notion of the immaturity of young people, and the pursuit of their personal happiness—the traditional position defended by Houard, which visualized love as an act of folly that vitiates consent. In the view of this 'Enlightened' author, as in that of the Catholic or Puritan moralists, marriages should unite individuals of the same social standing, with the agreement of their parents. The Enlightened élites of the eighteenth century dreamed of instituting the love-match, but they were incapable of doing this as long as their social power remained based on a material patrimony. The love-match was to cease to be a fantasy, in that social milieu, only when the essence of inherited capital became cultural—that is, in the twentieth century. The new aspirations were expressed for a long time before economic changes made possible their realization. However, the revolution of the conjugal system did not take place until after that of the economic system, for only then could the marriage founded on love be instituted without challenging the hierarchical structures of society.

A Sexual Revolution? A Dispute

The Argument For Revolution

EDWARD SHORTER

The Argument Against Revolution

LOUISE A. TILLY, JOAN W. SCOTT, and MIRIAM COHEN

Sexuality constitutes a final area in which family related change has been noted, beginning in the later eighteenth century and continuing, amid fits and starts, through the nineteenth century into our own day. The idea of a "sexual revolution" early in the modernization process suggests that a vital change in behavior and outlook occurred some time ago, although initially affecting only part of society. Subsequent "sexual revolutions," including the recent one in the 1960s, may be continuations of a modernization trend, more than real changes in direction. New sexual behavior had ambiguous implications for family life. On the one hand, it reflected new independence of young people from family controls. On the other, it may have heightened expectations within marriage, once marriage occurred, in ways consistent with the rise of romantic love.

One of the first decisive changes in the traditional outlook of the common man in Europe and North America may have concerned sex. A number of historians are now claiming that peasant society, at least in northern and western Europe, was quite prudish. Marriage occurred rather late, and premarital sex was frowned upon. (Here is another aspect of preindustrial family life that might raise important questions about the satisfactions provided.) During the eighteenth century, however, a number of changes began to occur. The age at which puberty was attained gradually lowered. Choirboys, for example, found their voices changing at around the age of fifteen instead of the traditional eighteen—to the detriment of sacred music. Undoubtedly, improved food supplies were largely responsible for this change, but new sexual expectations may have played a role as well, for scientists have discovered that psychological factors as well as a better diet are involved in bringing about an earlier onset of puberty. Earlier marriages became more common. In addition, the conception cycle changed. Instead of bunching the conception of children at a few peak periods during the year, particularly during the late spring, as was traditional in rural society, villagers began to space out the birth of children through the year, which at least implies more regular sexual intercourse. And, as the following selection outlines, other important changes in sexual behavior began in the eighteenth century and continued as the modernization process advanced.

Obviously, any judgment about sexual change must be in large part speculative. We know with a fair degree of certainty that the rate of illegitimate births increased; we can surmise the extent to which this represented a change in values, a new sense of the individual ego.

Edward Shorter confirms the impression that a basic revision of outlook was at least beginning among the common people in the eighteenth century, before the full onslaught of industrialization and urbanization. In seeking the causes of this revision, Shorter looks primarily to prior economic changes and the related extension of urban influences. These in turn altered family relationships by loosening traditional parental control and, perhaps, increasing the importance of sexual compatibility between husband and wife. (It must be remembered that the marriage age was dropping even as illegitimacy was on the rise.) This is a plausible explanation, but it leaves open the question of what caused the economic changes.

Even so, the recognition that lower-class attitudes began to "modernize" this early helps us approach the next issue, the impact of the industrial revolution. Here the central issue is whether the lower classes could adapt positively, or whether they were completely confused and alienated, possibly for a long time. The fact that some adaptation had already begun in response to more limited changes may help us to answer the question. If the common people were becoming more individualistic, if indeed they found greater pleasure in sex, perhaps they were at least partially prepared to face still greater changes.

The first selection raises two final points. It clearly took two to tango in the sexual revolution, but did the revolution have the same meaning for women as for men? Certainly, for women burdened with illegitimate, or even legitimate, children, it could have distinctive consequences. We do not yet know if men and women engaged in sex for the same motives (women, for example, may more normally have expected marriage to result, often being disappointed in the outcome) or with the same sense of pleasure or liberation. In the second selection, written in response to Shorter's argument, the situation of women is explained quite differently. New behavior is granted, along with a loosening of family controls; but goals (at least women's goals) are traditional, and only the altered economic and urban setting resulted in rising illegitimacy.

The debate over "modern" sexual behavior raises questions about the ongoing links between sexuality and modernization in Western society. We have faced further changes in sexual behavior since the onset of modernization. Are they part of a common association between sexual expression and the modern outlook? Or, as the Tilly, Scott, Cohen argument may imply, did a decisive change in women's sexual attitudes occur only more recently? How far will modernization take us in sexual liberation, and with what social and psychic results?

THE ARGUMENT FOR REVOLUTION

The central fact in the history of courtship over the last two centuries has been the enormous increase in sexual activity before marriage. Before 1800 it was unlikely that the typical young woman would have coitus with her partner—certainly not before an engagement had been sealed, and probably not as a fiancée, either. But after 1800 the percentage of young women who slept with their boyfriends or fiancés rose steadily, until in our own times it has become a majority. And recently there have been large increases especially among adolescents, in intercourse by *un*engaged women (if one can imagine such a thing).

Illegitimate births and premarital pregnancies give us the most reliable data for determining the incidence of sex before marriage. Of course, not all women who are sexually active before marriage bear children. Some practice contraception—at least to the extent of saying, as in France's Vendée, "Look out!" before their partners ejaculate. Others force an abortion or miscarry spontaneously, and still others are not yet entirely fecund. But assuming such factors remain more or less equal, there will be at least a general coincidence between the level of coitus among unmarried women and the rate at which they become pregnant. Provided that the other "intervening" variables (such as contraception) remain unchanged, we should be able to infer from a long-term rise in premarital conceptions a similar rise in sexual activity before marriage. . . .

1550–1650   A brief, relatively insignificant rise and fall in out-of-wedlock pregnancies took place, most likely caused by a similar rise and fall in premarital intercourse. Of all periods, this is the most poorly documented; exactly what was going on in the *vie intime* of young Europeans in the late sixteenth century remains largely a mystery. Various charts of illegitimacy show an unmistakable peak in the 1590s, especially in England. Evidence is present that premarital pregnancy underwent the same uphill-downhill course. There is nothing to indicate that more sexual intercourse caused this increase. We have neither qualitative testimonies (other than the usual lamentations that the young were becoming more "immoral") nor sufficient data on such "intervening" variables as fetal mortality or female health (fecundability) to let us point to intercourse by process of elimination. As for the years that followed, the notion of the Counter-reformed, Puritanical seventeenth century as a time of sexual

From Edward Shorter, *The Making of the Modern Family* (New York: Basic Books, 1975), pp. 80–84, 85, 95–96, 149–50, 165–67.

repression is so firmly entrenched that I shall give it a respectful nod here as the probable explanation for the charted decline between 1600 and 1650.

1750–1850   There was an enormous rise in illegitimacy and premarital pregnancy in the years of the French and Industrial revolutions. Late in the eighteenth century, the number of out-of-wedlock pregnancies began to sky-rocket in virtually every community we know about, often reaching three or four times the previous levels. In case after case, from interior Massachusetts to the Alpine uplands of Oberbayern, the number of infants conceived before marriage increased markedly. Indeed this is one of the central phenomena of modern demographic history. In a moment I shall suggest that this huge upsurge in part reflected a decline in abortion and an improvement in female health and hence reproductive biology. Primarily, however, it was the result of increasing sexual activity. . . .

I prefer to see the giant rise in out-of-wedlock pregnancy in the late eighteenth century as the principal phenomenon to be explained. It changed the lives of more people than any fluctuation in premarital sex had previously or has since (before the 1960s, at least). And it accords perfectly with a larger notion of social change that I am advancing here: that there was, once upon a time, such a thing as traditional society, which endured relatively unaltered for a number of centuries but which was finally destroyed and replaced by something else we call "modern society." I see our own dear modern times as entirely different from this world we have lost, especially in everything touching intimate life, and I believe this huge one-time change in premarital sexual behavior to be part of the transition from one to the other. . . .

In point of fact, the years 1750–1850 witnessed a crescendo of complaints about immoral sexual activity among the young. This amount of lamentation was unprecedented since the Reformation—before that time my knowledge falters—and it was not again to be attained until the 1920s. Doctor after sober doctor, senior administrator upon administrator, would turn from their normal weighty concerns about infant hygiene or local self-government to comment upon the sad state of sexual morality. What could have been going on in their minds? Had all these observers been seized by some collective delusion, some secular millenarianism dormant since the fifteenth century? Or were they in fact picking up, even in their self-inflated, self-righteous ways, a shift in the fabric of intimate life about them? I believe the second.

Observe some German examples. Bavarian administrators early in the nineteenth century became alarmed about dancing because they thought the walk home customarily meant a stopover for sexual intercourse. Women would appear unescorted at dance locales and wait there until they had been asked to dance or had found a male partner to escort them home; nine months later the fruits of these casual couplings would appear. But the good Bavarians didn't need dancing as an excuse for coitus, as Joseph Hazzi discovered around 1800 in an administrative tour of Oberbayern. In the Seefeld district: "Both sexes are so inclined to debauchery that you scarcely find a girl of twenty who's not already a mother." Around Marquartstein County this interest in sex nestled within a larger rebelliousness. The proverb "We'll have no lords" was popular among people who "get married enthusiastically and very early, produce lots of children, among whom sufficient illegitimate ones that this is considered much more a beneficial than a sinful deed." Officials in Oberfranken testified in 1833 that communities full of deflowered maidens were commonplace. "In the countryside a girl who has preserved her virgin purity to the age of twenty counts as exceptional, and is not at all esteemed for it by her contemporaries." In Unterfranken even the "middle classes" in rural areas, and certainly the laborers in cities, had by 1839 concluded "that the natural satisfaction of the sex drive is neither legally forbidden nor morally very reprehensible." By 1854 premarital sex had apparently become so commonplace that provincial officials were handwringing: "Every time single boys and girls go out dancing or to some other public entertainment they end up in bed. In places where male and female servants work side by side, sexual intercourse is a daily phenomenon; and Altötting County reports that it's not seen as sinful at all to have produced children before marriage." These are droplets in a torrent. Literate observers were shaken in southern Germany during the first half of the nineteenth century by what they deemed a sexual revolution, first among the youth of the lower classes and then finally even among those of their own class. . . .

To begin with, what evidence do we have of the infusion of romance into courtship before 1900? For one thing, people either started to say they were in love or to act in ways consistent with no other interpretation. After 1730 there was a big jump in the use of such words as "amour" and "passion" in the explanations that unmarried women gave to municipal officials [in] Grenoble of why they were pregnant, and there was a decline in the use of such terms as "amitié" that suggest a limited commitment.

In a small town in western France, to take another example, a young journeyman cabinetmaker impregnated the daughter of his employer in 1787, a banal event and in every way "traditional"—save for the young man's remaining in contact with the girl after his flight to avoid prosecution (the traditional seducer would have vanished without a trace), and save for the tenderness of the love letters he wrote. "My dearest, I embrace you with all my heart. I am unable to forget you. Everyday I think of you and hope you do the same for me. Tell me how you feel, if you want to make me happy. I remain your close companion. . . ." Note that the young man was not a peasant but an artisan; for . . . it was outside the agricultural middle class that the revolution begins.

Towards the mid-nineteenth century we learn the following of the coastal town of La Ciotat (Bouches-du-Rhône): "The young men are constantly letting partners with handsome dowries go begging. When they marry, it's ordinarily for inclination and not for advantage. They would be incapable of feigning sentiment they did not feel. Such is the case above all for the young lads who go to sea." So seafaring people, at least, were willing to sacrifice their pocketbooks for their affections. And if it wasn't love, how else may we explain that in a Gascon village, around 1911, "three mailmen became needed instead of two because the posts got so cluttered by all the magazines and post-cards the young men and women were in the habit of sending one another"? . . .

The uses of sex   In traditional society, sexuality mainly served instrumental objectives. That is, it helped the participants to achieve ulterior goals of a nonsexual nature rather than serving the exploration of the personality. For traditional unmarried women, especially, intercourse was a means to an end (such as having peace with the employer, or ratifying a marital alliance between two families) rather than an end in itself (sex as personal fulfillment). The testimony we have reviewed suggests that in Europe before 1800, people seldom had sexual intercourse before it was absolutely certain they would marry, and that sex served for them the larger ends of procreation and the continuation of the lineage, rather than being in itself an object of joy and delight. Otherwise the emotionless, passionless, affectionless courtship rituals we have observed would be incomprehensible.

With the first sexual revolution came a breakthrough in intimacy, a dismantling of the sex-role barriers that had hitherto kept men and women locked in watertight compartments with little hope of emotional exchange. The libido unfroze in the blast of the wish to be free. In the years after 1750, lower-class young men and women awakened to the fact that life involved more than just doing your duty in the eyes of the local social authorities and doing your work in the same way that your father had done it, and his father before him. People had personality needs that might conflict with the surrounding community's need for stability. Among these needs was "happiness," and among the cardinal ways of becoming happy was undertaking an emotional relationship with a person of the opposite sex. Such a relationship, of course, meant fooling around, for sex was an obvious extension of emotional intimacy. And so the first sexual revolution would be danced out in the stiff, awkward manner of people who had spent eons in immobility and who were just beginning to create for themselves a sympathetic world of symbols and signs, a culture congenial to romanticism.

The first sexual revolution of the late eighteenth century shifted supervision of courtship from the community as a whole to the peer groups of youth itself. Barriers to promiscuity there had to be—firewalls against the fulmination of all this erotic nitroglycerin that the onrush of sentiment had started agitating—but barriers within the context of a sub-culture generally sympathetic to self-discovery and intimacy. So there was a lot of sex, and because the youth organizations lacked much of the coercive power of the larger village networks, accidents happened, suitors jumped ship, and illegitimate children were born. Yet the coital partners were doubtless anxious to follow the standards of the larger peer groups of which they were a part.

The second sexual revolution of the 1960s seems to have removed even this feeble peer-group control over adolescent mating and dating. The wish to be free has frayed all the cables that used to tie the couple to surrounding social institutions. Self-realization—accomplished through sexual gratification—has taken command of courtship.

THE ARGUMENT AGAINST REVOLUTION

During the nineteenth century most commentators on the "condition of the working classes" attributed large families and frequent illegitimacy among the poor to social, economic, or moral pathology. For Engels overpopulated working-class families were the offspring of industrial capitalism. For Malthus they were evidence of imprudence, of an inability to make rational calculations. For both, as for many government investigators and social reformers, high rates of fertility among married and single workers were both indicators and causes of misery and deprivation. Since the nineteenth century, of course, there have been many debates about the effects of industrialization on the standard of living of workers and on their demographic behavior. There have been some studies of family size among occupational groups and there have been attempts to describe and explain changes in working-class fertility patterns. Most of these studies lack the explicit moralizing of the nineteenth-century commentators, although some implicitly retain those biases. Few, however, maintain that large families and numerous bastards were positive developments.

Now Edward Shorter has advanced such an argument. In an intriguing and provocative piece, Shorter speculates that "female emancipation" led to increased rates of legitimate and illegitimate fertility in

From Louise A. Tilly, Joan W. Scott and Miriam Cohen, "Women's Work and European Fertility Patterns," *Journal of Interdisciplinary History* VI: 3 (Winter, 1976), pp. 447–48, 471–73.

Western Europe at the end of the eighteenth century. His subject is not economic deprivation; indeed, that is an irrelevant consideration for him. Instead, he maintains that industrialization early led to the sexual emancipation of working-class women by offering employment opportunities outside the home. Work led to sexual liberation, according to Shorter, by revolutionizing women's attitudes about themselves: They became individualistic and self-seeking; they rebelled against traditional constraints and sought pleasure and fulfillment in uninhibited sexual activity. In the absence of birth control, heightened sexual activity inevitably meant more children. Indeed, toward the end of the nineteenth century, as information about contraception became available, fertility rates sharply declined.

Far from home, cut off from possible property ownership, no longer required by craft organizations to postpone marriage until the completion of long apprenticeships, and in difficult economic straits, the men and women in cottage, consumer, and service industries acted in what contemporaries called "improvident" ways: They married younger and did not control their fertility as compulsively as peasant and artisan families had tended to. Why? A number of related factors were involved. The abandonment of late marriage itself represented the relinquishing of the chief means that families had used to control fertility. Associated with this was a decline in the numbers of those who never married. Stearns has reminded us that in pre-industrial society fertility was controlled through the celibacy of a large minority of men and women. The likelihood that such celibacy could be enforced decreased with propertylessness and with migration; hence, the rates of partnerships of all sorts, including marriage, were likely to increase, and with them, the number of children born. The economic necessity which required both partners to work for the survival of the family led young mothers to relinquish the practice of nursing their own young. This, and high levels of infant mortality which also reduced the nursing period shortened the interval between successive births. The possibility of employment for young children encouraged families to continue high fertility strategies even as child mortality fell. Above all, however, high rates of infant mortality determined family strategies of high fertility. In order to guarantee the survival of one or two children, families experiencing high rates of infant mortality had traditionally produced many children. This continued to be the case.

Le Play's example of the Parisian carpenter's family well illustrates the pressures which led to high fertility. The carpenter's wife worked in the early years of her marriage. She sold fruits and vegetables at Les Halles and polished metal at home. In a period of eight years she bore six children. Four of them were bottle-fed, and all died before the age of 18 months. Bottle feeding (a necessity for a mother working away from home who could not afford or did not want to send her baby to a wet nurse) was undoubtedly a factor in the short interval between the births as well as in the deaths. This high rate of infant mortality made a strategy of high fertility appropriate, especially if a son were to live to inherit his father's membership in the carpentering trade, but also if two or three children were to survive to an age when they could earn wages and thus free their mother of the need to work.

Illegitimate fertility increased, too, because of a growth in the population of propertyless working men and women. In rural areas, geographically mobile men established relationships with women, became betrothed, engaged in intercourse, and then moved on. In cities, engagement often led to abandonment, or to a free union. In all cases, illegitimacy was a by-product. The migration of these "surplus" children, then, resulted in an even larger population of mobile men and of sexually vulnerable women, far from the protection of their families. The consequences of the increase in this population were increased incidence of abandoned pregnant women; increased prostitution of abandoned or unemployed women; increased incidence and duration of consensual or free union. All three of these alternatives produced illegitimate children.

Illegitimate and legitimate fertility rose simultaneously, then, because of a complex of changes stemming from declining mortality during the eighteenth century. These changes increased the numbers of young people physically and materially removed from their families and from work within the traditional household. They were also removed from the constraints on personal and marital behavior of property; for many of them, the link between legal marriage and property had been broken. There is little evidence to indicate, however, that changes in sexual attitudes, particularly those of women, preceded these developments. Instead, the various attempts at union whether successful or not, represented the pursuit of older goals, an endorsement of established male-female relationships. In every kind of situation, the woman's goal, at least, seems to have been to reestablish the family economy, the partnership of economic enterprise and of social and, perhaps, emotional sustenance. These women sought not sexual fulfillment, but economic cooperation and all of the other things which traditional marriage implied. That they often failed to find them, and that their attempts to establish a family took a variety of forms does not prove anything about their motivation. The form of male-female relationships was created not by the revolutionized sexual attitudes of the partners, but by a complex interaction of values and expectations and changing social and economic circumstances. And it is those circumstances that must be examined if rising rates of fertility are to be explained.

The New World of Children

J. H. PLUMB

Changes in attitudes and behavior toward children seem basic to the modernization process. This is not surprising, though historians are just uncovering the magnitude of the change; a new treatment of children would produce new personalities, and new personalities constitute the essence of modernization in its most encompassing form. The radical improvement in the outlook toward children, described in the following selection on eighteenth-century England, may seem surprising, for we constantly uncover in our own society signs of neglect and cruelty. In part, our continued derelictions reflect the fact that new principles of treatment were goals, not uniform practices. In part, they follow from the uneven social base for the "modernization" of child-rearing. In the eighteenth century the new standards were those of the upper and middle classes. The poor could not afford the new artifacts, such as toys and books. Indeed their changing sexual behavior suggests quite a different pattern for the young, involving greater freedom from parental control, a pattern which newly vigilant "proper" parents were eager to prevent in their own charges. Modernization, particularly in these early phases, was less a social than a class phenomenon.

Finally, our continued anguish over our failures toward children reflects the very attitudes that began to develop by the late eighteenth century. It is not far-fetched to say that, just as the new methods of child-rearing were designed to produce new kinds of guilt in children, so they guaranteed parental guilt. The parent was now morally responsible for the child, an intrinsically good creature, so it was next to impossible to be a consistently satisfactory parent in one's own eyes. The task was awesome, and it still is.

What caused the new approach to raising children? J. H. Plumb suggests the inspiration of people like John Locke, themselves guided by the scientific revolution. With new knowledge available, teaching became a matter of greater importance. Children had to be prepared more to be taught than to be controlled. But is this intellectual impulse an entirely satisfactory explanation? Why did so many parents change their habits in what was, for such a private matter as child-rearing, a surprisingly brief time? (Compare the childhood outlined below to that of just a century earlier, detailed in the selection by David Hunt.) It is clearly easier to describe what was happening than to discover basic motivations. What we can be sure of is that the new methods of treating children guaranteed further social change in the future.

The modernization of childhood was of course double-edged. Nothing shows the mixture of gain and loss in the new social framework more clearly. Children had a better world in many respects but also a host of new restrictions, including the simple fact of more watchful parents. Play itself was altered when new toys were designed to improve the child. We are still working out what implications our attitudes toward children have for the quality of life and the ability of man to be free.

There had been, however, towards the end of the seventeenth century, a perceptible new attitude—John Evelyn, long before Locke, had practised many of the Lockeian ideas on education on his own son, preferring a system of rewards, provocations, emulation and self-discipline to physical punishment or verbal chastisement. His whimsical friend, Aubrey, was also strongly against corporal punishment, although he allowed the use of thumbscrews as a last resort! Indeed, Locke's book encapsulates what was clearly a new and growing attitude towards child-rearing and education which was to improve the lot of the child in the eighteenth century.

Locke, although not opposed to corporal punishment as a final sanction, nor indeed for very young children of an age too tender to be reasoned with, in order to instil the necessary fear and awe that a child should have for an adult, strongly disapproved of beating once formal education had begun, just as he was equally opposed to bribing the child to work through material rewards.

> The *Rewards* and *Punishments* then, whereby we should keep children in order, are quite of another kind; and of that force, that when we can get them once to work, the Business, I think, is done, and the Difficulty is over. *Esteem* and *Disgrace* are, of all others, the most powerful Incentives to the Mind, when once it is brought to relish them. If you can once get into Children a Love of Credit, and an Apprehension of Shame and Disgrace, you have put into them the true principle. . . .

As well as arguing for a more liberal attitude towards the child, Locke also pleaded for a broader curriculum. He believed education should fit man for society, as well as equipping him with learning, hence he pressed not only for lessons in drawing, but also in French. Indeed, he opposed rigid grounding in English grammar and urged that Latin be taught by the direct method, as it would have been had it been a living language. . . .

Not only did this new attitude towards children begin to emerge among educationalists in the middle decades of the eighteenth century, but we can deduce also from the success of small private academies, from

From J.H. Plumb, "The New World of Children in Eighteenth-Century England," *Past and Present: A Journal of Historical Studies*, No. 67 (May 1975), pp. 67–93.

the development of a new kind of children's literature, and from the vastly increased expenditure on the amusements and pleasures of children, that parents, too, were no longer regarding their children as sprigs of old Adam whose wills had to be broken. Many had come to look upon their children as vehicles of social emulation; hence they began to project their own social attitudes as the moral imperatives of childhood. And so education for society became paramount. Owing to the growth of economic opportunity and social mobility, it was now less necessary to make a child accept its calling as a dictate of God. Locke's attitudes were replacing those of the catechism.

The repercussions on the world of children were very great. Society required accomplishment, and accomplishment required expenditure. The children's new world became a market that could be exploited. Few desires will empty a pocket quicker than social aspiration—and the main route was, then as now, through education, which combined social adornment with the opportunity of a more financially rewarding career for children. . . .

Parents were commercial targets through their children—they could, through the best of motives, be made to spend money on schools which they could scarcely afford, but there were other ways to the parents' pocket-books, educational games and industrial toys, which became increasingly available as the century progressed.

Books by which children could be taught had existed from the first days of printing—alphabets, grammars, and the like, but few, if any, were designed specifically for children. Authors and publishers made very little attempt to entice the young mind. Fairy stories, ballads, riddles and fables were intended as much for adults as for children. Indeed, Aesop was not specifically adapted for children until 1692, when Roger l'Estrange produced his edition.

As with so many cultural developments, the late seventeenth and early eighteenth centuries saw the beginnings of a changed attitude towards children's literature and methods of learning to read. In 1694 "J.G." published "A Play-book for children to allure them to read as soon as possible. Composed of small pages on purpose not to tire children and printed with a fair and pleasant letter. The matter and method plain and easier than any yet extant," which was, for once, a true statement in a blurb. The book has wide margins, large type; its language simple and concrete and mostly within the compass of a child's experience. The author states in his preface that he wished "to decoy Children in to reading." It did well enough to be reprinted in 1703, by which time a few other authors—notably William Ronksley—were attempting to find methods and materials more suitable for very young children. He believed in teaching by verse according to the metre of the Psalms—first week, words of one syllable, the next week words of two syllables, and so on. And he used jokes, riddles and proverbs to sugar his pills. Even so, his and other innovative children's books of Queen Anne's reign were designed, quite obviously, to be chanted, to be learnt by the ear, rather than by the eye. They were more for teachers and parents to teach with than books meant for a child's own enjoyment. Similar books were slow to appear and it is not until the 1740s that the change in style of children's literature becomes very marked. The entrepreneurial noses of Thomas Boreman and John Newbery twitched and scented a market for books that would be simple in production, enticing to the eye, and written specifically for children. Of course, it was not quite as simple as that. Children do not buy books, adults do.

So the new children's literature was designed to attract adults, to project an image of those virtues which parents wished to inculcate in their offspring, as well as to beguile the child. These alphabet and reading books, by their simplicity, also strengthened the confidence of parents in their ability to teach their children to read in the home. The new children's literature was aimed at the young, but only through the refraction of the parental eye. . . .

Education was public as well as private, and there was far more entertainment designed both to amuse and instruct, to which parents were encouraged to take their children by sharply reduced prices for them. Children were expected to be companions of their parents in ways which would have been impossible in the seventeenth century, because the attractions did not then exist. Exhibitions of curiosities; museums; zoos; puppet shows; circuses; lectures on science; panoramas of European cities; automata; horseless carriages; even human and animal monstrosities were available in provincial cities as well as in London. Sir Ashton Levers's Museum of Natural History at Leicester House, a typical eighteenth-century hotch-potch, advertised family tickets. A yearly season ticket for the entire family was quite expensive at five guineas, but it included both the tutor and the governess, and so was aimed at the rich. In April 1773 families of Leeds were regaled by Mr. Manuel of Turin with his display of automata which, as well as having an Indian lady in her chariot moving around the table at ten miles an hour, also contained the "Grand Turk, in the Seraglio dress, who walks about the table smoking his pipe in a surprising manner." All, of course, to the accompaniment of mechanical musical instruments. The prices were cheap enough, 1s. front seats, 6d. back, and servants at 4d. Mr. Manuel also sold fireworks as a sideline. After Mr. Manuel Mr. Pitt arrived with his principal marvel, a self-moving phaeton which travelled at six miles an hour, climbed hills, and started and stopped with the touch of a finger. He also brought along his electrifying machine, his camera obscura, his miraculous door which opened inside, outside, left or right by the turn of a key. All for one shilling. The phaeton either wore out, broke down, or at five hundredweight proved too expensive to move, for it was dropped by Pitt, who continued for some years to travel the Midland circuit, Nottingham, Coventry, and so on, but only with his scientific apparatus. Quite obviously he made a tolerable living.

On 10th August the attraction at Leeds was geographical rather than mechanical, when the model of the city and suburbs of Paris arrived at the Town Hall. It was extremely elaborate and eighteen feet square. Viewing started at 9:00 in the morning and closed at 8:00 in the evening, price, as usual, one shilling. In September a spectacular, double-column advertisement with woodcuts announced the arrival of Astley's circus, prices as usual a shilling for front seats, sixpence back, but Astley warned that boys trying to climb in would be taken care of by guards. He now also brought along with him his famous "Chronoscope": an apparatus for measuring the velocity of projectiles.

The emphasis was on marvels, curiosities that were new and remarkable, and usually mechanical or optical; hence many children were given a keen sense of a new and developing and changing world in which mechanical ingenuity, electricity and science in general played an active part—a totally different cultural atmosphere to that in which their grandfathers had lived. Their cultural horizons, too, were widened by the availability of music to listen to in festivals and concerts, the cheapness of musical instruments, and the plentiful supply of music teachers; the same is true of art. Art materials were to be found in every provincial town, and so were drawing masters, who taught in the home as well as in the school. Prints of old masters and modern artists were a commonplace of provincial as well as London life. Visually it was a far more exciting age for children than ever before. And they could travel. By the end of the century middle-class families were on the move, visiting country houses and ancient ruins, viewing the industrial wonders of Boulton and Watt, Wedgwood, Arkwright, and braving the dangers and dirt of coal-mines, sailing in splendid barges along the new canals, going off to the sea—to take the water externally and internally—an outburst of travel that is recorded in hundreds of illustrated books which depict children with their parents, enjoying, as they themselves enjoyed, the wonders of their world. The intellectual and cultural horizons of the middle-class child, and indeed of the lower middle-class child, had broadened vastly between 1680 and 1780, and this change was gathering momentum. Parents, more often than not, wanted their children with them, not only in the home but on holidays.

However, through most of the amusements ran the theme of self-improvement and self-education. The same is true of indoor games, as well as outdoor excursions. Playing cards had long been used to inculcate knowledge—largely geographical, historical or classical. One of the earliest packs of about 1700 taught carving lessons—hearts for joints of meat, diamonds for poultry, clubs for fish and spades for meat pies. But more often than not these were importations, usually from France. The eighteenth century witnessed a rapid increase in English educational playing cards, so that almost every variety of knowledge or educational entertainment could be found imprinted on their faces. The majority of booksellers, provincial as well as metropolitan, stocked them. Some cards were designed for the education of adults, or at least adolescents, but there were packs, very simply designed, for young children to play with and learn at the same time. One pack taught the first steps in music. . . .

A hundred years had brought about a remarkable change in the lives of middle- and lower middle-class children, and indeed of the aristocracy as well. From Locke onwards there had been a greater preoccupation with educational ideas; indeed, in the second half of the eighteenth century, stimulated by Rousseau, the advanced radicals—the Burghs, the Days, the Edgeworths, and the rest—had been deeply concerned. Many, particularly the Edgeworths, disapproved of the growing indulgence of parents towards their children, particularly the waste of money on useless toys. Maria Edgeworth denounced dolls and dolls' houses, had no use for rocking-horses, and strongly disapproved of baa-lambs, squeaky pigs and cuckoos, and all simple action toys. She was for a pencil and plain paper, toys which led to physical exercise—hoops, tops, battledores and a pair of scissors and paper for a girl to cut out her fancies; later boys should be given models of instruments used by manufacturers—spinning-wheels, looms, paper-mills, water-mills which, as I have said, were readily available. Maria Edgeworth resonates with modernity, but the interest in her long discussion of toys lies in the huge variety which obviously abounded in the 1790s—a variety not as extensive, of course, as today, but reflecting our world rather than that of seventeenth-century England. Indeed, wherever we turn in the world of children—clothes, pets, toys, education, sport, music and art, their world was richer, more varied, more intellectually and emotionally exciting than it had been in earlier generations.

And yet all was not gain. One must not paint too radiant a picture, too exciting a world. Mrs. Trimmer was there, so was Hannah More. One must remember the Fairchild family trooping off to view the corpse decomposing on the gibbet, the frightful treatment of William Cowper at Westminster, the horrors of Harrow and Eton and Winchester that drew boys into violent rebellion. Nor should we forget the dangers to children in the growing sentimentality about the innocence of the child which needed to be protected at all costs, nor the dangerous intellectual concept that regards each human life as recapitulating that of the human race, which firmly placed the child in Eden, but surrounded by serpents and cluttered with apples.

As a richer life in material objects became available to children, so did their private lives, in some aspects, become more rigidly disciplined.

The world of sex was to become, in the eighteenth century, a world of terror for children, and one which was to create appalling guilt and anxiety. We know little about the history of sexual attitudes. In eighteenth-century children's literature, adultery is mentioned, not approvingly, of course, but as a fact of life. In some tales for children men and women were discovered in bed together. This certainly would not have been allowed in Victorian literature for children. And such references were few, and vanish after the 1780s. In another respect, at least, there had been a disastrous development. In the sixteenth century Fallopius had encouraged masturbation in boys as a method of enlarging the penis, and Pepys, who had considerable guilt and shame about his fumbling of women, took masturbation in his stride, and indeed mentions with considerable pride that he had managed it without using his hand and with his eyes wide open. He did, it is true, wish it had not happened at midnight mass in the Chapel Royal, but that was his sole reaction. The early eighteenth century witnesses a total change of attitude. . . . By 1800 crimes of unbelievable cruelty were being practised on young boys in order to cure them, such as circumcision without, of course, anaesthetic. This development was not an English phenomenon. Dr. Tissot produced an equally alarming and equally popular book in Switzerland and France in 1760. And Kant denounces the practice with intense moral fervour in his *Über Pädagogik* (1803).

Chastity and abstinence, however, were imposed with an increasing verbal and, at times, physical, violence on the growing boy and girl. The practical results of this campaign were probably minimal, but the psychological danger to the sensitive was considerable, as we may see from the diaries of men so different in temperament as Samuel Johnson and William Ewart Gladstone. Childhood had become more radiant, but there were dark and lowering clouds. Children, in fact, had become objects: violence and noise, natural to children, were deplored, so was greed for food as well as lust. Obedience, sweetness, honesty, self-control were the qualities desired and inculcated. They were to stay firmly in Eden with their hands off the apples and deaf to the serpents. Fortunately the images that society creates for children rarely reflect the truth of actual life. If we turn from theory, from projected literary images, to the artifacts of childhood, then we can rest assured that children, both girls and boys, had, so long as they were middle-class, entered a far richer world. They had more to stimulate the eye, the ear and the mind, and that was pure gain.

The Rise of Modern Medicine

JEAN-PIERRE GOUBERT

Without question, changes in the attitudes and practices associated with health form a major part of the development of a modern mentality. We think of sickness as something to be cured scientifically; we define good health with growing rigor; and we worry about health increasingly. These changes in our approach to health began to take shape in the later eighteenth century.

The modernization of medicine and popular attitudes toward medicine are receiving growing attention as we seek to understand our own attitudes toward doctors, health, and death. In one sense, medicine seems a clear success story for modernization. Doctors uncovered more and more scientific information about the human body and how to treat it. People learned to use doctors. Health improved. And all was well in the best of all possible worlds.

The actual story, not surprisingly, is more complex. Doctors certainly represented modernization. As early as 1780, they claimed sole access to scientific truth, and they did indeed know that a lot of popular medical practices were dangerous. But their own knowledge of new treatments was limited throughout the nineteenth century. They had little to do with major health gains until the twentieth century (and, some would argue, even beyond), and the gains themselves, stemming mainly from improved nutrition, were not substantial. Consequently, doctors often relied on legal support to bolster their position, as when they used the state to ban unlicensed practitioners. Also, their attacks on the medical habits of the past were far from a complete success.

The following selection, dealing with doctors' attitudes in the late eighteenth century, captures a particularly dramatic early phase of the rise of modern medical attitudes. Based on state-sponsored surveys of doctors in 1786 and 1790, the selection therefore reflects official medical opinion above all. Although they had no new means for treating illness, doctors were mounting new claims to science and attacking other popular healers who could not make these claims. Their campaigns suggest the richness of popular medical culture, relating to the longstanding role of religious and superstitious faith in dealing with health problems.

In the long run, however gradually, the doctors won, although more than vestiges of popular cures and charlatanism remain. We now ask two related questions: How much has the doctors' victory improved health, and at what social and financial costs? And how have popular attitudes—our own attitudes, not just those of "the masses"—changed with regard to treatment for disease? Doctors have clearly taught us to expect more cures, and to pay more for them. But Jean-Pierre Goubert, a leading authority on the social history of medicine, asks whether or not the dilemma first suggested by the rise of modern medicine—doctors' claims to authority unsupported by corresponding scientific advance—continues to poison the modern outlook. Have modern people simply been encouraged to transfer older faiths and superstitions to new practitioners? What, indeed, is a "modernized" outlook toward health?

Goubert also suggests a major use for modernization history that has been applied to areas other than health. Take a basic paradigm in the early stages of modernization—in this case, doctors' claims to authority. Then assume that this paradigm still applies to modern society and is as fundamentally hollow as it was in the first place. The result of this kind of analysis suggests a need to adjust key portions of the modern outlook—to downgrade doctors for example. But it also suggests the difficulty of doing this—precisely because of the power of initial claims and assumptions. If someone believes that modern medicine has moved away from simple assertion of new scientific authority to a more complex and useful role in society, how could that person develop a different historical picture?

Aᴛ the end of the eighteenth century, the effectiveness of medicine—whether preventive or therapeutic—was not the indubitable fact it is today but, rather, a goal to be pursued, despite certain advances that had recently been made. Recourse to the physician, the surgeon ("the poor man's physician"), or the midwife remained the prerogative of a minority that asserted its enlightenment, even though a concerted effort was made by the medical elite and the royal government to train midwives or to provide care for the poor in times of "epidemic disease." For the most part, of course, the French population practiced self-medication; it also consulted quacks, bonesetters, and matrons, listened to ambulant charlatans, and followed the course of treatment prescribed by the sorcerer-healer of the village.

Although the enlightened physicians of the eighteenth century took much of their inspiration from Hippocrates and Galen, they had come to question the set patterns of their learned tradition and to stress the prime importance of firsthand observation. Yet one wonders whether they were also able to understand the practices of popular medicine and to grasp the causes of its expansion and increasingly broad appeal. In view of the profusion of written documents they felt obliged to pass on to posterity, and of their zeal in denouncing charlatanry, which they viewed (in the years around 1789) as one of the four evils afflicting the "art of healing," one might be carried along by their self-assurance and their unanimity. To decide this matter on the basis of concrete evidence, certain testimonies left by the physicians and surgeons of the time must be carefully analyzed. These testimonies are to be found in the replies to the official surveys

From Jean-Pierre Goubert, "The Art of Healing: Learned Medicine and Popular Medicine in the France of 1790," in Robert Forster and Orest Ranum, eds., *Medicine and Society in France* (Baltimore: Johns Hopkins University Press, 1980), pp. 1–2, 5–6, 8–9, 11–12, 18–19.

made in 1786 and 1790 and form the documentary basis of the present study.

For this reason it is important to stress the mythical character of the opposition between learned and popular medicine. If there was really a break between these two arts of healing, it was to be found at the end of the eighteenth century more at the level of collective notions than in the area of medical learning and social practice. In this respect, medicine was one, for all of its diversity and even its cleavages, except perhaps in the minds of the several thousand men who shared the social view of the Enlightenment. In fact, these two "worlds" of medicine were so close to each other that they were in constant contact, both hating and penetrating each other. For one and the same patient might well turn successively or simultaneously to a physician, to a surgeon, and also to his healer—to the Devil but also to the Lord.

Consequently, the questions asked of the representatives of the surgical profession by the Comité de Salubrité tell us something about the manner in which these men perceived the so-called popular medicine. Under these circumstances it would be absurd (even if it were possible) to try to measure the extension or the actual density of the network of charlatans. It would mean to accept the question asked in 1790 by the members of the Comité de Salubrité as entirely valid, without recognizing the fact that the committee transferred to a realm where it was not applicable a question that was valid for a preselected population, namely, the officially certified practitioners.

Actually, the question had been asked earlier by the controller general's office of the provincial administrators in a survey of 1786. This survey attempted to ascertain the medical statistics of the country as a whole and to assemble information concerning the professional quality of its physicians, surgeons, and midwives. The statistical analysis of the results of this survey concerning the physicians and surgeons (especially the latter), within the limits of northern France, leads to the following conclusion: if the vast majority of the French population, especially in rural areas, only rarely consulted a physician or a certified surgeon, it was not because the medical network was lacking in density. In other words, the "medical desert" evoked by certain correspondents of the Société Royale de Médicine does not correspond to the actual facts; it only expresses—and this is not surprising— the refusal of an elite to include in the medical profession the masses of "second string" surgeons and popular therapeutists. The success of "charlatanry" in the France of 1780–90 was indeed a matter of concern to the medical profession of that period; especially the success of the category of surgeons who regularly treated a more rural, less "enlightened," and generally more modest clientele than their colleagues, the physicians.

Physicians and Charlatans

How, then, could a well-designed "medical policy" fail to ensure the future of the profession and also bring relief to a suffering humanity? The physicians' discourse, whether in 1790, around 1900, or even after 1970, constantly expresses the same obsession: "to confound [sic] charlatanry and bring enlightenment to so useful an art. . . ."

In any case, and with respect to the late eighteenth century, the social border between "physician" and "charlatan," between learned and "popular" medicine, was not clearly drawn, however shocking this may seem to us. A few examples will briefly demonstrate this fact. The first set of testimonies is taken from the responses to the survey of the Comité de Salubrité concerning the practice of surgery (1790); the second comes from the survey of the kingdom's physicians and surgeons the intendants were ordered to conduct by the controller general's office in 1786.

At Montdidier the deputy surgeon reported "a charlatan admitted to the surgeons' guild." The deputy surgeon at Lyons-la-Forêt thundered against two "charlatans" who wanted to join the surgeons' guild. Better yet, the deputy surgeon of Tonnère notes among the "empirics" "only one or two experts in urine, although they are not masters of surgery." At Domfront, the deputy surgeon declared, speaking of "charlatans, empirics, and purveyors of nostrums": "there are many of them here, . . . even a physician and a surgeon who judge their patients' water by sight and give them medications from behind."

Whether admitted to a surgeons' guild or not, these "surgeons-empirics" appear to have been very numerous in rural France in 1790. And yet, if we are to believe the statements analyzed here, they were actually on the side of the patented surgeons and physicians, for they "borrowed" or sought official recognition, practiced a "natural" medicine based on bleeding, purging, emetics, and simple or composite remedies, and followed—albeit from a distance—the sociocultural model imposed from "above." Thus, the official surgeons found themselves in an understandable quandary: should they reject these semisurgeons, or should they try to absorb them? Officially, of course, the outcome was rejection, expressed again and again in the various royal edicts and declarations, in the name of *competence* and with a view to the *monopoly* over which henceforth the medical profession wanted to keep full control with the help of diplomas. This is why most of the deputy surgeons were distressed at their "inability to curb the country's empiricism. . . ."

The unanimity and ferocity with which the surgeons lashed out against their colleagues the "semisurgeons" are all the more understandable as the latter took many patients away from them, thereby threatening their livelihood and diminishing the practices of those who, often of modest origin, had been obliged to pay for their education, examinations, and admissions fees.

These studies show that the potential clientele of the surgeon (and of the physician as well) was not very considerable, nor even elastic, despite the demographic growth of eighteenth-century France. The existence of two cultures, the patients' need to trust their therapeutist, the existence of a "wall of money"—all of this contributed to making the ascendancy of the official medical profession much less extensive than it considered desirable. And it is because they sensed—not too clearly at times—the importance of such obstacles to their advancement that the patented physicians and surgeons avidly seized the opportunity held out to them by the state to be recognized as the obligatory source of help and as the sole "specialists" in human sickness. This explains to a large extent their crusade against "empirics," "charlatans," and "purveyors of nostrums.". . .

The majority of the surgeons (47 percent) denounced, first of all, the *itinerant* charlatans, but also those with a fixed residence, the "empirics" and "purveyors of nostrums." Among the settled charlatans were the "traditional village healers," and here the bonesetters occupied a prominent place. In fact, certain surgeons' guilds had admitted them and recognized their existence, to the keen regret of the surgeons of 1790, who already favored an unqualified monopoly. This, whether they admitted it or not, was the reason why they excluded the bonesetters from their guild.

The other practitioners cited (see table 1)—dentists, oculists, hernia experts, pedicurists—were excluded in a similar manner. The surgeons treated them as a kind of subcategory of the paramedical type, thus foreshadowing the official medicalization of these occupations and their eventual inclusion in the health professions.

In the second rank of the accused we find the representatives of charitable medical organizations. For the most part, these were ecclesiastics, the majority of them regular clergy, primarily—as one would expect—nuns, and the Gray Sisters in particular. Better tolerated as a group in consideration of their "estate," they were nonetheless almost always designated as empirics, even charlatans, and sometimes as purveyors of nostrums "of the worst kind." Such statements mark the dividing line that was supposed to separate those whose professional concern was with the body and with health from those whose professional concern was with the soul, with poverty, and with charity. It was, of course, in the name of the Enlightenment, in the name of their professional competence, and in the interest of the common good that the patented surgeons of 1790 rebelled against the interference of these "benefactors of the poor."

Lastly, the deputy surgeons leveled charges of charlatanry against certain of their colleagues, namely, in ascending order, physicians, apothecaries, and surgeons. To be exact, these accusations applied only to the more or less "empiric" "semisurgeons" of the countryside. The physi-

**Table 1—Gamut of "Charlatans," According to the Words
Used by Surgeons (77 Statements)**

Stated Category	Number of References	Percentage of Total
Charlatans and healers		
Bonesetters	11	
Dentists	6	
Oculists	5	
Hernia specialists	4	
Spice mongers	3	
Pedicurists	2	
Straighteners	2	
Redresser	1	
Restorer	1	
Total	35	47%
Representatives of charitable medical organizations		
Nuns	10	
Secular Clergy	8	
Monks	3	
Lay persons	2	
Total	23	30%
Members of the medical profession		
Surgeons	13	
Apothecaries	3	
Physicians	2	
Total	18	23%
	Total	100%

cians and apothecaries, for their part, were accused of encroachment, that is, of the illegal practice of surgery. This was no longer a matter of medical men lashing out against charlatans, but rather of infighting within the medical profession.

In the final analysis, the vocabulary used by the patented surgeons is remarkably narrow and confused: narrow to the extent that these surgeons perceived and designated the various types of charlatans in terms of their "enlightened" culture, and confused, since the term "charlatan," which in the surgeons' minds was highly charged with emotion, became a vengeful epithet used to encompass and to exclude. In other words, they did not seem to know what it meant.

The "charlatans" were thus considered, on the first count, as actual or potential criminals. According to the expressions of the surgeons' representatives, they constituted a "scourge of humanity," a "poisonous horde," a "[special] race," and a "sect of cannibals." The deputy surgeon of Tartas, steeped in physiocratic thinking, spelled out the meaning of this accusation: "charlatans and empirics contribute to the country's depopulation. . . ." This accusation also frequently flowed from the pens of intendants and subdelegates in their responses to the survey of 1786 and appears in the correspondence concerning "epidemic diseases," although it was leveled more often against the matrons and "so-called wise women." In this manner the charlatan, the empiric, and all nonprofessionals appeared to be eminently harmful, if we follow the opinions of the masters of surgery and physicians, who judged the learning of the "charlatans" totally irrational and more than inadequate, considering them "a separate race," "barbarians," and savages. It was in the name of a learned culture bent on asserting its superiority that the medical profession—and in this instance the surgeons in particular—loudly voiced its claim to the monopoly of heath care.

The second count of the accusation (mutilations, accidents caused by imprudence and incompetence) concretely expresses the grievances and the reproaches directed against the "charlatans" by the surgeons. The deputy surgeon at Nuits (Côte-d'Or) wrote in this connection: "We have women and men, both in our town and in the surrounding countryside, who meddle with treating the sick and giving them remedies. . . . We even have a woman oculist, well-versed in producing one-eyed and blind people, as well as individuals who claim that they can straighten cripples." At times some compassion is expressed for the "unfortunate ones who are *martyred* by the charlatans."

Given their animosity and their lack of understanding, the surgeons had no qualms at piling up the crimes and acts of malfeasance with which they charged the "charlatans." The logic underlying their hatred seems to proceed as follows: (1) the charlatan is incompetent, for he has not studied; (2) since he is incompetent, the charlatan causes accidents or, worse, commits crimes; and (3) under these conditions, charlatans are "knaves who dupe the people, . . . swindlers in fact, who try to mislead others about their health." All this because the learning of charlatans and healers did not proceed from a rational logic, founded upon a specific set of therapeutic procedures that were already seen as the only "scientific" ones!

Yet in the responses analyzed here the surgeons do not place all the blame on the regime, old or new. They felt—and explicitly said so—that the fundamental cause of charlatanry was to be found in the "credulity of the people," which, according to their testimony (9 out of 12), was more widespread in rural areas than in towns. The surgeons of Strasbourg, for example, stated: "The people of the countryside are more credulous than those of the towns." At Boiscommun and also at Cognac, the deputy surgeon felt that this popular credulity was due to the lack of enlightened education. At Mont-de-Marsan the local deputy depicted "a people impressed by the marvellous . . . devoid of the faculty of discernment," which for this reason is easily deceived by charlatans. Clearly, the various explanatory factors invoked by the provincial surgeons fit into the typical ideology of the adherents to the second Enlightenment. As we now know, these explanations did not correspond to the social realities in the specific area of literacy and primary education. Most importantly, however, the explanatory schema itself, proposed by diploma-holding and city-dwelling surgeons, is unconvincing, for a culture does not have to be founded on a narrow or short-sighted rationalism.

Pursuing their analysis of charlatanry, some of the surgeons saw it as more than a breach of trust committed by one kind of swindler or another. The deputy surgeon of Saint-Omer wrote, "The people . . . like to be deceived." According to the deputy surgeon of Tours, "It even seems that the wretched class derives a kind of satisfaction from being deceived. . . ." The deputy surgeon of Beaufort came to the following conclusion: "And with a heavy heart, we say to ourselves: the public wants to be deceived. So be it!" What more is needed to show the discouragement, or perhaps the conscious or unconscious wisdom, of the surgeons faced with a "new world," inhabited by "savages" who refused the benefits of the Enlightenment?

Finally, the surgeons whose responses are recorded have spoken of the deepest cause of their failure; but since they felt that they represented a rational, learned, and (therefore) superior culture, the only "true" culture, they were unable to carry their analysis very far. Here is one indication, found in the response sent by the surgeons' guild of Cognac: "The number of purveyors of nostrums is also very large. They talk of *chaple, vertaupe,* and a lot of other foolishness of this kind, which surely is not part of the *nomenclature of diseases. Chaple*, according to them, is any mucous tumor appearing anywhere on the body. Scrofulous humors are called *vertaupe* by them." Here we have the expression of "two interpretations of the world, two systems . . . that had become more alien to each other than ever before." These statements also manifest—notwithstanding the translation proposed by the "enlightened" surgeon—the dismissal of a popular nomenclature of diseases. At the very time when they asserted the need for observation unhampered by any preconceived system, the surgeons adamantly refused to consider a different language, a different body of knowledge, because they felt that these were tied to a "popular" culture inferior to their own.

The analysis of the responses to the surveys of 1786 and 1790 has provided a series of revealing testimonies about the mentality of the French medical profession concerning the relationship between learned and "popular" medicine. It has brought to light certain problems of interpretation involved in reading a set of documents of learned origin and character. First of all, it confirms the assumption that the ideology of the Enlightenment had reached the group of masters of surgery as a whole as well as their urban elite. When it came to "charlatanry," their "discourse" deviated very little from that of the "enlightened" correspondents of the Société Royale de Médicine or of certain Parisian master apothecaries. The irresistible ascent of surgery and pharmacy in professional and scientific terms was in part responsible for the establishment of closer ties between some of the surgeons and the physicians; it was a *rapprochement* that foreshadowed, albeit from afar, the eventual unification of the medical profession that was to take place in 1892.

The second testimony provided by the *corpus* examined here is this: better administrative techniques for taking a survey (which had been perfected in the course of the eighteenth century) tended to reinforce the preconceived notions of an elite that meant to stress its enlightenment. The medical elite also expressed, very forcefully indeed, its "will to power," its will to monopolize the vast field of health care, from which it excluded all nonprofessionals with a grim determination that was rooted in a centuries-old tradition and strengthened by the ideology of the Enlightenment.

Altogether, then, the medical elite clearly outlined the undertaking it was to pursue throughout the nineteenth and twentieth centuries, namely, a veritable crusade against charlatanry and a struggle to impose medical control upon the body social as a whole. During the 1780s a group of men, asserting their superiority, laid claim to the exclusive practice of an art that was itself considered the fruit of superior learning. This, among other things, explains the masculine image of the therapeutist in the discourse of the enlightened surgeons, not only on the level of the images projected (sorcerers were designated as such, but nothing was said about witches) but also on the level of social realities, as exemplified by the increasing numbers of physicians practicing obstetrics and surgeons demonstrating the techniques of delivery.

This was the attitude of a conquering power; it was also a lazy and ultimately unwarranted attitude, for it side-stepped the authentic problems raised by the existence of a popular culture, problems that must be faced by the historian as well as by the anthropologist or the physician. In our own time the scientific, professional, and social success of medicine and the medical profession is so great that in the present medical elite one can observe the reappearance of the feeling of superiority and the same self-assurance that pervades the enlightened texts of the eighteenth century. In order to stress the superiority of its learning, the medical profession has reduced or denied the veiled kinship, the mere nuance of difference, the sigh [of mutual attraction] that existed—and still exists— between "legitimate physicians and charlatans." And this nuance is due not only to the increasing (and that means both dangerous and beneficial) effectiveness of medical knowledge, but also to two different systems of understanding the world. It also involves the matter of personal identity. As for the denial of this nuance, it has its source in the peculiar relationships obtaining in the social and the natural order, where the first [group], once it has detached itself from the second, attains a sovereign position, thanks to mankind's adaptation to that segment that holds the tools of power.

The Insane in Modern Society

ANDREW SCULL

Beneath the obvious changes of an industrializing century, but closely related to them, important new attitudes toward the insane developed. In a society that increasingly stressed rationality, those who were not behaving rationally inevitably received new kinds of attention. The rise of modern medical attitudes, discussed in the previous selection, quickly spilled over into new claims regarding the treatment of the mentally disturbed. One of the most important areas of recent work in social history has, correspondingly, focused on the treatment of the insane as an index, and sometimes as a critique, of mainstream modern values.

Several historians have discovered the beginnings of a new outlook as early as the seventeenth and eighteenth centuries, when more rigorous concepts of rationality led to new and more restrictive notions of what "normal" behavior was. These led initially to a growing desire to close off the insane from the rest of society—a declining tolerance for deviance. Gradually this desire spread from theoreticians and institutional leaders to ordinary people, so that a growing demand for asylums—places where the insane could be shut away—arose by the nineteenth century. Changes in family forms, which made care for needy members more difficult as the family became a tighter emotional unit, contributed to this need for institutions as well.

The following passage discusses a further change in this approach, specific to the late eighteenth century and the nineteenth century. William Tuke's work began in the late 1700s, and was continued through the 1800s. Institutions for the insane began to move toward a more basic therapeutic effort in which the insane should be changed, not simply shut away. Society's belief in rational organization, and possibly its intolerance for those who could not conform, reached such a point that a belief in positive therapy became essential. On the surface, the resulting changes in institutional care pointed in more humanitarian directions. Brutal physical treatment declined. But some argue that the modern outlook produced its own, more binding fetters. When an insane person was not only to be separate, but to be pressed to change and conform, was he or she not being subjected to the most basic kind of constraint imaginable—all the more compelling because it was wrapped in a progressive package? Interestingly, during the nineteenth century new fears about lunacy and asylums arose, as ordinary people worried that their own sanity might be questioned.

The history of madness, once an offbeat subject, increasingly becomes part of an understanding of modern social trends. Modern people do rely on definitions of insanity as a measurement of their own normalcy, while concern about mental illness—which is growing in our own century—becomes a major part of the definition of health. Questions remain unanswered. It has proved almost impossible to assess whether mental illness itself increased in modern society, as opposed to official determination of this illness and resulting institutionalization—both of which definitely have increased. We do not know how much the new concern for mental illness denoted a real increase in problems of functioning. Nor do we know how much it reflected more rigorous definitions of sanity.

Questions of interpretation also remain. To some observers, the decline in the tolerance of madness and the effort to "remake" the internal conscience of the insane constitute major weaknesses of modern society. Recently, efforts to reduce institutionalization, to let more mentally troubled people operate in the mainstream, have reflected this view—along with the growing concern about the cost of institutionalization. Other observers continue to argue that institutionalization represented a major modern advance, even if a less purely humanitarian advance than was once believed. They note that problems of functioning become more dangerous amid the complexities of modern society. It does seem clear, however, that the insane themselves have hardly benefited from the modernization process, and they may have lost. And it seems possible that the modern outlook depends on marking off a fragile sanity by labeling difference as madness, thereby creating new intolerance of those who fall on the wrong side of the dividing line.

W̲e are all familiar with that traditional version of pyschiatric history which celebrates it as a not always continuous, but ultimately triumphal, procession toward the rational and humane forms of treatment presently practiced. In such accounts, the introduction of moral treatment always occupies a central place of honor: the legendary decision by Pinel to strike the chains from the raving maniacs in the Bicêtre; and the less dramatic but equally significant endeavors of William Tuke to provide humane care for insane Quakers at the York Retreat. It is with moral treatment that I shall be concerned in this essay. I shall try to explicate some of the central dimensions of its English version, and to explore some of its broader social roots and significance. For I take it that one of the more important contributions that a sociologist can make to the history of the psychiatry is to break down some of the parochialism that marks most treatments of the subject and to show some of its connections with larger social movements and processes.

From Andrew Scull, ed., *Madhouses, Mad-Doctors, and Madmen* (Philadelphia: University of Pennsylvania Press, 1981), pp. 105, 106, 107, 109–15.

Traditional Approaches to Madness

From a number of perspectives, I think Tuke's admirers are quite right to stress that his approach marked a serious rupture with the past, rather than simply a refinement and improvement of existing techniques. They go astray, however, when they accept at face value the account that Tuke and his followers provide of their activities. The advent of moral treatment is both something more and something less than the "triumph of humanism and of therapy, a recognition that kindness, reason, and tactful manipulation were more effective in dealing with the inmates of asylums than were fear, brutal coercion and restraint, and medical therapy." It will not do simply to assert that Tuke replaced immoral with moral therapy, or to attribute the reformers' achievements to their superior moral sensibilities while consigning their opponents to the status of moral lepers, men devoid of common decency and humanity.

On the contrary, the perception that the traditional way of coping with lunatics in madhouses (even such things as the use of whips and chains to maintain a semblance of order) were inherently cruel and inhumane is by no means as simple and self-evident a judgment as both the reformers and later generations came to believe. The practices of the eighteenth-century madhouse keepers seem so transparently callous and brutal that we tend to take this judgment as unproblematic, as immediately given to any and all who have occasion to view such actions. But cruelty, like deviance, "is not a quality which lies in behaviour itself, but in the interaction between the person who commits an act and those who respond to it." Consequently, whether or not a set of practices is perceived as inhumane depends, in large part, on the world view of the person who is doing the perceiving. Practices from which we now recoil in horror were once advocated by the most eminent physicians and cultured men of their day. That madmen were chained and whipped in asylums in the eighteenth century was well known at the time. How could it be otherwise when, throughout the century, the doors of Bethlem [Bedlam] were open to the public, and the inmates exhibited before the impertinent curiosity of sight-seers at a mere penny a time, and when every treatise on the management of the mad advocated such treatment? Certainly such practices were not something of which magistrates only became aware at the turn of the century. Yet it was only then that protests began to be heard that such treatment was cruel and inhumane.

To be sure, some of the treatment meted out to lunatics in private madhouses was the natural product of an unregulated free market in madness—the consequence of the unchecked cupidity of the least scrupulous, of the incentives to half starve and neglect pauper inmates, of the temptation to rely on force as the least troublesome form of control. But there is more to it than that. Even in situations where such factors were

obviously inapplicable, lunatics were treated in ways which later generations were to condemn as barbaric and counter-productive—in ways which
they (and we) find virtually incomprehensible and almost by default attribute to an underdeveloped moral sensibility, if not outright inhumanity.

The treatment of George III during his recurrent bouts of "mania"
perhaps makes this point most dramatically and unambiguously. No doubt
Francis Willis, who was charged with treating the king, earnestly sought
the monarch's recovery. But to modern eyes, he went about the task in a
distinctly peculiar fashion. In the words of the Countess Harcourt, "The
unhappy patient . . . was no longer treated as a human being. His body
was immediately encased in a machine which left no liberty of motion.
He was sometimes chained to a stake. He was frequently beaten and
starved, and at best he was kept in subjection by menacing and violent
language."

John Monro, the physician to Bethlem from 1751 to 1791 and one of
the two most eminent mad-doctors of the mid-eighteenth century, speaks
of madness as involving "a total suspension of every rational faculty";
just as Andrew Snape, almost half a century earlier, had lamented "those
unhappy People, who are bereft of the dearest Light, the Light of Reason." In a revealing passage, Snape then goes on to say,
"Distraction...divests the rational Soul of all its noble and distinguishing
Endowments, and sinks unhappy Man below the mute and senseless Part
of Creation: even brutal Instinct being a surer and safer guide than
disturb'd Reason, and every tame Species of Animals more sociable and
less hurtful than humanity thus unmann'd."

Eminent mad-doctors of the early nineteenth century continued to
adhere to this position, arguing that "if the possession of reason be the
proud attribute of man, its diseases must be ranked among our greatest
afflictions, since they sink us from our preeminence to a level with the
primal creatures."

I suggest that the resort to fear, force, and coercion is a tactic
entirely appropriate to the management of "brutes." Thus, when we look
at the treatment of the insane prior to "reform," we must realize, as
Foucault points out, that

> the negative fact that the madman is not treated like a "human being" has
> a very positive meaning. . . . For classicism, madness in its ultimate form is
> man in immediate relation to his animality. The day would come when
> from an evolutionary perspective this presence of animality in madness
> would be considered as the sign—indeed the very essence—of disease. In
> the classical period, on the contrary, it manifested the very fact that *the
> madman was not a sick man.* Animality, in fact, protected the lunatic from
> whatever might be fragile, precarious, or sickly in man. . . . Unchained
> animality could be mastered only by *discipline* and *brutalizing.*

The Rupture with the Past

It was this world view that the nineteenth-century reformers and, indeed, society as a whole were in the process of abandoning. Much of the reformers' revulsion on being exposed to conditions in contemporary madhouses derived from this changed perspective. For them, the lunatic was no longer an animal, stripped of all remnants of humanity. On the contrary, he remained in essence a man, a man lacking in self-restraint and order, but a man for all that. Moreover, the qualities which he lacked might and must be restored to him, so that he could once more function as a sober, rational citizen.

The beliefs which lie at the heart of the new approach to the insane—Tuke's moral treatment, as well as the less well-known equivalents developed by his contemporaries—differ so profoundly from those underlying traditional practices as to lend some credence to Michel Foucault's notion of a *rupture épistémologique*. At the core of the eighteenth-century approach, as we have seen, was its view that the essence of madness was the absence, or the total perversion, of reason. "In the new system of moral treatment," by contrast, "madmen are not held to be absolutely deprived of their reason." Tuke's whole system crucially depends upon "treating the patient as much in the manner of a rational being as the state of his mind will possibly allow"—a change so striking that it attracted much contemporary comment. In Sydney Smith's words, "It does not appear to them that because a man is mad upon one subject, that he is to be considered in a state of complete mental degradation, or insensible to feelings of gratitude."

The emphasis on the lunatic's sensitivity to many of the same inducements and emotions as other people was associated, whether as cause or consequence, with other equally profound alterations in his treatment. What was seen as perhaps the most striking, both at the time and subsequently, was the emphasis on minimizing external, physical coercion—an emphasis which has had much to do with the interpretation of moral treatment as unproblematically kind and humane. William Cullen articulated the eighteenth-century consensus when he contended that

> restraining the anger and violence of madmen is always necessary for preventing their hurting themselves or others; but this restraint is also to be considered as a remedy. Angry passions are always rendered more violent by the indulgence of the impetuous notions they produce; and even in madmen, the feeling of restraint will sometimes prevent the efforts which their passion would otherwise occasion. Restraint, therefore, is useful and ought to be complete.

Tuke's dissent from this position was sharp and unequivocal: "Neither chains nor corporal punishment are tolerated, on any pretext, in this

establishment." Less objectionable forms of restraint might be necessary
to prevent bodily injury, but they ought to be a last resort, and must
never be imposed solely for the convenience of the attendants. As a routine policy, those running an asylum ought "to endeavour to govern
rather by the influence of esteem than of severity." The insistence upon
"the superior efficacy . . . of a mild system of treatment," together with
the elimination of "gyves, chains, and manacles" had a profound effect
on contemporary reformers, who saw Tuke's success at the Retreat as
proof that the insane could be managed without what were now seen as
harshness and cruelty.

This was no kindness for kindness' sake. From its architecture to its
domestic arrangements, the Retreat was designed to encourage the
individual's own efforts to reassert his powers of self-control. For instead
of merely resting content with the outward control of those who were no
longer quite human (which had been the dominant concern of traditional
responses to the mad), moral treatment actively sought to *transform* the
lunatic, to remodel him into something approximating the bourgeois ideal
of the rational individual. From this viewpoint, the problem with external
coercion was that it could force outward conformity, but never the necessary internalization of moral standards. The change in aim mandated a
change in means. Granted, "it takes less trouble to fetter by means of
cords, than by assiduities of sympathy or affection." But "the natural tendency of such treatment is, to degrade the mind of the patient, and to
make him indifferent to those moral feelings, which, under judicious
direction and encouragement, are found capable, in no small degree, to
strengthen the power of self-restraint." On purely *instrumental* grounds,
then, "tenderness is better than torture, kindness more effectual than
constraint. . . . Nothing has a more favourable and controlling influence
over one who is disposed to or actually affected with melancholy or mania,
than an exhibition of friendship or philanthropy." Only thus could one
hope to reeducate the patient to discipline himself. By acting as though
"patients are considered capable of rational and honourable inducement,"
and by making use of the vital weapon of man's *desire for esteem* (which
even lunatics were now seen as sharing), inmates could be induced to collaborate in their own recapture by the forces of reason. "When properly
cultivated," the desire to look well in others' eyes "leads many to struggle
to conceal and overcome their morbid propensities: and, at least, materially assists them in confining their deviations within such bounds, as do
not make them obnoxious to the family."

The staff played a vital role in this process of reeducation: they must
"treat the patients on the fundamental principles of . . . kindness and consideration." Again, this was not because these were goods in themselves,
but because "whatever tends to promote the happiness of the patient, is
found to increase his desire to restrain himself, by exciting the wish not to

forfeit his enjoyments; and lessening the irritation of mind which too frequently accompanies mental derangement. . . . The comfort of the patients is therefore considered of the highest importance in a curative point of view."

Here, too, lay the value of work, the other major cornerstone of moral treatment, since "of all the modes by which patients may be induced to restraint themselves, regular employment is perhaps the most generally efficacious."

By all reasonable standards, the Retreat was an outstandingly successful experiment. It had demonstrated, to the reformers' satisfaction at least, that the supposedly continuous danger and frenzy to be anticipated from maniacs were the consequence of rather than the occasion for harsh and misguided methods of management and restraint; indeed, that this reputation was in large part the self-serving creation of the madhouse keepers. It apparently showed that the asylum could provide a comfortable and forgiving environment, where those who could not cope with the world could find respite, and where, in a familial atmosphere, they might be spared the neglect that would otherwise have been their lot. Perhaps even more impressive than this was the fact that, despite a conservative outlook which classified as cured no one who had to be readmitted to an asylum, the statistics collected during the Retreat's first fifteen years of operation seemed to show that moral treatment could restore a large proportion of cases to sanity.

The Social Roots of the New Approach

But if one must grant the importance of the changing conceptions of insanity and its appropriate treatment as an intervening cause in the rise of the lunacy reform movement, one must also recognize that ideas and conceptions of human nature do not change in a vacuum. They arise from a concrete basis in actual social relations. Put slightly differently, the ways men look at the world are conditioned by their activity in it. The question which we must therefore address—albeit briefly and somewhat speculatively— is what changes in the conditions of social existence prompted the changes we have just examined.

In a society still dominated by subsistence forms of agriculture, nature rather than man is the source of activity. Just as man's role in actively remaking the world is underdeveloped and scarcely perceived—favoring theological and supernatural rather than anthropocentric accounts of the physical and social environment—so too the possibilities for transforming man himself go largely unrecognized and the techniques for doing so remain strikingly primitive. In a world not humanly but divinely authored, "to attempt reform was not only to change men, but even more awesome, to change a universe responding to and reflecting God's will"—to embark on a course akin to sacrilege. And where the rationalizing impact of the marketplace is still weak, structures of domination tend to remain *extensive* rather than intensive—that is, the quality and character of the work force are taken as a given rather than as plastic and amenable to improvement through appropriate management and training.

But under the rationalization forced by competition, man's *active* role in the process presents itself ever more insistently to people's consciousness. This development is further accelerated by the rise of manufacturing—a form of human activity in which nature is relegated simply to a source of raw materials, to be worked on and transformed via active *human* intervention. More than that, economic competition and the factory system are the forcing house for a thoroughgoing transformation in the relation of man to man. For industrial capitalism demands "a reform of 'character' on the part of every single workman, since their previous character did not fit the new industrial system." Entrepreneurs concerned to "make such machines of men as cannot err" soon discover that physical threat and economic coercion will not suffice: men have to be taught to *internalize* the new attitudes and responses, to discipline themselves. Moreover, force under capitalism becomes an anachronism (perhaps even an anathema) save as a last resort. For one of the central achievements of the new economic system, one of its major advantages as a system of domination, is that it brings forth "a peculiar and mystifying . . . form of compulsion to labour for another that is purely economic and 'objective.'"

The insistence on the importance of the internalization of norms, the conception of how this was to be done, and even the nature of the norms which were to be internalized—in all these respects we can now see how the emerging attitude toward the insane paralleled contemporaneous shifts in the treatment of the normal and other deviant elements of the population. It coincides with and forms part of what Peter Gay has dubbed "the recovery of nerve"—a growing and quite novel sense that man was the master of his destiny and not the helpless victim of fate; and it has obvious links with the rise of "the materialist doctrine that people are the product of circumstance." "Is it not evident," asked James Burgh (and certainly it *was* to an ever-larger circle of his contemporaries), "that by management the human species may be moulded into any conceivable shape?" The implication was that one might "organize the empirical world in such a way that man develops an experience of and assumes a habit of that which is truly human."

This faith in the capacity for human improvement through social and environmental manipulation was translated in a variety of settings—factories, schools, prisons, asylums—into the development of a whole array of temporally coincident and structurally similar techniques of social discipline. Originating among the upper and middle classes, for example, there emerged the notion that the education and upbringing of children ought no longer to consist in "the suppression of evil, or the breaking of the will." With the growth of economic opportunity and social mobility, the old system of beating and intimidating the child to compel compliance came to be viewed as a blunt and unserviceable technique, for it badly prepared one's offspring for the pressures of the marketplace. The child needed to be taught to be "his own slave driver," and with this end in view, "developing the child's sense of emulation and shame" was to be preferred to "physical punishment or chastisement." John Locke, the theoretician of these changes, said,

> Beating is the worst, and therefore the last Means to be used in the Correction of Children. . . . The *Rewards* and *Punishments*, . . . whereby we should keep Children in order *are* of quite another kind. . . . *Esteem* and *Disgrace* are, of all others, the most powerful Incentives to the Mind, when it is once brought to relish them. If you can once get into Children a Love of Credit and an Apprehension of Shame and Disgrace, you have put into them the true principle.

The essential continuity of approach is equally manifest in the methods and assumptions of the early nineteenth-century prison reformers. Crime had been seen as the product of innate and immemorial wickedness and sin. Now, however, the criminal was reassimilated to the ranks of a common humanity. As Fine puts it, "The prisoner was to be treated as a person, *who possessed a reason in common with all other persons,* in contrast to animals and objects. However hardened the prisoner was, beneath the surface of his or her criminality an irreducible reason still remained." In consequence, as lunatics were for Tuke, they were "defective mechanisms" that could be "remoulded" through their confinement in a penitentiary designed as "a machine for the social production of guilt." And for such purposes (again the parallel with moral treatment is clear) prison reformers plainly perceived that "gentle discipline is more efficacious than severity."

The new practices, which had their origins in the wider transformation of English society, were shared, developed further, and given a somewhat different theoretical articulation in the context of the lunatic asylum. As in the wider world, so too in the lunatic asylum: one could no longer be content with the old emphasis on an externally imposed and alien order, which ensured that madness was controlled, yet which could never produce self-restraint. Control must come from within, which meant that physical violence, now dysfunctional, became abhorrent. The realization of the power that was latent in the ability to manipulate the environment and of the possibility of radically transforming the individual's "nature" was translated in the context of madness into a wholly new stress on the importance of cure. It represents a major structural support of the new ethic of rehabilitation. As the market made the individual "responsible" for his success or failure, so the environment in the lunatic asylum was designed to create a synthetic link between action and consequences, such that the madman could not escape the recognition that he alone was responsible for the punishment which he received. The insane were to be restored to reason by a system of rewards and punishment not essentially different from those used to teach a young child to obey the dictates of "civilized" morality. Just as the peasantry who formed the new industrial work force were to be taught the "rational" self-interest essential if the market system were to work, the lunatics, too, were to be made over in the image of bourgeois rationality: defective human mechanisms were to be repaired so that they could once more compete in the marketplace. And finally, just as hard work and self-discipline were the keys to the success of the urban bourgeoiseie, from whose ranks Tuke came, so his moral treatment propounded these same qualities as the means of reclaiming the insane.

The Middle Class in France

THEODORE ZELDIN

The rise of middle-class values was a key development in nineteenth-century society. Indeed, modernization, insofar as it involves changes in mentality, coincides substantially with middle-classness. Middle-class people were the first to commit themselves to beliefs in science, progress and other familiar modern cultural symbols. They were also leaders in developing modern family styles and new ideas about leisure and work. Almost everyone is familiar with aspects of middle-class gains, for they have touched our lives deeply, whether we are middle class, aspire to be, or wish we were not. We know about the virtues of the self-made man, the ethic of competitive achievement.

The following selection deals with various segments of the middle class in nineteenth century France—a period in which the middle class left a growing mark on French politics and society. It paints, inevitably, a complex picture. The middle class was not a single grouping, joined in all particulars. Professional people like doctors used claims to new knowledge as one basis for their social position—in a way already suggested in the earlier selection by Jean-Pierre Goubert. Businessmen, however, stressed their wealth and property, and they could clash with professional people. Businessmen themselves were divided among the venturesome and the timid, the defensive small shopkeeper and the eager entrepreneur. We will see echoes of these divisions much later in European history—for example, in the constituency of the Nazi movement in Germany.

The middle class is, then, a complex animal. It is also, at least in the French case, less clearly "modern" in this period than might be expected. Older values linger strongly. Even doctors rely on a more traditional, cultured life style as well as their professional claims. The French middle class may have been particularly conservative, despite its frequent link with revolutionary political activity. But the point that the middle class had difficulty in articulating a totally new set of values is probably valid beyond the French case. The class itself was not entirely new. It was not in firm command of the social structure. The nineteenth century did not see a total triumph of a pure, progressive middle-class mentality. Even in its hostility to the lower classes, the middle class mixed older judgments about social hierarchy with the more distinctive sense that the poor were poor because of their own faults. A realistic picture of middle-class complexity, against common stereotypes, raises important questions about the real nature of nineteenth century modernization and about middle-class commitment to it.

Nothing is more difficult to define than bourgeois, and it must be accepted at the outset that the notion is necessarily a vague one. In 1950, when polls were held in France and the U.S.A. asking people what classes they belonged to, 5.4 per cent of the Americans said upper, 45.2 per cent said middle, 10.6 per cent working, 0.8 per cent farming, 4 per cent lower, 6.5 per cent other and 27.5 per cent gave no answer. But in France 7.9 per cent said they were bourgeois, 22.5 per cent middle, 27.1 per cent working, 13.7 per cent peasants, 7.5 per cent poor, 2.3 per cent other and 19 per cent no answer. As with their political parties, so with their social status, the French give more complicated answers. 32.3 per cent of the professional, business and higher administrative people questioned called themselves bourgeois, but 57.6 per cent claimed to be middle class and 5.3 per cent working class. Likewise, 5 per cent of the artisans and skilled workers thought they were bourgeois, 36.4 per cent middle class and 52.9 per cent working class. The bourgeoisie is a peculiarly French category—as is the peasantry, for few American or British farmers deny membership of the larger working world simply because they live by agriculture. It is impossible to say how many people one is taking about when one discusses the bourgeoisie. Does one mean the electors of Louis-Philippe's 'bourgeois monarchy'—200,000 males? But one knows, from the way he was overthrown, how arbitrary this distinction was and how it excluded at least as many of comparable social rank. Does one mean those who had servants? There were about a million servants in 1900, but would the fall in their number paradoxically mean that the size of the bourgeoisie diminished in the twentieth century? Does one mean those who had some inherited capital or income? That gives about 15 per cent of the population, but one should bear in mind that the average value of inheritances was about sixteen times higher in Paris than in the Ariège in 1900 (but falling to three times in 1934) so that the significance of private income varied enormously in different regions and that its distribution changed rapidly in the twentieth century. Does one mean those who had enough capital to pay for their funerals? The figure in Paris in the 1840s was 17 per cent.

Perhaps the best-known attempt to explain the significance of the word was made in 1925 by Edmond Goblot, a professor of philosophy at Lyon. His analysis fits in with what four-fifths of the Frenchmen questioned in 1950 stated was the principal criterion which determined class: style of life. Goblot insists that it is not wealth that makes a man a bourgeois, but the way that wealth is acquired and the way it is spent. There are rich people who are not bourgeois, and there are poor ones who are accepted as belonging to the bourgeoisie. A bourgeois must spend his

From Theodore Zeldin, *France 1848–1945*, Vol. 1 (Oxford: Oxford University Press, 1973), pp. 13–18, 41–42, 66–68.

money to maintain a certain decorum in his clothes, his accommodation and his food. This does not require large sums. The bourgeois spent less money than the worker on food. What distinguished him was that he served his food differently, with a table cloth laid symetrically, and placed in a special room, not in the kitchen. He had to have a *salon*, furnished with a piano, paintings, candelabras, clocks and bibelots, in which to receive visitors and to show that he possessed a surplus of wealth, dedicated to cultured living, beyond the basic necessities. The rest of his house could be of Spartan simplicity and often was, because he had to spend his money on other things, to keep up his status. He had to pay for his children to go to secondary school, to enable them to take up professions to keep them bourgeois. If they became artisans, he would lose his self-respect. A bourgeois had to be able to perform his job in bourgeois costume, so that manual or dirty physical work was unacceptable. That is why there was such a sharp social distinction between the shopkeeper, who served customers himself, and the wholesaler, who by giving orders and never touching his goods could therefore claim to be a bourgeois. There were indeed wholesalers who refused to receive retailers in their homes. All this implied that the bourgeois gave much effort to distinguishing himself from the masses. He cultivated *distinction*, which involved a special kind of politeness, laying stress on giving a good impression. He had to show taste, which meant knowing what was *correct*, and inclining therefore to conservatism and understatement. That is why for so long the bourgeois wore a black uniform, pointing out his precise rank only with details of cut and cloth. He did not aim to outdo other bourgeois but to keep up with them: moderation and the traditional virtues were his guide. Do as others do: that was the level he worked up to. Do not be common: that was the barrier he had to maintain.

Education and the family were two of the principal concerns of the bourgeois and he spent a lot of his money on them. He had to equip his sons with the *baccalauréat* [a secondary-education degree] and his daughters with a dowry. He laid stress on the acquisition of *culture générale*, which distinguished him from mechanics and artisans; by the twentieth century he may have quickly forgotten his Latin but at least he could speak classical French. He did not allow his wife to work, until 1914 at least, but used her to cultivate the domestic virtues of which he made himself the champion. He linked morality with chastity, fidelity and duty. Even when he asserted his independence against the Church, his quarrel with it was about politics, not about ethics.

However, there are difficulties about this kind of definition of the bourgeoisie. One could buy oneself in or out of the class within a couple of generations. The distinction between bourgeois and noble was not absolutely clear. Those who had been bourgeois long enough, and were rich enough, married into the nobility, which gladly welcomed their hefty dowries. The richest industrialists and financiers—like Schneider, whose four daughters all married noblemen and whose grandson married an Orleans—were rapidly absorbed into the nobility. Those who could not wait made themselves noble by a do-it-yourself process: they just assumed titles, a process which became much easier once the republic was pro-claimed. The number of nobles paradoxically rose after 1789. There were about three times as many people falsely parading titles in the twentieth century as there were genuine nobles. Two thousand claimed to have papal titles, but between 1831 and 1906 the pope granted only 300 titles. And it should be remembered that many of the genuine nobles had legally bought their titles before the Revolution, by purchasing state offices. The bourgeoisie and the aristocracy had much in common; what differed now was that movement betwen the classes was easier and more rapid. The distinctions were less firm and therefore there was more room for snobb-ish rejection. Noble exclusiveness was a matter of show. It strongly resembled the *distinction* the bourgeoisie cultivated. And the bourgeoisie adopted many of the ideals associated with the aristocracy. Though they praised work, their ideal was also to live off a private income, to have a house in the country, and divide their time between it and the town in exactly the same way as the aristocracy. Though they began as revolutionaries—like the eighteenth-century nobility—many of them, by the end of the nineteenth, had accepted Catholicism as a mark of respec-tability. Their attitude to commerce was aristocratic. They adopted aristo-cratic attitudes towards social status. The aristocracy for its part did not disdain to work in the bourgeois civil service: the departments of finance and justice and the army were particularly smart. The aristocracy joined the bourgeoisie in business and industry, particularly banks, insurance, railways, mines and steel, where the boards of directors often contained between a third and a quarter of noblemen. The nobles went into agricul-ture in a massive way after 1830, but many bourgeois also had farms. Possibly the nobles claimed a peculiar quality and had as their special ideal *prowess*—as opposed to bourgeois moderation. They claimed this could not be acquired but could only be inherited; but the bourgeoisie also laid great stress on family qualities. Both were obsessed by making marriages of the right kind, and their politeness differed no more than their clothes. The argument therefore that the nineteenth-century bourgeois cultivated ideals radically different from the aristocracy needs to be qualified. The nobles were former bourgeois and the bourgeoisie were moving up. They may have differed before they reached the top, when they were climbing, but they adopted many of the nobles' values when they could.

In the same way the values of the bourgeoisie were shared by many of those beneath them in the social scale. The gradations were equally blurred here. The bourgeois was supposedly distinguished from the worker by his education, but this was a distinction made more definitely by the academic members of it: there were many members of the provincial bourgeoisie who managed their properties and held influential positions in business without having a *baccalauréat*. Likewise there were *bacheliers*, especially in town, who were the sons of workers and small shopkeepers, but the possession of the supposedly distinctive bourgeois education did not make them bourgeois: many entered business or the civil service, but married into the class they came from and remained in it. The son of the *instituteur* [teacher] often climbed up in the social hierarchy, but the relation of class and education was complex and not automatic. The *lycée* [classical secondary school] was not an exclusively bourgeois institution, and indeed some bourgeois refused to send their daughters to it because they would be contaminated by lower-class girls. The masses did not distinguish as clearly between secondary and primary education as did the professors, and among the illiterate, any sign of learning made a man a bourgeois. Supposedly, the bourgeoisie represented the triumph of merit but they were quick to entrench their privileges in their families with the same determination as the aristocracy. The passion for thrift and for property was shared by the peasants and the artisans. The taste for culture was not a bourgeois prerogative: indeed it was precisely for his false interest and conservative philistinism that the bourgeois was attacked. Though the bourgeois went to the theatre, so did artisans, clerks and even some workers, and it was they who probably in even greater numbers flocked to the painting Salons. The bourgeois kept his wife at home and gave her a servant to do the housework; but the worker called his wife *la bourgeoise* precisely because she was often not a wage earner either. The dowry was a universal institution with all but paupers, until it was whittled away, from the bottom of the social scale upwards, by inflation and depression between the wars. . . .

Success in medicine was, to many doctors, only a means to an end. Their ideal of the good life, while including service to the community, also often involved activity in other spheres, and in particular the arts. French doctors were famous for their dedication to hobbies, and one can see the place these had in their lives if one looks at some of the leading luminaries. Hippolyte Hérard (1819–1913), president of the Academy of Medicine, gave as much effort to his piano playing to the point of almost having two careers: 'was not Aesculapius the son of Apollo?' Albert Robin (1847–1928), who became a member of the Academy of Medicine at forty, also ran the metallurgical factory he inherited from his father and was a reviewer for the *New York Herald* for many years, which did not stop him publishing over 400 articles in medical journals and being a consultant to the Tsar of Russia. He, by the way, had been cut off by his father when he originally refused to enter the family business, and he had worked his way through medical school on his own. Louis Brocq (1856–1928) was another who was cut off for refusing to be a barrister like his father and his brother. . . . When he became famous as a doctor the father relented, reconciliation took place, and he spent his annual holidays at home in Agen. But Brocq's passion was collecting: he had paintings by Monet, Pissarro, Sisley, Renoir and Degas. Jean Halleé (1868–1951) came of a long line of painters going back to the seventeenth century, though some members of his family turned to medicine in the nineteenth. He was a family doctor in the Fauborg Saint Germain where his family had lived for 300 years. He painted, exhibited, travelled abroad and between his two country houses. French doctors have long had a very flourishing painting society, with large exhibitions; they have been critics and patrons of the arts. An extraordinarily large number of writers have been trained as doctors, and not a few of them have then used their knowledge to attack the profession they forsook or could not find a place in, for its powerlessness and credulity.

Two tentative conclusions may be suggested. The prestige of science and the conquests of medicine placed the doctors in key positions in society, but, like the clergy, their knowledge and their medicine [were] challenged. Their exclusiveness produced a hostility or jealousy against them which was the counterpart to the anticlericalism which the clergy aroused. This is a factor which needs to be weighed in any discussion of the domination of the bourgeoisie. Each section of this class raised itself up by a monopoly which gave them power and enemies at the same time. Bourgeois society was riddled with a vast number of different anticlerical-isms. In these many-sided conflicts, not everybody knew who was his worst enemy. Secondly, the doctors demonstrate, as the other occupa-tions to be discussed will also, that the prestige of technical knowledge in any one subject was seldom accepted as being, by itself, an adequate mark of success. The ideal of general culture remained the final crowning of life. Hence the preoccupation with the arts and letters which was so com-mon. It will be argued in due course that perhaps one ought to talk not of the domination of France by the bourgeoisie, nor even by money, but of the unacknowledged role of the intellectuals. . . .

The memoirs left by some of the northern textile manufacturers are much more about their families than about their firms. They stress the activity of their women in their businesses, and not only by the introduc-tion of a proportion of the initial capital and by joining the name of their father's to that of their husband's firm. 'One should not fail to recog-nise,' wrote one of them, 'the important role the women [of the nineteenth century] played in the home which they animated with their permanent presence. They had absolute control—that goes without saying—of the running of the house, but at a time when the business or the workshop and the home were built as one, they participated in the professional duties of their husbands at the same time as they gave a a great deal of attention to the education of their children. It was on this close collaboration of the head of the firm and his wife that the astonishingly rapid rise of industry in Roubaix-Tourcoing in the early nineteenth century was built.' The historian of the Motte-Clarrisse family (of whom there were 1,622 alive in this single branch in 1952) finds 'the family spirit' evident from the very first extant letter in its archives. Parents expected and obtained obedience. 'Believe in my affection', wrote a father to his daughter in 1869, 'as I believe in your submission and your assiduity in your duties.' Children were asked to pray for the dead members of their dynasty, as for the living. All were required to attend weekly family dinners which were raised almost to the status of religious ceremonies or as one Motte called them 'compulsory festivals'. Madame Motte-Bredart's Sunday lunches began with a sung grace and the litanies of the Virgin were recited before dessert. Mutual aid among members of this family was the practical consequence of their close-knit life. It was the closeness, the secrecy and the exclusiveness that stimulated accusations of oligarchy. But these families were not entirely self-sufficient. Though they nearly always went into the business, lack of ability or inclination sometimes meant that they could not run them on their own. They often delegated a great deal of power to managers, who, in many cases, were then married into the families. There are not infrequent cases of new firms being set up for young men in association with foremen who had proved their worth.

Prudence characterised their economic policy. One Motte went on a pilgrimage in 1836 'to obtain illumination from the Holy Ghost so that we should never undertake anything in business above our strength, lest we should be troubled by hazardous speculations'. His wife's favourite saying was 'Economy is the first profit'. The rule against borrowing was sometimes written into their articles of association. They carried this into their private lives, where simplicity and austerity were severely practised and sentimentality rigorously excluded. One twentieth-century magnate, who was brought up in this textile world, recalls the bedroom of his parents furnished 'worse than a hotel for commercial travellers'. They rose early, worked hours as long as those they imposed on their employees, and very often thought of little besides their work. On the whole, they avoided higher education and they were stauncher patrons of the Church than of the arts.

However, these generalisations about the notables in textiles ignore many exceptions. From time to time these families threw up individuals who were innovators, who broke with tradition (within limits), and who brought about expansion and modernisation. Alfred Motte, for example, born in 1852, and set up in business by his relatives, proceeded to establish at least four other firms. He was a veritable industrial impresario, but he concealed his work behind the traditional façade of family firms. Each of his new companies was set up in association with a manager, who was in charge of its daily running while Motte gave general supervision. Motte broke with the habit of specialising in only one branch of textiles; he was a great believer in industrial enterprise and in the legitimacy of competition and natural selection between firms. Family firms, that is to say, could be vigorous as well as defensive. The well-known textile firms of Alsace, in contrast to those of the north, often were. Their Protestantism set them even further apart from the rest of society. They were among the few supporters of free trade. This was not simply because they were optimistic but because as specialists in printing cloth they worked much more for the export market. Jules Siegfried, father of the famous writer, was among the most colourful and enterprising of these Alsatians. He became a millionaire at twenty-nine by seeing that the American Civil War would cut off France's supply of cotton: he went to India and imported from there. His activity as a cotton merchant took on an international scale. He travelled widely and sent his sons on world tours. He admired the U.S.A. and Britain as exponents of industrial initiative and he despised civil servants who were content with fixed salaries, engineers whom he thought of as pure theorists, and professors, for he had no use for books or culture. When his son André showed academic inclinations, he urged him to become Director of the School of Political Sciences, not simply its employee, for he understood only the success that brought power. His motto was 'to live is to act'—and he had it engraved even on his cuff-links. But it is interesting to see why he did not become a Rockefeller. He confined himself to cotton, a branch of industry where he felt he knew what he was doing. There were limits to his ambition. At forty-four he retired from business giving his firm to his younger brother and devoting himself to politics and social work. He refused to marry 'well' and preferred the daughter of a Protestant pastor who turned him further in the direction of public service. He left his children to make their own way in the world, as he had done.

However, these textile dynasties formed only a small proportion of the employers in this industry. The bulk, in the middle of the nineteenth century, were merchant-manufacturers still using artisan labour and just beginning to turn to mechanised weaving in factories. Such men had yet to establish themselves: they had often begun as dyers, or cloth merchants in small towns. Few rose very fast, for the self-made man was an exception in textiles. They did not set the pace: their humble origins made them continue to see their future in small, regional, if not purely local, terms. They preserved the mentality of the retailer.

The Changing Nature of Protest

CHARLES TILLY, LOUISE TILLY, and RICHARD TILLY

By the end of the Middle Ages, the common people of western Europe had developed a standard form of protest—they rioted against deteriorating economic conditions and against more general encroachments on their rights. With the onset of modernization many groups stepped up their rate of protest but did not initially change its nature. Protest still largely took the form of riots in the name of past rights and standards, a reaction against changes imposed by the outside world. The protesters sought the restoration of a previous price level or of previous taxation rates or of previous rights to the land or to guild protection. Some of the most dramatic passages in nineteenth-century history, such as the French revolutions of 1830 and 1848, were based on the common people's reaction against change. Typically, the groups most involved were not new factory workers, but peasants or artisans, who still had a sense of traditional community and past values on which to base protest as a reaction.

But protest did change, often suddenly for some groups, as people learned that the trends of modernization could not be confronted head on. Instead it was discovered that these trends might be used for compensatory gains such as a higher standard of living or new political rights. The following selection, focusing on France before and after 1850, stresses the contrasts between the old and the new protest in form and duration; in basic orientation, seeking to master change rather than reacting to it; and above all in the scale of organization. New or modern protest becomes distinctively political in its attempt to use the state, though earlier protesters had manifested their own sense of politics.

The new kind of protest could be vigorous, bitter, and certainly violent, but for the most part it worked within the framework of a modernizing society rather than rebelling against it. Expanding rights—to vote, to demonstrate, to strike—encouraged more frequent protest than ever before. But in the advanced industrial nations, including France, it usually fell short of outright revolution, though the rise of anarchism, socialism, and communism produced more avowed revolutionaries than ever before. There are many reasons for the decline of revolution; one of them may be that, although they had learned to ask for more within the modern scheme of values, protesters were no longer seeking a distinctive set of values of their own.

Yet we must ask whether or not motivations changed as much as did the form of protest. In the following selection, protest is labeled very neatly, but organization is stressed more than human content. Many people may have accepted large-scale organization as a necessity of modern life, while still harboring traditional sentiments. Others may have turned away from the most overt forms of protest because massive organization was itself unacceptable. The human meaning is more difficult to find in modern protest than it is in traditional protest—which may caution us against accepting too simple a categorization or too optimistic an assessment of the ability of protest to express grievances in modern society.

[The] vast series of changes in French social structure reshaped the struggle for political power in three fundamental ways. First, position in the national structure of power came to matter far more than local for practically every purpose. Second, the struggle increasingly took the form of contention or coalition among formal organizations specialized in the pursuit of particular interests; communal groups virtually disappeared from politics. Third, new contenders for power emerged as the class structure and the organizational structure evolved. The rise of organizations speaking for segments of the industrial working class was the most important single movement. Other bids for power came from representatives of assorted groups of peasants, of youths, of schoolteachers, of Catholic employers, of government employees. Furthermore, as long-organized groups such as landholders and churchmen contended for power, they adopted the new associational style.

As in other western countries, the political parties which emerged to full activity in Third Republic France compounded diverse interests. The Radicals, the Socialists—and, for that matter, the Radical Socialists—long represented curious melanges of the French electorate. But, compared with her neighbors, France always had a remarkable susceptibility to party fragmentation, an exceptional openness to new parties representing new or old but separate political interests, a considerable tendency for parties to slim down to a single major interest. The Parti Ouvrier Français, the Parti Social Français, the Boulangists, the Christian Democrats, the Communists, the Poujadists represent different phases of this specialization.

Fragmentation was the normal condition of French parliaments, alliance among fragments the parliamentary game. Genuine threats to the parliamentary system came less from this kind of splintering than from the occasional appearance of an important political force acting outside the parliamentary arena: the Ligue des Patriotes, the Croix de Feu, Algerian nationalists, sometimes the Gaullists or the Communists. Inside or outside parliament, the twentieth-century political struggle pitted associations representing relatively narrow segments of the population against each

From Charles Tilly, Louise Tilly, and Richard Tilly, *The Rebellious Century, 1830–1930* (Cambridge, Mass.: Harvard University Press), pp. 44–55.

other and aligned them with or against the regime. Interest-group politics emerged in France.

Our review of social change in France has pointed up spurts of industrialization, urbanization, and demographic transformation after 1850, after 1920 and—preeminently—after 1945; they contrast with crises and reversals at the times of the Franco-Prussian War, the two world wars, and the depression of the 1930s. These are but ripples in a fast-flowing stream. An urban-industrial class structure gradually emerged from a class structure based on land and locality. The new structure relied on control of capital and labor rather than on landed wealth. It separated owners and managers of large formal organizations (factories, governments, schools) from their employees. It emphasized position in the national labor market over local attachments, and gave exceptional rewards to technical expertise. Periods of urban-industrial growth accelerated this transformation of the class structure.

The centralization of politics through the growth of a massive and powerful state apparatus continued trends established centuries before, although the advent of Louis Napoleon after 1848 and the extension of controls over the economy in the 1940s speeded the process. The nationalization of politics through the shift of power and participation to an arena far larger than local went on more or less continuously, but the political mobilization of 1848, of the early Third Republic, of the popular Front, and of the years just after World War II probably drew men into involvement in national politics faster than at other times. The shift of collective action—both political and nonpolitical—from communal to associational bases proceeded inexorably over the entire period, especially during those same periods of political mobilization. These changes transformed the struggle for power, and thus transformed the character of collective violence.

How? Most immediately by changing the collective actions characteristically producing violence. Group violence ordinarily grows out of collective actions which are not intrinsically violent—festivals, meetings, strikes, demonstrations, and so on. Without them the collective violence could hardly occur. People who do not take part in them can hardly get involved in the violence. The groups engaging in collective action with any regularity usually consist of populations perceiving and pursuing a common set of interests. And collective action on any considerable scale requires coordination, communication, and solidarity extending beyond the moment of action itself. The urbanization and industrialization and political rearrangement of France from the Revolution onward utterly transformed the composition of the groups capable of collective action, their internal organization, their interests, their occasions for collective action, the nature of their opponents, and the quality of collective action itself. The transformation of collective action transformed violence.

Again, how? It is easy to illustrate and hard to analyze. The classic French tax rebellion, for example, took two forms, singly or in combination: first, a group of taxpayers attacked the matériel of tax collection, typically by smashing tollgates and burning assessment records; second, many of the residents of a community greeted the tax collector by blocking his way, by beating him, or by running him out of town; if he brought an armed force the villagers fought them. A typical small version of the tax rebellion occurred at St. Germain (Haute-Vienne) in August 1830. Local tax collectors stopped a carter to check his load and collect their toll. A crowd of men, women, and children "armed with picks and with stones" surrounded them, shouted against the tax, and led away man and wagon from the helpless revenue men. This elementary form of resistance sometimes compounded into widespread and grave rebellion, as in the years before the Fronde, during the early Revolution, and (for the last time) in 1849.

Although the sheer difficulty of paying when times were hard certainly had something to do with this common form of resistance to the state, it is important to see how regularly and directly it centered on the very legitimacy of the tax. Not long before the Revolution of 1830, the *procureur général* of the judicial district of Poitiers reported that "seditious posters" had been appearing in the city of Fontenay (Vendée); "the content of the posters is always to forbid the payment of taxes before the ministers who voted the budget are brought to trial." The same sort of campaign was gathering strength in other parts of France at that time, and continued through the Revolution; often it operated secretly and without violence, but now and then it showed up in public confrontation. The tax rebellion developed in the sixteenth century, flourished in the seventeenth, recurred in 1789, 1830, or 1848 as new revolutionary officials sought to reimpose the state's authority; it vanished after 1849. Its history traced the government's long struggle to secure both obedience and income.

Gabriel Ardant has identified the general conditions for waves of fiscal revolts in France: a sharp increase in the central government's demands for cash; a sharp decrease in the market for products of rural industry or agriculture (hence in the ability of villagers to convert their surplus into cash); or, more serious, both at once. He has also pointed their clustering in areas of "closed economy"—not necessarily poor, but little involved in production for the market, typically composed of self-sufficient farms. As he sums it up for the Massif Central:

> The proportion of the population in agriculture remains relatively large. No doubt some industries have grown up in the Massif Central near the coalfields, but the coalfields themselves are less productive than those of the

North and the East. Furthermore, the factories do not have the advantage of channels of communication comparable to the networks of rivers and canals in the North and the East. In any case, industries like agriculture are far from the important markets of the North, the East and the Parisian region. From all this comes a larger tendency than elsewhere to live in a closed economy. Thus we can explain that the regions of the Massif Central have been perpetual zones of fiscal rebellion, that movements like those of the Croquans have periodically reappeared in Limousin, Perigord and Quercy, that in 1848 and 1849 the resistance to taxation developed in these same provinces. In our own time the Poujadist movement started out from Haut-Quercy (now the department of Lot), and the first departments affected were the adjacent ones, the locales of fiscal sedition under the old regime.

Tax revolts grouped together in time and space, primarily because the changes in national policy which incited them affected many localities sharing common characteristics at more or less the same time. The largest nineteenth-century bursts of tax revolts came in 1830, when the officials of the new monarchy sought to reimpose taxes on the provinces; in 1841, when the new Minister of Finances tried a special census as a step toward reorganizing the whole inequitable tax system; and in 1848 and 1849, when another revolutionary government tried to put its fiscal affairs in order.

The tax rebellion often succeeded in the short run. The tax man fled, the tollgates fell. Its success, its timing, its personnel, its very form, however, depended on the solidarity of small, local groups of taxpayers and on the vulnerability of a system of control which relied on agents dispatched from cities into treacherous hinterlands. While individual Frenchmen have shrewdly finagled and dissimulated to avoid taxes up to our own day, their capacity for collective resistance to the tax collector sank fast after the middle of the nineteenth century. When anti-tax movements revived with wine-growers after 1900, small distillers in the 1930s, or shopkeepers in the 1950s, the groups that joined the combat were no longer the taxpayers of a single commune, then of the next, but specialized regional and national associations responding to centralized direction. Marcelin Albert's Comité de Défense Viticole (in the first period), Henri Dorgères' Comités de Défence Paysanne (in the second), and Pierre Poujade's Union de Défense des Commerçants et Artisans (in the third) all adopted the defensive stance of earlier tax rebels, right down to their titles. All left violence aplenty in their wakes, but in these cases the defensive actions and the violence came after the deliberate, strenuous organization of protest groups through substantial sections of small-town France.

Changing Forms of Collective Action

Around the middle of the nineteenth century, both the scale and organizational complexity of the collective actions that normally produced violence—hence of violent action itself—increased rapidly and decisively. That happened for two related reasons: first, the scale and organizational complexity of the groups contending for power also increased rapidly and decisively, the expanding organization of industrial workers being the most notable; and second, communal groups dropped out of the struggle as the new associations, and new groups organized associationally, joined it. The organizational revolution reorganized violence.

There is something more, something the tax rebellion alone cannot reveal. Consider for a moment the point of view of the state. From that perspective the predominant forms of collective violence in France during the first half of the nineteenth century were *defensive*: tax rebellions fended off state employees; food riots beat back outside merchants; attacks on machines repelled technical innovations. The demonstrations, strikes, and rebellions which grew in importance over the century had a much larger *offensive* component; their participants reached for recognition, for a larger share, for greater power.

The crux of the contrast is the relation of the participants to organization at the national scale: the national market, the national culture, and, preeminently, the national state. In the earlier, defensive phase most of the participants were resisting the claims of national structures, especially the state. In the latter, offensive phase most of the participants were bidding for power over the operation of these national structures. In between the nation won out.

We can be more exact. Suppose by "violence" we mean damage or seizure of persons or objects. Suppose by "collective" we mean that a substantial number of people act together. . . . In that case, "collective violence" will ordinarily grow out of some prior collective action which is not intrinsically violent: a meeting, a ceremony, a strike. A question about the causes of collective violence immediately breaks into two questions. Why do these forms of collective action occur? Why do they sometimes—but not always—end in violence?

The nationalization of politics and of economic life in France divided the major forms of collective action which commonly produced violence into three main categories. They waxed and waned successively. The first we will call *competitive* collective action. Competitive actions which once produced a good deal of violence include feuds, acts of rivalry between adjoining villages, recurrent ritual encounters of competing groups of artisans. Although each of these had a distinctive form, by the nineteenth century national observers tended to lump their violent forms together as *rixes*: brawls. The report of the Royal Gendarmerie for the Department of the Rhône in June 1830 expressed alarm that:

> in the arrondissement of Villefranche the young men of its communes, having had some earlier conflicts, get together on holidays, Sundays, and days of fairs in groups of several communes, one against another, and fight tooth and nail; but if the Gendarmerie tries to intervene in those fights to restore good order, the combatants close ranks against the gendarmes, whom they often treat improperly, even making so bold as to attack them with stones, clubs, etc.

Such battles are the most visible form of a general phenomenon: the constant contention among communal groups within small-scale, local political systems. They predominated, statistically at least, in France before statemakers such as Mazarin and Colbert began pressing the claims of the national state and the national economy over local commitments and resources.

That bitter struggle of the statemakers for control over the general population and its resources promoted defensive, backward-looking conflicts between different groups of local people, on the one hand, and agents of the nation, on the other. . . . The word *reactive* describes them. The tax rebellion, the food riot, violent resistance to conscription, machine-breaking, and invasions of enclosed land rose and fell in their own rhythms. They often occurred in the course of transfers of power which our comfortable retrospect permits us to treat as progressive revolutions. Yet they had in common a tendency to involve communal groups jostled and outraged by the commotion of statemaking. This does not mean in the least that the actions of the groups involved were blind or incoherent. In October 1848 we find that the prefect of the Seine-Inférieure had first suspended exports of grains and potatoes because of a food shortage and then lifted the suspension:

> Strong opposition arose at once. Groups gathered on the quay d'Ile about 10 A.M., near some ships which were loading. One of these ships, *le Blé*, was boarded by fifty workers, who started to unload the sacks of potatoes which were its cargo. They had hadly gotten fifty sacks onto the quay when they went to another ship, the English sloop *The Brothers*, which was completely loaded and preparing to sail from the outer corner of the quay. The workers climbed onto the ship themselves, towed the ship toward the bridge, and moored it in the basin, without any resistance from the crew. But the English captains raised their flags to protest against the visits their ships were receiving.

The National Guard came to repossess the ships from the workers; after some scuffling they expelled the workers; then the ships sailed under armed guard. Only in the general pattern of such disturbances does their essential character emerge. They embodied resistance to the growth of a national market exercising priority over local needs and traditions. This was the pattern: the disturbances were clustered in areas torn between the needs of the local population and the demands of the national market; they followed a well-defined routine in which the actors assumed the places of the authorities but melted away when the authorities took the approved action, even if people remained hungry. Yet each incident, including the boarding of ships in Rouen, tended to display a kind of coherence and conscious intent which fits ill with the word usually applied: riot. From the point of view of the statemakers, such actions can only be ill-considered and disorderly; from the point of view of the participant, they are justice itself.

The state and the national market eventually triumphed. Their most difficult battles had been won . . . by 1868; by 1968, they belonged to a fading historical memory. From the period of those eighteenth- and nineteenth-century victories by the state, *proactive* forms of collective action became the standard settings for collective violence. They are "proactive" rather than "reactive" because at least one group is making claims for rights, privileges, or resources not previously enjoyed. The deliberate attempt to seize control of the state is proactive. So are the majority of demonstrations and strikes. Daniel Guérin, a leftwing author, recollects a famous encounter between the far left and the far right. The setting is Paris, February 1934:

> Toward 10 P.M., a column of marchers comes from the rue Royale, filling the whole width of the street, carrying tricolor flags. In the middle of the street gentlemen of mature and respectable appearance, with their ribbons of the Legion of Honor, shout the "Marseillaise." They don't look like rioters. Along the sidewalks, all around them, young workers in sweaters and caps sing the "Internationale." Neither of the two kinds of choristers seems inconvenienced by the presence of the other or bothered by the bizarre cacophony. Instead they give the impression of demonstrating together against the power and the police. Someone tells me they are veterans, some from the right, others from extreme left. But most of the kids who are thundering the Red hymn aren't old enough to have been in the war.
>
> The parade, not having been able to reach or cross the bridge, doesn't stay forever on the Place de la Concorde. And pretty soon the Place is taken over by scattered curiosity-seekers, come to see the damage left by the riot. But suddenly toward 11:30, the black curtain of demonstrators (which was still visible in the distance, on the bridge) rushes toward us in disorder. Under the influence it seems, of a colonel of gendarmerie who, posing as History, roars "Follow me! Forward!," two columns of cops start to attack. One comes out of Cour-la-Reine toward the Champs-Elysées; the other passes between the horses of Marly where the demonstrators built a

bit of barricade at the beginning of the evening, and tries to clean out the bushes of the Champs-Elysées in the direction of the Théâtre des Ambassadeurs. A crackle of gunfire breaks out. A mad panic comes over the bystanders. I have just enough time to put my bicycle on my shoulder, to run just like everyone else, as fast as my legs will carry me, to cross as best I can (given the weight of my machine) the half-barricade at the entrance to the Champs-Elysées, and at a full run try to make it to the avenue Gabriel. Bullets crash into the glass of the streetlights, which break into fragments. Next to me, people fall on their backs, all four limbs thrashing. Others crawl below the line of fire. A young man, a little farther along, complains about a burn on his ear; he touches it with his hand, which fills with blood.

On that February night thousands of individual experiences compounded into a grave conflict. Seventeen persons died and at least two thousand were wounded. As a more or less direct consequence, the Daladier government fell. Yet the events began with nonviolent, proactive demands for power.

This sort of collective action differs from the reactive varieties in important ways: in pivoting on attempts to control, rather than resist, different segments of the national structure; by involving relatively complex special-purpose associations rather than communal groups; through a great articulation of objectives, programs, and demands.

These characteristics imply further contrasts with reactive conflicts. One is a lesser dependency on natural congregations such as markets, church services, and festivals in favor of deliberate assemblies and shows of strength (since special-purpose associations rarely draw all their members from the same round of life but are often effective at calling together a diverse membership at crucial moments). Another is a tendency of the disturbances to be large and short. Communal groups, once committed to a conflict, rarely mobilize large numbers of men, rarely have leaders with the authority to negotiate quick compromise settlements, and rarely can call off the action rapidly and effectively; it may also be true (as it has often been argued) that communal groups have an exceptional capacity to hold out in the face of adversity. Associational groups, on the other hand, tend to become involved in violence as an outgrowth of brief, coordinated mass actions which are not intrinsically violent. Still another contrast between reactive and proactive movements is a prevalence of indignation about the loss of specific rights and privileges in the reactive cases, as compared with a greater emphasis in proactive cases on rights due as a consequence of general principles.

Two features of the shift from competitive to reactive to proactive forms of collective action as prime settings for violence stand out: the change in organization of the participants, and the change in locus of the conflict. First, the groups taking part in collective action become bigger, more complicated, more bureaucratized, more specifically committed to some public program or ideology, more open to new members prepared to support the group's special goals; earlier we called this a transfer from communal to associational bases for collective action. Second, the locus of the conflicts involved moves away from the purely local toward the national, even the international, scale; although by 1830 Frenchmen were making national revolutions and demonstrating in support of Poland, the bulk of violent conflict aligned local groups on essentially local issues; by the 1930s national issues and national antagonists took precedence. From a national perspective this change seemed to involve a "politicization" of conflict.

The trouble with that way of stating it is the fact that the competitive and reactive forms of collective action also grew out of well-developed struggles for power, out of political conflicts on a smaller scale. The tax rebellion, the food riot, the invasion of fields, and even the artisans' brawl pivoted on local questions of rights, duties, and power. For that reason, we would be better off speaking of a "nationalization" of conflict, integrally related to the nationalization of political life. In our own day we may have to speak of a further stage of "internationalization."

It is wrong to picture competitive, reactive, and proactive collective action as three distinct, exclusive stages. That image has two defects. First, some communal groups gradually acquire associational characteristics, yet retain their capacity for collective action throughout the process: a city's traditional elite joins a national pressure group; a religious community becomes a corporation. During the transformation their characteristic *forms* of collective action, and thus of collective violence, also change. Second, the proactive forms of collective action emerged early in those sectors of French social life in which the national structures emerged early: major cities, areas of advanced industry, the hinterland of Paris, and so on. At the center of the centralized French system, men had begun struggling for control of the state and the national market centuries before their brothers at the periphery stopped fighting the expansion of the state and the market. The rapid nineteenth-century transition from predominantly reactive to predominantly proactive forms of collective action resembled the movement from one terrain to another rather than the passage of a guarded frontier. We might visualize the statistical distribution of violence emerging from each of the major forms of collective action as that shown in Figure 1.

In the absence of reasonable criteria for the "amount" of collective violence and of reasonable data for the period before the nineteenth century, the exact shapes of the curves represent no more than informed speculation. The biggest speculation is that the volume of reactive violence swelled rapidly during the heroic statemaking of Louis XIII and Louix XIV. We know that popular rebellions of a reactive form abounded at that time, but too little work has been done on conflicts well before and

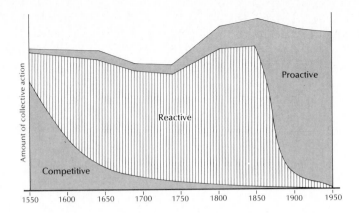

Figure 1.   Hypothetical Evolution of Collective Action in France

well after the Fronde to verify the general timing. The graph rests on a
firmer factual footing in stating that reactive conflicts rose to a
nineteenth-century peak, instead of gradually diminishing. The real point
of the diagram, however, is to portray the slow displacement of competitive by reactive forms of collective action as the French state extended its
claims, and the rapid displacement of reactive by proactive collective
action during the nineteenth-century nationalization of the struggle for
power.

PART 3

Mature Industrial Society 1850-1918

Detail from "Over London by Rail," a wood engraving by Gustave Dore, from Jerrold's *London: A Pilgrimage*, London, 1872.

Mature Industrial Society

With industrialization well established in central and western Europe, some of the more dramatic social dislocations eased in the later nineteenth century, if only because a smaller percentage of the population was moving from countryside to city—that is, from a traditional to a dynamic environment. Major problems of adaptation remained, however; rural people had only just begun to be converted to new values. Many workers were still new to the factory setting. Even some older workers, who had successfully preserved elements of a traditional approach to work during the early stages of industrialization, had major problems of adjustment as industrialization became more firmly entrenched.

And the nature of industrial society continued to change. For factory workers and artisans, the introduction of new techniques and the rise of big business organizations created obvious difficulties. Women in many social classes felt the impact of change more acutely in this period than ever before. In the early industrial revolution, middle-class women preserved many traditional goals. They worked closely with their husbands in business and expected to bear many children. Working-class women faced a less familiar situation, particularly when they worked outside the home; but again their outlook probably remained fairly traditional. They expected to marry, after which the vast majority would stop working outside the home to define their lives through service to their families. In the later nineteenth century a declining birthrate gave women more free time, and as most women were now exposed to schooling—a minority to advanced schooling—rising levels of education produced new expectations. In some cases expectations outstripped opportunity because the definition of a woman's "place" changed only slowly. Particularly, in the middle class, problems of adjustment became increasingly obvious. By the 1900s, one result was an intense feminist movement in many countries.

The late nineteenth century, in which modern technological and organizational structures were well established (though still evolving), was probably the key period of change for women and workers. Before this—with some exceptions such as lower-class sexual behavior—many traditional values had been preserved, even in radically new settings. But was this new round of change really modernization, to be lumped with earlier alterations of mentality among, say, middle-class men? Here is a clear test for the frequent claim that modernization is a catchall, without a sufficient linkage among various kinds of change.

Many of the attitudes formed during this period of maturing industrialization proved quite durable. Although many workers were new to their situation and the nature of industrial life continued to change, a recognizable working-class culture began to emerge—one major outgrowth of the general modernization process that endures in most respects to the present day. Durable changes in the nature of protest form the aspect of the new popular culture. Many of the new ambiguities in women's lives also persisted. At the same time, the broader popular culture was changing in other directions familiar to us today. In the later nineteenth century, a new interest in sports arose, soon to become a consuming passion for many people.

The outlines of modern society were becoming clearer. Most people in western Europe were now accustomed to change, so questions arising from the sheer confrontation between tradition and innovation gave way to more subtle issues. Was the new interest in leisure, for example, an expression of modern man's alienation, his desire to escape monotonous labor and recover, if only vicariously, some of the aggression and passion of his primitive ancestors? Or was the rise of leisure a more positive sign, an indication of growing affluence and leisure time and an expression of the desire to develop new fields of individual achievement? The changing position of youth might be seen as an application of modern values to a new age group or as an expression of stress caused by modern institutions and family life, forcing isolation of age segments that did not readily fit the mold. Similar questions apply to more familiar topics: Did the rise of socialism signify a growing belief in progress and an orderly political process on the part of working people? Or did it betoken the institutionalization of class warfare and periodic acts of violence? Was imperialism the product of a confident, dynamic society or of a society that translated its insecurity into aggression abroad? With change established as an inescapable part of modern life, the need to assess its meaning became paramount.

BIBLIOGRAPHY

The history of women is beginning to receive considerable attention. J. A. Banks has written *Prosperity and Parenthood: A Study of Family Planning among the Victorian Middle Classes* (New York, 1954), and with Oliver Banks, *Feminism and Family Planning* (Liverpool, 1964). Good general introductions to recent writing on the history of women are Martha Vicinus, ed., *Suffer and Be Still: Women in the Victorian Age* (Bloomington, Ind., 1972), and *A Widening Sphere: Changing Roles of Victorian Women* (Bloomington, Ind., 1977). Other valuable collections are Lois Banner and Mary Hartman, *Clio's Consciousness Raised* (New York, 1974), and Renate Budenthal and Claudia Koonz, eds., *Becoming Visible: Women in European History* (New York, 1976). Bonnie G. Smith, *Ladies of the Leisure Class: The Bourgeoises of Northern France in the 19th Century* (Princeton, 1981) is a vital monograph. Some key trends among working-class women are discussed in Margaret Hewitt, *Wives and Mothers in Victorian Industry* (New York, 1958). William L. O'Neill, *Woman Movement: Feminism in the United States and England* (Chicago, 1969), is a good brief survey of this important movement at the turn of the century. An important survey is Joan Scott and Louise Tilly, *Women, Work and Family* (New York, 1978).

Studies that deal with workers, as opposed to formal protest movements by labor, are not overabundant. For Britain, E. P. Thompson, *The Making of the English Working Class* (New York, 1964), Eric J. Hobsbawm, *Labouring Men: Studies in the History of Labour* (New York, 1964), and John Foster, *Class Struggle and the Industrial Revolution* (New York, 1975) are works of major importance; for the years around 1900, see also Standish Meacham, *A Life Apart: The English Working Class 1890–1914* (Cambridge, Mass., 1977). Daniel Walkowitz and Peter N. Stearns, eds. *Workers in the Industrial Revolution* (New Brunswick, N.J., 1974) covers several countries; see also Stearns, *Lives of Labor: Work in Maturing Industrial Society* (New York, 1975). On France, see Michael Hanagan, *The Logic of Solidarity: Artisans and Industrial Workers in Three French Towns 1871–1914* (Urbana, 1980). A fine German case study is David Crew, *Town in the Ruhr: A Social History of Bochum 1860–1914* (New York, 1979). A recent survey, with good bibliography, is Dick Geary, *European Labour Protest 1848–1939* (New York, 1981). To follow continuities in working-class culture into our own time, see John H. Goldthorpe et al., *The Affluent Worker in the Class Structure* (New York, 1969). See also Robert Blauner, *Alienation and Freedom: The Factory Worker and His Industry* (Chicago, 1964).

Carlo M. Cipolla, *Literacy and Development in the West* (Baltimore, 1969), and Geoffrey H. Bantock, *Culture, Industrialization and Education* (New York, 1969), provide a general background for the modern history of education. See also Fritz Ringer, *Education and Society in Modern Europe* (Bloomington, Ind., 1979). For France, Michalina Vaughan and Margaret S. Archer, *Social Conflict and Educational Change in England and France, 1798–1848* (New York, 1971), is good on the early period. E. H. Reisner, *Nationalism ad Education since 1789* (New York, 1923), deals with another important theme, the inculcation of nationalist values through the schools. F. Ponteil, *Histoire de l'enseignement en France* (Paris, 1966), is a fine French survey. On rural education, Roger Thabault, *Education and Change in a Village Community* (New York, 1971). On schoolteachers, a recent study of Germany is useful: Antony LaVopa, *Prussian Schoolteachers, Profession and Office 1763–1848* (Chapel Hill, 1980). English education has been extensively studied; see B. Simon, *Studies in the History of Education, 1780–1920* (London, 1960), and Howard C. Barnard, *A Short History of English Education* (New York, 1955). R. D. Altick, *The English Common Reader: A Social History of the Mass Reading Public, 1800–1900* (Chicago, 1957), deals with the uses of growing literacy. See also Harvey Graff, ed., *Literacy and Social Development in the West* (Cambridge, Eng., 1982).

Key studies in the history of crime are: J. J. Tobias, *Crime and Industrial Society in the 19th Century* (New York, 1976); Howard Zehr, *Crime and the Development of Modern Society* (Totowa, N.J., 1978); Abdul Lodhi and Charles Tilly, "Urbanization, Crime and Collective Violence in 19th-Century France," *American Journal of Sociology* 49 (1973), 296–318; and V. A. C. Gatrell, Bruce Lenman and Geoffrey Parker, *Crime and the Law; The Social History of Crime in Western Europe since 1500* (London, 1980). Louis Chevalier, *Dangerous Classes and Laboring Classes* (New York, 1972) deals with perceptions, rather than firm statistics; also interesting is Mary S. Hartman, *Victorian Murderesses* (New York, 1975). Michel Foucault, *Discipline and Punish: The Birth of the Prison* trans. Alan Sheridan (New York, 1977) is an important interpretation. For some of the changes in twentieth-century criminal patterns that so complicate a modernization model for this topic, see F. H. McClintock and N. Howard Avison, *Crime in England and Wales* (New York, 1969).

The history of leisure is another of the important subjects that have until recently not been given much attention by serious historians. For a brief general interpretation, see Michael Marrus, *The Rise of Leisure* (St. Louis, 1976), and *The Emergence of Leisure* (New York, 1974). Peter C. McIntosh, *Sport in Society* (New York, 1963), and *Physical Education in England since 1800* (London, 1969), are useful. See also James Walvin, *Football—the People's Game* (London, 1975) and *Leisure and Society, 1830–1950* (London, 1978); Richard Mandell, *The First Modern Olympics* (Berkeley, 1976). Hugh Cunningham, *Leisure in the Industrial Revolution* (New York, 1980) has a rich bibliography. On France, see Richard Holt, *Sport and Society in Modern France* (Hamden, Conn., 1981).

Age groups are just beginning to catch historical interest. See, for the United States, Joseph Kett, *Rites of Passage: Adolescence in America, 1790 to the Present* (New York, 1977). Peter N. Stearns, *Old Age in European Society* (New York, 1977), deals with another important group. A set of oral histories on English adolescence is Thea Thompson, *Edwardian Childhoods* (London, 1982); see also J. A. Mangan, *Athleticism in the Victorian and Edwardian Public School* (Cambridge, Eng., 1981).

Middle-Class Women

PATRICIA BRANCA

There has never been much question that the middle-class woman of the nineteenth century was in a novel position, but there has been great debate over what the novelty consisted of. Some historians see the woman trapped in an essentially idle domestic role, praised for her purity and lack of sexual desire, pampered as an ornament, but given no effective life functions other than demonstrating a few social graces and bearing children. They note that this woman was part of some positive changes. The middle class pioneered in birth control, though this can be seen as a decision by sexless women to limit their responsibilities still further or by harried husbands to reduce the drain on the family budget. From the middle class, unquestionably, came women reformers and ultimately feminists, but they are seen as rebels against the middle-class way of life, its vacuity and boredom, not as positive products of it. Indeed, in this view, the Victorian woman has only a negative impact on modernization, symbolizing values and constraints against which really modern women had to fight and must fight still.

Patricia Branca takes a different view. Dealing with British women around 1850, at the height of Victorianism, she admits the primacy of the household for women, but sees the middle-class wife and mother as a key agent of change. Far from functionless, she was burdened with huge responsibilities, many of which were newly defined. Motherhood, for example, became much more arduous with fathers at work outside the home. Moreover, with a new sense of concern for children's health and well-being, changes in the concept of the child became central to the life of adult women. As mothers and housewives, women worked in novel urban surroundings, amid intense criticism for failures ranging from sloppiness to inadequate child care. On the whole, despite great anxiety, women met the challenge by applying much the same mentality that their husbands were developing in the business and professional worlds. Above all, this fostered a desire to gain new dominion over their lot. Birth control, stressed again as a middle-class innovation, here stems from women's modernized outlook, their openness to new techniques, and their desire for satisfactory self-expression.

Ending with the late nineteenth century, Branca leaves open the question of women's future. Would they be able to apply their modernized mentality to a wider sphere, or did their horizons remain too purely domestic even to cope with the implications of birth control itself in reducing the domestic function? Was their modernization, in other words, part of the larger social process, or was it distinctly female, leaving women changed but still trapped in a set of gender roles that would find them ill prepared for the twentieth century? In recent decades, more obvious changes in women's situation have occurred than took place in the nineteenth century, but Branca would view such changes largely as a continuation of the modernization begun in the Victorian era, not simply a rebellion against this era as many believe.

The Victorian woman's life would never be quite the same with the birth of her first child. Most of her thoughts, her worries, and her energies would revolve around her child, and with each child the responsibilities grew more and more intense. She did not feel confident in the adequacy of her maternal instincts and so she worried continually about her child and its care. Her major concern was for the child's health. With every sickness of childhood, the mother's anxieties heightened. Even the most basic aspects of child care, for example, feeding and discipline, were to create serious problems for her. She continually sought advice on the best method of care for her child. But in the end, as was the case with her own health, there was very little she could do to improve the child's situation given the limited means available and the traditionalism which still maintained a strong hold on this part of her life.

With each new birth, the Victorian mother experienced many anxious moments wondering if the babe would live or die. The fate of thousands of infants dying prematurely every year was to become a burning issue in Victorian society. The outcry against the needless tragedy of infant mortality continued throughout the century. The sentiment expressed was similar to that concerning the state of maternal mortality, but more intense because of the greater numbers involved and the helplessness of the victim. A declining sense of fatalism and a growing determination that this tragedy need not be, were again much in evidence. A typical reaction was that of Dr. Alfred Fennings, author of *Every Mother's Book: or the Child's Best Doctor* who noted that

The OMNISCIENT GOD never intended that nearly half the babies born in this country should die as they now do, before they are five years old. Carelessness . . . and a general ignorance of simple and safe remedies to cure their peculiar diseases have been the fatal causes.

Dr. R. Hall Bakewell, who wrote a series of articles on "Infant Mortality, and Its Causes" for *The British Mothers' Journal*, was of the same belief.

We cannot deny that there must be something wrong in the management of children during the early years. Children are not sent into the world to die, they are sent to live to a natural term of man's life; and a system by which one-fifth of all who are born never see the first anniversary of their birth, must be radically wrong somewhere.

These are just two examples of the growing concern over infant care. There were hundreds of books published and articles written specifically on child care. The books were widely publicized: for example, Dr.

From Patricia Branca, *Silent Sisterhood: Middle-Class Women in the Victorian Home* (Pittsburgh, Pa.: Carnegie-Mellon University Press 1975), pp. 95–96, 108–09, 114, 137–38, 144–53.

Fennings' book was advertised regularly in *The Mothers' Friend*, a monthly magazine. One of the advertisements made the following claim:

> Do not let your children die. Fennings' *Every Mother's Book* contains every-thing a mother ought to know about her child's Feeding, Teething, Sleep-ing, Weaning, also Hints, Cautions, Remedies for all diseases, and Secrets worth 500 Guineas. Mothers and Fathers, save your child's life by reading it. Its instructions have already saved thousands.

However, in spite of the intense concern, in spite of the sage advice, infant mortality remained a perplexing problem for the Victorian mother. The infant deathbed scene so popular with the religious writers, the grief of a bereaved mother at the loss of her child, which was a regular feature in many of the women's magazines, reflected grim reality. . . .

> doctors, who gave it eight calomel powders, applied one leech to the chest, one blister to the chest, six mustard plasters, and gave it antimony wine and other medicines in abundance. Yet the poor thing died!' The friend in amazement replied, "Died! It would have been a miracle if it had lived."

It is difficult to say when women sought medical attention for a sick child. Judging from the mortality rates it would appear that it was not often enough or soon enough. Traditional ideas about childhood illnesses were still very strong, as indicated by Dr. Bakewell in his last article on infant mortality. His warning was that

> I would caution my readers against the notion, too prevalent among moth-ers, that ailments will get well of themselves when the child has cut all its teeth. Very frequently we see children suffering from scrofulous and other constitutional diseases, who are undergoing no treatment, because their mothers 'fancy' it is nothing but the teeth.

He also noted that many children died of bronchitis because their mothers failed to take them to a physician soon enough. Mothers ignorant of the disease treated it as a cold, but even a delay of twenty-four hours could make the case hopeless because of the rapid progress of the disease in infants. But in many cases even when a doctor's advice was sought it was of little use, because of the lack of knowledge of pediatric care. Traditionalism and the state of medical practice supplemented each other.

Hence the growing concern about children's health enhanced anx-ieties on the mothers' part and at the same time, in public discussions, produced a barrage of criticisms of maternal care. Not yet would the con-cern produce the kind of knowledge about the infant's health and care that was needed. As with the advice on women's health, the advice for child care was too general, based in fact on the same three principles of general health: regulation of diet, proper clothing and plenty of fresh air and exercise. There was little concrete assistance for the mother faced with serious illness and the prospect of frequent infant death. The middle-class mother, no longer resigned to infant mortality, had to feel an acute sense of helplessness and frustration when she realized that despite her efforts and intentions the fate of her child was still so very precarious.

Along with the growing concern for the physical health of the child a profound interest developed in securing the child's mental and moral health. Here too a new attitude toward children was beginning to make strong inroads among the middle-class by mid-century and was to alter child-rearing methods significantly by the end of the century. The child was beginning to be viewed as an individual with very particular needs which only a loving mother could fulfill. The ramifications of this new concept of the child for the Victorian mother were indeed great, as they increased her responsibilities to the child even more. . . .

The deliberate limitation of family size was one of the principal contributions of middle-class women to the modernization process of women generally. This decision flowed not only from the new definitions of childhood and motherhood; it represented the only means available in the mid-nineteenth century of resolving several key problems arising from the new situation and new consciousness of women. As manager of the household the middle-class woman, confronted with limited means, was acutely aware of the expenses involved in maintaining her children in the new fashion. Also birth control was the most practical means of coping with the unresolved problems of maternal mortality.

The positive aspects of the decision to control births were perhaps the most compelling for the middle-class woman. As we will see, the middle-class woman's new image of self involved a new sexuality—one of more intense personal enjoyment. In order to maximize sexual enjoyment, it was necessary to prevent the traditional consequences of sex—pregnancy. Through the adoption of birth control the middle-class woman found the most important ingredient to liberation. . . .

It is probable that the most significant devices involved in the middle-class birth rate decline were the sponge, the douche, and the vaginal diaphragm. One cannot ignore the fact that all the other methods—abstinence, *coitus interruptus*, and the condom— were well-known before the nineteenth century, yet it was not until the introduction and development of the three new methods of birth control that the birth rate began to drop significantly. The fact that the newer methods were designed for the female at a time when she was beginning to exert more and more control over her body also cannot be ignored. Just as the woman rejected the fatalistic attitude related to pain in childbirth and sought chloroform, just as she rejected the fatalistic attitude toward the discomfort and burden of nursing and sought artificial feeding methods, so she rejected the fatalistic attitude to the inevitability of pregnancy and sought contraceptive devices. Is it mere coincidence that as the burdens and responsibilities of motherhood increased the demand for and production of birth control methods particularly for the woman also increased? Overall, the array of available contraceptive devices makes it abundantly clear that the woman was an important factor in the decision-making process. This is not to imply that the husband had no part to play, though the advertisement for the Check Pessary suggested that this might sometimes be the case. The mutuality of decision-making so commonly invoked by the marriage manuals may well have operated in this area. We can reasonably be sure that the woman was no passive partner and that her changing values and situation—even more than economic factors—heavily influenced the decision taken, whether by husband and wife together or, as was technically possible, by the wife alone.

The Victorian middle-class woman experienced dramatic changes in her role as mother. She challenged the traditional attitude toward infant mortality and maternal mortality by seeking advice on better care for herself and the child. Unfortunately, until very late in the nineteenth century, the challenge was successful only in so far as she was able to limit the number of children she had, and thereby lessen the risk of death for herself and her child. Here again, the development of birth control is a vital feature of the history of Victorian motherhood.

The Victorian woman took her role as mother seriously. She realized the importance of the new emphasis on the intimate relationship of mother to child, which added significantly not only to the physical work involved with child care, but also to the mental strain on the mother's part. She assumed complete responsibility for the future health and happiness of her child. The new birth control methods aided her in meeting her responsibilities as mother and helped eliminate an important threat to her life and health. . . .

After an examination of some of the more important aspects in the life of the middle-class woman, one begins seriously to question if the Victorian woman, as she has so long been depicted, ever really existed. Certainly, the woman whose life was characterized as leisurely, dependent, prudish, and boring was not the married middle-class woman of the nineteenth century. Whether or not the image applies to upper-class women remains to be investigated, and it is a task worth undertaking in nineteenth-century English social history. The woman portrayed in this study perhaps lacked some of the glamor and romantic flavor of the woman in the image. However her life, viewed in terms of realities, in terms of the problems she encountered, gives the Victorian woman more meaning and substance than ever before. Within the context of the family, her role was not only functional but central and crucial. One could not possibly understand anything about the Victorian family without understanding the woman in the family, who nurtured it, who managed it, who comforted it. In her role as mistress of the house, in her relationship with domestics and most importantly, in her role as mother, the middle-class woman of the nineteenth century defined herself.

Yet the middle-class woman's historical role transcended the boundaries of the family during the nineteenth century, for she was caught up in the broader transformation of English society. In her daily functions she began to develop attitudes and behavior patterns that form part of the process of modernization. The evolution was incomplete, even well after the 1880s, for the middle-class woman retained important links with traditional values. And assessment in these terms is complicated by the failure, heretofore, to apply any but economic criteria of modernization to the history of women. Nevertheless, the stresses and problems with which this study has been concerned cannot be understood without relating them to a more fundamental evolution, in which middle-class women led the way. If other women, many of them unmarried, seem as individuals closer to a modern set of values during the nineteenth century, the married middle-class women constituted the first large category to undergo the modernization process, precisely because they applied it within the context of the family.

Before proceeding with this discussion, it is necessary to elaborate the precise definition of modernization. Modernization involves industrialization and urbanization on a broad scale. Concentrated population centers replace isolated rural communities as the normal human environment. The nature of work obviously changes and the bulk of the populace is removed from the land. And modernization brings about not only changes in work and style of living, but also a new attitude of mind, which in the long run is probably its more significant feature.

Modern man has conventionally been defined as possessing a mentality that, for the most part, is open to innovation and new experiences. This involves belief in planning and organization in every aspect of life, in the benefits of science and technology, and a conviction that one's environment was calculable, that it could be improved. The modern mind rejects fatalism, and it is present- and future-oriented rather than backward-looking. Characterization of modern man in many ways defines the new middle-class man of the nineteenth century, and in combination the modernization theme and progressive middle-class values are familiar enough. But what about modern woman? Since this study claimed from the outset that the Victorian middle-class woman was the first modern woman, it is necessary to apply the definition of modernization to her life. Did she follow the same pattern? Did she share the same outlook?

The process of modernization was never a voluntary process for women (nor was it for men). It was more a result of outside forces, the new pressures of urban industrial society coming together and making their impact in the nineteenth century, first on the values of the middle class. More than her upper-class sister or her working-class sister, the middle-class woman, in order to maintain herself in this period of great transition, had to adapt to new economic means and a new environment. The working- and upper-class woman long maintained more traditional life styles. For example, the upper-class woman never encountered the economic pressures which continually perplexed the middle-class woman in her effort to maintain an appropriate living standard. The upper-class woman could still afford her retinue of servants and enjoy the society and seasons of the fashionable world during most of the nineteenth century. While the working-class woman shared more of the experiences of the middle-class woman, on the whole, and was certainly deeply affected by industrialization, her life was restricted by a number of factors. Her material means were long insufficient to enable her to alter greatly her lot in life. Her education and outlook were not the same as those of the middle-class woman. Her attitudes toward ordering her home and children remained tradition-bound for the greater part of the nineteenth century. In some respects, in the initial reaction to industrialization the working-class woman developed a special function in preserving as many traditional familial values as possible, to cushion the shock of change. In contrast, the middle-class woman was ultimately able not only to react to change but to initiate some changes on her own. The primary impulse toward modernization stemmed from the middle-class woman's accession to a modest level of prosperity which ultimately brought about a new life style—a lifestyle defined by middle-class values and goals—which neither imitated the aristocracy or attempted to throw up purely traditional defenses against change within the family.

The impact of urban living was profound for the middle-class woman of the nineteenth century. The problems of urbanization—overcrowding, polluted waters and air—were not of great concern for upper-class women, who maintained control of the better sections of the city during most of the century. Also the upper-class woman was able to maintain her traditional rural ties by keeping a place in the country. However, urban society was the only life for the new middle-class woman and in this she shared many of the problems of urbanization with the working-class woman. But in contrast to the ability of many working-class wives to recreate a supportive family network, the middle-class woman was more on her own. Admittedly, until a serious investigation is made into the demographic changes of the middle class in the nineteenth century, we have to rely upon impressionistic evidence. It appears from the literature of the day that one of the special problems for the middle-class woman was the frequent changing of residence. The results of this constant state of flux was that the middle-class woman had no sense of roots, no sense of belonging to an established community, and often lacked strong extended family ties. It is interesting to note that in all the various sources used for this study, there is no mention of any type of family relationship beyond the nuclear family. Never once was there a reference to the role of grandparents, aunts, uncles, or cousins. This lack of relationships beyond the immediate family was particularly striking in the discussions on pregnancy. It would seem likely that at this very important event in a woman's life she would have her mother or sister or some other close relative assist her. However, the middle-class woman was advised to seek the aid of a friendly neighbor. The absence of guidance from experienced kin could have accounted for the middle-class woman's need for such fundamental advice on child care. Also the middle-class woman would be able to innovate in child-rearing more easily without the more tradition-bound influence of her mother. She was certainly freer to adopt artificial feeding methods and contraceptive techniques.

Another important aspect of the modernization process in the lives of married middle-class women, which must be viewed as both cause and result, was the declining influence of religion in their lives. Historians have generally accepted and documented the overall decline of religion in the nineteenth century. It is well known that the returns of the Religious Census of 1851 indicated severe limitations in the numbers attending church, for approximately half the population was not present at religious services. Contemporaries claimed that widespread absenteeism was due mainly to a waning of religion among the working class, and subsequent historians have generally accepted this position. However, more recently, it has been noted that "there was proportionately as much conscious unbelief, if not indifference, in the Victorian middle-class as amongst the workers. . . ." Yet even if this point is accepted it is tempting to assume that indifference was confined to men only; and the image of the Victorian middle-class woman as extremely pious and religious continues to persist. However, there were some indications of changes in women's outlook during the nineteenth century which suggest, at least, a growing modification of traditional religious beliefs. There is no need to claim complete separation or a defined anti-religious sentiment; but religion lost some of its meaning for middle-class women.

One indication of the declining influence of religion was the increasing secularism of the material read by women. In the early years of the century, the printed matter for women was primarily of a religious nature. By the second half of the century, the literature was almost completely lacking in religious inspiration. The few religious magazines, such as *The British Mothers' Magazine*, constantly bemoaned the decline of religion among the fairer sex. One example of the new trend of secularism was found in the editorial policy of the very popular *Englishwoman's Domestic Magazine*, which stated that it was the policy of the magazine to exclude all religious composition from its pages. It would not answer any theological questions, or even publish poetry of a religious nature. Looking through the hundreds of magazines printed in the nineteenth century for women, one is left with the impression that women were more concerned with the condition of their wash or the nature of their complexions than the state of their souls.

In sum, middle-class women shared with other groups many of the general pressures of urbanization. They shared also a decline of religious interest, and this may have had a distinctive impact on them because of their exposure to secular reading materials. Their ability to modernize was particularly enhanced by an unusually nucleated family structure and by the ability to forge a standard of living above the subsistence level. Other causes may have been involved, for we are in a better position to describe the modernization process than to assess the reasons for its special applicability to middle-class women, but even this short list suffices to explain why middle-class women were able to innovate in response to new pressures.

But not all middle-class women could adapt. Even for most, as we shall see, modernization should not be regarded as a triumphant conquest of progress over tradition but as a painful, often confusing, reaction to change. Some women could not manage even this, especially given the real physical burdens that still defined their lot. As with most social groups, middle-class women divided between adapters and nonadapters, although we are not yet in a position to suggest the size of the latter group and the boundary line is admittedly unclear.

The rapidity and vastness of change could cause a sense of bewilderment, which was especially difficult for many women to cope with because they had very little outlet for their tensions. The growing sense of insecurity seen in the many letters asking for advice is one sign of the tensions modern society produced in the life of the middle-class woman. Forced into the mainstream of a new style of living, the middle-class woman developed anxieties, as we have suggested in the study of her various roles in the family. The changing concept of motherhood is a case in point. The middle-class woman believed that she could be a better mother so she ventured new methods of child-rearing. However, she was still very insecure about the new ways; hence the continual seeking of advice, perhaps as a source of reassurance In some respects aspirations changed more rapidly than reality, as in the desire for better health or for an orderly improvement in the standard of living, which added frustrations to anxieties.

Not surprisingly, given the tensions of initial modernization, some symptoms of disturbance emerged among some middle-class women. There is evidence that some women sought refuge in alcohol and drugs. The subject of alcoholism among women was discussed a number of times, indicating that it was a serious problem for some. In 1870, a letter appeared in the *EDM* from "A Sufferer of Low Spirits," asking advice from other women on her problem with depression and alcohol. Especially in the health manuals, women were often warned about the ill effects of alcohol. In the manual, *The New Home; Or Wedded Life*, the story was told of a young girl who came to realize the folly of taking a little gin, or brandy, or beer everytime she was low, overworked, or simply out of sorts. The relief it offered was very brief, but the destruction it wrought upon her health was lasting. Another indication that women might have resorted to alcohol is suggested by the article "Intemperance in Women, with Special Reference to its Effects on the Reproductive System," which appeared in *The British Medical Journal.* The author noted that one of the principal causes of alcoholism among women was domestic problems.

Drugs were commonly used in the nineteenth century and were readily available, as was seen in the discussion of infant mortality. There is, again, no direct evidence about the use of drugs by women, but some contemporary observers noted a problem here too. For example, Dr. Robert Dick, in his health manual, made the following observation on the need of drugs by women:

> Many women would pass the most indifferent night; many would be inadequate to the task or duty of entertaining their guests or meeting their friends; in others the chagrins of life would prey too severely; regrets and disappointments and painful reminiscents would visit them too acutely did they not deaden the poignancy of suffering, actual or remembered, by the 'drowsy syrups'; . . . or by something analogous.

He remarked that many women, because of the pressures of society, needed artificial sedatives or stimulants, such as opium, morphia, hyoscyamus, prussic acid, camphor, musk and valerian. Further indication of the probability of considerable drug use comes in the many home remedies found in the manuals and periodicals for headaches or sleeplessness which included strong dosages of drugs. The following is a preparation recommended for use as a sedative: orange flower water—2 oz., laurel water—1 oz., syrup of poppies—½ oz., acetate of morphia—½ grain. A teaspoon of the above was to be taken every hour.

All of this, obviously involves impressionistic evidence. There is no reason to suggest that alcoholism or abuse of drugs were the normal lot of middle-class women or even that they necessarily followed from the tensions of modernization in every case. The extent of the phenomena cannot presently be determined, but they must be taken into account both because they suggest an interesting group of women who could not cope with their lot and because they emphasize some of the pressures that women more generally encountered during the period.

The more durable impact of modernization on the life of the middle-class woman can be seen more directly by looking back upon the discussion of mistress of the house. It was shown that the middle-class woman's most important considerations here were time and money. She never seemed to have enough of either, so they required of her careful planning and organization. Admittedly, she was not totally successful in meeting these requirements, but she did display a willingness to accept and try the new concepts. She was the major purchaser of the proliferating manuals that proclaimed the new science of domestic economy. She seemed to realize that she had novel problems which required new solutions.

One of the clearest illustrations of the middle-class woman's willingness to participate in the mainstream of modern society was her acceptance of innovation and technology into her home. The sewing machine is one very important example. Objections were voiced concerning the sewing machine, similar in many ways to the objections roused early in the century over the introduction of machines into industry. There was a lament that the sewing machines would destroy the long-valued skill of hand sewing—that element of personal touch associated with the craft and womanhood. However, the criticism was never persuasive enough to deter the middle-class woman as she readily adopted this new invention and eagerly sought information on it. No doubt the primary reason women welcomed this advance in technology was necessity. There were just so many hours in the day, and so much time to spend on sewing. With the sewing machine, the middle-class woman was able efficiently and economically to come to terms with both problems. However, one cannot neglect the fact that she was willing to give up, almost overnight, a long tradition of hand sewing in favor of a machine which did take away much of the personal touch. One could further suggest that the sewing machine was, in some ways, an expression of the woman's growing sense of individualism within the household. In buying the machine she acquired a new piece of property that was hers, as well as one that worked primarily to her own benefit. This does not mean that she was the heroine of passive consumerism as depicted in the conventional image—the manifestation of the paraphernalia of gentility—but in her own sphere she was trying to define herself, as well as make her life easier, in new ways.

Viewed in the light of modernization, the familiar list of other household innovations that gained ground in the later nineteenth century assumes new importance. One could argue that if the middle-class woman had not been so receptive to innovation, the process of modernization, which depended on mechanization, could not have progressed as rapidly as it did. As was noted in the earlier discussion of the mistress of the house, the middle-class woman was the prime consumer of many of the new products of industrialization. She was the only woman who both needed and could afford the advances in technology. The upper-class woman with her retinue of servants did not necessarily need the innovations, while the working-class women could not afford them. Other major industries, such as advertising and women's magazines, depended heavily on the middle-class woman as consumer. In other words, because of her new attitudes and her decision-making power, the middle-class woman emerged as a significant force for consumer-related economic development.

There are other aspects of the process of modernization in the life of the middle-class woman which are not as easy to recognize but equally significant. In the discussion on health it was shown that the middle-class woman was intimately involved with many of the changing attitudes now associated with modernization, such as sanitation. Also, the middle-class woman more and more rejected the traditional, fatalistic attitude toward death, especially where infant and maternal mortality were concerned. By seeking advice about her health and that of her children, she demonstrated the belief that her world could be ordered and improved. She expressed a growing reliance on science; first through her purchase of health manuals which were generally written by doctors, and second by her increasing use of doctors to tend to her health problems. There was some evidence that she clung more to traditional ways in this particular aspect of her life than as mistress of the house. The reliance on quack medicines was certainly based to a great extent on tradition, but we have noted that the key to success for many of the patent medicines in the nineteenth century was the claim to innovation and scientific expertise, most often in the forms of bogus testimonials from doctors. It was also pointed out that one major reason for apparently traditionalist behavior lay with the reluctance of the medical profession to implement available innovations rather than with the woman.

The Victorian woman's personal life was profoundly altered by modernization. This was seen very clearly in her receptiveness to chloroform, artificial feeding and contraceptive devices. In all three cases, especially the last, there was evidence of the middle-class woman's growing desire to order her own personal comfort, thereby demonstrating a sense of strong personal autonomy. In the discussion of contraception the development of a modern mentality was most evident. Women accepted contraceptive devices for selfish reasons in part, to insure their own physical well-being by limiting the number of children they bore, and to increase their opportunities for sexual pleasure and gratification.

There were, of course, ambiguities in "modern" attitudes themselves. For example, the woman's desire for greater personal autonomy was juxtaposed with the equally modern notion that as mother she should devote herself intensively to the care and attention of her child. This is a dilemma in the modernization of women that has even yet to be resolved. And these and other modern attitudes did not win complete acceptance by the 1870s, for the hold of traditional values was still strong. The period covered in this study emerges as an important transitional stage. The advent of birth control is perhaps the most obvious sign of the development of new attitudes, and by releasing some energies from traditional functions it sets the stage for other developments. But we can now see that this change was part of a larger modernization package, which saw the middle-class woman seeking to define herself, albeit with the family, as an individual and to gain new control over her body.

The changes in behavior and outlook that did occur in this transitional period were both marked and confused by the constant carping from contemporary publicists, which has in turn tended to mislead historians dealing with Victorian women. Contemporary observers found the middle-class woman a convenient vehicle for criticism of modernity generally. They sensed her desire for new things and therefore exaggerated her indulgence in luxuries. Many critics, some of the strongest of which came from among the religious spokesmen, found an audience among middle-class women themselves. This undoubtedly reflected an uncertainty among many of these women about the new ways, even as they largely persisted in them. There was also some unintended coincidence involved: reading matter that was sought primarily for recipes or patterns often contained a lament over the decline of true womanhood. And this raises again the question of the impact of the criticism in heightening the middle-class woman's sense of insecurity and anxiety. Victorian society, in terms of its official culture, was very demanding of its women. It expected them to be perfect ladies, perfect wives, and perfect mothers. The Victorian woman was to have an observing eye, a calculating head, a skilful hand, concise speech, a gentle step, external tidiness and internal purity. She was expected to exercise constant patience and forebearance, in spite of narrow means, inconvenient houses, crying children and preoccupied husbands. Her responsibilities were indeed overwhelming, and if she failed she had only herself to blame:

> . . . on you *fair* and amiable creature who was born to assuage our sufferings, dispel care, wipe away the tears of grief and to exalt all our enjoyments, much more depends than you commonly imagine. For, if we so frequently remark that marriages of attachment end in anything but cordiality and happiness,—if it be obvious that indifference has crept in where all was once love and respect,—it is (we are sorry to state) but too probable that the lady has originated this fearful change. The angel has become a demon of domestic strife.

To be sure, middle-class men encountered some criticism of their life style as well, but it was never as intense as that directed against women. For women, the adverse public culture could not only cause feelings of guilt about new patterns of behavior but could inhibit a consciousness of the significance of this behavior. Women were seeking more autonomy and control but they may not fully have realized their own goals, because they lacked public sanction. Here is another complicating factor that requires consideration in an understanding of the modernization of women.

Clearly, the middle class needs renewed attention if we are to grasp the dynamics of change in nineteenth-century Britain, and indeed elsewhere. The study of Victorian women suggests that the middle class had not only its own life style but a complex series of problems that have rarely been appreciated in the cursory treatment the class has received from historians. Its men have been too often dismissed as exploiters or conquerors; its women as useless ornaments barely deserving a serious history. In fact, while the social historian cannot point to the stark misery that has lent drama to many of the treatments of the working class, the problems with which the middle class was grappling have at least as much enduring significance. Aspirations were often unmet in a life that remained rigorous in many ways. The class did advance, and Victorian women did benefit from the modernization process. But the changes were hard-won, for new ideas were the product neither of leisure nor of luxury. Most middle-class women had enough margin to avoid taking refuge in traditional family functions alone, but they suffered considerable anxiety as they tried to develop a new life style. That many of the behavior patterns they developed ultimately became part of the modernization of women more generally is a tribute to their ingenuity as well as their influence. But the complexities of the transitional period have enduring significance as well, for they have by no means been shaken off. Here is where middle-class women, like the middle class as a whole, deserve a careful historical assessment, and not merely a characterization.

Crime and Modern Society

VINCENT McHALE and ERIC A. JOHNSON

Crime, as an aspect of how society functions, is commanding increased attention among historians. The following selection deals with crime patterns in Prussia between 1880 and 1914, when German society was changing rapidly with the rise of industrialization and the rapid growth of cities. The selection deals with shifts in crime rates from one geographical area to another, and with changes in the incidence of various kinds of crime. Thus it finds a shift from rural to urban high crime incidence, and an increase in crimes against property compared to those committed against people.

It has proved difficult to associate crime patterns with any general theory of modernization. The following selection takes up a number of theories about modern crime; these theories can be compared to theories about protest patterns discussed in the earlier selection by the Tillys. Most blanket explanations, including those which assume that cities automatically generate higher crime, prove faulty. However, several points can be noted. First, any image of rural society which assumes low levels of crime—because rural life was so tightly knit or satisfying—is incorrect. Crime could be significant in rural areas. Second, modernization made crime more visible and increased concern about it. At times, a belief in rising crime actually contradicted the facts. Modern people have grown sensitive about crime, a sensitivity that expresses some real problems but also some larger insecurities about urban life and the urban poor. Third, there is no large trend in crime rates that would allow us to say, for example, that the more modern a society becomes, the more crime it has. In the past several decades, crime rates have tended to rise in most Western countries, including of course the United States. But in several cases—Britain, the United States, and France—crime rates stabilized or actually went down around 1900, as people became more accustomed to urban life and discipline and as police work improved.

Most societies did, however, undergo a period of dislocation, associated with particularly rapid urban growth, in which crime rates rose. This period in Germany falls around 1900. This period of major crime increase cannot be associated simply with poverty or even with the existence of large cities, for cities had been growing earlier in Germany without these effects. Apparently the strangeness of urban life to new immigrants, when they are sufficiently numerous, causes a breakdown in established restraints, leading to more crime. At this point also the tendency for crimes against property to increase with particular rapidity suggests a "modern" outlook that sees crime somewhat more as a means for personal gain, less as an expression for personal tensions, than is true in the crime balance in more traditional societies.

However, this period of tension does not necessarily persist, precisely because it is linked to a stage in urbanization and not to city life itself. It does help produce the enduring anxiety about crime that seems part of modern life. It helps explain the movement of middle-class people to suburbs, where they hoped to be freer from the criminal element; and it conditioned many judgments of working-class and immigrant (Polish, in the German case) life. These effects could be more durable than the crime wave itself.

This approach to modern crime in terms of periodic waves, rather than some straightforward trend, has been clearly demonstrated in many nineteenth-century cases—as in the present study of Germany. Does it also help us to understand contemporary crime? Has the increase in crime in recent decades resulted from some new relationship between crime and modern life? Does it compare at all to the surge that accompanied high levels of urban growth during the industrial revolution? Is it a new trend, or another expression of cyclical patterns of crime that may not be closely tied to broader trends of modernization? Historians' study of crime does not suggest any simple pattern; indeed, one of their principal contributions is to complicate some common assumptions about modern crime.

Theorizing About Crime in 19th-Century Europe

Crime was an important topic of both governmental and popular concern in 19th-century Europe. Increases in crime during this period were believed by many to stem directly from the social changes brought about by the complex processes of urban-industrial development. Among the determinants of crime were thought to be the conditions of poverty, low levels of education, population density and crowding, urbanism, and migration. Several pioneering efforts with mixed results were made to assess the empirical validity of these notions.

Theorizing about the effects of urban-industrial development on the propensity for crime and other forms of social pathologies can best be described as a loose patchwork of arguments and hypotheses. The subject of crime and its relationship to the emergence of industrial society has been a controversial one for the social historian of 19th-century Europe. First, there are those arguments which posit that various forms of criminal behavior, social disorganization, and collective protest are functional alternatives—all being associated with the same general types of environments within a society. The basic assumption is that manifestations of

From Vincent McHale and Eric A. Johnson, "Urbanization, Industrialization and Crime in Imperial Germany," *Social Science History* Vol. 1, No. 1 (Fall, 1976), pp. 46–48, 69–71 and Vol. 1, No. 2 (Winter, 1977), pp. 228–31, 237, 240, 242, 244.

social rebellion such as crime must be viewed as part of a continuum of deviant behavior, and thus we would expect to find the incidence of criminality and social unrest to be highly interrelated phenomena in 19th-century Europe.

The second major category of propositions involves a series of structural arguments which have linked high levels of crime to the conditions of urbanism and population density in an industrializing society. It is argued that urban and non-urban areas differ fundamentally in their structural and organizational features, especially in terms of social homogeneity and the degree of interdependence. The criminogenic effects of urban life are seen not only as the result of greater social friction brought on by congested living conditions, poor housing, and material shortages, but the increasing scale and complexity of such environments make it easier for the criminal to escape detection, and thus provide a strong temptation for deprived sectors of the population to engage in criminal and other types of anti-social behavior. According to this perspective, the level of crime would tend to vary positively with the level of urban-industrial development across society.

Closely associated with these structural explanations have been so-called "tension" arguments relating crime to the dislocations growing out of urban-industrial change. Both urbanization and industrialization as dynamic societal processes over time lead to greater physical mobility for the individual. As individuals are uprooted by change and are thrust into new social environments where new rules of behavior prevail, traditional regulatory institutions and social sanctions tend to become ineffective, making it less costly for individuals to adopt deviant patterns of behavior. Thus the high rate of internal migration in 19th-century European societies has been viewed as a source of social strain which was associated with an increase in crime and other forms of social disorganization.

Change can also result in new sets of norms and values along with new patterns of consumption that may actually provoke an increase in criminal activity. Finally, one must also consider the problem of social unrest in relation to heightened tensions between "ascending" and "descending" groups, especially in those areas where the basic structure of rewards in society has been fundamentally altered by urban-industrial change.

The last type of explanation we will consider involves what is generally termed the "immiseration" theory of crime. It was a widely held belief that crime was a natural social consequence of the poverty, deprivation, and immiseration brought on by the spread of capitalist development in 19th-century European society. However, early attempts to link the incidence of crime to inequalities in wealth were inconclusive, for it appeared as if both the conditions of poverty and affluence had strong criminogenic potential.

Many early studies attempted to show that the poor were more crime prone because of their deprived social condition. An opposing school of thought rejected any relationship between crime and economic hardship, and considered the incidence of criminal activity to be the work of a hardened criminal class in society. Several longitudinal studies also attempted to relate movements in the level of crime to the fluctuations of various economic indicators.

The East-West Axis in Prussian Development

The source of regional variations in the Prussian crime rate during the 1880's must be sought in the contrasting developmental experience of the eastern districts over the course of the 19th-century. Prior to the decade of the 1880's, these districts had experienced a substantial growth in population due to a higher fertility rate and also due to higher levels of in-migration. Between 1815 and 1870, the northern and eastern territories of Prussia did quite well economically, as agricultural areas in general prospered. During this time, however, there was a concerted movement toward agricultural consolidation in these areas which resulted in the rise of a large "property-less" proletariat. Hamerow reports that in eastern Prussia, "in the course of some sixty years of agrarian reform, the proportion of those, whether noble or peasant, whose properties were sufficiently large to provide economic security and independence, declined from 39 to 26 percent of the rural population." This change was not an insignificant one because over 50 percent of the population living in these districts was located in rural areas and had been engaged in husbandry or other agricultural activities. The long period of agricultural prosperity, which nevertheless brought with it problems for those with properties which were too small to be economically viable, resulted in reversal and decline for many rural elements. This pattern of growth followed by decline bears some resemblance to the conditions preceding widespread social rebellion. . . . The higher levels of crime observed in these areas may have been a symptom of social discontent that was further exacerbated by the regional effects of agricultural consolidation.

Agricultural problems, however, represent only one of many possible reasons for the higher levels of social unrest and crime in the districts east of the Elbe at this time. It was not only the peasant population that was adversely affected by developmental change in these territories, but also the artisan class which was relatively large compared to the rest of Prussia. The abolition of the guild system and the near impossibility of competing with factory production must have presented grave threats to these elements. In addition to the sorry economic plight of the eastern peasantry and artisanry, still other factors were at work which may have been in part responsible for the higher level of criminal activity. In contrast to the rest of Germany, there was an extremely high degree of social stratification in these areas which hindered upward mobility, and must have led to a sense of frustration for the majority of the populace.

There is also evidence indicating that the lower and middle classes in the eastern districts were poorly represented in city and local government, in the army corps, and in the state bureaucracy when comparisons are made with the rest of Imperial Germany. These classes had fewer and weaker organizations (both political and economic) representing their interests. In the urban-industrial areas of the west and south, conditions may not have been much better, but at least these elements had a growing trade union movement and relatively stronger progressive organizations. In contrast, the eastern artisan no longer had the guild system to look after his interests, and the eastern peasantry often did not even have the privilege of voting for the party of their choice because pressures were exerted by local Junkers to vote conservative. Under-represented both politically and economically, and faced with fewer opportunities for social advancement, many of these deprived elements in the eastern territories must have felt they had little stake in the emerging industrial system of the 1880's.

Summary and Assessment: The 1880's

Our analysis of crime and socioeconomic conditions in Prussia during the mid-1880's suggests a different pattern of relationships from the one uncovered by Tilly and Lodhi in 19th-century France. They posited that the best explanation of crime was a structural one (urbanity), and they argued strongly against dislocation or tension theories (e.g. urbanization). Instead of finding a positive relationship between the level of urbanity and the level of crime in Prussia during the 1880's we found the opposite—namely, a mild but distinct negative relationship. As our data did not show much of a relationship between crime and urbanization either, we were forced to probe further into the question of the etiology of crime and its relationship to developmental change in 19th-century German society.

What we eventually concluded was that the Tilly and Lodhi model is underspecified for Germany, and that the best explanation for spatial variations in crime during this period was a wealth related one—the level of crime appeared to vary inversely with the level of wealth in any given district. Furthermore, if one controlled for the level of urban-industrial development in computing the wealth indicator, one finds an even higher correlation between wealth and crime during this period.

Another important factor which we observed at this time was the great degree to which crime varied along an east-west axis in Prussia. The eastern border districts had the highest crime rates for all of Imperial Germany in the mid-1880's, and the western [more urban] districts had, by and large, the lowest crime rates. In our attempt to explain these regional differences, we underscored the importance of developmental imbalance, and such factors as the higher degree of social stratification, ethnic diversity, and poverty in the eastern areas.

In our earlier investigations, it was observed that the rate of criminality varied greatly between the eastern and western parts of Prussia during the mid-1880s. In a attempt to explain these regional differences, we stressed the conditions of ethnic diversity, social stratification, wealth inequalities, and problems of agriculture in eastern Prussia. . . .

[By 1900] we note . . . the level of crime in the eastern districts was no longer exceptionally high relative to the rest of Prussia. In the years between 1900 and 1914, high levels of criminality appeared in areas which had relatively low rates of crime in previous decades. In particular, the highly urbanized and industrialized districts of Berlin and Brandenburg and the districts in the Rhine-Ruhr area (e.g., Düsseldorf and Köln) were characterized by higher levels of criminal activity. Why crime shifted from east to west in Prussia, and why it rose dramatically in districts like the ones just mentioned are the primary concerns of this analysis. The answers to these questions hopefully will tell us more than merely what the new correlates of crime in a new period of German history are: they will also enable us to gain more general insight into the relationship between urban-industrial development and manifest social discontent.

Why did high rates of crime (especially crimes committed against property, state, religious, and public laws) emerge after the turn of the century in areas of greatest urban-industrial development in Prussia? The possible explanations for this transformation are manifold. . . . The following analysis will demonstrate that neither social anomie nor area wealth (or lack of it) were direct correlates of crime in turn of the century Prussia. The explanation for the growth of crime in urbanized western and central Prussia and its decline in the northeastern region is attributable to other factors—namely the spread of education, the break up of the heavy Polish concentrations in East Elbia through internal migration, and to the new conditions associated with the urban environment in turn of the century Germany (e.g., heightened family discord, personal and financial insecurity, and rising socio-political protest and strike activity).

In the early period [the 1880s], crime had little relationship to urbanity. The correlations were negative, but insignificant. Even with tests for various kinds of curvilinear relationships, no significant association emerged. In contrast, the association between crime and urbanity in 1900 was positive and quite high. Whereas property crime and state crime became highly associated with urbanity in the later period, personal crime remained totally unrelated to urbanity over the entire period.

Although it is easy to document that the urban areas of Germany became highly crime ridden in the years prior to World War I, it is not a simple matter to explain why this was the case. Was this condition an inevitable outgrowth of the industrial revolution; or was it caused by a multiplicity of factors, some of which were specific to Germany at this particular stage of development? It can be argued that the processes of urban-industrial change have the potential for creating imbalances in society in that the structural conditions of living are changed along with an alteration in norms and social roles. Whether or not these processes engender antisocial behavior would seem to depend to a large degree upon the mechanisms of adjustment available to the society.

By the turn of the century, there are many indications that urban Germany had adapted less smoothly to the changes brought about by the industrial revolution than had rural Germany. Urban Germany increasingly became the center of personal and family difficulties and unhappiness, social and political protest, and financial insecurity—all of which could have been assumed to have had an impact on the level of criminality.

Although it has been argued previously that anomie measures are not to be considered direct causes of crime, it is reasonable to conclude that such factors were at best symptoms of the social malaise existing in urban Germany at this time. When such conditions of anomie are accompanied by other destabilizing influences (e.g., political discord, financial woes, etc.), they may have helped to create the kind of environment where crime flourished.

Another important factor which must be considered was the close association between urbanity and socio-political protest which became manifest by the turn of the century. Although the urban areas of Germany had long been centers of radical politics, the growth of urban-based political opposition was staggering after 1890. The Social Democratic Party (SPD) grew from approximately 2 percent of the electorate in 1871 to about 33 percent in 1912, the last election year of the period. There is little evidence to support the view that this growth also coincided with an acceptance of German society as it then existed. On the contrary, the years between 1900 and 1914 were marked by a wave of urban-based collective violence and strike activity of far greater magnitude than in the past.

Urban discontent was also reflected in the growth of industrial strike activity after the turn of the century. The correlation between the rate of strike activity and urbanity remained at a very high level ($r > .80$) for all of the years between 1899 and 1913. Despite the fact that the official working class party (SPD) had managed to become the largest single party in the Reichstag, and the German worker was better paid than previously, the needs of the urban populace apparently had not been met. They had very little "voice" in the government decision-making process, and prime economic goals such as the eight-hour work day were not granted to them. An entrenched political elite, dominated by large landowners and big business and led by an unaccountable ministry, retained its hold over the political process.

The data presented in this study suggest that there is nothing inherent in city life that necessitates such high levels of discontent; nor is there any reason to believe that urban-industrial growth (by disorienting newcomers, by breaking down traditional norms and social ties, etc.) precipitates crime. Urbanization and industrialization do not cause crime, but they may redistribute it across society. Our evidence does not permit a general theory which fastens urbanity as the principal cause of crime in nineteenth-century Europe. Crime in Germany had a negative association with urbanity in the years prior to 1900. A more reasonable argument is for us to consider the relationship between urbanity and crime in the context of different stages of societal development. Urbanity appears to be positively related to crime during or immediately after the period in which the society has experienced the greatest increase in urban-industrial change, but this positive relationship need not endure as other stages of development are reached and new mechanisms of social and political adjustment emerge. We assume that there are likely to be important thresholds in the relationship between urbanity and crime.

Lodhi and Tilly also found that crime in nineteenth-century France was highly associated with urbanity. In many ways, France of the 1850s and 1860s—the time period Lodhi and Tilly studied in depth—was similar to Germany in the period 1895 to 1914. . . . In the years after 1860, the rate of urban growth declined substantially. Based on the previous discussion of German urban growth, such rapid growth rates came later to Germany—about the time when crime shifted from a mildly negative association with urbanity to a strongly positive one. Had Lodhi and Tilly studied crime at an earlier (or perhaps even later) period in France, their findings might have been quite different.

The evidence presented in this study shows that structural theories which view crime as a natural consequence of urban life are wanting. The city or the farming village can harbor grievous discontent and crime at one time and not at another. Dislocation theories are equally unacceptable. The rate of crime does not grow as a linear function of urban-industrial development. Personal crime, in fact, has no relationship to development at all. Urban-industrial development, to be sure, puts strain on society. In its earlier stages this may be more threatening to those in the more traditional sectors of society; but, after periods of tremendous growth and change, the burden probably falls heavier on the urban populace.

Conclusions

The literature on crime and industrial society in nineteenth-century Europe is full of simple hypotheses linking crime to a variety of societal factors. Our findings indicate that the relationships between crime and urban-industrial development in Imperial Germany were complex. We have also documented how the relevance of certain factors in relation to crime changed over time. We have demonstrated how the path of crime in Prussia can be divided into two distinct phases. The first phase lasted from the mid-1880s to the turn of the century; the second phase began about 1900 and persisted until the beginning of World War I. During these two periods, the locational bases of crime, particularly property crime, shifted significantly across the surface of Prussia. Although the reasons for this shift were manifold and complex, they do lead us to conclude that the locational bases of crime in nineteenth-century industrial society were significantly related to situations of high societal stress.

In the mid-1880s, it was not the urban-industrial areas that were experiencing stress in Germany, but the rural areas of eastern Prussia. The cities seemed to be capable of managing growth, and migration was largely short-distance moves from rural areas to nearby towns. After the turn of the century, we note that societal stress lessens in the eastern region because of depopulation and social change, and becomes more pronounced in the swollen urban-industrial centers. This is also the period when long distance migrations become more important.

Much research needs to be done on the bases of crime in nineteenth-century Europe before we can piece together a more comprehensive theory involving the effects of societal change on social deviance. We recognize the deficiencies inherent in the statistics, and the almost insurmountable problems of cross-national comparisons. In the short run, within-nation studies are likely to be the most fruitful in terms of documenting the diversity of patterns that are likely to have existed during this period. Our plea is for a recognition of complexity, and a hope that those interested in such studies will move away from simple and naive theories which are likely to obscure rather than illuminate.

New Leisure: Sports

WILLIAM J. BAKER

Popular patterns of recreation were severely disrupted during the first phase of the industrial revolution. The confusion of movement from the countryside to city, which weakened festival traditions, and a concerted middle-class attack on leisure forms that wasted time or fostered violence or immorality were the most obvious causes of the decline of many familiar games and dances. New, individualistic recreations, such as heightened sexual activity, may have played a role as well.

The later nineteenth century saw a major revival of popular leisure, a revival that in many ways continues to the present. Upper and lower classes both benefited from rising prosperity and more time free from work. A modern expectation began to emerge that each day should have some leisure time set aside, and that leisure outlets should provide enough variety so that a person could choose whatever activity he or she liked.

The new leisure interests were not random, however. Some older interests, such as folk dancing, never fully revived. Dancing was increasingly associated with sexuality and with youth. On the positive side, sports commanded far more leisure attention than had previously been the case.

Why did the importance of sports increase? The following selection, focusing on Britain where most modern sports began, suggests that both lower and upper classes had their own reasons for new sports interests. It also suggests that the nature of sports had changed. Sports obviously were a prime example of the new commercial potential of mass leisure pursuits. Did sports also provide contact with more primitive human impulses, a thirst for violence, which continued despite the modernization of other aspects of life? Or was the basic nature of sports changed? The popularity of team sports might suggest a correspondence with the growing organization and bureaucratization of working life. Perhaps sports have become a key element in modern leisure because they reinforce basic modern values, not because they contrast with them. Certainly the fact that sports like soccer football have spread rapidly across Europe to most of the rest of the world suggests that sports wield a power in modern life that requires serious analysis if we are to understand how our basic values differ from those of the past.

The French painter Eugène Delacroix captured the spirit of the nineteenth century in his romantic *Liberty Leading the People*. Liberty is a woman of goddess proportions. The People range from affluent middle class to the laboring poor, from the young to the very old. All appear confident but determined. All are militantly moving forward to claim the rights of full citizenship. They are people for whom the combined effects of industrialization and the French Revolution have broken the grip long held on European society by priests, kings, and aristocrats. For the first time ever, the masses began to concern themselves with politics, economic and social policies, education, and recreational activities of their own choosing. . . .

Exodus from the countryside into the cities, begun early in the Industrial Revolution, accelerated. By 1900 city dwellers accounted for about three-quarters of all British citizens, more than half of the German population, and just under half of traditionally rural France. Even the United States, with a western frontier still largely unsettled, doubled its urban population within the three decades following the Civil War.

Economic opportunity was by no means the sole magnet drawing people from the countryside. Cities offered variety, excitement, and anonymity. But freedom from the restrictions of rural family and village life soon proved to be a mixed blessing. The cost of urban independence was a loss of ties that came from shared assumptions and common experience. City schools, churches, social and civic groups, and labor unions satisfied some of the need to be part of a well-defined community. Sports clubs and teams served similar functions. Sponsored by clubs, schools, and universities, numerous new team sports became organized as antidotes to the individualistic tendencies of modern city life.

Team sports also reflected the nationalistic, patriotic tendencies of the age. Individuals found a sense of self-importance as parts of a larger whole—a nation, club, or team. As one youngster in the novel *Tom Brown's Schooldays* (1857) said of the team game of cricket, "The discipline and reliance in one another which it teaches is so valuable, I think. It ought to be an unselfish game. It merges the individual in the eleven; he doesn't play that he may win, but that his side may." Tom Brown heartily agreed: "That's very true and that's why football and cricket, now one comes to think of it, are such much better games than fives or hare and hounds, or any others where the object is to come in first or to win for oneself and not that one's side may win." Although individual sports also became highly organized in the second half of the nineteenth century, team sports peculiarly suited the temper of the times.

From William J. Baker, *Sports in the Western World* (Totowa, N.J.: Rowman and Littlefield, 1982), pp. 115–127.

Moreover, team sports appealed to city spectators repelled by the brutalities of the prize ring, and bored by the lack of variety offered by footraces, boat races, and horse races. The fast, intricate movements of soccer, rugby, and American football presented a kind of coordinated complexity akin to the character of city life. Spacious cricket and baseball fields, on the other hand, evoked pleasant pastoral images reminiscent of the recent rural past. Seldom absent from the history of sports, spectators in the nineteenth century became a central feature of the sporting scene.

Most modern organized team and individual sports originated in Victorian England, just at the time when the British Empire stretched to the four corners of the earth. Sport as well as commerce followed the flag to distant places such as South Africa, India, New Zealand, and Canada. In a less orderly fashion, British industrial advisers, merchants, sailors, and tourists enthusiastically introduced their sports around the world—to Hungarians as well as Frenchmen, in Russia as well as the United States. Britain's imperial involvement in world affairs facilitated the rapid geographical spread of sports in the late nineteenth century.

In industrialized Britain and the United States, especially, several factors coalesced to encourage sports participation and spectatorship. Rising wages and a shortened workweek (half-day Saturdays at first) allowed laborers to make their way to new parks, playgrounds, and sports fields. City tram systems, first drawn by horses and later by electricity, provided transportation. Cheap train service carried both players and spectators to games in other cities. Newspapers exploited innovative print technology to publicize forthcoming events, and then they gave instant reportage by means of new telegraph and telephone systems. Editors soon discovered that more sports coverage meant higher circulation figures, particularly with the arrival of yet another nineteenth-century invention, photography. By 1900 some sportswriters were pecking away at a new contraption called a typewriter.

Technological advances also played a major role in sports equipment. Tougher iron and steel went into the making of goals for soccer, rugby and American football, ice hockey, and basketball, and for golf clubs, ice skates, bicycle frames, gymnastic equipment, spiked shoes, and face masks, not to mention the construction of sturdy stadiums. Vulcanized rubber provided resilient, air-filled balls of all shapes and sizes and pneumatic tires for bicycles and harness-racing rigs. Mechanical sewing machines turned out uniforms at a pace and low cost never before possible; new synthetic dyes added touches of color to the fabrics. Most important of all, perhaps, was the invention of the incandescent light bulb. By the mid-1880s indoor gymnasiums and sports arenas began scheduling evening prizefights, gymnastic classes, wrestling matches, and pedestrian contests under electric lights rather than by the earlier inadequate, foul-smelling gas lamps and torches. Outdoor night games lay several decades in the future, but by 1900 electric light had revolutionized the social life of the cities. Amid all the strategic factors affecting sports in the nineteenth century, technology stood tall.

Of all the team sports that became organized in the nineteenth century, football was the most international in appeal and diverse in form. Nourished in England's prestigious "public" (private) schools, the old plebeian game split into two distinct styles of play. Association (soccer) football featured kicking and controlling the ball with the feet, without the use of hands; rugby football entailed handling as well as kicking, tackling as well as running with the ball. These distinctions emerged slowly, amid much controversy, and in the end appealed to quite different segments of British society. The simpler of the two games, soccer, attracted mass participation and spectator audiences. Especially in the industrial Midlands and northern England, professional soccer became a spectacle of unrivaled popularity. During the last decade of the century, some northern rugby teams also went professional, but the rugby game remained largely a middle-class and aristocratic sport dominated by the elite public schools and universities and their graduates.

Made in Britain, both games were quickly exported. Rugby became established largely in British colonies throughout the Empire, but soccer spread like wildfire in all of Europe and South America. By 1900 soccer football was well on the way to becoming the most internationally popular game in the world. For a brief time it was the dominant campus game in the United States, only to be replaced momentarily by the rugby code, then transformed into a unique American version of football. From the outset the varieties of football were numerous.

Schoolboy Games

While restrictions of space, time, and local ordinances kept common folk from playing their traditional game of football in England's newly industrialized towns, schoolboys at institutions such as Eton, Harrow, Westminster, Winchester, Charterhouse, Shrewsbury, and Rugby made the game their own. Called "public schools" because they had been founded in the distant past as charitable institutions for the education of bright but poor boys, these schools by the turn of the nineteenth century were anything but public. Rich parents happily paid large sums to have their sons exposed to the niceties of Latin and Greek, the advantages of useful connections, and the possibilities of maturation in a loosely structured environment. Life at the public schools was coarse and often brutal. Discipline was lax. Boys mostly governed themselves by means of their own pecking order of authority: older boys bullied newcomers mercilessly. On the playing fields as well as in the dormitories, the future leaders of

England learned to exert their personalities and thus to wield power over the younger, weaker, or more timid members of their society.

Games admirably served those purposes. In the early autumn and late spring, boys rowed and played cricket. For the major part of the school year, however, their attention turned to football. Each school, physically isolated from the others, developed its own style and rules of play, usually in accordance with the grounds available. The two London schools, Westminster and Charterhouse, had only long brick-covered cloisters. Their football games therefore featured much pushing and shoving but no tackling; "dribbling" (controlling the ball with the feet) but no long, high kicks; some handling but no passing of the ball. At Winchester, too, rough and constricted grounds dictated a controlled kicking game. A perennially muddy field set in a basin at Harrow made for an even slower game with a large, heavy ball. Slower still was the Eton "Wall Game," played on a field 120 yards long and only 6 yards wide, with a brick wall forming one of the sidelines. About twenty boys on each team shoved, kicked, and clawed for the ball, attempting to propel it to the "goal": a small garden door at one end of the field, and old tree stump at the other. Appropriately, the knotted mass of bodies was called a "bully."

At Rugby School, where more spacious, lush fields were available for play, an altogether different style of football evolved. According to legend, a young Rugbeian named William Webb Ellis in 1823 seized the ball in his hands and ran with it, thus inventing the distinctive game of Rugby football. In truth, that account is misleading. Well before 1823 Rugby boys customarily caught the ball in midair and kicked it back to their opponents, but not until the late 1830s did the running and tackling style of Rugby play become common. In *Tom Brown's Schooldays* (1857), Thomas Hughes penned a famous description of football as he and his Rugby mates played it around 1840. Massive teams struggled in the "scrum," pushing and "hacking" (kicking each other's shins), cracking skulls on skulls, flailing elbows into ribs. Rugby football still had a long way to go before it became a game of dash and spectacular runs.

The headmaster of Rugby School from 1828 to 1842, Dr. Thomas Arnold unintentionally encouraged the distinctive Rugby game. Intent on reforming the old lax and aristocratic nature of the public school, Arnold welcomed sons of professional and business families. He forbade traditional aristocratic field sports such as hunting, shooting, and fishing (which in fact meant poaching from the fields and streams of farmers in the Rugby area), replacing them with team sports. A contemporary headmaster of Shrewsbury School, Samuel Butler, denounced football as a game "more fit for farm boys and labourers than young gentlemen," but at Dr. Arnold's Rugby School football was encouraged as a means of instilling manly virtues. Geographically removed from the other public schools, Rugby boys devised a unique style of "running in" with the ball for a "touchdown." By the early 1840s their game was commonly acknowledged as an odd deviant of the football being played elsewhere.

While Rugby went its own way, Eton schoolboys came up with a new "Field Game" of football. Necessity forced the invention. In 1827 the rough Wall Game at Eton produced a free-for-all, and Eton's officials banned the Wall Game for ten years. Not to be denied their play, Eton schoolboys turned to a nearby open field and invented a wide-open game in which more kicking and running for the ball replaced the old thickly massed "bully." By 1840 Eton, Harrow, and all the other public schools except Rugby played a style of football roughly equivalent to the future soccer game. Yet all these various forms of football were confined to intraschool competition. Not until the 1850s, when a network of railways made travel easy, did teams represent their schools in competition with other schools.

At Oxford and Cambridge, where cricket, rowing, and field hockey were the traditional university sports, chaos reigned when boys turned to the football field. "The result was dire confusion," according to one contemporary, "as every man played the rules he had been accustomed to at his public school." Before each game, captains of the opposing teams had to negotiate the number of men per team, whether or not handling and running with the ball would be allowed, whether hacking and holding were permissible, and on and on. More time was spent negotiating the rules than in playing the game itself.

A codification of the rules was necessary. In 1845 a group of Rugby boys produced the first-ever written rules for football. Three years later a group of fourteen Cambridge undergraduates spent seven hours debating a set of "Cambridge Rules." According to one participant, "the Eton man howled at the Rugby man for handling the ball." Outnumbered Old Rugbeians momentarily had to play a style of game totally different from their schoolboy days. The handwriting was on the wall: Rugby football was simply unacceptable to the majority of footballers in mid-nineteenth-century England. In the 1850s public school and university graduates founded several football clubs in Sheffield and London; except for the Blackheath and Harlequin clubs (London), all played the Eton and Harrow kind of kicking game.

Finally in 1863 the impasse became fixed. While American Union and Confederate armies clashed three thousand miles away, English footballers fought their own serious though less dangerous version of civil war. On 26 October 1863 captains and representatives of several London and suburban clubs met to form the Football Association "for the regulation of the game of football." According to the rules agreed upon by the majority, no player could run with the ball. No tripping, hacking, holding, or pushing would be tolerated, and throwing or passing the ball to another player was forbidden. Actually, some handling of the ball was still permissible: "If a player makes a fair catch, he shall be entitled to a free kick, provided he claims it by making a mark with his heel at once." Not until 1870 did the Football Association altogether abolish touching the ball with the hands.

Despite further refinements, however, the year 1863 is a red-letter date in the history of football, for in that year was formed the first national organization and the first set of rules governing the game throughout an entire country. The term Football Association soon became abbreviated to "Assoc.," whence came the word "soccer." Most important, the rules laid down by the Football Association decisively alienated the advocates of the "carrying game," preventing a single, all-inclusive game of football in Britain and the world.

In 1871 the rugby equivalent of the Football Association, the Rugby Football Union, was formed. Two London clubs, Blackheath and Richmond, organized the meeting of twenty-two club representatives. They took only two hours to reach an agreement on the principles and title of their group, which has remained the central authority of rugby football in Britain to the present. Within two months of the formation of the Rugby Football Union, an English team played its first international match against Scotland; during the following decade Irish and Welsh international teams began competing. Similarly prestigious, the annual university match between Oxford and Cambridge began in 1872.

During the 1870s the Rugby Football union abolished "hacking," reduced the size of teams to the now standard number of fifteen, and began counting points for touchdowns ("tries") as well as field goals. In the 1880s the style of the game changed dramatically, from a sluggish mauling in the scrum to exciting open maneuvers and sharp passes (laterals). Yet the social basis of the game remained the same: respectably middle and upper class. Whereas Dr. Arnold of Rugby granted team sports an important but subordinate role in the inculcation of gentlemanly Christian character, headmasters of late-Victorian public schools turned games into a fetish. With the expansive British Empire beckoning public-schooled-trained army officers and administrators, Greek verbs and Latin authors paled beside the manly courage that one supposedly learned on the football field. Thus the rugby game remained faithful to its schoolboy, amateur, upper-class roots. Association football took an altogether different turn.

Football Mania

For a time, gentlemen of leisure dominated the Football Association as well as the Rugby Football Union. During the 1870s the two leading soccer figures, first as players and then as officers on the F.A. governing committee, were C. W. Alcock and A. F. Kinnaird. Alcock was a Harrow man, a quick, agile athlete, and an energetic writer who explained and extolled Association football. A red-bearded Old Etonian, Kinnaird was a fierce competitor on the field and a shrewd negotiator on matters of policy: he was a future banker, peer, and Lord High Commissioner of the Church of Scotland.

This upper-class leadership reflected the composition of the dominant teams in the 1870s. In 1872 the first F.A. Cup (championship) was won by the Wanderers, a team totally composed of public school and university men. Between 1872 and 1882 the Wanderers claimed five cups, the Old Etonians two, and other similar "old boy" organizations the remaining four. Yet their days in the limelight were numbered. C. W. Alcock said more than he intended when he observed in the *Football Annual* for 1878: "What was ten or fifteen years ago the recreation of a few has now become the pursuit of thousands." Soon thousands of common people seized the game of soccer football out of the hands of the privileged few and made it their own. During the last quarter of the nineteenth century, soccer became the "people's" game.

Increased leisure time, extra spending money, and new public facilities made the takeover possible. Once mid-century legislation limited the working hours of women and children in textile factories, aggressive labor unions set to work on shortening the traditional six-day work week of male adults. By the 1870s most factories, mines, and workshops closed down at noon on Saturday. Simultaneously, wages handsomely increased for most British laborers. New city trams furnished cheap and easy transportation to newly established public parks in town, or to open fields beyond the suburbs. Saturday afternoon became a time of family outings for picnics and games.

Soccer was a game made to order. Compared to rugby football, soccer was a simple game of few rules, requiring little practice, coaching, or study. Cricket was similarly attractive, but cricket required a certain kind of ball, a bat, and wickets. Soccer could be played with any kind of ball, even with a round piece of wood or tin can. Most important, people of all ages, sizes, and abilities could play. Quickness and agility, not brute strength, counted most on the soccer field, but even the slowest and most awkward player could derive pleasure from it. More than any other team sport in Victorian England, soccer was (as one journalist put it) a "democratic game . . . within easy reach of absolutely everyone."

From casual, fun-filled play came organized teams. When the F.A. Cup competition was established in 1871, only fifty clubs belonged to the Association; by 1900 almost 10,000 had joined. Most traced their roots to the 1870s and 1880s. Some, like Burnley, Derby County, Sheffield Wednesday, and Tottenham Hotspur, were offshoots of cricket clubs.

Many others originated in churches, local branches of the YMCA, or temperance societies. Both Aston Villa and the Bolton Wanderers originated in 1874 as church teams; from 1875 to 1880 Birmingham City, Everton, Burnley, and Wolverhampton clubs were formed out of similar religious and philanthropic organizations. Local schools also fielded teams, such as the Blackburn Rovers, Leicester City, and Sunderland. The names Stoke City, Manchester United, Arsenal, and West Ham United betray their origins at the hands of industrial workers and labor organizers eager to play. Except for London-based Tottenham Hotspur, Arsenal, and West Ham United, all these new clubs sprang up in the industrial Midlands and northern England, where a massive growth of population had occurred in the nineteenth century.

Southern gentlemanly organizers of the Football Association might well have taken alarm when an obscure club from the Lancashire mill town of Darwen reached the fourth round of eliminations for the F.A. Cup in 1879. Not one of Darwen's players could claim even a white-collar occupation, much less a public-school background. All were young working men from local factories whose incomes were so marginal that they had to solicit public contributions in order to pay their train fares to London for a playoff game against Old Etonians, their social opposites. Unfortunately, the game ended in a draw, 5–5. Darwen returned home, passed the hat once more, and made their way back to London the following week. Perverse were the furies that produced yet another draw, 2–2. Finally on their third expensive trek to London, Darwen succumbed. Yet in defeat they served notice of a new and vigorous working-class participation in the game to the north, beyond the pale of southern refinement.

Four years later the promise was fulfilled. The Cup Final of 1883 pitted the Blackburn Olympics against another team of Old Etonians. Captained by a master plumber, the Blackburn squad included three weavers, a spinner, a dental assistant, a picture framer, and an iron-foundry worker. They beat the upper-class Old Etonians in overtime. The dike was broken, never to be repaired. From 1883 to 1914 northern working-class teams won every F.A. Cup except one. Even the one exception, the Tottenham Hotspurs who won the Cup in 1901, was a team comprised of three Englishmen from the industrial north, five Scotsmen, two Welshmen, and an Irishman.

In the rise of those northern clubs lay the origins of professional soccer. Working-class footballers were simply unable to take time off their jobs to practice and travel unless their expenses were paid. Even expenses were forbidden by the amateur officers of the Football Association, but payments soon went under the table. In semiprofessional fashion northern footballers went from one town to another taking employment for their football as well as for their industrial skills. Scotsmen especially capitalized on this arrangement. Jobs were scarce in

Scotland, and Scottish footballers happily crossed the border to sell their services to the highest bidder in northern England. They offered a fast-paced team concept of short, accurate passes, a style vastly different and far more effective than the traditional English pattern of individualistic ball control and field-length "dribbling." Like recent American baseball players in Japan, Scottish footballers were recruited and paid handsomely.

London officers of the Football Association avoided the issue as long as they could. In 1884, however, William Sudell of Preston, whose northern team was in the Cup finals, publicly admitted that he paid not only his players' expenses but also small salaries. While other northern owners and players gave understanding nods, howls of protest arose from southern public-school quarters. F.A. officials threatened to ban the Preston team from further championship play, but Sudell in turn called a meeting of Lancashire clubs to form a breakaway professional organization. Led by C. W. Alcock, the F.A. committee reluctantly backed down. One Old Boy declared that it was "degrading for respectable men to play with professionals"; Alcock countered that it was hardly "immoral to work for a living." Following a long and heated debate, in 1885 the Football Association reached a compromise, whereby separate amateur and professional leagues could operate within the same organization.

The day of competitive amateur soccer, at the national level, was past. One team, the Corinthians, was formed by selecting the best players from all the leading amateur clubs in London, and they survived into the twentieth century as a team of amateurs who could beat most professional squads. But they were exceptional. As a rule, amateur clubs soon found that they could no longer compete successfully with the professionals. Most refused to try, some doggedly persisted, but with dismal success. At the turn of the century public-school amateurs established their own F.A. Amateur Cup, only to languish in mediocrity and low crowd appeal. For soccer excellence and spectator excitement, one had to look to the industrial north, where soccer became a business.

Factory owners, rich with their industrial profits, applied their managerial skills to the game, pumping expanding profits into new stadiums, equipment, uniforms, and salaries. The heavier the investment, the less could they afford to continue in the traditional amateur pattern of scheduling impromptu games during the season leading up to the more orderly Cup playoffs. Thus in 1888 they enthusiastically endorsed a proposal by William McGregor, director of the Aston Villa (Birmingham) club, for a number of professional teams to organize themselves into a Football League for the purpose of regularly scheduling home and away games. Twelve teams joined—six from the northern county of Lancashire, six others from Midlands counties, none from London. Following suit, the Irish League was formed in 1890 and the Scottish League in

1891. Finally, in 1894 teams from London and counties to the south formed the Southern League.

Spectators flocked to the stadiums in droves to see their favorite teams, especially in the industrial cities. Professional soccer matches provided color and excitement for an otherwise drab existence of factory routine and cramped working-class ghettos. Only nightly pubs and music halls competed with Saturday afternoon football for laborers' entertainment. Workers who had recently come to the city from rural villages found a feeling of identity as they gathered and cheered "their" team with their fellow workers. For Cup Finals in London they also traveled *en masse* by train, singing songs, wearing colorful scarves, drinking, and generally delighting in the new-found comradeship. Attendance figures bear witness to the football mania that swept the country toward the end of the nineteenth century. From the 2,000 spectators who watched the first F.A. Cup Final in 1872, the number jumped to 25,000 in 1892, and to more than 110,000 in 1901.

Little wonder that the game attracted working-class players. Not only would they be paid for playing a game they enjoyed, a professional football career also offered a chance of social recognition. In class-structured Victorian England, politics, commerce, and higher education were beyond the reach of sons of mill workers and miners. On the football field, on the other hand, they could compete on even terms regardless of background or wealth, even to the extent of soundly defeating the old upper-class amateur teams.

Yet salaries were low by modern standards. By 1900 the average wage of a professional soccer player was nearly two pounds a week, about the same as a skilled artisan, but the inflated salaries of a few exceptional players hid the fact that younger, lesser known footballers received a pittance for their efforts. Worse still, after professionalism became publicly accepted, owners legislated stern managerial policies. Once a player signed with a club, he was registered on its books by the Football Association, thereby forfeiting his right to bargain for a better contract with any other club until his owner granted an official release. Like American baseball owners with their "reserve clause," professional soccer owners ruled with an iron hand.

In tightening their grip they squeezed the old public-school originators of soccer right out of their places of authority. In the early 1890s rugby football appeared to be headed in a similar direction. Although not as popular as soccer, rugby also appealed to northern working-class communities. Taking a cue from their soccer counterparts, several Yorkshire rugby clubs in 1893 submitted a formal request to the Rugby Football Union that "players be allowed compensation for bona fide loss of time." But rugby officials, incensed at the turn taken by Association football, dug in their heels. In 1894 they declared that professionalism was "contrary to the true interest of the game and its spirit" and announced that "only clubs composed entirely of amateurs shall be eligible for membership" in the R.F.U. At an impasse, twenty representatives of northern rugby clubs gathered at Huddersfield, a mill town situated between the industrial centers of Manchester and Leeds; in August 1895 they formed the Northern Rugby Football Union.

That northern professional branch of rugby football (soon renamed the Rugby Football League, a name that still holds) altered the rules and style of the game to make it faster and more attractive to paying customers. But while amateur rugby continued to thrive in the public schools, the universities, and Old-Boy clubs in London and the southern counties, professional rugby remained provincially isolated in northern industrial towns. At the end of the nineteenth century English football—soccer as well as rugby—accurately reflected a nation socially divided. On just one point did the upper classes and the masses resemble each other. They all fiercely defended and zealously promoted their respective versions of football.

Modern Leisure, Middle-Class Style

PETER BAILEY

The following selection stresses some special characteristics of the late-nineteenth century conversion to leisure. The focus is on the middle class, rather than the undifferentiated masses. Middle-class leisure behavior definitely changed, but the older middle-class emphasis on respectability and utility was not entirely abandoned. One reason for the rise of sports, for example, was because they—more than more frivolous leisure forms—could be justified in terms of moral values and a positive relationship to work. Because the middle class remained extremely influential in determining values for society at large, this distinctive approach to leisure affected more than just the middle class.

The middle-class position on leisure helps explain why modern leisure, or at least some of it, was esteemed not because it contrasted with work, but because it seemed to parallel work. Sports, in their modern form, provided rules, competition, and specialization just as work did.

Of course, important elements of the middle-class leisure outlook in the later nineteenth century were transitional. That is, they justified leisure to a class that had previously taken its satisfaction from work alone. Once the middle class became more accustomed to leisure it might broaden its horizons further. Certainly some elements of the middle-class leisure approach—for example, attendance at uplifting lectures as a recreational form—declined after the nineteenth century. But the initial middle-class approach raises some questions about leisure even in our own day. Does part of a specifically modern definition of leisure rest on middle-class values of self-improvement and utility? Have the lower classes managed to avoid this particular definition of the basis for recreation? And to the extent that the middle-class approach continues to be part of modern leisure forms, are the value and spontaneity of modern leisure reduced? The late nineteenth-century middle class began to glory in new leisure opportunities, but it set some definite limits on the nature of these opportunities. Some observers believe that these limits continue to affect leisure today, even among many people who insist that they have shaken off "Victorian" restraints in the pursuit of pleasure.

In the years around the mid-century the Victorians entered a new leisure world. The Ten Hours Act of 1847 and the Great Exhibition at the Crystal Palace in 1851 were both in their various ways the concrete and symbolic pivots of this change whereby leisure in its modern form became progressively more plentiful, more visible, more sought after and more controversial. Something of the impact of this phenomenon (and the tensions it generated) is well caught in a leading article in 'The Times', 20 June 1876, which remarked tetchily on the importunate demands of 'Modern Amusements':

> The space we ourselves are from time to time compelled to surrender to this class of subject is in itself not the least proof of the importance they have attained . . . a mingled mass of perfectly legitimate pleasures ever thrusting themselves forward in a variety of shapes, some known, some unknown, to our more easily contented ancestors, and all together making continually increasing demands upon our time, upon our money, and not least, upon our strength and powers of endurance.

It is a point of considerable importance that it was the middle classes who were the most substantial beneficiaries of the new bounty. Like their inferiors they were entering into the process of developing a new culture within the unique matrix of a maturing urban industrial society, and from the mid-century on leisure and its activities became a significant area of social innovation and fulfillment for the Victorian bourgeoisie. The increasingly prominent role of recreation in middle-class life, its effects upon the bourgeois identity, the debate which such changes generated—all these features of the new leisure world held important implications for campaigns to improve the recreations of the working classes.

Leisure and its enjoyments were hardly a mid-Victorian invention, but contemporaries were frequently moved to draw a contrast between the more abundant leisure of their own day and the meagre commons of previous decades. The middle classes of the older provincial centres of England had enjoyed a cultural life of considerable vigour and sociability in the late eighteenth century, and many of its institutions, if not perhaps its original élan, had survived into the early Victorian period. In the new towns too, middle-class life had not been all jejeune: Banford was as impressed by the literary and musical interests of the Lancashire middle classes in the 1840s as he was by those of the workers: a Bolton lawyer who took articles in the 1830s recalled that hard work had taken its reward in leisure hours enlivened by a constant round of amateur dramatics, discussion clubs, much dancing, singing and athletic exercise, together with

From Peter Bailey, *Leisure and Class in Victorian England* (Toronto: University of Toronto Press, 1978), pp. 58–62, 63–67, 71–73.

the relaxations of fireside and garden. Such a life-style could not have
been unique to Bolton's John Taylor, but the more general recollection of
middle and late Victorians was of an immediate past which was grey and
joyless. 'We must remember', wrote the novelist Walter Besant, 'how
very little play went on even among the comfortable and opulent classes
in those days . . . dullness and a serious view of life seemed inseparable.'
It has been well said that the Victorian bourgeoisie had had their own
'bleak age' to endure.

Relief came with greater economic security and the time, services
and commodities that it could buy. Though the business world was still
visited by periodic crises after 1850, fluctuations became less severe and
the remarkable expansion of the economy in the third quarter of the century did much to cushion middle-class incomes against irreparable re-
verses; even when growth and prosperity seemed to suffer a more general
contraction from the mid-1870s on, the finances of a substantial element
in the Victorian bourgeoisie proved solid enough to resist serious curtail-
ment of expenditure and consumption. Such good fortune was being
actively enjoyed by the 1850s. Men who had weathered the various exigencies of previous decades could afford to rest awhile on a comfortable
plateau of prosperity, accompanied by wives whose domestic duties were
taken care of by a growing army of servants. Constant attention to business was no longer necessary for the successful, and a mellowing process
suffused their lives. We may take the Ashworth brothers of Bolton as an
example. In the 1840s they had struggled through a period of uncertain
profits; in the 1850s they felt secure enough to delegate the running of
their mill to subordinates and allow themselves a series of travelling
holidays. . . .

There were always new recruits for the single-minded pursuit of
money, but the second or later generations of successful business families
were less disposed to answer its imperatives. The younger Gurneys of
Norwich were 'rather more inclined to stand before the fire with their
hands in the fronts of very good riding breeches' than to attend daily at
the bank. The 'Saturday Review' remarked in the 1860s how rapidly the
'habit of enjoyment' had spread among the young. 'It is', the journal
maintained, 'an axiom with many young people that they have a right to
be always amused, or to be always going to be amused.' Certainly the
middle-class young (of whom more were surviving into early adulthood)
enjoyed more free time than their elders had done, for the increasing
emphasis upon public school and, to a lesser extent, university education
as indispensable requirements for middle-class gentility meant a prolonged
freedom from the immediate pressures of earning a living. Eventually put
to work in the family firm the son and heir often continued to exploit the
generosity of the paterfamilias—'stretching his legs under the governor's
mahogany'—and apply himself more to play than business. This much is

clear from a lively debate on the 'young man of the day' in the correspondence columns of the 'Daily Telegraph' in the late 1860s.

The 'habit of enjoyment' was diffused and encouraged through major improvements in communications. By the early 1850s the major lines in the British rail system were completed or under construction. Rail travel stimulated a general public curiosity and helped break down regional insularities of mind and practice. 'The typical John Bull', said the 'Cornhill Magazine', 'is fast becoming a legendary personage; his vegetative life and stationary habits and local prejudices are all disappearing beneath the stimulating influence of the railway, the telegraph and the great cities.' Of parallel importance was the growth of the cheap press and the increase in newspaper advertising; the tax on advertising was abolished in 1853, the newspaper duty of 4d a copy went in 1855 and six years later the duty on paper was removed. Escott recorded the effects:

> The cheap press, with its ubiquitous correspondents and historians of all contemporary ranks and occurrences in the body politic, has transformed the severely domesticated Briton of both sexes, of all ages, who belonged to a bygone generation, into an eager, actively enquiring, socially omniscient citizen of the world, ever on the outlook for new excitements, habitually demanding social pleasure in fresh forms.

What were the particular forms that social pleasure took? Certainly a great deal of it took place within the ambit of the home and family. The proliferation of newspapers was part of a general flood of literature which kept the middle-class public well supplied with its periodicals and three-decker novels, either for solitary reading (perhaps during the new 'enforced' leisure of the railway journey) or to be read aloud to the family group. Cheap sheet music was also published in increasing abundance from the 1840s; mechanical refinement and improved production methods provided suburban villas with moderately priced pianos upon which the ladies of the house could display their talents—music was a fashionable, indeed necessary, accomplishment for girls. There were many other new diversions for the drawing room besides reading and music. The 'Saturday Review' found 'the cleverness and the laziness of the age aptly typified . . . by its ingenious contrivances for getting rid of an evening'. Within the home these contrivances might consist of private theatricals, quizzes and games newly devised for the middle-class family market, or older pastimes such as draughts and billiards—the latter now restored to respectability within the new canon of 'domestic athletics'. Cheap service and gains in space and comfort in the middle-class home allowed of the increasing vogue for entertaining guests, particularly at the dinner party, whose growing extravagance was a prime indicator of rising consumption levels among a class increasingly divorcing itself from its heredity of thrift and frugality. Gardens were also part of the improved amenities of domestic life; here the family and its guests could play a set of lawn tennis (an invention of the 1870s) or take a game of croquet—as E. L. Woodward pointed out, 'Alice in Wonderland' affords a convincing demonstration that every middle-class child could be expected to know the rules.

The mid-Victorian middle classes were not, however, permanently home-bound in their recreations, though they did in general take their public pleasures en famille. The railway gave them in particular a new mobility in leisure, and the regular spate of advice and reports in the press in the summer months testified to the growing habit and ritual of the annual holiday. Old-fashioned watering places were neglected for the attractions of new seaside holiday resorts. Travel horizons broadened, and by the 1860s Thomas Cook was running excursions, not only to the Continent but to the USA and the Holy Land. 'The quietest sort of people', so the 'Saturday Review' observed, 'are uncomfortable unless they, at least once a year, tie themselves together in batches and go prowling over the tops of unexplored Alps.' Recreation out of doors was generally brisker than the gentilities of domestic leisure as a London lawyer and socialite recorded in his diary in 1861:

> Muscular Christianity, the Volunteer movement, and alpine climbing are in the ascendant. The affected Dandy of past years is unknown. If he exists, he is despised. The standard or average English gentleman of the present day must at least show vigour of body, if he cannot display vigour of mind.

Sport or, more specifically, organised games gave expression to this predilection for the physical. The newly codified games spread from the reformed public schools to the universities, and thence into adult life; national bodies for the supervision and co-ordination of the major new sports were formed in the 1860s and 1870s under middle-class auspices. The Volunteer force, established in 1859 in the face of threatening noises from the French, also contributed to this particular impetus and direction in middle-class recreation: the local corps promoted the cause of physical fitness and the sports meetings which enlivened the drills often became the basis for the formation of permanent athletics clubs. In addition the fund-raising activities of bazaars and fêtes gave an outlet for the leisure energies and talents of the womenfolk. Though middle-class involvement declined considerably after only a few years, the movement was an important leisure stimulus—one contemporary credited the Volunteers with 'fostering a love of outdoor life that has been utterly wanting among the great middle-classes for a century'. Certainly the strainings of amateur athletes and part-time soldiers provided occasions for new leisure festivals for middle-class families: the Oxford and Cambridge athletics meet, the Eton and Harrow cricket match, the Volunteers' annual reviews, rifle meets and sports tournaments at Brighton, Wimbledon and in the counties—all were significant additions to the social calendar.

Public amusements of a less strenuous kind were also plentiful; so much so that Stephen Fiske, an American who worked in London in the 1860s, found the English at play anything but the traditional dullards that other visitors had judged them (Froissart's tag 'they take their pleasures sadly after their fashion' was another cliché of commentaries on national manners). Wrote Fiske:

> Taking the average Englishman and the average Frenchman, the former goes oftener to the theatres, has more holidays, laughs more, and spends more evenings where something besides a drink and smoke are to be had for his money, than the latter; and yet the average Frenchman is mistakenly held up to us as a devotee of amusement.

These conclusions were based upon Fiske's experience as a theatre manager in a capital city which was sucking up the theatrical talent of the provinces and thriving on a tourist traffic built upon the excursion boom of 1851. Providing one was not in search of diversion on a Sunday—Taine found himself ready for suicide after his first sabbath in London—there was no gainsaying the long-standing vitality of the metropolis as an entertainment centre.

Mid-Victorian Bolton certainly provides clear evidence that the middle classes in one large manufacturing town knew a real expansion of leisure and recreation. Bolton's growing population enjoyed general prosperity in these years—the relative diversification of her industries and her specialisation in better quality textiles enabled her to survive the cotton famine of the early 1860s better than most Lancashire towns—and the middle classes showed a substantial increase in numbers and wealth. The 'Chronicle' in the late 1850s considered the local bourgeoisie 'scanty' compared with other large towns, but correspondents pointed to the recent wave of professional and commercial men now assuming middle-class status in Bolton, plus a disturbing new breed of 'fast' young men. The 'Chronicle' was pleased to see the leisure energies of these novitiates absorbed by the new passion for outdoor sports and the pull of the Volunteer movement, thus dispelling its fears that increasing affectation of manners must lead to effeminacy. But refinement was as fashionable as athleticism and found its expression in exclusive subscription concerts at the Baths Assembly Rooms and 'select and gorgeous' dinner parties in private houses. Pub society had ceased to be respectable. John Taylor took the teetotal pledge and pursued his love of debate in a private club which met at members' houses—the pledge was hardly fashionable but the retreat to the drawing room was. Middle-class homes grew more palatial and one local builder at least made his fortune providing new residences for wealthy Boltonians at Southport on the Lancashire coast. Southport was the fashionable resort town for the north-west, but the biographies of

Bolton worthies show how much further their excursions ranged, from Scotland to the Continent.

Yet amid this vitality one soon detects a persistent sense of dissatisfaction and unease on the part of both observers and participants in this new leisure world. Analysing the palsied progress of a middle-class dinner party, Trollope concluded that the pursuit of leisure in England was as laborious, affected and dull as foreign observers persistently made it out to be, and it was the spectacle of bourgeois 'enjoyments' that moved Matthew Arnold to ask: 'Can any life be imagined more hideous, more dismal, more unenviable?' By taking account of the problems of leisure as well as its gratifications we can more readily understand the fundamental novelty of its presence in Victorian life.

The problem of leisure for the Victorian middle-classes was a many-sided one. In the first place they were discovering that recreation in the railway age meant planning and preparation; time-tables meant an increasing preoccupation with time-budgeting and the co-ordination of people and services. In a moment of disenchantment with modern 'holydays' 'The Times' complained that the search for enjoyment was often fatuous: 'It is work, and it is tiring work . . . it involves a perpetual attention to time, and all the anxieties and irritations of that responsibility.' Even when the respite of true leisure was reached, its satisfactions were impaired by that compulsive regard for the precise and purposive ordering of time that nagged the creatures of an industrial society. 'There is', remarked the 'Saturday Review', 'a sort of mechanical style in our joys.'

A further cluster of difficulties lay in the very nature of bourgeois culture itself. As a class whose immediate history celebrated the virtues of unremitting industry, the Victorian middle class had only an attenuated leisure tradition to draw upon, so that the new life-space they had won for themselves was something of an embarrassment—'We really do not know how to amuse ourselves', was the 'Saturday Review's' admission in an article on 'Pleasure Taking', 4 June 1870. The leisure of the aristocracy and the gentry—the aboriginal leisure class of history—was rooted in the husbandry of their landed estates and nourished by a high amateur tradition in the civilised arts; the leisure of the common people still echoed with the collective rituals of the folk community and the craft workshop, and evinced a ready taste for pleasure. Yet it was these associations which had made leisure such a suspect quantity in bourgeois ideology; in a work-oriented value system leisure represented the irresponsible preoccupations of a parasitic ruling class or the reckless carousing of an irrational working class. Though the bourgeoisie had none the less at times been enamoured of the aristocratic style, the clash of political and economic interests and the structures of the evangelical revival had severely reduced its attractions during the early Victorian period. By the same process certain once universally honoured convivialities were also now disallowed, but the question of their replacement could no longer be ignored, as the 'Saturday Review' explained in a piece on evening amusements, 4 January 1862:

> It is a very fine thing to have cured ourselves of the boosing [sic] habits of our ancestors; but there is no doubt that the moral conquest has left a formidable void in our social existence . . . the gentlemen used to be drunk, and are now sober; and the mistress of the house, who got rid of them in the drinking days, has to bear the burden of their reformation, and find amusements to beguile the weary hours of sobriety.

A wide range of modified or newly contrived recreations were pressed into service to fill the void, but it was difficult to infuse such ad hoc devices with much spontaneity, particularly since the exercise of choice was heavily constrained by that need for moral legitimation which characterised bourgeois leisure in these early years of new growth. As another commentator noted:

> A lingering asceticism of sentiment, a relic of the superstition which looked upon the body as the source of sin, still affects our modes of thought. . . . We do not proscribe amusement as previous generations have done, nor do we go heartily into them, as Paganism did and the Latin races do; but we indulge in them and apologise for them. We take some of our more pleasant and more needful recreations with a half suspicion that they are only half right.

A further discomfiture came from the apprehension that the freedoms of modern leisure might prove too great a test of the individual's capacity for responsible self-direction, in the absence of that mutual public vigilance that policed the life of the small community. The temptation to delinquency was thought to be most acute for the young, particularly among the army of rootless young office workers in the great urban centres. 'The immense size and total unlocalisation of life', wrote a correspondent to the 'Daily Telegraph', 'tend to make the career of a young man excessively individual . . . he loses the fear of censure that is the guiding idea of much life in smaller places.' Compared to the disciplined structure of the workplace and the home, leisure appeared to some a normative as well as a cultural void.

There were other tensions which attended the middle-class pursuit of leisure, but enough has been said already to demonstrate its ambivalence in bourgeois life. Moral integrity and the code of respectability which defined its public face were essential constituents of middle-class identity and class consciousness. Resting on basically religious sanctions reinforced by the teachings of political economy, bourgeois morality had, in the first half of the century, provided its class with an effective platform from which to challenge the aristocracy and subordinate the lower orders.

From the turn of the mid-century the new and extensive bonus of leisure time threatened to subvert the internal discipline of the middle-class world by its invitation to indolence and prodigality. Unwilling or unable to deny the claims and attractions of leisure, yet anxious to maintain a sturdy and coherent code of values amid rapid innovation and social change, the Victorian middle classes sought a rationale which would relieve them of the need to apologise for their pleasures, yet still keep them within the bounds of moral fitness. 'Many people', observed the 'Saturday Review', 7 April 1877, 'are manifestly incapable of enjoying repose and light diversion except on the understanding that they have a right to do so.'

The question received considerable attention in the periodical press, particularly during the summer holiday season, when the correct disposal of such a conspicuous slab of free time called special attention to the ethics of leisure. A representative piece appeared in the 'Cornhill Magazine' for September 1867, written by Peter W. Clayden. Entitled Off for the holidays: the rationale of recreation, it moved on from the usual breezy bon voyage to the summer holidaymaker, to a consideration of the nature, method and purpose of recreation, 'a subject only now beginning to be understood'. The author emphasises how modes of life had been transformed by Britain's industrial progress. In response to the demands of modern civilisation, Englishmen had developed 'magnificent nervous organisations' which gave them an expanded capacity for work. This enabled them to continue to exploit the opportunities of the nineteenth-century world, but the cost of the new regimen was high:

> Our great-grandfathers ambled along with an almost restful movement; we rush along at high pressure, with fearful wear and noise. Their work was almost play compared with ours. . . . A kind of necessity is upon us, even at home, much more in our spheres of duty or activity, and all continuous necessity is a strain.

Readers could therefore rest assured that holidays and recreation were necessary, as relief from this strain; they allowed 'the rebound of an elastic nature from the repression and constraint of civilised life'. The rebound was best absorbed in recreation which afforded a total change of pace, direction and environment, for 'work and play, like day and night, are opposites, and the widest unlikeness between them is the truest completeness of each.' According to this principle therefore, men were encouraged to seek recreations which proveded the greatest contrast to their normal occupations, and the article sought to free holidaymakers of the oppressive fears of ridicule which too often confounded this stratagem:

> We are dreadfully afraid of making ourselves ridiculous before one another. Public opinion . . . persistently merges the man in his profession, keeps him

perpetually on the pedestal of his status, and will on no account allow him to descend from it.

Such strictures could be safely ignored, according to Clayden's dispensations.

Thus did one writer try to relieve some of the misgivings which attended the modern pursuit of leisure; there were, however, some important qualifications to be made. Mere rest was not true recreation, neither was amusement: 'amusement merely occupies or diverts, while recreation, as the word itself indicates, renews and recreates.' Work and play were best dissociated in time, locus and content—'renewal and recreation proceed on the principle of antithesis'—but their functions were complementary. In this way recreation was validated primarily as an adjunct to work and its ideal represented in terms of the vigour and purposiveness appropriate to work. Play, explained Clayden, was change of work as much as change from work. The sentiment became a commonplace under the imprimatur of Gladstone, who maintained that recreation was nought but change of employment, exemplifying the ideal in his retreat from the toils of office to the arduous pleasures of tree-felling on his estate at Hawarden.

For all his purposeful tone Clayden was alive to the potential of leisure for the intellectual and cultural enrichment of the individual, but many writers were only prepared to justify leisure in its utilitarian role. Writing in the 'Nineteenth Century', G. J. Romanes put the matter succinctly:

> Recreation is, or ought to be, not a pastime entered upon for the sake of pleasure which it affords, but an act of duty undertaken for the sake of the subsequent power which it generates, and the subsequent profit which it ensures. . . .

Accordingly, the recreations which recommended themselves to respectable tastes were those with some manifest moral or improving content. Much that took place in the home was naturally so blessed, but the new family games on the market took care to combine 'innocent amusement with instruction'—a formula met with in Greenwood's Round Games (Questions For Our Sunday Tea Table, Bible Quartets, Scientific Quartets) which earned the endorsement of the 'Bolton Chronicle'. The fusing of recreation with instruction had been exemplified in the Great Exhibition and the improving mixture was dispensed in penny packets in public lectures and readings across the country. Albert Smith drew huge crowds in the 1850s with his lectures on the ascent of Mont Blanc, illustrated with lantern slides and the equipment used on the expedition. The retelling of an heroic exploit, the information on a foreign country which was now within reach of the excursionist and the excitement of a night out proved an irresistible combination. Travel was generally regarded as wholesome: 'To have seen a mountain', averred the 'Chronicle', 'is a great step in a man's education.' There was thus a great deal of recreation that came within the pale by virtue of educational rather than spiritual content, though there was a felicitous combination of both in oratorios, whose considerable popularity in these years was attributed to 'the prevalent religious sentiment of the English middle classes'. Because of its non-representational character, music was generally thought to be the least corruptible of the arts; even so, we may recall that Haweis had warned of the need to refer it to moral touchstones.

The concern for moral legitimation remained a powerful determinant of middle-class choice in leisure, but it was not the only or necessarily the prime motivation, for recreations answered a variety of needs, and though the Victorian bourgeoisie plainly suffered under some vexing inhibitions in their pursuit of leisure they none the less proved capable of exploiting its dynamic properties. This is evident, for example, in their new enthusiasm for organised games, a set of recreations which met the tests of moral propriety while serving as an important medium for advancing middle-class social aspirations.

Charles Kingsley's exaltation of muscular Christianity provided the necessary moral gloss for organised games. As a country vicar in the 1840s Kingsley had championed physical health:

> The body, the temple of the living God. . . . There has always seemed to me something impious in the neglect of personal health, strength and beauty, which the religious and sometimes clergymen of these days affect. I could not do half the little good I do do here if it were not for that strength and activity which some consider coarse and degrading.

Thus he had done much to dispel the suspicions of the body as a source of sin, a staple of evangelical teaching which Clayden and others had identified as an impediment to physical enjoyment. Kingsley urged his young audiences 'to carry into them [games] the principles of honour and religion', declaring bodily health a matter of personal responsibility to God and duty to one's country. Neglect of what he came to call 'the science of health' would, he maintained, render Englishmen 'incapable, unhappy, like a Byzantine Greek, filled up with some sort of pap'. Herbert Spencer acknowledged Kingsley's leading role in registering the importance of bodily exercise, and himself used the language and imperatives of religion in emphasising that 'the preservation of health is a duty . . . all breaches of the laws of health are physical sins.' Kingsley's novels gave currency to such ideals, and inspired a whole school of imitators who were, in the words of the 'Saturday Review', 'continually ready to build a model hero, very good and very strong . . . and free from faults and fat'. As 'The Times' remarked drily of the spread of athleticism: 'When you can at the same time enjoy yourself and feel the consciousness that you are doing a moral action, it is difficult to refrain.'

Popular Education: Peasants into Frenchmen

EUGEN WEBER

Many of the dramas associated with modernization occurred in conjunction with the intriguing, difficult, and ambiguous process by which education was forced on the rural population. At one level, the state served as the compelling agent, breaking local traditions, from language to religion, in favor of the very essence of a modernized mentality: belief in progress, in science, in a new idea of work and personal advancement. At another level, peasants developed a new interest in education in response to broad structural pressures around them, such as the rise of market agriculture with its concomitant need for new technical knowledge. In between was a host of mediating factors, including changing concepts of the child (over which state and peasant long warred) and that curious new creature, the schoolteacher. Education spread largely from the top of society downward—which explains why in America the process has been dubbed a matter of "social control" by many recent historians. But it was also colored by new and old interests of the constituents, who could see some value in certain kinds of change, and by the intermediary groups involved.

It is not surprising that the peasantry adapted to modern values and institutions more slowly than any other social group. Peasants maintained contact with many traditions, including religion. Their adaptability was further limited because many younger, enterprising peasants migrated to the cities. Yet peasants were pressed to change their outlook and way of life, and the national education systems that developed in the later nineteenth century played a major role in this change. Many peasants who for many years had refused to send their children to school finally did yield. Their understanding of the possible value of education reflected their changing circumstances. Small-town artisans had quickly seized on education as a means of social mobility, often seeking new skills to compensate for the diminishing utility of traditional craft training. Peasants, however, had to undergo a more fundamental shift in values to make a similar transition. The intense economic problems in agriculture from the 1870s onward helped expedite this shift.

As education was accepted, further changes were inevitable. Everywhere, the state and the upper classes sought to use education to shape the lower classes into obedient, productive citizens. They preached national loyalty. They also emphasized the value of science and technology; in France after the 1870s, they actively attacked religion. Most schoolteachers eagerly supported these positions, for their own prestige was enhanced by associating themselves with progressive forces. So peasants were exposed to many new ideas. In a real sense, at least in France, education brought them into contact with the concepts of the

Enlightenment. Although they did not necessarily accept all they learned, they could hardly avoid questioning traditional ideas. For some, education became a truly radical force.

The following passage surveys the major facets of the establishment of mass education in the French countryside under the Third Republic, particularly after 1880. It clearly delineates the destructive power of education; old ways of thinking and speaking were rooted out, though not without difficulty. Yet the result was not a clear victory for modernization. Peasants were not uniformly transformed into secular, progressive, individualistic citizens. Instead they were encouraged to transfer loyalty and blind faith from religion to the nation, a process with immense political and diplomatic consequences. That transfer also suggests a more qualified change in the thinking of the peasantry itself. Modernization has entailed unprecedented involvement of the masses with the broader society, but is this because the outlook of the masses has really changed or because the state and the ruling classes have found new ways to manipulate it?

The school, notably the village school, compulsory and free, has been credited with the ultimate acculturation process that made the French people French—finally civilized them, as many nineteenth-century educators liked to say. The schoolteachers, in their worn, dark suits, appear as the militia of the new age, harbingers of enlightenment and of the Republican message that reconciled the benighted masses with a new world, superior in wellbeing and democracy. Observers have pointed out that there were schools before the 1880's, and have quarreled with implicit assumptions or explicit statements that there was no popular education under the Ancien Régime. But we shall see that the now-classic image of a profound change of pace, tone, and impact under the Third Republic is roughly correct if it is placed in the proper context.

The context matters because schools did in fact exist before [1881], indeed were numerous; and so, to a large extent, did free education. What made the Republic's laws so effective was not just that they required all children to attend school and granted them the right to do so free. It was the attendant circumstances that made adequate facilities and teachers more accessible; that provided roads on which children could get to school; that, above all, made school meaningful and profitable, once what the school offered made sense in terms of altered values and perceptions...

The schools that priests or laymen ran for the poorer classes before the last quarter of the nineteenth century tended, in the nature of things,

From Eugen Weber, *Peasants into Frenchmen: The Modernization of Rural France, 1870–1914* (Stanford, Ca.: Stanford University Press, 1976), pp. 303–38.

to put first things first. First things were those the masters thought important: the ability to gabble the catechism or a part of the Latin service. The teaching of even elementary reading, writing, and arithmetic was rare before the Revolution, reflected the prefect of Yonne in 1810, and teachers were little interested in "broad public education, I mean the sort concerning the greatest number of people." In any case, a great many teachers taught whatever they taught with limited competence. Until 1816, no title or proof of competence was required from a teacher. . . .

It takes a real effort today to conceive such an educational system, one in which both teacher and taught were ignorant of the material they were dealing with, and in which the capacity to draw letters or pronounce them completely outweighed any capacity to comprehend. Letters, words, and sentences were formulas and spells. "No child understands what he reads," reported a school inspector from Var in 1864. And in Brittany the inspectors noted that, though the children read along with fair fluency, "no child can give account of what he has read or translate it into Breton; hence there is no proof that anything is understood." In such circumstances, Latin was no more difficult, no more incomprehensible than French, and many a bright village child "learned" Latin in this fashion and left school full of bits of scripture, canticles, and the catechism, "rattling along in Latin like a phonograph, without understanding a word of it," and capable of writing in four different hands, accomplishments most impressive to his illiterate parents. . . .

From 1833 onward the government, supported by a steadily growing vested interest, bent itself to advance and develop public education. Nationally, the conscripts affected by the law of 1833 showed a much smaller measure of illiteracy than their forebears. And in an illiterate department like Corrèze, the change was equally evident. The proportion of conscripts who knew the elements of reading rose from 14.3 percent in 1829 to 31.9 percent in 1855, 34.8 percent in 1860, 41 percent in 1865, 50 percent in 1868, and 62 percent in 1875. By 1863 only about one-fifth of the children between seven and thirteen received no instruction whatever. What we want to know is the kind of instruction that was given and who got it. The evidence suggests, and so does common sense, that urban areas had more schools than rural areas, that these schools were more regularly attended by more of the local children, and that the quality of the teaching in them was better. By 1876 nearly 800,000 of 4.5 million school-age children were still not registered in any school. Most of these belonged to rural communes; and many who were registered hardly ever attended class. This was the enduring problem.

The next great change came in the 1880's. It would have come earlier had the Minister of Education Victor Duruy had the chance to develop the plans he elaborated in 1867. But he did not, and most of his initiatives remained in the project stage. Hence the importance of the reforms introduced by Jules Ferry. In 1881 all fees and tuition charges in public elementary schools were abolished. In 1882 enrollment in a public or private school was made compulsory. In 1883 every village or hamlet with more than 20 school-age children was required to maintain a public elementary school. In 1885 subsidies were allotted for the building and maintenance of schools and for the pay of teachers. In 1886 an elementary teaching program was instituted, along with elaborate provisions for inspection and control. . . .

One reason for the slow progress in eliminating illiteracy, strangely ignored by even the best accounts of education in France, was the fact that so many adults—and consequently children—did not speak French. As we have seen in 1863 by official tally some 7.5 million people, a fifth of the population, did not know the language. And as we have also seen even that figure is questionable. The actual number was probably much larger, particularly if one includes those whose notions of the language were extremely vague.

The greatest problem faced by the public schools in the 8,381 non-French-speaking communes, and in a good few of the other 29,129 where French was said to be in general use, was how to teach the language to children who never or hardly ever heard it. The oft-repeated claim that they were learning their mother tongue could hardly have rung true to those whose mothers did not understand a word of it. "The children [of Lauragais] don't have to learn simply how to read and write," commented M. F. Pariset in 1867. "They have to learn how to do so in French, that is, in another language than the one they know." The result was that, for a lot of them, the instruction received in school "leaves no more trace than Latin leaves on most of those who graduate from secondary school. The child . . . returns to patois when he gets home. French is for him an erudite language, which he forgets quickly, never speaking it." Officially, the problem was faced by denying its existence and forcing even those who could scarcely master a few words to proclaim, as in a catechism, that what *should* be true was true and what they *knew* to be true was not: "(l) We call mother tongue the tongue that is spoken by our parents, and in particular by our mothers; spoken also by our fellow citizens and by the persons who inhabit the same *pays* as us. (2) Our mother tongue is French." So read an army examination manual in 1875. Unofficially, the schools continued to struggle to make the slogan true. Teaching French, "our beautiful and noble mother tongue," asserted Ferdinand Buisson, the leading light of Republican education in the 1880's, "is the chief work of the elementary school—a labor of patriotic character." The labor proved long and hard. . . .

French was gaining ground. But not so much through persecution as through the peasants' growing appreciation of the usefulness of a less parochial language and of the skills learned in the schools. Universal military service both spread the use of French and made at least a smattering of it important to more people. The introduction and spread of kindergartens—*salles d'asile*—to relieve teachers of the care of three- and four-year-olds given into their charge familiarized very young children with authority figures who spoke French rather than the mother's language.

Most important of all, perhaps, more girls were being schooled, more girls and women learned French, more mothers could speak French to their children if they chose to do so. Women had willy-nilly perpetuated local speech. Girls had been left untaught at the village level much longer than in bourgs and towns, a fact that the available statistics hardly mirror at all. Only in 1867 were communes over 500 souls required to provide a girls school (they had been required to provide schools for boys in 1833), and it took some time before the results of this law were felt. In any case, girls schools were generally run by members of religious orders, and their standards remained quite low until the 1880's. Nor did the girls have the benefit of military service as a refresher course in French and "civilization." It follows that the school laws of the 1880's had the broadest impact on the literacy and schooling of girls, both of which had lagged far behind. And that when the results came to be felt in the 1890's, the women's cultural role in th family would suddenly change and, with it, attitudes to schooling and to the use of French.

There was another great problem that had to be mastered before French could truly be made the national language: the teacher's own poor knowledge of the language that he had to teach. "Most teachers don't know French," complained a report of 1803 in Ardèche. Half a century later things had hardly improved. A special summer refresher course for teachers held in 1839 at Privas reported great success: when it ended those who began with 60 to 80 mistakes in a page of dictation made only 25 to 40 errors when the exercise was repeated. Through the 1840's and 1850's many teachers still found it difficult to spell or to form a proper sentence. . . .

Neither students nor teachers read enough to be familiar with, let alone teach, French literature. In Basses-Pyrénées we hear that cultivated people knew French (1874). But what kind of French? A year later the normal school at Lescar reported having problems with the language because "even the cultivated who speak it don't speak it very well, and that's all the students have heard when they have heard it." In Dordogne in the same year, 1875, examiners for the teaching diploma were warned to make sure that every teacher *"knows at least how to write his language correctly."* (To be certain the point got across, the warning was underlined.) In the Landes in 1876 student teachers and their mentors had mastered the language only shakily. "Many masters read no better than their students," and in explaining a reading both sides offered plain absurdities. At the Avignon normal school, also in 1876, "the master himself knows French badly." At Perpignan in 1878 student teachers read and understood French badly; they were used to Catalan and only great efforts could "familiarize them with French." Much the same thing in Puy-de-Dôme in 1877: "Detestable local accent," and patois hindering everyone. The reports of 1881 carry similar criticisms. The teachers don't do very well in French because they have been insufficiently prepared to handle it (Lot-et-Garonne). The teachers are insecure in their use of French; they lack solid training in using it on their own account (Basses-Pyrénées). Even many of the normal school teachers are local men who have never left the department; they retain the local accent and habits, and pass them on to their students (Aveyron).

In short, with few exceptions teachers were merely peasant lads who hoped to improve their condition or wanted to escape military service. Only in extraordinary circumstances would a man who expected to inherit property have wasted his time on something that until the 1880's brought little profit or prestige. The reports amassed in the government's survey of the state of primary instruction in 1864 show that student teachers came from the "working class" and from families of small farmers chiefly interested in getting an exemption from military service for their sons (Dordogne, Eure, Savoy); that they were recruited from the poor families of the countryside (Lot-et-Garonne); that they had the defective pronunciation and habits of the peasants (Calvados). A motion of the governing board of the normal school of Montpellier encapsulates the problem in blunt terms: "Whereas the department's . . . wealth offers young men of intelligence and a little money careers much more profitable than that of elementary teaching and which they in fact prefer; whereas the students of the normal school are recruited only among the poor inhabitants of the mountain areas in the department's north and west. . . ." Even as late as 1881 we hear that recruitment came easily in the poorer regions; but that in wealthy ones, where families had few children, only those who were useless in the fields were sent to normal schools. Many must have gone off with the greatest reluctance to what we could generously describe as miserable holes, far worse than barracks. "A sorry, mean, and shabby dump materially and morally" was how one report described the normal school at Parthenay (Deux-Sèvres) in 1882. "Intellectually nonexistent, depressing on all counts, it forms or deforms poor young peasants to become poor old teachers."

Also, we may add, acolytes of the priest. "Elementary education properly understood . . . is the fraternal union of presbytery and school," pronounced Rector Denain at an awards ceremony in 1862. Just how fraternal, the readers of Flaubert's *Bouvard and Pécuchet* could learn. "The teacher is no more than a mnemotechnical auxiliary of the priest," complained Félix Pécaut, less mellifluously than the rector. Yet by then things had improved since the day when the teacher's first duty was to assist the priest, sing all the offices, sweep the church once a week, dust and polish the ornaments, see that the bells were rung and the clock was wound, and finally keep school and instruct the children according to the true faith. But inspectors in the day of Marshal MacMahon still checked to make sure that "teachers show themselves useful auxiliaries of the priests." The peasants greatly appreciated teachers when it came to practical matters such as surveying land and measuring properties, remembered a beginner of those days; but their subjection to the priests was horrid. One need not wonder at the consistent devotion of teachers after the 16th of May to a Republic that emancipated them from their humiliating bondage. One need not wonder either that it should take something of a revolution—in training and consequently in outlook—for the village school-teacher to blossom into the dynamic missionary illustrated in our books.

But before teachers could take on the role of missionaries, they had to learn to live the part. Too many teachers "dress like peasants, think like peasants. They are peasants who have a slightly different trade." They mixed with the villagers, went off to fairs with them; there was no distance here and certainly no respect. "One has a lot of trouble to make them give up such habits." The 1880's saw a campaign to turn these browbeaten peasants into models of the new enlightened style. Above all, they were not to go around "dressed in smocks, caps, and sabots, keeping their heads covered in class like their students . . . as uncivilized as the populations in whose midst they live." In their persons and in their actions teachers were expected to maintain standards that would reflect their elevated functions and their representative role.

Though pay improved somewhat, such standards were difficult to maintain. Beginning teachers earned 700 francs a year in 1881, 800 ten years later, and 900 between 1897 and 1905, when the starting salary was raised to 1,100 francs. The highest pay doubled in the same period. By the turn of the century, after withholdings for pensions and other things, country teachers at last earned as much as a miner and more than a Paris laundress or a textile worker. But they had to "dress suitably," and to keep up at least outwardly a style of living that went with their position as *fonctionnaries d'Etat* (1889) and aspiring notables. That they were willing and able to make the attempt was due to the training inculcated by the reformed normal schools. . . .

As early as 1865 the teachers' growing influence rated an official warning. Teachers were running the affairs of negligent, often illiterate mayors. They had become legal advisers to the villagers; lent farmers money, wrote their letters, and surveyed their fields; had "become occult powers." Their prestige was great, their status in the community almost "sacerdotal." Most alarming of all, warned the sub-prefect of Joigny (Yonne), teachers were even beginning to go into politics. Hardly the browbeaten figure that Flaubert etched.

Such forebodings became serious fact when village teachers, trained to greater competence and new self-respect, became the licensed representatives of the Republic. By the 1890's they not only ran the administration in almost all the communes, but also in some instances worked as correspondents for the local newspapers, earning a useful increment in salary and prestige. A theme that recurs frequently in political accounts is the observation that the local schoolteacher "had turned the commune round politically by his influence on the young." The teacher was the municipal lamppost, the *bec de gaz municipal,* a half-friendly but suggestive nickname. The political influence attributed to him was probably a reflection of shifts that we have seen to have had more complex roots. But even if exaggerated, such reports attest to the growing role of the man whose light, however dim, glowed strongly on his parish.

This could not have happened as long as schools remained irrelevant to a great many people; and this they did into the last quarter of the century. Most peasants wanted their children to work and contribute to the family budget. If they sent them to school at all, it was usually for the sole purpose of getting them past their first communion, a crucial rite of passage. Once that was accomplished, the child was withdrawn. Parents send their children to school for a few winter months before their communion, grumbled a Breton teacher in 1861, and that short time was almost exclusively devoted to learning the catechism, an awkward business since the children could not read. For this reason communions were made as early as possible, between the ages of ten and twelve. As a result school enrollments of children past that age diminished sharply, and children soon forgot the little they had learned, mostly by rote, lapsing once again into a "state of complete ignorance."

In any case the country school provided little stimulus to learning for its pupils, not even the challenge of exposure to more motivated students. Parents in comfortable circumstances who were willing and able to keep their children in school for a time preferred to send them to the bourg or to a boarding school. More important, the offspring of wealthier parents, aware that schooling would play a part in their later activities, assimilated more and retained more of what they learned. The parents took more interest in their work. Thus the children of the poor had access to poorer schools, less time to attend them, and far less reason to make the most of such opportunity than their better-off mates.

Some poorer families kept their children out of school under the pressure of local landowners who did not want their future work force to be subverted or diminished by even a modicum of book-learning. More were discouraged by the distance the children had to cover to get to school and by the state of the roads. Where the peasants lived in small, dispersed settlements or in isolated houses the problem was twice as difficult. One village in Finistère refused to build a school because "the distance from the hamlets to the center does not permit farmers to send their children there. In summer they need them to watch the cattle; in winter they could not get to school because of the bad state of the roads." Another, in Ille-et-Vilaine, pointed out that though the present school seemed to have cramped quarters, the space was adequate because no child could make his way to school before the age of eight or nine, which cut the potential attendance by half. In Sarthe the rural roads were too bad for children to negotiate in the winter months; in Maurienne, Tarentaise, and Savoy generally, only the twelve- or thirteen-year-old child had the stamina to get to school regularly. At that point they left! Not especially surprising, considering that they might have had to cover three to five miles on foot each way or use a boat to get there. In the Lannion district of Côtes-du-Nord where, in 1877, one child in three was not enrolled in a school though nearly every parish had one, the figures show that distance from isolated farms and hamlets made a significant difference, with the loneliest cantons averaging only half the enrollment of the others. . . .

Where and when children were registered in school, what matters, after all, is not their enrollment as such, but their attendance. This varied with the region and its ways, but tended generally to be restricted to the winter months. As actual or potential workers, children were free for school only when there was no work. In the Limousin they did not say that a child had been in school for three years but that he had three winters in school. He entered it in December, after the chestnuts had been gathered and the migrants he had helped replace had returned home, and left in late March or early April when the migrants set off again. Similarly, in Côte-d'Or and the Jura, which had more elementary schools for their outlying villages and hamlets than most departments, children usually had to work much of the year, and attended class for only a few months in the winter, forgetting in the interval whatever they had learned. The only ones who benefited from schooling were the sons of those with sufficient means to do without their help. In the Doubs, on the other hand, winter is hard and long. This kept the children in school longer, and they picked up more. Yet even children who did not help their parents left school in March or April. In Lozère children attended school four months a year at most. After Easter, only infants were left; schools were either closed down or turned into day nurseries (1877). In Manche parents were happy to leave children in school during the years when they would only get underfoot around the house, but wanted to withdraw them as soon as they were able-bodied, precisely when they would be at their most teachable (1892). Alain Corbin concludes that child labor disappeared only slowly, between the 1870's and the late 1880's. By the end of the century, at any rate, inspectors could note a greater regularity in school attendance in the winter. Continued complaints of irregularity now referred to the rest of the year. Grumbles were bitter, but standards had been raised. . . .

We hear of a large Périgord village, with a quota of 20 scholarships, whose school in mid-century was attended by only three paying and three non-paying pupils. It was not enough to admit the needy free. In 1884 Georges Clemenceau met a peasant in a field with his son, and asked him why the child was not in school. "Will you give him a private income?," the peasant answered. The child who went to school had to bring a log for the fire, or a few sous instead. He had to provide his own ink, pen, and paper for writing—and though a slate could be used, the results were less than satisfactory. "A great number of children admitted to schools free get no benefit because they cannot acquire the indispensable books and class materials," read a report of 1875. "The well-off send their children away to school," reported a teacher from Tarn in the 1860's. "The poor don't send them to the elementary schools, because it costs 18–24 francs a year plus books, paper, etc., which can raise the cost to 30 francs." So, even if tuition was free, the child attending school, a useless mouth around the household board, was an expense. The "inexplicable inertia," the "indifference" that perplexed and annoyed apostles of the school, was in good part due to poverty—a lack of cash so great that, as a pastor in the Pyrenees explained in 1861, "even if the school fees were only 50 cents, they would still be a painful subject of anxiety and concern for the farmer." We must conclude, with a correspondent from Gironde, that "it is not enough for schooling to be free; the child's work must bring in some revenue to cover his keep or simply because the family needs it."

But the same report held out the hope of change: "The remedy to this state of things lies in public opinion. Even the most ignorant portion of the masses begins to understand that instruction is useful to all [and not just to their betters]. Country people know now that reading, writing, and arithmetic are means of rising in the world." Let us say at least that they began to know it. Free education had been gratuitous, that is, seemingly useless, to the children of the poor because it did not serve any needs that their parents could discern. The remitting of fees did not prove a critical factor in rural school attendance. There is no good evidence that the poor children who were admitted as free students attended school more diligently as a result; indeed, often they attended less regularly than the paying students. The crux of school attendance lay in the social practice: when going to school was the thing to do, all would do it. It also lay in the dawning comprehension, related to changing circumstances, that instruction was useful. With this realization, even lack of means would not deter many from sending their children to school.

We have arrived at the fundamental cause of that "indifference" to book learning that Philippe Ariès, like Destutt de Tracy before him, finds indigenous to the countryside. The urban poor had occasion to use the skills picked up in parish schools and to observe the opportunities of improving their position with that learning. In the countryside, such skills brought little profit, their absence small disadvantage, and there were fewer chinks in the armor of misery through which curiosity or enterprise could find escape. The *Statistique* of Vendée, regretting in 1844 that the department's inhabitants "showed little inclination for the study of sciences and polite literature, or for the culture of fine arts," sounds ridiculous until it shows that it understands why this was not surprising: "Far from the sources of inspiration and taste, they were rarely in a position to know their value or [to find] any object of emulation." Objects of emulation were scarce in the countryside, sources of inspiration even scarcer.

School was perceived as useless and what it taught had little relation to local life and needs. The teacher taught the metric system when *toises, cordes,* and *pouces* were in current use; counted money in francs when prices were in *louis* and *écus.* French was of little use when everyone spoke patois and official announcements were made by a public crier in the local speech. Anyway, the school did not teach *French*, but arid rules of grammar. In short, school had no practical application. It was a luxury at best, a form of more or less conspicuous consumption. Corbin has pointed out the significant role that all this played in the lack of interest displayed by parents and children. When Martin Nadaud's father wanted to send him to school, neighbors and relatives argued that for a country child school learning was useless, enabling him merely to make a few letters and carry books at mass. Teachers and school inspectors failed to persuade the peasants that reading and writing had any value in themselves. And parents found their reticence justified by the slight difference in the situation of those who attended school and of those who did not. When Ferdinand Buisson linked poor school attendance to a lack of concern for the moral benefits that children could derive, he was in the great (abstract) tradition. Yet show people a practical benefit that they could understand, and the problem would shrink to manageable proportions. Rural inhabitants, explained a village mayor, were "only very vaguely conscious of an intellectual or moral culture that has no immediate or tangible relation to pecuniary profit." That seemed to make sense. Before a man could want his child to go to school, he would have to abandon "the gross material interests" that were all he understood. Not so. It was when the school mobilized those interests that men began to care.

In darkest Finistère, while the other local councils squirmed uncomfortably before the requirements imposed by Guizot's education law of 1833, the council of Audierne alone voiced a positive response. Since most children in the little port "belong to families of sailors and soldiers, and are destined, like their fathers, to defend the fatherland [on] sea or land, where they can expect no advancement if they lack basic instruction and cannot read, write, or reckon sums," the council decided that "a school appears necessary." Not all municipalities enjoyed such enlightened majorities and many . . . placed the personal interests of men who could fend for their children's schooling above the training of potential competitors or social rebels. But the connection between practical interest and school, when it became apparent, was a potent force.

A number of individuals had overcome the disadvantage of illiteracy by self-education. Others, faced with the need to keep accounts, devised private systems of notation. By their nature, such records were not likely to survive; but we do know about a Loire mariner who, around 1830, kept track of his expenses by drawing the objects of his outlays or figures of little men accompanied by ciphers to show francs and sous. Clearly, mariners were involved in trade and in commercial transactions long before the peasants of the isolated countryside had reason to engage in such activities. Yet by the 1870's even sharecroppers in Brittany were being pressed to keep accounts. Manuscripts of the accounts maintained by two illiterate sharecroppers in Finistère have survived to show the new need for records. Each man separately seems to have devised a system of figurative notation to identify purchases (rope, horseshoe, horse collar), hired help (a man with a spade to dig up a field or an expensive sawyer), the number of horses or cattle sold, and coins (*sol, réal, écu*). These rough records, with their crude, ingenious shapes reminiscent of children's drawings, were preserved by offspring who went to school. The very treasuring of them as artifacts suggests the reasoning that led to that decision.

My point is that it needed personal experience to persuade people of the usefulness of education. Certain migrants had learned this, and we have seen how they and their children recognized at an early date "the value of instruction and the profit one can derive from it in the great centers." Through the second half of the century, school attendance in migrant Creuse was far better than in neighboring Haute-Vienne and Corrèze—higher by 7 percent and 12 percent, respectively, in 1876. Another spur to schooling came from the military law of 1872, not only because it abolished the purchase of substitutes, but also because it provided advantages for men who could read and write and threatened illiterate conscripts with an additional year of service. The school authorities made haste to refer to these facets of the law to persuade parents to send their children to school. In Isère a poster was even displayed in every schoolroom, and teachers were required to read and discuss it at least every two weeks, presumably arguing that the fulfillment of one patriotic duty could help lighten the burden of another.

But another army was growing, as important as the regular one—the body of public and private employees, access to which was opened by the school certificate, the certificate of elementary studies. The little school of

Roger Thabault's Mazières put its graduates into the numerous jobs that opened up there (and elsewhere), with economic, social, and political development: the town's 15 civil servants in 1876 had become 25 in 1886, and there were seven railway employees as well. Ambition was encouraged by propaganda. "A good primary education allows one to secure a post in several state services," the student was told in a first-year civics text published in 1880. "The government servant has a secure position. That is why government posts are in great demand." They were. Given the chance, many peasants wanted to stop being peasants, to change to something else. In 1899, 40 former natives of the little village of Soye in Doubs, population 444, worked as functionaries elsewhere, and 14 inhabitants worked as domestics in town. The prefecture of Seine received 50,000 applications for 400 openings in its department.

Other times had seen the growth of a state bureaucracy that triggered the expansion of education to fill the available posts. Such educational booms, however, had been restricted to relatively high social groups. Under the Third Republic the means for those too humble to have gotten their share of the educational pie were made available just when the ends (i.e., the jobs) emerged to reinforce and justify their use. Around the 1880's even rural laborers began to lend attention to the schools. As the number of jobs expanded and getting one became more than an idle dream, the education that would help secure such prestigious jobs became important. Even more so the certificate to which it led. Scattered encomiums to its practical uses appear in the late 1870's. By 1880 Pécaut could report that the school certificate "is slowly being accepted. Families realize that this small diploma can be of use for several kinds of jobs; hence they consent ever more frequently to leave their children in school for a longer time." Schools were still badly housed, still far from home, but children now were made to attend even when they lived six km away, because "the idea of the utility and the necessity of elementary schooling" had caught on so well.

The recognition of new possibilities and of the school as a key to their exploitation was in full evidence by the 1890's. By 1894 practically every child in a village of Lower Provence that had been almost totally illiterate a generation earlier was attending school, even those who lived one and a half hours' walk away. In the southwest the image of little boys doing their homework of an evening by the light of the dying embers became a reality. Municipal councils voted rewards for teachers whose pupils won the coveted certificate. Families became avid for it; they celebrated when a child got one; too many failures could become issues raised at council meetings. In a natural evolution, the school certificate, significant because of the material advantages it could help secure, became an end in itself. "It is an honor to get it," wrote a little girl (and wrote it very badly: "être ademise s'est un honneur d'avoir son certificat d'étude"), about what popular parlance dubbed the "Santificat." The passing of the examination became an eminent occasion, competing in importance with the first communion. Men who had taken it in the 1880's remembered the questions that they had to answer, had every detail of their examination day graven in their memories. To take one example among many, here is Charles Moureu, member of the Academy of Medicine and professor at the Collège de France, speaking at the graduation ceremony of his native village in the Pyrenees in 1911: "I could if I wanted to recite by heart the exact details of the problem that turned on the things Peter and Nicholas bought and sold."

There were of course more immediate gains: there would be no more need to go to the nearest town to consult a solicitor or a notary when one wanted to draw up a simple bill or promissory note, make out a receipt, settle an account in arrears, or merely write a letter, explained a thirteen-year-old schoolboy in the Aube. The literate man did not have to reveal his friendships, his secrets, his affairs to some third party. *And* he could better himself—in local politics, or teaching, or the army (whence he returned with a pension and decorations, achieving a position "that places him above the vulgar crowd").

The vulgar crowd was full of the sort of peasants whose stereotyped image filled current literature: they spoke ungrammatically, used characteristic locutions, mishandled the small vocabulary at their command, and "do not look more intelligent than other peasant farmers around them." The only escape from this was education, which taught order, cleanliness, efficiency, success, and *civilization.* Official reports coupled poor education with rude, brutal ways. Where schooling did not take hold, "ways are coarse, characters are violent, excitable, and hotheaded, troubles and brawls are frequent." The school was supposed to improve manners and customs, and soothe the savage breast. The polite forms it inculcated "softened the savagery and harshness natural to peasants." Improved behavior and morality would be attributed to the effects of schooling. Schools set out "to modify the habits of bodily hygiene and cleanliness, social and domestic manners, and the way of looking at things and judging them." Savage children were taught new manners: how to greet strangers, how to knock on doors, how to behave in decent company. "A bourgeois farts when his belly is empty; a Breton [peasant] burps when his belly is full," declared a proverb that seems to confuse urban and rural differences with race. Children were taught that propriety prohibited either manifestation; and also that cleanliness was an essential part of wisdom.

The schools played a crucial role in forcing children to keep clean(er), but the teachers had to struggle mightily to that end. Hair, nails, and ears were subject to regular review; the waterpump was pressed into frequent use; the state of clothes, like the standards of the child's behavior out of school, received critical attention and constant reproof. Study, ran the text of one exercise, "fills the mind, corrects false prejudices, helps us order speech and writing, teaches love of work and improves capacity for business and for jobs." What does study tell us? Among other things: cold baths are dangerous; the observance of festivals is a religious duty; labor abuses the body less than pleasure; justice protects the good and punishes the wicked; tobacco is a poison, a useless expenditure that destroys one's memory, and those who use it to excess live in a sort of dream, their eye dead, incapable of paying attention to anything, indifferent and selfish. And then there was the lesson of Jules and Julie, who are rich and therefore do not work at school; and who, having learned nothing, are embarrassed later by their ignorance, blushing with shame when people laugh at them for the mistakes they make when speaking. Only the schools could "change primitive conditions," declared Arduoin-Dumazet. The primitive conditions themselves were changing, and schools helped their charges to adapt to this.

Of course they did more—or they did it more broadly. If we are prepared to set up categories with well-drawn limits, society educates and school instructs. The school imparts particular kinds of learned knowledge, society inculcates the conclusions of experience assimilated over a span of time. But such a view, applicable to specific skills and subjects, has to be altered when the instruction offered by the school directs itself to realms that are at variance with social education (as in the case of language or measures), or that social education ignores (as in the case of patriotism). In other words, the schools provide a complementary, even a counter-education, because the education of the local society does not coincide with that needed to create a national one. This is where schooling becomes a major agent of acculturation: shaping individuals to fit into societies and cultures broader than their own, and persuading them that these broader realms are their own, as much as the [local] *pays* they really know and more so.

The great problem of modern societies, or so François Guizot considered in his *Memoirs*, is the governance of minds. Guizot had done his best to make elementary education "a guarantee of order and social stability." In its first article, his law of 1833 defined the instruction it was intended to provide: the teaching of reading, writing, and arithmetic would furnish essential skills; the teaching of French and of the metric system would implant or increase the sense of unity under French nationhood; moral and religious instruction would serve social and spiritual needs.

What these social needs were is laid out clearly in various writings, both official and unofficial. "Instructing the people," explained an anonymus writer of 1861, "is to condition them to understand and appreciate the beneficence of the government." Eight years later, the inspecteur d'Académie of Montauban concurred: "The people must learn from education all the reasons they have for appreciating their condition." A first-year civics textbook set out to perform this task:

> *Society* (summary): (1) French society is ruled by just laws, because it is a democratic society. (2) All the French are equal in their rights; but there are inequalities between us that stem from nature or from wealth. (3) These inequalities cannot disappear. (4) Man works to become rich; if he lacked this hope, work would cease and France would decline. It is therefore necessary that each of us should be able to keep the money he has earned.

The ideals of the educators were to be fulfilled at least in part.

Schools taught potent lessons of morality focused on duty, effort, and seriousness of purpose. Hard work and rectitude were bound to bring improvements, internal and external. You must be just and honest. The Roman Camillus refuses to take a town by treachery: the people of the town become the allies of Rome. Never forget that no end, however useful, can justify injustice. Progress is good, routine is bad. "Routine consits in refusing to make any improvement and in following the methods of our ancestors." Progress was new schools, fire companies, municipal bands. It was Monsieur Tardieu, mayor of Brive, who built a bridge that permitted people to sell their goods in the market on the other side of the river, and thus increased the prosperity of his town: "The Brivois perceived the possibilities of gain, and the more they worked, the richer they got." A Vosges village teacher's report of 1889 echoes what he taught and what his students learned: "The farmers are better educated and understand that they have to break with their routine, if they want to earn more. In 1870 they only did what they had seen their forebears doing."

"Believe in progress with a sincere and ardent faith. . . . Never forget that the history of all civilization is a perpetual glorification of work." Perhaps it is true that men are seldom so harmlessly employed as when their energies are bent on making money. "Work draws men together and prepares the reign of peace." "Work is the instrument of all progress." Francinet and his little friends are told the story of the sago tree, which feeds a man during a whole year in return for only a few hours' work, but in so doing, destroys his moral values. Conclusion: "Work is moralizing and instructive par excellence. But man only resigns himself to constant and regular labor under the pressure of need." One rises in the world by work, order, thrift: "Not all at once, of course. My father had nothing, I have something; my children, if they do like me, will double, triple what I leave behind. My grandchildren will be gentlemen. This is how one rises in the world." The speaker is the shoemaker Grégoire, hero of several little moral tales in a collection published by Ernest Lavisse in 1887. They war against idleness, indolence and thriftlessness, and make their point with lots of solid detail ("his charming wife brought a dowry of 5,000 francs; he had 3,000 . . ."), with useful explanations of things like bankruptcy law and fraud, and not least, with a profoundly realistic sense of values.

Such is the tale of Pierre, who, called to serve in the 1870 war, escapes death when a German bullet is deflected by two five-franc pieces sent him by his father and his brother as tokens of their affection. Decorated with the military medal, which the proud father frames and garnishes with flowers, Pierre "will go every year to draw the 100 francs to which his medal entitles him until his death, and place the money in the savings bank." Both family affection and heroism are expressed and regarded not only in elevated feelings but in concrete terms: a thoroughly sensible view. No wonder that patriotism was advocated in similar terms. The fatherland was a source of funds for road repairs, subsidies, school scholarships and police protection against thieves—"one great family of which we are all a part, and which we must defend always."

We come here to the greatest function of the modern school: to teach not so much useful skills as a new patriotism beyond the limits naturally acknowledged by its charges. The revolutionaries of 1789 had replaced old terms like schoolmaster, regent, and rector, with *instituteur*, because the teacher was intended to *institute* the nation. But the desired effect, that elusive unity of spirit, was recognized as lacking in the 1860's and 1870's as it had been four score years before.

School was a great socializing agent, wrote a village teacher from Gard in 1861. It had to teach children national and patriotic sentiments, explain what the state did for them and why it exacted taxes and military service, and show them their true interest in the fatherland. It seems that there was a great deal to do. The theme remained a constant preoccupation of eminent educators. Twenty years after this, student teachers "must above all be told . . . that their first duty is to make [their charges] love and understand the fatherland." Another ten years, and the high aim is again repeated, that a "national pedagogy" might yet become the soul of popular education. The school is "an instrument of unity," an "answer to dangerous centrifugal tendencies," and of course the "keystone of national defense."

First, the national pedagogy. "The fatherland is not your village, your province, it is all of France. The fatherland is like a great family." This was not learned without some telescoping. "Your fatherland is you," wrote a thirteen-year-old schoolboy dutifully in 1878. "It is your family, it is your people [*les tiens*], in a word it is France, your country."

"The fatherland is the *pays* where we are born," wrote another, "where our parents are born and our dearest thoughts lie; it is not only the *pays* we live in, but the region [*contrée*] we inhabit; our fatherland is France." The exercise was a sort of catechism designed to teach the child that it was his duty to defend the fatherland, to shed his blood or die for the commonweal ("When France is threatened, your duty is to take up arms and fly to her rescue"), to obey the government, to perform military service, to work, learn, pay taxes, and so on.

At the very start of school, children were taught that their first duty was to defend their country as soldiers. The army—and this was important, considering the past and enduring hostility to soldiers and soldiering—"is composed of our brothers or parents" or relatives. Commencement speeches recalled this sacred duty in ritual terms—our boys will defend the soil of the fatherland. The whole school program turned on expanding the theme. Gymnastics were meant "to develop in the child the idea of discipline, and and prepare him . . . to be a good soldier and a good Frenchman." Children sang stirring songs like the "Flag of France," the "Lost Sentry," and "La Marseillaise." Compositions on the theme were ordered up, with title and content provided: "Letter of a Young Soldier to His Parents. He tells them that he has fought against the enemies of the fatherland, has been wounded . . . and is proud (as they must be too) that he has shed his blood for the fatherland." And teachers reported with satisfaction how they implanted the love of the fatherland by evoking "those memories that attach our hearts to the fatherland" from history, and then "develop[ed] this sentiment by showing France strong and powerful when united." . . .

But the effects of school went further. In the first place, the literary or written language children learned in schools was as alien to the spoken tongue as spoken French itself was to their native dialect. In other words, schools began their work by propagating an artificial language, and this was true even for French-speakers. They did this largely through the discipline of dictations, "the instrument of a learned and universal language" beyond the local ken. As a result, many students learned to express themselves freely and easily in speech, but had difficulty when it came to writing or to expressing thought in an idiom close to that of the written word. We can glimpse this best in the surviving files of gendarmerie reports, which are often drawn up in a stilted administrative style and relate even simple events in an awkward and convoluted manner.

A striking result of this (much worse in areas estranged by dialect) was that "for months or years [the children] give no sign of intelligence, merely imitate what they see done." Just as legislation can create crime by fiat, so education created stupidity by setting standards of communication that many found difficult to attain. "Our children cannot find, and indeed have no way to find, enough French words to express their thoughts,'' reported a Cantal teacher. The result was a divorce between school learning, often acquired by rote, and assimilation, which helped slow down the progress of the schools. Memorization saved the trouble of "having to translate one's thought into correct French." It also divorced word from reality. Many children "can spell, but syllables have no meaning for them; can read, but fail to understand what they read, or to recognize in writing some words they know but whose orthography is alien," or to identify words learned in French with the objects around them. "You will learn it, this language of well-bred people, and you will speak it some day," promised a prize-giver in Dordogne in 1897. The future tense used in such improbable circumstances suggests a possible reason why, by 1907, the number of illiterate conscripts seems to have been slightly higher than in the immediate past. The absolute banning of the native tongue, which had been helpful in teaching French as a second language, inhibited the learning of idiomatic French and impeded its full assimilation.

This is not to say that French did not make great strides forward. It did. But writing remained a socially privileged form of expression, and the French of the schools and of the dictations was an alienating as well as an integrative force. Perhaps that was what a school inspector meant when, looking back from 1897, he declared: "Ignorance used to precede school; today on the contrary it follows schooling."

Of course there were (from the school's point of view) positive results; and these two went beyond the immediately obvious. The symbolism of images learned at school created a whole new language and provided common points of reference that straddled regional boundaries exactly as national patriotism was meant to do. Where local dialect and locutions insulated and preserved, the lessons of the school, standardized throughout France, taught a unifying idiom. In Ain, the Ardennes, Vendée, all children became familiar with references or identities that could thereafter be used by the authorities, the press, and the politicians to appeal to them as a single body. Lessons emphasizing certain associations bound generations together. The Kings of France were the older sons of the Church, time was the river that carried all in its waters, a poet was a favorite of the muses, Touraine was the garden of France, and Joan of Arc the shepherdess of Lorraine. Local saws and proverbs were replaced by nationally valid ones, regional locutions by others learned in books: castles in Spain rose above local ruins, and golden calves bleated more loudly than the stabled ones. The very mythology of ambition was now illustrated by landscapes that education had suggested, more stirring than the humbler ones at hand and by this time no less familiar. These are only aspects of the wide-ranging process of standardization that helped create and reinforce French unity, while contributing to the disintegration of rival allegiances.

The cultural underpinnings of rural society, already battered by material changes, were further weakened by shifting values. First of all, manual labor was devalued—or better still, the natural aversion to its drudgery was reinforced. The elementary schools, designed to form citizens, neglected producers. The school glorified labor as a moral value, but ignored work as an everyday form of culture. The well-established contrast between the plucky, mettlesome spirit of the *courageux* and the idle *fainéant*—the one hardworking, especially or only with his hands, the other avoiding manual labor—was translated into scholastic terms. Soon, the idle boy was the one likely to be the most pressed into hard physical labor, the plucky boy the one most enterprising with his books. It made good sense, for the rewards of work now came to those not doing what had once been recognized as work, But it opened a crack—one more—in age-old solidarities.

In a great many homes, illiterate adults depended on small children to carry out what were becoming essential tasks—accounting, correspondence, taking notes, reading aloud pertinent documents or newspaper items. And new literacies at whatever level made new ideas accessible, especially to the young, to whom certain profound changes in the political climate of country districts were now attributed. In any case, the relationship between school and social claims was not ignored in their own time: "The Republic has founded schools," sang Montéhus, the revolutionary chansonnier, "so that now the people have learned how to count. The people have had enough of the pauper's mite; they want an accounting, and not charity!" More important, where, as in Brittany, a determined campaign taught new generations French, "children and parents form two worlds apart, so separated in spirit, so estranged by speech, that there is no more community of ideas and feelings, hence no intimacy. Often as a matter of fact, any kind of relationship becomes impossible." This is both exaggerated and suggestive of a generation gap more easily discerned in modern societies than in traditional ones. But even granting the exaggeration, the corrosive effects of one sort of education on a society based on another kind are undeniable.

Like migration, politics, and economic development, schools brought suggestions of alternative values and hierarchies; and of commitments to other bodies than the local group. They eased individuals out of the latter's grip and shattered the hold of unchallenged cultural and political creeds—but only to train their votaries for another faith.

Workers in Modern Society: Two Cases

I. British Construction Workers

RICHARD PRICE

II. Rubber and Cable Workers in Bezons, France

LENARD R. BERLANSTEIN

What was the position of the working class as European society became
more modern? From the beginnings of the industrial revolution until quite
recently, the manufacturing labor force has grown rather steadily—it is, therefore,
an important part of modern society numerically. At the same time, the workers'
position in the overall power structure of society was weakened by their lack of
property and the challenge to many traditional skills. Some workers reacted by
trying to cling to as many traditional patterns of behavior as possible, particularly
during the early decades of industrialization, when some workers could directly
recall village and guild traditions of work and leisure. But gradually, workers
began to change, at least in part. They learned to protest in new ways, and to
develop new goals. They also developed new patterns of consumption and family
life.

Some historians see the essence of a modern working-class in the new protest forms. Pointing to the situations and groups most capable of militancy, they
assert that this militancy went to the heart of the industrial power balance. Workers were not simply interested in better pay or shorter hours; they wanted to
determine their own working lives. The following selection deals with a particularly vigorous period of British working-class protest just before World War I.
Strike rates were high, and many skilled workers attacked timid union leaders and
the give and take of collective bargaining. Some invoked doctrines of syndicalism, which called for worker control of the units of production along with highly
democratic unions. Historian Richard Price sees these new worker demands as
part of an ongoing development in the class warfare, the struggle for power in the
workplace, endemic to a capitalist society.

Other historians, recognizing the importance of radical groups and of
periods of militancy, also consider other kinds of worker adaptation to modern
conditions. Indeed, some stress ways in which workers tried to imitate middle-
class habits, a process known as *embourgeoisement*. The second selection does not
take this simple path, but focuses on another distinct working-class culture at the
turn of the century—one that cannot be described primarily in terms of militancy.
These French factory workers lacked the trade union traditions of the workers

Price discusses, and they were not skilled artisans, which may have shaped a different set of expectations about the workplace. What did modernization mean to these workers in terms of political behavior, family life, and general outlook?

Price and Berlanstein do agree on three important points. Both acknowledge that workers were moving away from purely traditional attitudes and behavior. Both see workers as different from the middle class in certain key respects—a fact that complicates any picture of the trends of modern society by introducing lasting class distinctions. And both point to the years around 1900 as crucial in working-class development. By this date, experience with the industrial process had blunted the worst shocks of industrialization. At the same time, new organizational forms—the corporation, or the large construction crew—and new technology posed important challenges to the working class. British construction workers were clearly reacting in part to some of these changes which threatened established skills.

But clearly there is important dispute about what the essential trends in modern working-class development are. Some differences relate to the stop-and-go quality of technological change and to fluctuations in material conditions—workers calm at one point, might be irate five years later. Some differences unquestionably reflect variations stemming from place and type of employment setting. But differences also flow from the aspects of the worker experience considered—whether family life is evaluated along with strike action—and from the extent to which militant workers are taken to represent the whole class. These differences affect the judgment of what workers were in the recent past, and they also relate to continuing disputes about the position of workers today.

In addition to the factor of class, the selections raise another question vital to our understanding the modernization process: Has modern society reduced pleasure in work? Even as job satisfaction declines, a modern mentality may find compensations, in better living standards or new family behavior. Nevertheless, this is a potentially major qualification to any equation of modernization and progress, even for workers who are not profoundly militant. It involves an assumption that the quality of work was once higher (which Laslett, for example, does suggest in an earlier selection). Without question, workers around 1900, though their levels of discontent varied, were facing huge work adjustments. Does working-class modernization center around adjustments to a work situation that is not only beyond workers' control, but increasingly devoid of satisfaction?

BRITISH CONSTRUCTION WORKERS

The key to understanding the unique character of the unrest lay in the perfect symbiosis it represented between past and present. It was from the interaction between the challenges of the present and the traditions of the past that the labour militancy emerged; it was precisely because the past infused the present that the labour unrest gained its particularly threatening and purposeful force. Tradition in no way bred confusion about contemporary developments but was, rather, a central and vital ingredient to understanding and grappling with new realities. Only on the basis of their particular histories of work control struggle could those militant segments of the working class (and . . . they covered the whole spectrum of industrial experience) actually make their journey. There was nothing new about the issues that formed the core of militancy's attention and anger; all were to be found in some form or another at earlier periods. What was new were the impediments to the realisation and articulation of those issues—impediments which included the trade unions, economist collective bargaining and, ultimately, the corporatist social welfare state. Their presence lifted the old, 'traditional' struggle to a new level of experience, transformed it from a struggle at the workplace to one which finally had to confront national structures and institutions. This was why the militancy was unique, why it cannot be patronisingly dismissed as just another stage of simple union militancy, why its significance cannot be gauged by the measurement of statistical indices of any sort.

The labour militancy grew out of the historical struggle for work control; it was that same struggle writ larger than before because the obstacles it had to confront were more immense than those of previous days. The national perspectives of industrial relations inevitably lifted the contest out of isolated local foci into the realm of the nation as a whole. In its industrial setting, then, tradition fused with, informed and heightened a militancy that was stimulated by the contemporary context. But in order more properly to understand the dynamic that created the labour unrest, it is necessary to locate it precisely within those structures that formed the reality of the contemporary world and the transforming links between past and present. And it is here that the themes of corporatism are of most interpretive use, for they enable us to comprehend the central benchmark of this period's militancy which was to be in revolt against the very institutions and procedures that represented the Labour Movement's

From Richard Price, *Masters, Unions and Men* (Cambridge, Eng.: Cambridge University Press, 1980), pp. 240–245, 249–250, 258–260.

achievement. From the growing disillusionment with Labour Party policies to the commonplace rejection of officially negotiated industrial agreements, all sections of the Labour Movement experienced some variant of
this problem. Nor was this alienation simply a function of natural diver-
gence inherent to the collective organisation of diverse and competing
groups and strategies. What raised it above those kinds of mundanely
simple precepts was the depth of its intensity—as manifested by the ideological presence of syndicalism—and its contribution to, and coincidence
with, the wider and general crisis in British society. The revolt of labour
was a revolt against the institutions and tactics that worked for the incor-
poration of labour into society and although that must not be taken to
imply a continuously high level of self-conscious action, it is only within
that general analytical framework that we can make any real sense of the
phenomenon. In the industrial sphere, it was the first time a crisis of capitalism had been accompanied with a demonstration of the modern
dilemma of collective bargaining systems: that is, the inherent contradiction between their labour management function and their inability to
address the central issues that created the need for that function. Sooner
or later, the economist articulation of worker aspirations and the economist focus of industrial relations systems run into the basic reality that
industrial struggle is a struggle for control and authority at work; the strain
that results between the image and the reality cannot forever be contained
and ultimately threatens to reveal the illusion for what it really is. It was
this point of consciousness that had been reached in the labour unrest.

The Structure of Militancy

The basis of labour militancy lay in the fact that, for a variety of con-
junctural reasons, this period saw a climacteric collision between the disciplinary impulses of the industrial relations system and work control.
Richard Hyman has explained the essence of the problem in terms which
precisely describe the process at work in Edwardian England:

> The ordinary employee, perpetually subject to the oppressive and exploita-
> tive relations of capitalist wage-labour is always liable to overturn some
> aspect of existing 'industrial legality.' The union's function is to 'keep the
> faith'. . . . It is precisely at the point when existing structures of capitalist
> domination are under pressure, when the frontier of control is being forced
> forward, that the potentially conservative role of trade unionism, as the
> defender of industrial legality, is a most serious danger.

An exhaustive study of this relationship in American steel and auto industries has conclusively shown how a piecemeal and successive rollback of

work control gains that had been achieved in the early years of mass unionisation was a consequence of the creation of collective bargaining systems. Paralleling this decline of labour power over managerial rights and prerogatives was the enhanced status and influence of union leadership. Such developments as the replacement of strike enforcement with conciliation and arbitration rendered the rank and file increasingly dependent upon the union leadership; worker devices to restrict managerial decisions were rolled back with union participation. A division of responsibility assigned to the unions the job of problem solving whose function was not to challenge managerial authority but to ensure the smooth working of industry.

We have already noted that, from the 1890s, a similar process was at work in Britain—this, after all, was the equivalent historical period to the late 1930s and early 1940s in US labour relations. But a direct parallel from that period might be useful to illustrate the kinds of frustrations that must eventually find an outlet. Once the boilermakers became enmeshed in a collective bargaining structure, there was a progressive negotiating away of apprenticeship restrictions. After some hard bargaining caused by the employers' desire for a removal of all limitations, the 1894 agreement set the apprentice-journeyman ratio at 1:4 in return for a union commitment not to enroll apprentices until their fourth year. And in 1901, for reasons that will remain obscure until the union opens its records, the leadership accepted the removal of this restriction. This may have been a wise or unwise decision, but its main interest lies in the way in which the agreement was bludgeoned through the union. On the first vote, the membership rejected the agreement but the union ordered a new referendum on the spurious grounds that too few votes had been cast. Only 3300 more votes were cast on this second ballot but the result was what the leadership desired and no more trips to the polling booth were necessary. Like the pattern noted by Richard Herding amongst the American unions and as with [other] collective agreements . . . this agreement weakened the workers' power whilst elevating that of the union. It was explained that 'it is not their [employers] intention to overstock the yards with Apprentices, and if the Boilermakers' Society finds it necessary to prefer a complaint respecting the number, this must be done through the Secretaries of the [union and] . . . the Shipbuilding Employers' Federation.'

Even as it grew, then, the industrial relations systems were creating the conditions and spawning the unrest that was to detonate with such ferocity from 1909. The dispersion of legitimate power and authority away from the workplace and into the body of the corporate structures of the system created a vacuum into which 'shop systems of domination and resistance . . . [develop] in their own right.' These 'informal' groupings, characteristic of all collective bargaining systems, focus around work control issues, pose 'a continuous and growing challenge to managerial authority, and a source of industrial unrest' that explodes as violently against the unions as it does against management. It was just this process that was involved in the growth of 'formal' workshop organisations in Britain from the 1890s: that is, from the moment that the contradiction emerged between union-oriented economist collective bargaining and the continuing reality of workplace struggles for authority. Drawing upon the firmly established historical tradition of work group solidarity, it was during the 1890s that this tradition was obliged to express itself in formal organisation precisely because it was denied a recognised and authoritative position with the union or industrial relations structures.

The growing prominence of the shop steward was one manifestation of this development. Although the office had existed for many years before, it was only at this point that it added to its other duties the role of representative of rank and file interests against those of the official structures. In Building, where they were known to the rule books as early as the 1840s, we may see the first glimmerings of their modern role during the masons' strike of 1877–78, but formal rank and file organisation does not seem to have begun until 1911 with the creation of a syndicalist Consolidation Committee whose main support derived from the London bricklayers. Unlike the engineering stewards, who were integrated into the union structure in 1917, those in building have only recently attained official recognition. In shipbuilding, the boilermakers' district delegates were inhibited by their subordination to the Executive to ever develop into rank and file leaders. But the very nature of their work had accustomed platers and riveters to work group organisation and coincident with the growth of executive power in the early eighties complaints began to be heard about 'inner circles' who 'meet in the yard and decree what shall be the price paid on certain jobs, which has been in some cases exorbitant.' By the early 1900s, these 'platers' socials' became formalised into Vigilance Committees about which one would like to know more. On the Clyde, for example, the local Vigilance Committee was reported to have 'abused' officials, distributed circulars, survived the amazing smears levelled at it in the Monthly Reports, and successfully defied executive attempts to secure its dissolution.

This flurry of rank and file organisation extending throughout industry was of great significance in understanding the historical dynamics of the labour unrest. It represented that synthesis of past and present which gave the militancy its portentous force; for these organisational efforts signified a challenge to the established authority systems that are based upon an older tradition of work group activity which aimed to exert a control over the productive process. Like the wider, less organised militancy of which they were a part, formal rank and file organisation came into being at the point where the 'traditional' aspirations of the workforce were being denied or restrained by the system. And it was precisely here that the relevance of the past infused the present with a revolutionary force because, in the contemporary context, those traditional aims could not be achieved without an alteration and re-arrangement of the whole structures of industrial relations and—potentially—those of the whole social system. The case of the Durham miners' opposition to the eight hour day can be seen to illustrate the point. Like the non-union issue in building, resistance to the three-shift implications of an eight hour day had a long tradition behind it whose rationale was based upon its threatened disruption of the miners' ability to control safety conditions, wage levels and division of time between home and work. But the traditional nature of the issue spoke only to the eternity of the tussle for authority in the pits and the influence that transformed the question from its 'traditional' context to one that led to an attack upon the authority structures of the union was the workings of collective bargaining itself. As with the Shipbuilding Trades Agreement of the same year, negotiations were carried out in secret; when the agreement was published it was found that the Executive had reversed its previous policy without seeking any mandate from the rank and file and had accepted the eight hour day. These inescapable features of 'responsible' union negotiation combined with the face workers' traditional resistance to any weakening of their ability to control working conditions and led ineluctably to a rank and file revolt against the Executive and the union itself.

Like most such revolts, this one failed, but that is decidedly beside the point; its importance lies in the disclosure that it was exactly the interaction of the past upon the present that permitted militancy to move beyond the limited aims of opposing this or that wage settlement or conciliation decision towards an attack upon the whole system that made those decisions. The hostility to conciliation, the concern with non-union men, the rejection of executive authority were not isolated, discrete outbursts of an inchoate, dispersed militancy. All were integrally related, and seen to be related, as different parts of the same problem: how were the rank and file to re-assert their control and authority over decision making at the point of production (as over the labour supply) or at the point of the bargaining procedures (as in the conciliation boards)?

It was inevitable, therefore, that conciliation should not remain the only target of hostility. Entrapped by conciliation and no-strike clauses, with their unions as the under-keepers, the men were led to focus their particular attention upon the roles and actions of their unions and executives. The carpenters and joiners (whose hostility to conciliation was, perhaps, the strongest of all the building trades) had reached a clear appreciation of this relationship by 1911. The point was made in one resolution that: 'Our Society, being founded on democratic principles, it should be ruled and governed by the members as a whole, and not be a few who are self-appointed, such as our representatives on the National

Board are at present.' But letters and resolutions were of little avail against the arrogance of power in the Amalgamated Society. In 1912, it was reported—and not denied—that the union had participated in changes in the conciliation procedures that violated union rules and that although this was recognised by the Executive there had been no thought of consulting the membership. In 1913, the union went even further when its General Council ordered the Executive not to grant trade benefits until all conciliation procedures had been worked through and elevated any conciliation decision into the status of an executive order.

The constant reminders that the rank and file were barren of legitimate authority and power occasioned a dialectical response that issued in the slogan and practice of 'direct action.' Standing in complete opposition to the 'time-serving' devices of the system, direct action expressed the traditional form of industrial action in the industry which aimed at success by the sudden and total paralysis of jobs. But direct action was more than just the translation of traditional methods into syndicalist prose; it couched in a modern guise the continuing relevance of autonomous regulation and negotiation by imposition to the conditions in which the men found themselves. Given the presence of no-strike clauses, procrastinating conciliation procedures, immovable and unresponsive industrial relations structures, autonomous regulation was, in fact, the only viable alternative open to the men. An assertion of autonomous regulation, however, now implied something more than it had done in earlier days, for it involved confronting the union as well as the employer. In its claims for a share in the control of the productive process, autonomous regulation had always contained a radical, incipiently revolutionary, core which the contemporary escalation in the price of conflict allowed to become extant. Its revival in the form of direct action represented the impact of the present to politicise and radicalise tradition and, conversely, the adaptation of the tradition to fit modern circumstances. Syndicalism was the vocabulary which translated autonomous regulation from a limited expression of resistance to managerial authority to a radical challenge to the whole gamut of established authority. Thus, it was possible for an article on the delays and failures of the conciliation boards to end by asserting that: 'By direct action we can bring pressure to bear upon the capitalist class without the aid of intermediaries of any description . . . working in concert we can bring about the expropriation of the capitalist class.'

The lockout and strike of 1914 represented a tipping of the tightrope balance that unionism had to walk between persuading its memberships to accept unpopular decisions and policies whilst maintaining their credibility within the system of industrial relations. It marked the realisation of the problem that had been articulated by building union officials in London at the very moment of their full recognition as agents of collective bargaining:

> It will be altogether useless for us to go back to our constituents and report
> to them to this effect [i.e. a year delay in the wages advance], because we ...
> should just merely be deposed—they would take proceedings on their own
> lines and would have nothing to do with us anymore. . . . We have incurred
> a great deal of odium by adopting the line of policy which we have done
> already. . . . We have got enough to do to square them on that score [i.e.
> 9½d per hour instead of 10d] without having to square them with regard to
> anything else.

The events of the two years previous to 1914 and, in particular, the last
six months of 1913 revealed that the system as a whole was slowly grind-
ing to a halt. Meetings of employers, unions and conciliation boards
might continue to follow their normal schedule but increasingly they bore
little relationship to what would actually happen at the worksite; quite simply, their writs no longer ran. Between May 1913 and January 1914 there
were at least forty-eight strikes in London: all were unofficial and, as far as
one can judge, all violated the conciliation procedures. There were seventeen strikes affecting twenty firms against sub-contracted non-union labour
and 'nearly all these cases have occurred without notice being given either
to the employer or to the [conciliation board].' Although there was some
feeling amongst the employers that certain union officials were not as
innocent in these matters as they claimed, the unions' protestations that
they were powerless to do anything about these conflicts were generally
recognised to be true. Throughout the last part of 1913, there were frequent and constant meetings between the employers' association and the
unions where the same theme was echoed again and again. 'What was the
use of an Agreement if the parties thereto repudiated responsibility for
control of its [sic] members,' the plasterers were asked in September
1913. In the same month the [union] confessed that 'the officials had no
power over their members' in respect to the non-union question. The
masons' union, too, was unable to retain a control over their members on
this same matter:

> The whole of this trouble has arisen because individual members, or groups
> . . . have felt themselves at liberty to take exception to the presence of
> non-union workmen in the same employ . . . regardless of the agreement
> existing between their unions and the Employers' Association . . . that no
> exception shall be taken . . . and also that, to avoid stoppage of work, any
> dispute shall be brought before a Conciliation Board.

The lockout—which the [employers] had resolved to declare unless
they obtained a guarantee that strikes would cease—was about a loss of
control by both unions and the employers and it is hardly surprising,
therefore, that the first three months or so were dominated by the
employers' presentation of the document and the demand for a monetary
guarantee against strikes over the non-union issue. Both were attempts to

ensure the reassertion of *union* discipline: 'The employers had no desire to permanently adopt the principle of individual guarantee; it was only adopted whilst a collective guarantee was withheld.' It would be a great mistake to regard the document as either the central issue or as designed to 'do injury to the fabric of trade unionism.' The last thing the employers desired was a collapse of official trade unionism. Indeed, it was just the way to revive the credibility of the official union structures. Any notion that employer policy was motivated by a crude, simplistic anti-unionism is quickly disabused by the constant contacts between employers and unions that were maintained in the period whilst negotiations were in abeyance and by the immediate withdrawal of the document and monetary guarantee once the unions had agreed to a system of fines against those who breached the rules. 1914 is, therefore, very different from the earlier lockouts. . . . All were about authority and control and all occurred when industrial discipline had broken down, but none of the earlier instances had involved the reassertion of union control and authority.

The real arena of struggle in 1914 was between competing conceptions of industrial authority and discipline. The employers and unions were concerned to reaffirm the legitimate authority of the established procedures and structures and were obliged to confront a rank and file searching to assert their sovereign authority. The different paradigms proposed by the rank and file revealed, once again, the inter-marriage of past and present. The almost eerie revival of hostility to the contracting system and the efforts to secure direct labour contracts betokened no harking back to the golden days before 1833 but, rather, the enduring persistence of this form of the class struggle. And it was hardly surprising, therefore, that the forgotten tradition of autonomous regulation should also re-emerge from the shadows of the past to play a central role in the dispute. Cole and Mellor articulated the issue as it appeared to take shape when the national lockout loomed near in July:

> As a result of the threatened lockout there will come a united claim from the organised workers in the building industry for absolute freedom of action on any job . . . to down tools against their worst enemy—every disability clause must go. In future the men must work on the strict understanding that it is their right to decide what kind of man they shall count as fit to associate with.

But this same sentiment had been expressed from the very beginning of the dispute in January when a delegate meeting resolved that the autocratic behaviour of the employers had voided all rules and that the workers should therefore formulate their own conditions of work. District and Management Committees were called upon to appoint sub-committees to draw up rules 'that will be . . . the means of governing all in the industry. . . . [The opportunity now existed] for the men of all sections to make arrangements for their own work, without considering the opinions of others. All desired improvements can now be made without the interference by the capitalists or by Trade Union officials.' Such an attitude . . . went beyond a merely negative rejection of official authority to an attempt to change the authority structures themselves by the re-assertion of rank and file control over negotiations and decision making. Autonomous regulation—direct action—demanded no less and thus the stage was set for the tussle that marked the whole course of the dispute between the efforts of the rank and file to subordinate the official structures to their authority and the stubborn refusal of the officials to so surrender their power.

RUBBER AND CABLE WORKERS IN BEZONS, FRANCE

While textbooks continue to portray the nineteenth century as the Age of Liberalism, Nationalism, or Revolution, historians now recognize another great impersonal force which touched more people than did these, and perhaps more deeply. This was proletarianization, the reduction of formerly propertied people to the status of wage earners. Social historians and demographers of pre-industrial Europe have demonstrated how most aspects of private life were organized about the preservation or extension of a patrimony, whether in land, a business, or intangible property, like the skills of a craftsman. The emergence of a propertyless group of people through population growth and capital accumulation helped to undermine the fragile equilibrium in this property-centered social order and created the possibility for new patterns of comportment. It hardly needs to be stated that in attempting to understand the causes and consequences of proletarianization, historians have an ambitious agenda before them.

The present study will consider the growth of a factory population in Bezons (Val d'Oise), a small town eight miles west of Paris. This case study immediately presents two features which distinguish it from others that have been examined so far. The factory workers were not at all isolated in a region of peasant agriculture. They took work on the edge of a great metropolis, and in an area of intensive industrial expansion and concentration. Secondly, we will be dealing with an unskilled labor force. Not only did the laborers, male and female, lack a sense of craft, but they

From Lenard R. Berlanstein, "The Formation of a Factory Labor Force: Rubber and Cable Workers in Bezons, France (1860–1914)," *Journal of Social History*, Vol. 15, No.2 (Winter 1981), pp. 163, 165, 166–168, 171, 172, 173–176, 178–181.

could not even identify with a particular kind of labor, as miners did. These features should provide new perspectives on the proletarianization process. To be sure, Bezons was not the scene of infamous confrontations between labor and capital nor the home of a socialist leader with national stature, but it did witness complex transformations in the workers' community that established itself there.

At this point, it might seem reasonable to conclude that the rubber factory managed to attract only a floating population which could never have established a coherent community of workers. The unskilled work they performed, their history of mobility, their cultural deficiencies—a third of the Bretons could not sign their marriage acts—might make them prime candidates for the label of *lumpenproletarians* in the eyes of some scholars. Still others might expect that these laborers were peasants-in-a-factory, who had no intention of remaining very long in the plant, but rather hoped to scrape together the cash to acquire land. Then they would either remain as cultivators in the Paris region or return—better off than they had left—to the homeland. In fact, neither of these hypotheses held true for Bezons's factory workers; or, if they obtained for some individuals, neither alternative characterized the labor force as a whole. The tax records of Bezons show that the factory laborers rarely acquired land. Only 5 *journaliers* became land-owners in Bezons, and their total holdings amounted to less than a hectare. Since land was inexpensive in this still-rural commune (the municipality was paying less than two francs a meter for good residential land) the failure of workers to possess much probably indicates that ownership had a low priority with them. This was not because workers intended to return home with their hoarded wages or because, as sub-proletarians, they drifted aimlessly from one job to another. An outstanding feature of the rubber workers' comportment was their tendency to settle down in Bezons. Establishing roots is not usually associated with unskilled migrants to large factories, but this is what many factory workers in Bezons did.

Far from being on their way to somewhere else or to some other status, an impressive portion of Rattier's workers stayed as laborers in Bezons. The persistence rate for married males between census periods of 1876 and 1881 was 65.4 per cent, and 53.2 per cent between 1876 and 1886. While unmarried male workers were much less stable, thirty per cent for the five-year period, they formed only a small portion of the labor force. The married rubber workers were, thus, considerably more rooted than all residents, including propertied ones, in Bochum, Germany, a rapidly industrializing town with a persistence rate of 44 per cent over a decade. And in American cities of the nineteenth century only a third of the wage earners could be expected to remain in a city for a decade. Another demonstration of the workers' residential stability comes from records concerning the Assistance-to-the-Aged Act of 1905. The average time that 17 septuagenarian workers (or their widows) had spent in Bezons was 18.6 years. Rejecting the label "sub-proletariat" for newcomers to the industrial scene, Michelle Perrot has suggested that they "aspired to roots and to security of employment and retirement." The case of Bezons's factory workers certainly confirms Perrot's insight. Propertyless before their arrival, these laborers seemed to develop a commitment to industrial employment and even to a particular company. Such a finding is significant, but to recognize the workers' commitment is not to understand why it developed. Indeed, we shall have to delve into work conditions and community structures in order to place the workers' stability in its proper perspective.

Whatever the bases for this residential persistence, the workers' material conditions were probably not among them. True, the daily wages of 3.5 francs for men and two francs for women were higher than what they could earn in Brittany or Flanders. But they could have had similar wages elsewhere in the Paris region, and, in any case, their earnings were not sufficient to keep workers out of the household cycle of poverty. The records of the commune's parsimonious charity board are useless for gauging the extent of material deprivation, but one can form an impression from the lists of indigent students which appeared in the municipal council deliberations. In 1880, a third of the primary school pupils belonged to impoverished families, and factory workers headed all but one of these households. Moreover, work in Rattier's plant was dangerous and disagreeable. Complicated machines with few safeguards, cluttered shops, and inexperience resulting from frequent changes in job assignments made for numerous and sometimes vicious accidents. A local newspaper claimed that the plant suffered 125 accidents within a month. According to a doctor who studied the effects of the vulcanization process, hardly a worker escaped disturbing reactions to the sulfur fumes. State authorities were even more concerned about the noisome effects of benzene compounds on laborers. No doubt, the best feature of factory employment was the steady work it offered. Rattier's plant apparently did not suffer many large layoffs. Even during the economic crisis of 1882, when neighboring Argenteuil was providing relief to its workers, a municipal councillor noted (with exaggeration) that "the workers of Bezons prosper while the inhabitants around them are in despair."

The harsh work conditions were aggravated by the fact that Bezons was unprepared to receive so many poor immigrants and never took much collective action to upgrade their situation. Nor is there evidence that Rattier provided any of the services (housing, schooling, job training) that the large mining and steel companies used to attract workers—apparently he did not have to do so. Bezons's newly created health board found that over half of the housing stock was below its loose standards in 1865, just when factory workers were arriving. By 1870, the building workers and quarry owners began to put up tenements of sorts. They did so in the extreme east of the commune, about two to three kilometers from the traditional center. What became a veritable "workers' hamlet" was isolated, marshy, all but inaccessible in bad winter weather, and virtually devoid of essential services. The municipal council recognized that this area lacked access to drinking water even as tenants suffered from diseases originating (they thought) in the undrained ditches near their lodgings. These conditions were soon reflected in the workers' health statistics, especially in the incidence of infant mortality. This averaged a very high 281 deaths per thousand live births between 1865 and 1885. The fact that the commune was without a resident midwife at times surely contributed to the abnormal number of deaths.

The isolation and "village" modes of comportment of Bezons's factory workers did not survive intact into the twentieth century. The harshness of their material existence began to ease a bit, and even before the change in living standards was evident, new patterns of behavior and belief appeared. One can say that the rubber and cable workers began to participate in an urban, working-class culture; but the situation was somewhat more complex than this. Discovering their identity as workers and a sense of collective interests went hand-in-hand with individual efforts to take advantage of the slender opportunities for personal advancement open to them. To examine Bezons's workers from 1890 to the First World War is to find them attempting to integrate themselves into the socio-economic order in multifarious ways.

One consequence of this industrial growth was a substantial improvement in material conditions over the early days of rubber production. The last decade of the nineteenth century, in particular, was a time of improved earnings. The daily wages for male *journaliers* had been four francs in the 1880s but rose to 5.5 francs by 1901. Moreover, when the S.I.T. had large orders to fill, it hired on a bi-monthly basis rather than daily, a practice much appreciated by the laborers themselves and envied by the skilled metal workers. The cable workers usually earned half a franc more than unskilled hands in metal construction works and a franc more than the quarry workers of the region. Perhaps the fact that the S.I.T. had few competitors and operated on lucrative public contracts allowed it to be somewhat more generous to its workers. After the start of the new century, wages ceased their rapid climb, and workers may have lost some ground to inflation, even if monetary renumerations gained somewhat and the work day was cut from eleven to ten hours.

Industrial expansion engendered not only better living conditions but also marked changes in patterns of sociability and, inevitably, new perspectives and loyalties. The rubber workers' isolation in a "village with a factory" gave way to multi-faceted contacts with a wider community of laborers, especially skilled and semi-skilled metal workers. Arriving from

Lille, Nantes, Brest, Paris and other large cities, these metal workers brought perspectives which had not yet penetrated very deeply into the factory labor force of Bezons. We can measure their growing contacts by examining the witnesses to cable workers' marriage acts. Whereas friends and relatives had almost always been fellow factory laborers before 1890, in the years 1890–1910, 41.2 per cent were metal workers and 12.4 per cent were other sorts of workers (electricians, tramway employees, building laborers). In the twentieth century, it became a commonplace for a *journalière* [female laborer] to marry a mechanic or a fitter. The metal workers also became neighbors of the rubber-plant laborers as wage-earners' residences spilled beyond the "hamlet" and moved toward the center and the northern periphery of the commune. It was probably from these urbanized, skilled workers that the factory laborers began to learn that they were "workers" as much as Bretons or Flemings.

The scope of the ensuing cultural transformation is suggested by significant shifts in demographic comportments. The selection of brides who were the same age or older than the groom dropped to half its earlier level (10.0 per cent). At the same time, the average age of women who married rubber workers declined to 22.1 years, only a bit above the age of metal workers' brides (21.7 years). During this first decade of the twentieth century, a third of the factory workers' brides were below the age of twenty; very few had been so young before 1890. Provincial endogamy, once so strong an impulse, lost its force as well. Its precise extent is hard to measure since there is no way to determine how many Bretons married natives of Bezons born to Breton parents. However, the portion of Bretons who took brides from their province fell from over eighty per cent to 31.4 per cent between 1889 and 1910. Intermarriage among Flemings, always less than among Bretons, virtually disappeared. The new calculations and sensibilities surrounding marriage which these data reflect also brought a new openness to concubinage arrangements. In the decade before World War I, the cable workers, male and female, were as likely as fitters, mechanics, carpenters, seamstresses, and laundresses to be parents of recognized, illegitimate infants. Concubinage was indubitably a working-class variant on family life, and there could be no more certain a demonstration of the abandonment of village culture for working-class norms than the increasing practice of concubinage among the factory population.

The religious faith—or conformity—of rubber workers was surely under attack when their isolation broke down. Their attachment to Catholic rituals began its decline even before the Dreyfus Affair made anticlericalism the common coin of advanced republicans and socialists. In the twentieth century, the factory workers were only slightly more "conformist" than the skilled workers. Pockets of piety remained: a number of rubber workers had their children renew their communions year after year. This was a small sub-group, though. For the most part, cable workers now behaved much as other workers did. It is worth noting that this evolution in outlook followed not so much their proletarianization as their urbanization.

Such shifts in community structures and values could not have occurred without tensions, and some of these must have been experienced within the family as integenerational conflicts. Unfortunately, we possess very few documents on private life, but surely it was no accident that the local socialist press turned its attention to the working-class family at the turn of the century. Several issues lamented troubles between parents and children and proclaimed that "obedience ought to be based on love, not authority." In 1901, the paper reported the suicide of a twenty-year-old youth because of conflicts with his father. The concerns of the journal hint at the private manifestations of a major change in the workers' way of life.

Thus far, we have presented evidence of changes among cable workers that point in the direction of class formation: the building of a common understanding among wage-earners based on their common experience. The factory workers were also integrating themselves into the socio-economic order in a more individualistic way. Workers and their families took advantage of the few opportunities for social promotion that were accessible to them. The census of 1911 demonstrates quite clearly that the majority of sons (age fifteen or older) who resided with their parents were not condemned to occupy the very lowest rung on the social scale. The records of the Assistance-to-the-Aged Program show about the same pattern for children who no longer lived in Bezons. Many sons moved into the metal trades and other crafts requiring some skills. While these boys had certainly not escaped from the harsh conditions to which all workers were subjected, they did have an earning capacity at least a third higher than their unskilled fathers. This advance, small though it was, could require family sacrifices. The more skilled metal workers had to pass through a period of training which paid very little, and parents had to accept such earnings for a year or more. The vocational ambitions of some young Bezonnais were clear by 1894, when the municipal council of Argenteuil complained that too many youths from Bezons were attending its evening design classes. An enrollment list from 1899 shows 46 young apprentices from Bezons seeking to supplement their vocational instruction.

The ascension of nearly a fifth of the workers' sons into white collar positions is still more notable. Nine of the youths living in Bezons even managed to become accountant-bookkeepers (*comptables*). Acquiring the numerical skills, softer manners, and finer clothing needed for their positions could not have been easy and must have been accomplished with family support. These occupational ambitions were absent in the early

Table 1
Occupations of Children, Age 15 and Older,
of Day Laborers in Bezons (1911)

Children Residing with Parents

	Sons		Daughters	
Occupations	No.	%	No.	%
No occupation	5	5.4	3	4.8
Unskilled	28	30.4	40	64.5
Apprentice	8	8.7	1	1.6
Skilled & Semi-Skilled				
Metal	25	27.1		
Building	3	3.3		
Other	5	5.4	13	21.0
Sales or Clerical	18	19.6	5	8.1
	92	99.9	62	100.0

Children Not Residing in Bezons

	Sons		Daughters	
Occupations	No.	%	No.	%
No occupation	1	5.3	8	36.3
Unskilled	6	31.6	8	36.3
Apprentice	0		0	
Skilled & Semi-Skilled				
Metal	5	26.3		
Building	1	5.3		
Other	3	15.8	4	18.2
Sales and Clerical	3	15.8	2	9.1
	19	100.1	22	99.9

years of Rattier's plant. Though Bezons's population had doubled with the implantation of the factory, the municipality had been able to accommodate whatever increased demand for schooling there was in the original facilities. Many workers had put their children out to work at the age of 10 or 11 as cowherds for the many dairymen (*nourisseurs*) in the vicinity. Only when education became compulsory did schoolrooms become inadequate. By the twentieth century, the factory workers were supporting at least a small degree of upward mobility. The search for steady work at subsistence wages, which had first brought the laborers to Bezons, was no longer their sole concern.

How did integration into a urban, working-class culture affect the factory workers' political consciousness and their potential for collective protest? Were they able to act in solidarity with other wage earners or to confront public authorities and their employer with independent demands?

We can answer these questions affirmatively, but it is necessary to add that the factory laborers did not turn Bezons into a "workers' town," nor did they challenge the existing social, political, and economic order aggressively. However, this moderation was not the consequence of a lingering "village" culture; it was a matter of pragmatic adjustments to the political structures and managerial policies that necessarily shaped the workers' responses to public and work-related issues. Stopping short of militancy, the cable workers were still able to mobilize in support of parties and organizations that furthered their interests.

If strike initiatives were rare this was not because the workers were unskilled rural migrants, happy for any job at all and, thus, incapable of organizing protests. That might have been the case in the 1870s, but, as we have seen, the mentality of the workers had evolved significantly by the twentieth century. The S.I.T. workers' relatively high wages were surely one reason for the disinclination or inability to strike. They were earning as much as unskilled laborers in Paris and more than most in the immediate vicinity. As such, the cable workers were a sort of "privileged" minority, and the company could easily have found laborers to replace strikers. Moreover, the workers were dealing with a flexible management which sought to defuse rancorous situations. While the local socialist press excoriated the owners of metal firms for arbitrary dismissals, harassment of unionized workers, or speed-ups, they had nothing of this sort to say abut the managers of the S.I.T. Indeed, [manager] Vitte seems to have been exceptional in his willingness to hear grievances and avoid confrontations. For example, when the workers' leader, Roblot, died in 1902, his fellow laborers wanted the day off to attend his funeral. Most employers would doubtless have resisted any show of sympathy for a socialist leader, but Vitte agreed to release his workers in the late afternoon so they could be at the funeral—a civil one. Surely it was this flexibility which allowed Vitte to dominate the municipal council as well as curtail the potential for strikes.

Just as the factory workers resisted pressure to vote according to their employers' wishes, they were also unwilling to surrender their organizational independence. A decisive confrontation on this issue came in 1906. Early in that year, the S.I.T. directors in Paris decided to suppress the policy of giving bonuses to workers after filling a large contract. The laborers sent a delegation to the headquarters . . . and convinced the officers to reverse their decision. Impressed by the efficacy of organizing, the workers moved to unionize. By March there were at least 400 members, according to the Radical-Socialist press. Vitte saw this as a chance to establish a company union and consolidate his hold over workers' opinion. However, the newly formed union split under this pressure. A small company union was established, but most workers remained with the independent one. By 1910, the company union no longer existed, but the "red" union did (though we have no information on its size).

Clearly, the number or intensity of strikes would not be a full measure of the rubber workers' independence.

In the end, Bezons's factory proletarians reflected rather well the contours of workers' movements in the industrialized towns surrounding the capital. Laborers in other parts of the *banlieue* may have been more skilled, less recently integrated into a working-class culture, or faced with more intransigent employers, but their involvement with class institutions was not, on the whole, more sophisticated than that of the cable workers. In Saint-Denis, for example, the commune with the highest portion of wage-earners in France, municipal socialism was slow to develop deep roots. After an unexpected socialist victory in 1892, the city hall returned to the hands of Radicals until 1912. It was not until this year that social-ists captured Puteaux, a birthplace of the French automobile industry. In Argenteuil, the most industrialized city in the department of the Seine et Oise, the municipal council was dominated by Radical Socialists continu-ously until World War I. A socialist militant proclaimed in 1902 that only a fifth of the workers in Argenteuil had any idea what socialism was, and even this may have been an exaggeration. When the POSR ran its own list in the municipal election of 1904, it received only 150 votes. The spotty unionization of the S.I.T. workers was not very different from that of their more skilled neighbors. Mechanics, fitters, and assemblers had worked in Argenteuil since at least the 1850s, but they did not begin to organize until the turn of the century, the same period when a union appeared among the S.I.T. workers. Once begun, the progress of unioni-zation was not rapid. The syndicalist press noted in 1907 that Argenteuil had over 4000 wage-earners but hardly 150 union members; only 110 of the 900 metal workers were unionized at this time of expanding collective activity, and the building trades of the town were only beginning to organ-ize. It is true that metal workers did strike somewhat more frequently and intensively than the rubber laborers, but special circumstances explain this disparity. The mechanics of Argenteuil faced more aggressive employers, a dilution of skills, and changing hiring practices. Moreover, the wages of these metal workers were considerably below the earnings of their Parisian counterparts, and workers from the capital were instrumental in promoting strikes as a means of equalizing income. These special conditions did not exist to encourage work-stoppages among cable workers. Placed in the perspective of workers in the immediate region, the class activity of Bezons's factory proletarians does not seem especially underdeveloped. Within two generations they had evolved from peasants-in-the-factory into an industrial proletariat as "mature" as most in the region.

"Perhaps it was finally in the last third of the nineteenth century that a true proletariat came into being in France?" Jean-Marie Mayeur's rhe-torical question underscores the lack of spontaneity entailed in the complex social, economic, and psychological changes that had to occur before a "modern industrial labor force" emerged. Resistance to the factory was one of the strongest impulses among artisans and domestic workers. This meant that immigrants from the countryside regularly filled the unskilled positions in the factory. Whether they came willingly, as in Bezons, or reluctantly, as in Carmaux, these new laborers were far from participating in a working-class culture by the mere fact of industrial employment. Uprooted though they were from the village and cut off entirely from agricultural labor, the "peasants in a factory" showed a remarkable ability to reestablish the moral order of the milieu they had left behind. It took a generation of factory employment, rising material standards, and above all, contacts with thoroughly urbanized laborers to undermine the habits of rural immigrants. With the case of Bezons in mind, time-honored assumptions about the traumas, tensions, and dislocations entailed in the formation of a factory labor force ring false. A factory proletariat quietly materialized in this town.

The rubber and cable workers underwent a dual process of proletarianization: reduction to the status of rural wage-earners brought them to seek industrial employment; then, they eventually took on the features of an urban labor force. However, the consequence of this process was not a class-conscious militancy. Nor should we jump to the opposite conclusion, that with the loss of their traditional identities, these unskilled workers faced the industrial order in a state of hopelessness, demoralization, or inertia. Clearly, the reaction of Bezons's factory workers to proletarianization was characterized far more by adaptation and acculturation than by alienation. An idealized past or future had little place in their history.

Youth and History

JOHN R. GILLIS

Adolescence as a precise concept was one of the many social discoveries of the nineteenth century. John Gillis, in the following selection, details the reasons for the discovery of adolescence and the framework for life which it set. The definition of adolescence, a middle-class concern, relates closely to new attitudes toward children and toward the importance of education. It had a demographic base in the massive new numbers of young people, the product of previous population upheaval. The potentially looser framework of urban life, and the visibility of less inhibited sexual and other behavior among young working-class people, provided an impetus for this new interest. The middle class would use its heightened sensitivity to adolescence to try to discipline young people—not only its own young but workers whose activities increasingly fell into rigorous categories of juvenile delinquency. The discovery of adolescence, then, should not be confused with gains for actual adolescents; in many ways, Gillis suggests, the lot of actual youth had been freer before adolescence was invented. He stresses, particularly, changes in the role of leisure for young people, leading to more structured activities and away from the outlets of preindustrial society. These changes could affect even the broader society; the rise of sport, following from the new school experience, is a key example.

Was the new attitude toward adolescence a permanent feature of modernization or a brief reaction to the first impact of industrial life? The twentieth century has seen some relaxation of sexual strictures, certainly, and possibly a diminution of the concern with preparing adolescents to be men, apart from the world of women. And the numerical importance of adolescence declines steadily as the population becomes older. But adolescent rebellion has been a recurrent feature of twentieth-century life. Some of the confusions the developed about adolescence in nineteenth century are now visible for a slightly younger age group. The tendency of modern society to define groups by age and to encourage an age-stratified, even age-segregated, pattern of life seems unabated. So, it might be argued, is a tendency to see each stage of life as one in which distinctive controls and institutional structures are necessary. Evaluating the significance of adolescence in the modernization process and in the balance of advantages and disadvantages of modernization, continues to spark debate.

The failed revolutions of 1848 marked a turning point in the political history of youth, effectively terminating Europe's first period of student unrest and ending the independent role of the young within the working-class movements as well. Not until 1900 would youth again take to the public stage, and then in very different forms and in support of new causes. The traditions of radicalism and bohemianism survived to renew themselves in the socialist youth movements and the artistic avant-garde of the turn of the century, but at that point they were joined, and even overshadowed, by a new set of youth movements that tended to be focused on the narrower spectrum of youth we now call "adolescence." Not only were the new organizations younger in constituency, but their sense of fraternity was both more nationalistic and socially conservative. By 1900 the symbol of youth as a regenerative force was shifting from left to right, revealing the changed status of the young in European society.

In England we can detect this process beginning in the 1850s, starting with the upper and middle classes and then gradually trickling down to the lower orders. During the Crimean War one of the traditional festivals of Misrule, Guy Fawkes Night, became the occasion for outbursts of patriotic venom. The effigy of Czar Nicholas replaced that of Guy on the November bonfires, and although such substitutions were not new—Napoleon, too, had been burned at the beginning of the century—the accompanying enthusiasm for juvenile marching and drilling in the name of Queen and Country was unprecedented. . . .

In England, traditional dancing, mumming, and hunt festivals had been in decline since the 1850s. Manning found that by 1900 not only were the occasions once presided over by young men and women being abandoned to children of a much younger age, but that the class composition of the participants was also changing. This was true of the First of May in Oxford itself, where the crowning of a king and queen, once entered into by youth of all social ranks, had become the rite of the very lowest of youths, the poor chimney sweeps, who managed to keep the tradition only with difficulty in the face of harassment by city officials. The profane version of the hymns sung on May Morning from the top of the Magdalen College tower had long since been expurgated, making the whole occasion more the quaint tourist attraction it is today than the boisterous revel it had been earlier in the nineteenth century. Festivals like the Whit Hunt in Oxfordshire's Wychwood Forest were also a thing of the past, perpetuated at the turn of the century by gypsies and other "undesirables," but no longer respectable as far as the mass of the rural population was concerned. Morris dancing and the mumming associated with it had fallen into such decline that it took the attentions of urban

From John R. Gillis, *Youth and History* (New York: Academic Press, 1974), pp. 95–118.

folklorists to revive them. From photographs taken in the 1860s, Percy Manning had been able to identify two former dancers, whom he encouraged to teach songs and steps to younger men. But even Manning's desire for authenticity was not strong enough to displace his Victorian sense of decorum and when his dancers made their first appearance in Oxford in 1899, not only were their lyrics clean of the good-humored profanity, but the antics of the traditional Lord of Misrule were missing.

The tendency for youth to lose its autonomy and become an instrument of adult interests was resisted most strongly among the laboring poor. Yet, by 1900, traditions of Misrule were dying in the better sorts of working-class neighborhoods, revealing changes there that paralleled what was happening to middle- and upper-class youth. Behind both the decline of the journeymen's movements and the disappearance of student radicalism lay deeper transformations that not only eased the demographic and economic strains that had been a cause of troubled youth earlier in the century, but altered the life-cycle itself in such a way as to bring forth new forms of fraternity in the place of old. Youth's loss of political and social independence reflected the fact that a significant segment of that life-phase, the adolescent years 14–18, was becoming increasingly dependent. While older youth retained much of its earlier autonomy, becoming even more identified with the status of adulthood, this younger age-group was losing access to the economy and society of adults as it became increasingly subject to parental and other institutional controls. The moral autonomy attributed to youth by earlier generations was giving way to new kinds of conformity associated with a more mindless kind of physical vitality. In turn, this was reflected in the public image of the young, changing from Delacroix's rebels on the barricades, youth at war with society, to the late-nineteenth-century recruiting posters, glorifying youth at war for their society.

The discovery of adolescence belonged essentially to the middle classes, the first group, apart from the aristocracy, to experience a drop in child mortality and the consequences this entailed. The nobility was able to absorb larger numbers of surviving children, because of both its greater wealth and the firm tradition of primogeniture that allocated subordinate roles to younger sons. The middle classes, particularly their professional elements, having no comparable resources and not wishing to penalize the last born, turned to family limitation as the only way to relieve their burden. Although the actuality of the two-child family was still some way off, the English middle classes, and other groups claimant to that social status, were beginning to adopt it as an ideal in the 1860s and 1870s as a means of bringing into line with their incomes the growing expense of raising and educating children. Among this group, the situation of the early nineteenth century, with its superfluity of sons and daughters, was thereby gradually ameliorated; and instead of each successive generation being larger than the next, each was now smaller among those groups practicing family limitation.

Family strategy had changed from one of high to one of low fertility, altering parental attitudes toward the children in the process. Increasingly, each individual child was treated (according to sex) without prejudice to his or her place in the birth order. "Give the boys a good education and a start in life," wrote J. E. Panton in 1889, "and provide the girls with £150 a year, either when they marry or at your own death, and you have done your duty by your children. The girls cannot starve on that income, and neither would they be prey of any fortune hunter; but no one has a right to bring children into the world in the ranks of the upper middle class and do less." The consuming concern that had previously been reserved for the very young child appears to have been extended to older youth as well, not simply out of sentimentality but with the realization that the investment in long, expensive education should be carefully planned and conscientiously protected, rather than left to chance as had so often been the case in the first half of the century.

One aspect of this new care and concern for older children was the longer period of dependence that youth was now subjected to. Girls of the middle classes were kept at home until marriage, tightly supervised by their parents until they passed safely into the bosom of another family. An interest in female education was growing in the second half of the nineteenth century, partly as a result of surplus young women for whom marriage did not beckon; but this was still suspect among a group who believed that "love of home, of children, and of domestic duties are the only passions they [women] feel." Boys had greater autonomy, but their careers were also being carefully supervised by the parents, who, recognizing the decline in traditional kinds of apprenticeship, were taking a much greater interest in secondary education. Even businessmen, for whom classical education had previously held little attraction, were increasingly concerned to gain for their sons the benefits of schooling to 16 or 17, even when they expected the lads to join theirs or some other business. James Templeton, master of the Mission House School in Exeter, told the English Schools Commission of 1868: "Instead of what I heard in my younger days, a parent saying, 'I have done very well in the world. I was only six or twelve months at school,' the acknowledgment of such a man will now be, 'I had no such advantages or opportunities in my early life; I should like my son to be something of an educated man, and to have far greater advantages than I have had.'" A similar trend was noticeable on the Continent, where the decline of apprenticeship was also the product of parental desires to see their children have not only the intellectual but the social benefits of elite schooling

The *Edinburgh Review* wrote in 1876 of an upper middle class which was "conscious that its retention of the advantages which it enjoys is still dependent on the mental activity by which they were gained; and keenly alive to the aesthetic and intellectual pleasures, the upper middle class seems the least likely of all to neglect its own educational concerns." The Schools Commission found them likely to keep their children in school the longest, to 18 or 19, and then to send them on to the university. But even the less well-to-do of the middle classes showed a similar concern, motivated by a desire to attain a similar privileged status. An ironmonger, Edmund Edmundson, testified in 1868 that because the traditions of apprenticeship had recently decayed, tradesmen's traditional prejudice against Latin education was diminishing. "The fact is, if a boy is not well educated he cannot keep his position in society. Society twenty years ago, as I recollect it, was a totally different thing to what it is now." The bias of the self-made man, never so strong to begin with on the Continent, was giving way all over Europe as the middle classes became increasingly dependent on the schools to guarantee a future for their progeny.

Smaller numbers of children encouraged longer coresidency, particularly on the Continent, where secondary education was organized around the day school. The growth of secondary education in the second half of the nineteenth century had made secondary schools locally available even in moderately-sized towns, making the need for boarding out while going to school much less prevalent than it had been earlier. Improved transportation facilitated the movement of pupils within urban areas where neighborhoods were not served by their own schools, and thus, by 1900, most French and German secondary students were living with their parents, leaving home only when they went on to the university or entered careers. Even in England, where the boarding tradition was continued and expanded during the second half of the century, longer vacations and better transportation were making contact between parents and their children much more frequent.

Whether a child was sent away to school or not, parents were assuming a much greater role in the supervision of the entire training process of each of their sons and daughters. German fathers were notorious for the strictness with which they oversaw their sons' training. They cloistered both boys and girls within the narrow confines of the home, allowing them only limited contact with the world outside, and then only for the purposes of formal training and education. The age of the partriarchal household, with its multiple economic and civil functions, was past by 1870, many of the prerogatives of the father having been usurped by factory, state, and school. Yet, the authority of the fathers persisted in what often seemed an outdated, tyrannical manner. Hans Heinrich Muchow has perceived a cultural lag operating in the fathers' slowness to adjust to the transition from the large multifunctional household to the small nuclear family unit: "Out of habit, he held onto the role, however, and thus pressed down on the nuclear family as a superfather [Übervater], especially on the growing children, who from the nursery onwards were subject to every impulse of their paternal master." Little wonder that the sons of the German middle class looked back on the earlier semi-dependent traditions of youth, especially the *Wanderjahr*, with a certain nostalgia. Trapped during their teen years between the tyranny of the home and the demands of the rigorous German academic school, the *Gymnasium*, they had lost contact with the sustaining force of the old peer-group structure and the autonomy which that represented.

In England, parental concern was no less intense or comprehensive, but, there, an alternative to fatherly tyranny offered itself. On the Continent, boarding schools and military academies remained the monopoly of the aristocracy, while in England this tradition was broadened to include a growing part of the middle class. The reform and expansion of the boarding (public) schools was a key instrument of the compromise between middle-class aspirations and aristocratic values that took place in the mid-Victorian period. The attractions to the social climbers were obvious: "In the great schools, which possess famous traditions, and in which the pupils come for the most part from the houses of gentlemen, there is a tone of manners and a sentiment of honour which goes far to neutralize the disadvantages of too early withdrawal from the shelter of home." For parents who were worried about sending their children away at an age that demanded care and protection, there was the assurance that "the master in this case stands in the parent's place, and to do his work properly ought to be clothed with all the parent's authority." Whether a boy remained at home for his schooling or was sent away to a boarding institution was obviously less important to the European middle classes than were the social controls associated with that education. The universal result was a state of dependence longer than that experienced by the previous generation: in effect, the creation of a new stage of life corresponding to what we now call "adolescence.". . .

Low mortality and low fertility made adolescence possible, but the real crucible of the age-group's social and psychological qualities was the elite secondary school. In England, the invention of adolescence was the unintended product of the reform of the public schools, whose beginnings are usually associated with the era of Thomas Arnold's tenure as headmaster at Rugby, 1827–1839. Arnold and the other reformers of his generation were the products of that earlier era of troubled youth, whose own training had been precocious and who themselves had known nothing like the adolescent stage of life that was to ensue from their reforms. . . .

Arnold proclaimed his calling as educator to be that of the keeper of the whole person: "He must adjust the respective claims of bodily and mental exercise, of different kinds of intellectual labour; he must consider every part of his pupil's nature, physical, intellectual, and moral; regarding the cultivation of the last, however, as paramount to that of either of the others." Arnold wished to turn out young men characterized by intellectual toughness, moral earnestness, and deep spiritual conviction. The feelings he wished to develop were not those of childish emotion but noble idealism. His own upbringing accustomed him to thinking in terms of precocious behavior and when he asked himself the question "Can the change from childhood to manhood be hastened in the case of boys and young men without exhausting prematurely the faculties either of body or mind?" his answer was staunchly affirmative. The object of a Rugby education was, he wrote, "if possible to form Christian men, for Christian boys I can scarcely make."

The philosophy of "boys will be boys" had no place in Arnold's world, one still so close to the conditions that encouraged precocity among the young earlier in the century. "If the change from childhood to manhood can be hastened safely, it ought to be hastened; and it is a sin in everyone not to hasten it," remained his educational philosophy to the end. As an admirer of tradition, Arnold did not attempt to destroy the structure of peer group. Instead, he turned the traditional hegemony of the older over the younger boys to his own advantage, purging the prefectorial system and the fagging of their violence, modifying both to fit the new, more paternal discipline of the schools. It will be remembered that in the early-nineteenth-century school, boys had virtually governed themselves, controlling their members through group pressure that tolerated an excess of bullying. When masters tampered with these rights of self-rule, they did so at their own risk, often provoking the kind of rebellion that was a frequent event in school histories throughout the first half of the nineteenth century. Nineteenth-century schoolmasters were infamous for their use of the whip, and reign by corporal punishment certainly did not end with the beginnings of reform. Nevertheless, the relationship between students and masters was both milder and more intimate. Repressive force was reduced by a system of almost fatherly supervision, aimed at preventing abuses rather than punishing them. And so it could be reported in 1864 that "the relationship between Masters and boys is closer and more friendly than it used to be. . . . Flogging, which twenty years ago was resorted to as a matter of course for the most trifling offenses, is now in general used sparingly, and applied only to serious ones. More attention is paid to religious teaching . . . and more reliance is placed on a sense of duty.". . .

Sport was taking over many of the functions of the rite of passage once reserved to Latin language study, for it, too, ensured the separation of boys from the world of women during the critical transition from childhood to adulthood. There was an important social change involved in this substitution, however. The model of the earlier Latin school was the monastery; the ideal of the public school was increasingly military. Women were to be avoided by adolescents because femininity was now associated with weakness, emotion, and unreliability. So strong was the avoidance of female traits by 1860 that men no longer dared embrace in public and tears were shed only in private. A whole series of male clubs sprang up to shield men from women. Some, like the Young Men's Christian Association, founded in 1844, drew their inspiration from the temperate evangelical fellowships of the late eighteenth and early nineteenth centuries; but, for the upper classes it was more likely to be hard-drinking, hard-riding organizations that attracted them. Despite their Victorian exteriors, these upperclass fraternal groups tended to uphold a double standard with respect to social morality, including sexuality. As males, they reserved for themselves the right of access to drink, gambling, and prostitution, rationalizing these things as "natural" to men and "unnatural" to women.

"God made man in His image, not in an imaginatory Virgin Mary's image," explained Charles Kinglsey, one of the so-called "muscular Christians" for whom traits of sensitivity or domesticity in a man were a kind of sin against nature and society. And, of course, what could better preserve the differences between the sexes than the military?—thus a partial explanation for the popularity of the rifle clubs and cadet corps in the second half of the century. Here male and national chauvinism blended neatly in a spartan model of boyhood that permitted no deviation. Boys who did not play the game or march in step were looked upon as misfits. Uniforms, whether athletic or military, underlined the growing intolerance of individuality that characterized late-nineteenth-century schooling in both England and Germany. Max Weber, looking back on the enormous impact of student fraternities on German life, wrote of the false understanding of freedom that these engendered:

> The "academic freedom" of dueling, drinking, and class cutting stems from a time when other kinds of freedom did not exist in Germany and when only the stratum of literati and candidates for office was privileged in such liberties. The inroad, however, which these conventions have made upon the bearing of the "academically certified man" of Germany cannot be eliminated even today.

He praised the English for educating their sons to a broader definition of rights, but he might well have listened to those in England who warned of the trend toward mindless conformity that was the product of the philosophy, "boys will be boys." To George Trevelyan the results were clear:

> What else can be expected, when a young man at the age his grandfather was fighting in the Peninsula or preparing to stand for a borough, is still

hanging on at school, with his mind half taken up with Latin verses, and the other half divided between his score in the cricket field and his score at the pastry-cook's?

Increasing concern with the physical elements of boyhood brought parents and educators face to face with sexuality, the taboo subject of the earlier generation. By the 1870s the subject of "puberty" was being discussed openly in both medical books and parents' manuals; and a decade later, even the conservative Oxford Clerical Association declared for "frankness" in the catechising of its young confirmees. Recognition of the sexuality of adolescence did not mean, however, a liberalization of Victorian attitudes. On the contrary, the tendency of writers was to blame parents for being too careless, allowing their sons to pick up bad habits from both peers and servants. Warned Elizabeth Blackwell: "The physical growth of youth, the new powers, the various symptoms which make the transition from childhood into young man- and womanhood are often alarming to the individual. Yet this important period of life is entered upon, strange to say, as a general rule, without parental guidance." If parents could not deal with it, then other institutions would. The cloistered sex-segregated schools were the best guarantee against sexual deviation, but Dr. William Acton also praised the efforts of the Young Men's Christian Association and the Volunteer Movement to impose continence: "I am convinced that much of the incontinence of the present day could be avoided by finding amusement, instruction, and recreation for the young men of large towns."

Contemporaries recognized that the high age of marriage among the middle classes (29.9 years for English professional males in the period 1840–1870) represented an enormous challenge to supervision and control, not just of relations with the opposite sex but of those between boys and boys. It was admitted by Acton and others that "a schoolmaster should be alive to the excessive danger of platonic attachments that sometimes become fashionable in a school, especially between boys of very different ages." As Robert Graves was to experience later, social attributes that were normal in the outside world were forfeited in favor of loyalty to the male group. Boys were forced even to abandon normal sex roles. "In English preparatory and public schools romance is necessarily homosexual," Graves noted. "The opposite sex is despised and treated as something obscene. . . . For every one born homosexual, at least ten permanent pseudo-homosexuals were made by the public school system; nine of these ten as honourable chaste and sentimental as I was."

For most, the regression to this form of innocent affection was but a temporary detour on the way to adult heterosexuality. Headmaster G. H. Rendall was probably accurate in his assessment that "my boys are amorous, but seldom erotic." Yet, while it is unclear whether the schools produced more than their share of adult homosexuals, almost complete isolation from the opposite sex had the effect of transforming the facts of genitality into a forbidden secret world, exposure to which had a traumatic effect on young asexuals like Graves. Confrontation with the effects of puberty was more unexpected and, therefore, more traumatic than today. At 17 Graves had his first real introduction to love play: "An Irish girl staying at the same pension made love to me in a way that, I see now, was really very sweet. It frightened me so much, I could have killed her."

Headmasters looked upon the peer group as a means of controlling sexual delinquency, both because it was the least expensive way of extending their own control and because they, like Arnold, sensed the power of "public opinion" among the boys themselves. Problems arose from the fact that group pressures became so strongly organized that any kind of individualism was immediately taken as a sign of sexual vice. A sure sign of "self abuse" (masturbation) was physical weakness: "Muscles underdeveloped, the eye is sunken and heavy, the complexion is sallow and pasty, or covered with spots of acne, the hands are damp and cold, the skin moist." How many innocents undergoing the physical change associated with adolescence, a growth spurt that was now coming earlier and more rapidly among the middle classes, must have been terrified by these symptoms of normal development? But even more telling was any failure to play the game or to march in step with the group, a sure sign of secret sin.

> The boy shuns the society of others, creeps about alone, joins with repugnance in the amusements of his schoolfellows. He cannot look anyone in the face, and becomes careless in dress and uncleanly in person. His intellect becomes sluggish and enfeebled, and if his evil habits are persisted in he may end in become a drivelling idiot or a peevish valetudinarian.

Thus, what were historically-evolved social norms of a particular class became enshrined in medical and psychological literature as the "natural" attributes of adolescence. The transmutation, through institutional imperatives, of social values into natural laws suited the new materialist outlook of the middle classes in the second half of the nineteenth century. One of William Acton's correspondents, writing to him concerning ways of convincing the younger generation of the dangers of incontinence, expressed the universal desire to find in science a new legitimation of old social controls: "It would be the greatest encouragement to know that physical science confirms the dictates of revelation." Conformity, self-denial, and dependence—all essentially functions of the kind of upbringing that was peculiar to a particular class—had become positivistic standards of human behavior by which an upper class could assure itself of its inherent superiority to the lower orders. The fact that children of the working class were independent and resistant to institutional controls was now proof of their inferiority.

However pleased the middle classes were with their invention, they were also aware of its difficulties, particularly the emotional deficits that arose out of so much investment in the artificial world of the school. "Left entirely to themselves they [adolescents] tend to disorder and triviality, and controlled too much by adults they tend to lose zest and spontaneity," wrote G. Stanley Hall. His conclusions were not unlike those

Stephen Spender arrived at some 50 years later, when, reviewing English adolescence, he wrote that the schools taught "boys to take themselves seriously as functions of an institution, before they take themselves seriously as persons or individuals." England's schoolboys possessed a composure and polish that surprised and delighted most foreign visitors, but beneath this surface lay considerable turmoil and self-doubt, the product of an education that gave little attention to personality and emotional development. Robert Graves, who was particularly sensitive to this deficit in his own training, wrote of how the total institution was arranged, so that boys came to view themselves as possessed of no personal rights as such, but only of statuses granted to them as privileges. "A new boy had no privileges at all; a boy in his second term might wear a knitted tie instead of a plain one; and a boy in his second year might wear coloured socks." A sturdy individualist like Graves was able to subvert the rules of Charterhouse School and develop a personal identity apart from its hierarchy, but most of his fellow students were not so fortunate. "School life becomes reality, and home life the illusion"; and boys whose whole lives had been built around team sports and fraternity life were naturally insecure in the company of the opposite sex. Moving on to university, the army, or the professions—all still exclusively male institutions—it was understandable that they should seek to allay their anxiety about this aspect of adulthood by perpetuating schoolboy comradery well past their own years of adolescence.

The most famous fictional schoolboy of the mid-century, Tom Brown, had been eager to get on with life. "If I can't be at Rugby, I want to be at work in the world, and not dawdling away three years at Oxford," he told his tutor. But in the end he accepted advice of the kind that was to become conventional by 1900: "Don't be in a hurry about finding your work in the world for yourself. You are not old enough to judge for yourself yet, but just look about you in the place you find yourself in, and try to make things a little better and honester there." The gap between Arnold's generation and that of the schoolmasters who followed them can be measured here. David Newsome has summarized it best: "The worst educational feature of the earlier ideal was the tendency to make boys into men too soon, the worst feature of the other, paradoxically, was that in its efforts to achieve manliness by stressing the cardinal importance of playing games, it fell into the opposite error of failing to make boys into men at all."

By century's end, schoolmasters all over Europe could congratulate themselves on the good order of their pupils. Never had the schoolboy been so at peace with the world, so accepting of his social deprivation, so apathetic toward his civil status. Although young fools might still play their pranks on a November night or dance on May mornings, middle-class boys did not ordinarily don the masks of Misrule except in a patriotic or conservative cause. Yet, beneath this surface calm many thought they detected an inner storm. The association of emotional turmoil with transition from childhood, which can be traced back at least to the writings of

Rousseau, had by 1900 found a prominent place in medical and psychological literature. The image of the schoolboy had shifted from trouble-maker to troubled, particularly in Germany, where the relationship of the school to the home only increased the problems of prolonged dependence.

The day-*Gymnasium* lacked those features of a total institution which distinguished the English public school. In Germany, the middle-class family retained control of social learning, the school monopolized intellectual training, and both civic and sexual education were left at dispute between them. This uneasy allocation was the subject of increasing controversy at century's end. The demographic and economic situation of the German bourgeoisie was much like that of its English counterpart, except that it placed greater emphasis on academic success because of the greater prestige conferred on formal educational attainment in that society. There appears to have been the same growing pressure on adolescents to meet parental expectations and thus justify the growing investment in education. In contrast to the English public school, however, the German *Gymnasium* was less well-equipped to deal with the phenomenon of "boyhood" that this produced. Lacking the characteristics of a total institution, it had greater difficulty in shaping youth to conform to its elite goals. There were no sports or extracurricular activities to cope with the social and emotional side-effects of prolonged dependence; and thus the school appeared to many of its inmates as an arid brain-factory, unable to meet the needs of the young. A rash of student suicides in the 1890s caused Ludwig Gurlitt to ask: "Can there by any graver charge against a school system than these frequent student suicides? Is it not grisly and horrible if a child voluntarily renounces seeing the light of the sun, voluntarily separates himself from his parents and brothers and sisters, from all the joys, hopes, and desires of his young life, because he doubts himself and no longer can bear the compulsions of school?"

The family, on the other hand, was organized in an authoritarian way around its own private affairs and was also poorly equipped to deal with the larger tasks of youthful development. Sexual learning remained in a kind of no-man's land, attended to by neither parents nor schoolmasters, despite the growing anxiety about the onset of puberty. Deprived of youth's traditional agency of sexual education, the peer group, German middle-class boys and girls found their stage of dependency an extraordinarily lonely, disturbing experience. By 1900 this social experience was translating itself into literary expression, with the novels of Thomas Mann, Hermann Hesse, and Robert Musil exploring the inner turmoil of adolescence. Similar concerns were reflected in the work of the German and Austrian psychological schools, including, of course, Freud and his followers. And their definition of the "problematic" character of adolescence was then influencing views in both England and the United States, particularly in the latter, where G. Stanley Hall published his massive *Adolescence, Its Psychology and Its Relation to Physiology, Anthropology, Sociology, Sex, Crime, Religion, and Education* in 1904. Adolescence, wrote Hall, was one of the most important blessings that civilization had bestowed; and yet its promise was also its danger. A stage of life withdrawn from adult pursuits was desirable, but it also exposed the young to idleness and depravity. "Modern life is hard, and in many respects increasingly so, on youth. Home, school, church, fail to recognize its nature and needs and, perhaps most of all, its perils."

PART 4

The Twentieth Century
1918–Present

For one week in 1933, the Granada Cinema in London was entirely staffed by women because its managers had noted most suggestions came from women.

The Twentieth Century

Analysis of European society in the past 70 years must handle two themes. In the first place, a number of vital developments were rather specific to Europe—including the rise of major political movements like Nazism and communism that had few echoes on our side of the Atlantic. After 1945, Europe underwent something of a revival in which it began to surpass the United States in certain ways, including economic performance. Specifically European history, then, dictates that we be attentive to important currents that touched on and drew from ordinary people. At the same time, modernization continued in Europe. Even Nazism, when its adherents gained power, continued the concentration of economic organization and increased the process of social mobility—both measures of modernization. Recent European history illustrates the modern as well as the European theme; an understanding of contemporary Europe must include both themes.

Contemporary Europe began to emerge from the strictures of its past during the horror of the First World War. The war severely damaged Europe's morale. Staggering death tolls distorted the population structure. Economic dislocations induced, or at least intensified, two decades of economic insecurity, culminating in the Great Depression. The war set other disturbing trends in motion. For example, Great Britain's crime rates in the early 1920s began to rise and have continued to mount to the present day, although they have not reached the levels of the late eighteenth century. It is not hard to portray twentieth-century European history in gloomy terms, compared with the nineteenth century. Certainly any history that focuses on the two decades between the world wars must stress the extreme social and political chaos that prevailed throughout most of the continent.

Europe's recovery after World War II showed a continuation of some earlier features of modernization. In certain ways, countries like France were able to realize older goals, like intense productive work, more fully than they had before the war. Europe contrasted interestingly with the United States, where concern about work values increased by the 1970s. However, European modernization also developed some new features. As in the United States, the role of women changed markedly. Attitudes concerning health and medicine showed new features, resulting among other things in a novel approach toward death. In these respects, and also as regards leisure behavior, Europeans moved farther away from nineteenth-century patterns than Americans did.

Some observers believe that the whole society that has emerged since the 1940s is radically new; they call it "postindustrial" or "postmodern." Has the basic process of modernization given way to some new set of values and institutions? The modernization process is probably still continuing, despite admittedly great changes in many areas ranging from technology to the world's diplomatic structure. But the question deserves serious consideration, particularly with regard to the lives and outlooks of the major segments of European society. The status of the family, for example, suggests that, although nineteenth-century patterns differed from traditional ones (as in the "modernization" of childhood), today's society is heading in a different direction. In general, the increasingly common references to "postindustrial" society raise the question of whether we have entered a new period *within* the modernization process or whether we are developing, so soon after modernization began, yet another social framework.

It is certain that Europe continues to change rapidly and that, within a recognizably common range, its developing blend of the old and the new differs, in some cases, from other advanced industrial countries. Compared with the United States, Europe is less violent. European family life is more stable, despite important changes in family values. At the same time, Europeans express less religious belief and engage less commonly in religious practice. Politics in Europe tends toward greater diversity and extremes. The possibilities for social mobility in Europe and the United States are approximately equal, but because Europeans tend less to emphasize it, European society at least appears to be more stratified. Similarly, the position of women may seem more rigidly controlled (in some countries it is demonstrably inferior in law); but how great are the real differences between Europe and the United States in this area?

It is not easy to determine major trends in the very recent past, and the essays that follow cover only a few of many possible topics. We do, however, have something of a head start in interpreting key features in the development of contemporary European society. We know some of the basic responses to earlier modernization. We can compare recent patterns with these responses to see if ordinary Europeans are reinforcing values established earlier or creating new ones. We can even try to assess the strengths and weaknesses of the society Europeans have developed.

BIBLIOGRAPHY

Most of the many studies of Nazism deal purely with the movement itself. Alan L. Bullock, *Hitler, a Study in Tyranny,* rev. ed. (New York, 1964), well exceeds the confines of biography and is an excellent survey. Karl D. Bracher, *The German Dictatorship: The Origins, Structure and Effects of National Socialism,* trans. Jean Steinberg (New York, 1970), deals extensively with the bases of Nazi strength. Ernst Nolte, *The Three Faces of Fascism* (New York, 1966), is an ambitious interpretation, but is written mainly from the standpoint of intellectual history. A valuable specific study of Nazism's causes and impact in a small German town is W. L. Allen, *The Nazi Seizure of Power* (Chicago, 1955). See also Herman Lebovics, *Social Conservatism and the Middle Classes in Germany* (Princeton, 1969), Peter Pulzer, *Anti-Semitism in Germany and Austria* (New York, 1964), and Jürgen Kocka, *White Collar Workers in America 1890-1940: Political History in International Perspective* (Beverly Hills, 1980). For recent interpretations of the effect of Nazism on German society, see Ralf Dahrandorf, *Society and Democracy in Germany* (New York, 1969), and David Schoenbaum, *Hitler's Social Revolution* (New York, 1968). Hannah Arendt, *The Origins of Totalitarianism* (New York,

1973) is an important interpretive statement.

Seymour Lipset, *Political Man, the Social Bases of Politics* (New York, 1959), studies the variety of modern political attitudes from a liberal viewpoint. John E. Goldthorpe et al., *The Affluent Worker: Political Attitudes and Behavior* (New York, 1968), based on data from a detailed study of the British working class, offers important interpretations of workers' political values. On French communism, see Robert Wohl, *French Communism in the Making* (Stanford, 1966); on recent changes in communism, see George Schwab, ed., *Eurocommunism* (Westport, Conn., 1981).

Probably the most sensitive study of modern women, with careful attention to historical background, is Simone de Beauvoir, *The Second Sex*, trans. H. M. Parshley (New York, 1953). See also Betty Friedan, *The Feminine Mystique* (New York, 1953). A vigorous survey is Evelyne Sullerot, *Woman, Society and Change* (New York, 1971); see also R. Patai, *Women in the Modern World* (New York, 1967); Patricia Branca, *Women in Europe since 1750* (London, 1978); and S. B. Kameran and A. J. Kahn, eds., *Family Policy: Government and Families in Fourteen Countries* (New York, 1978).

On the twentieth-century family, Colin Rosser and Christopher Harris, *The Family and Social Change* (New York, 1965), is an excellent detailed survey based on a study of a Welsh city. See also P. Willmott and M. Young, *Family and Class in a London Suburb* (New York, 1960). Michael Anderson, *Family Structure in Nineteenth-Century Lancashire* (New York, 1971), offers valuable background material. Richard Sennett, *Families Against the City* (Cambridge, Mass., 1970), based on a study of a Chicago neighborhood, is a pessimistic view of modern family trends that deserves comparison with the European studies. J. H. Goldthorpe et al., *The Affluent Worker in the Class Structure* (New York, 1969), specifically contests Ferdynand Zweig's thesis of growing working-class contentment, but the study barely touches on family relationships. An important thesis, derived from France, is J. Donzelot, *The Policing of Families* (New York, 1979); this book echoes the arguments presented in the Lasch selection, though with even greater pessimism about the autonomy of the contemporary family.

New work and leisure behaviors are discussed in Stanley Hoffmann, ed., *In Search of France* (Cambridge, Mass., 1963) and John Ardagh, *The New French Revolution* (New York, 1969). Michael Young and Peter Willmott, *The Symmetrical Family* (London, 1976), focus on work values while offering an important theory on the contemporary family's place in modern history.

Studies of the modern history of death include John McManners, *Death and the Enlightenment* (Oxford, 1981); David E. Stannard, *The Puritan Way of Death* (New York, 1977) and *Death in America* (Philadelphia, 1975). Related studies of health attitudes include Ivan Ilich, *Medical Nemesis: The Expropriation of Health* (New York, 1976) and René Dubos, *The Mirage of Health* (New York, 1959).

Nazism and the Lower Middle Class

HEINRICH AUGUST WINKLER

The rise of Nazism in Germany, and of similar movements in other countries, is the outstanding characteristic of the two decades between the world wars. How could such a movement take shape and win substantial support? Social scientists have developed a number of approaches to deal with the phenomenon. Some see Nazism and other totalitarian movements as endemic to the condition of modern man. Robbed of traditional values (such as religion) and close community ties, modern man stands alone and fearful; he easily yields to the solidarity and discipline of movements such as Nazism. Others view Nazism as a specifically German phenomenon, seeking in the German past an acceptance of authority and militarism. Still others emphasize more temporary factors, maintaining that Nazism was the product of a massive and unexpected defeat in war and of a variety of severe economic pressures, all of which had much greater impact in Germany than elsewhere. Even amid unprecedented social and political stress, Nazism did not really gain popularity until the Great Depression.

Interpretation of support for Nazism is further complicated by the sheer opportunism of the movement, which tried to appeal to almost all groups and was quite capable of switching stands to win support. Relatedly, the reasons Nazism won popularity differ considerably from the results of Nazism in practice. No one has yet clearly assessed the extent to which Nazi anti-Semitism and aggressive nationalism won support; all we know for sure is that these ideologies did not deter the Nazi voters. But Nazism's promises of support for farmers and small business, its suggestion of a return to a more traditional Germany, were directly contradicted by the actions of the regime once it gained power. It has even been argued that, horrible though it was, the Nazis ultimately helped make Germany more genuinely modern and therefore less susceptible to similar movements after Nazism itself was defeated in war.

The following selection points to the conditions and outlook of small businessmen as a crucial ingredient in the growing popularity of Nazism after 1930. It also stresses a larger social context in Germany, in which a modern economy had arisen without destroying key ingredients of a premodern social structure that included a powerful traditional aristocracy. Some historians would accept this kind of social analysis as part of the explanation for Nazism, but would also look at less clearly social factors, such as the German national character and characteristic ideology. Some historians would also point to other social groups, along with the property-owning lower middle class, who contributed to Nazi success; rarely can a major political movement be explained solely in terms of one-class adherence.

Nevertheless, in seizing on the lower middle class Heinrich Winkler is dealing not only with a major ingredient of Nazism, but with an important social group in the larger modernization process. The industrial revolution initially expanded the ranks of small tradesmen. They displayed a distinct and rather conservative version of the larger middle-class ideology, including a vigorous desire to remain separate from the working class and working-class politics. Later industrialization attacked this same group via new business forms. A new lower middle class arose simultaneously, composed of clerks and salespeople who owned no property. These developments altered both the position and the attitudes of small businessmen in many countries. This aspect of modernization—creating a major social group and then attacking it—is being repeated in our own day as the position of factory workers is eroded in the advanced industrial societies of Western Europe and the United States. Consequently, the reactions of the traditional lower middle class—called *Mittelstand* in Germany—have a bearing on an understanding of modernization beyond the interwar years themselves.

Yet Winkler emerges with an ironic conclusion about the old lower middle class itself. Further development of the industrial economy, in part encouraged by the Nazis when they were in power, changed the situation of the small businessman and integrated him within modern society in new ways. Winkler's analysis—unlike some more foreboding analyses of German character which hint that the beast might still be lurking—suggests a literal repeat of Nazism is unlikely in Germany.

T he revolution of November 1918 forced the artisans and the retailers to reappraise their political options. No doubt, only a tiny minority of impoverished small businessmen felt sympathy with the revolution or supported it actively. For the bulk of the *Bürgerlich* population, the paramount interest was the restoration of law and order. Their organizations hence pleaded for the immediate election of a National Assembly. When the election took place, on January 19, 1919, most small businessmen voted for the left-wing liberal German Democratic party (DDP). The reason was obviously not a late conversion to the cause of liberalism but a tactical consideration. The DDP was the presumptive coalition partner of the Social Democrats; a strong liberal party was thus seen as the best guarantee against socialist experiments.

The vote for the DDP was the beginning of a long migration through the party system of the Weimar Republic—a migration from left to right. After years of social and political unrest, of revolutionary and counterrevolutionary assaults on the Republic, middle-class sympathies shifted in the Reichstag election of 1920 to Gustav Stresemann's German People's party (DVP), a right-wing liberal party with an originally monarchist

From Heinrich August Winkler, "From Social Protectionism to National Socialism: The German Small-Business Movement in Comparative Perspective," *The Journal of Modern History*, Vol. 48, No. 1 (March, 1976), pp. 7–18.

tendency. In May and December 1924, they turned to the extremely conservative and avowedly antidemocratic party, the German National People's party (DNVP). After the rampant inflation and the Rhineland crisis of 1923, and after renewed Communist insurrections and Hitler's Munich putsch, a majority of the middle-class voters were prepared to protest against the parliamentary system as such. The vote for the DNVP was an expression of political nostalgia. The middle classes were longing for the world of the *Obrigkeitsstaat*, the authoritarian system of the Empire.

The DDP lost popularity for the same reason which had made it so appealing in 1919: its alliance with the Social Democrats. For a brief time, the DDP appeared to be indispensable, but it soon became a political liability. The German People's party disappointed the small businessmen because of its undeniable dependence on powerful industrial circles. It did not serve as a bridge between the interests of small and big business. Neither the industrialists nor the artisans and shopkeepers realized that they needed each other politically. The DNVP, while more successful than the right-wing liberals in combining heterogeneous interests, also had dominant groups: the agrarians and certain exponents of heavy industry. Thus, after a brief flirtation, the craftsmen and shopkeepers who had identified themselves with the Nationalists became disillusioned once again. It was particularly artisans and landlords who turned, in the mid-twenties, to a pure interest-type party, the Business party (Wirtschaftspartei), which in 1925 was renamed the Reichspartei des deutschen Mittelstands.

The growing alienation between the small businessmen and the traditional nonsocialist parties has to be seen against the background of the process of industrial concentration which culminated in the second half of the 1920s. The more corporations extended their power, the more helpless the small-scale producers felt. Feeling squeezed between big business and big labor, many small businessmen voted for the Business party in order to protest against the political and economic system of postwar Germany. The Business party never polled more than 4.5 percent of the total vote (1928), but it was highly symptomatic of small business's disgust with political parties. By mobilizing resentment against parliamentary democracy, the Business party helped prepare the ground for the biggest mass movement of the 1930s, the National Socialists.

The Weimar party system continued to reflect the social segmentation so characteristic of the Empire. The logic of the parliamentary system called for social integration within the parties, but there was, in the last analysis, only one party which learned this lesson sufficiently well: Hitler's extremely antiparliamentary NSDAP. In the mid-twenties, however, it was by no means clear that this party would win massive middle-class support. The pseudosocialist rhetoric of the Nazis, especially strong in the formative years of the party, frightened off industrialists, small businessmen, and peasants. The combination of nationalism and socialism as it was proclaimed by Hitler's party was only attractive to white-collar workers, members of paramilitary leagues, and some intellectuals. For many years the *Bürgertum* took the Nazis—as a right-wing handicraft weekly in Hanover put it in 1924—for "bolshevik poison in a black-white-red wrapping."

The shift finally came in 1930. It took a basic change in Nazi propaganda and a panic, caused by the great economic depression, to bring about heavy *mittelständisch* support for Hitler's movement. As early as 1927, the Nazis had tried to shed their proletarian image and to woo leading industrialists in private and the lower middle classes in public. During the years of stabilization between 1924 and 1929 they were not very successful. After the outbreak of the economic crisis they intensified their efforts to win middle-class support. Their "socialism" was now interpreted as just another version of the party's slogan, "Service not self" (*Gemeinnutz vor Eigennutz*). As the small-business organization of the party, the Kampfbund des gewerblichen Mittelstandes, put it in December 1932, socialism meant the "deproletarianization of the German worker." "The purpose of the socialist idea is the creation of property for those who have none. This means that Adolf Hitler's socialism contrasts most sharply with the mendacious pseudosocialism of the Marxists which aims at the expropriation of the Proprietors."

The attraction of the Nazis for the lower middle classes—and it was these groups that provided the Nazis' strength in the elections—cannot be explained by a single element in the Nazi ideology. Neither their extreme nationalism nor their violent anti-Semitism accounts for the rise of the NSDAP after 1930. Both issues were, though in differing degree, traditional aspects of right-wing movements in Germany. My proposition is that the combination of two elements made the Nazis so appealing to the lower middle classes: first, their persistent adoption of the protectionist demands of the lower middle classes and, second, their readiness to eliminate radically all ideologies, institutions, and groups which the lower middle classes blamed for their miseries.

Thus, the craftsmen were promised compulsory guilds and obligatory masters' examinations, and the shopkeepers were attracted by the campaign against "Jewish" department stores. The peasants were told that they would become the "first estate" in the Third Reich and that the goal of autarky made it necessary to introduce higher tariffs for agricultural products. The civil servants, emotionally linked with the tradition of a strong authoritarian state and deeply embittered by Chancellor Brüning's deflationary policy of salary cutting, expected Hitler to restore law and order and to recognize their vested place in the social hierarchy. The white-collar workers were the group which was most afraid of proletarianization. As mentioned before, they had been treated as a special group, separated from the working class in German social security laws since 1911. In their majority, they regarded themselves as part of the *Bürgertum.* No political party appealed more convincingly to their status concerns than the Nazi party. No group was more impressed by the specific Nazi combination of leveling and hierarchy than the white-collar workers, who felt both resentment toward the old elites and superiority toward the *Proletarier.*

The promise to eliminate the enemies of the *Mittelstand* aimed not only at the Communists but at the specter of "Marxism" as a whole, including the trade unions and the Social Democratic party. Moreover, no party was more convincing when it came to promising the destruction of parliamentarism, political parties, and majority rule than the Nazis. The preservation of the existing social order and the liquidation of its political superstructure, which obviously no longer guaranteed the status quo, was the service the Nazis were expected to perform for the German middle class. It was this very same promise which motivated leading industrialists, particularly in the coal and iron sector, Prussian Junkers, and conservative politicians to support, directly or indirectly, Hitler's seizure of power. This was just as crucial a contribution to his final success on January 30, 1933 as the millions of votes for the Nazi party. The conservative Kartell still functioned in 1933.

Nazism and fascism have been described as an "extremism of the center." Lipset, who first formulated this proposition, maintains that mainly former voters of the liberal parties turned to the Nazis. This is true, but it should not be overlooked that most of these voters had already shifted to the conservative camp before they eventually supported the Nazi party. Though [the] strategy and tactics of the Nazis differed clearly from the traditional conservative right, their attacks were predominantly directed against the left. If there was a mass basis for right-wing extremism, it was the middle classes.

But fascism was not simply a form of middle-class extremism. (I should add, at this point, that I regard nazism as a Fascist movement, though its violent anti-Semitism was not shared by the Italian Fascists and is, in fact, not a "necessary" element of Fascist ideology.) Fascism, if I may use the generalizing term, has to be analyzed on three different levels, depending on whether its social basis, the expectations of the traditional power elites, or the strategic objectives of its leadership are being considered. Fascism cannot be adequately described by unveiling the economic interests of its social basis and of the groups which supported it either financially of through collaboration after the seizure of power. The Fascist power elite acted with remarkable independence. Its final goals were not economic ones. Its domestic alliances had only a tactical character. It wooed those social forces which were indispensable for the achievement of its final objectives: in the case of the Nazis, hegemonial expansion without discernible limitations, and an inexorable fight against the Jews—*Lebensraum* and *Lösung der Judenfrage.* Other interests were unhesitatingly subordinated to this particular "primacy of politics."

It is well known that, in the last analysis, the *Mittelstand* belonged to the dupes of the movement it had helped to bring into power. Some of the traditional demands of the craftsmen and shopkeepers, such as obligatory masters' examination, the compulsory guilds, and prohibitive measures in favor of the retail trade, were fulfilled. With regard to the surtax on the turnover in department stores and to other discriminations against large-scale retail business, the Nazis continued the small-business politics of the presidential governments of the early thirties. But the Nazis never began the promised destruction of department stores and postponed action on the abolition of the consumers' cooperatives until 1941. Both types of enterprises proved to be useful instruments in regulating the distribution of goods. But more importantly, during the first years of the Third Reich, a liquidation of the larger retail enterprises would have meant an unacceptable increase in unemployment. The corporatist order, of which the craftsmen were particularly in favor, never came into being. Bureaucracy as well as big business thwarted all plans that would have led to a new parastate hierarchy and to economic stagnation.

The few concessions to small-business interests which were actually achieved were due more to the pressure of the conservative allies of the Nazis than to the Nazi party itself. After the proclamation of the Four-Year Plan in 1936, it turned out that small business was not seen as particularly essential to the war effort. The economic weight of small business sank, handicrafts and retail trade were "combed out," the chambers of handicrafts as instruments of corporate self-administration were dissolved under the impact of total war, and Nazi propagandists blamed the *gewerblicher Mittelstand* for its notorious selfishness. When in 1941 the Reichsstand des deutschen Handwerks complained about the allegedly ruinous competition between the construction industry and the construction crafts, Heinrich Himmler, the *Reichsführer SS,* comforted the craftsmen by pointing to the social opportunities offered to them in the newly conquered territories in eastern Europe. No *Lebensraum* perspective, however, could compensate for the material losses of small business. A privileged position in the Third Reich was only available to those who were indispensable for rearmament and war. The *Mittelstand* did not belong in this category.

Social protectionism for small business was no German invention. Discriminatory measures against department stores were taken in other countries too. France was the first when she introduced a special tax on large retail turnover. Further interventions of that kind followed at the end of the nineteenth and the beginning of the twentieth century. Under the impact of the great Depression, a law was passed which made the expansion of certain types of large-scale retail business illegal. Belgium and Switzerland chose similar forms of protection for small retail business. Handicraft chambers exist not only in Germany but also in some other countries; France introduced that institution in 1925. Only the reestablished artisan guilds, the *Innungen*, with their roots in the Middle Ages, can be seen as a specifically German phenomenon.

It is certainly not the guilds, however, that account for the difference between the political behavior of the *gewerblicher Mittelstand* in Germany and that in other European countries. In Germany, social protectionism was an integral part of an authoritarian system of mutual social reinsurance. The protection of small businessmen was intended to promote their identification with the existing social and political order. This was generally a successful strategy. The bulk of the craftsmen and shopkeepers became interested, in the wake of social protectionism, in the preservation of a nonparliamentary authoritarian state which sheltered them against the danger of being outvoted by consumers and workers. Soon after the revolution of 1918, the Empire began to look to small business as paradise lost.

The antidemocratic tendency of the *gewerblicher Mittelstand* was a cause as well as a consequence of the longevity of the *ancien régime* in Germany. In countries with a long democratic tradition—and this means, in most cases, countries that had experienced a successful middle-class revolution—protest movements of small business did not take an openly antidemocratic or Fascist but rather a populist direction. This applies in particular to the movement around Pierre Poujade in France during the 1950s. The attacks of the Union de défense des commerçants et artisans centered on department stores, banks, corporations, and unions; they were directed against the economic and political establishment as a whole. At the same time, the Poujadists claimed to be the true heirs of the French Revolution of 1789. Poujadism was late-Jacobin radicalism, nostalgic and backward, but certainly not totalitarian, as were the Fascist movements of the interwar years. The petit bourgeois allegiance to the ideals of the Revolution has solid material roots. By enabling the wealthier peasants to buy land, the French Revolution had indirectly also strengthened small shopkeepers and craftsmen. There was no large "industrial reserve army," formed from a rural proletariat, which could have been absorbed by big industrial enterprises. The retardation and incompleteness of the Industrial Revolution meant the lasting predominance of small-scale production in France. Moreover, the Revolution had destroyed that social class which in Germany helped to form the antidemocratic *Mittelstandsbewegung:* the feudal aristocracy. It was, thus, the Revolution which in the last analysis determined the political development and the ideology of small business in France—a development and an ideology which clearly differed from those of the *gewerblicher Mittelstand* in Germany.

The development of small business in Britain and the United States was basically different, but at least in America some parallels to the French case exist. The classical countries of capitalism have produced political cultures which have not offered many opportunities for openly protectionist *Mittelstand* politics or for a protectionist *Mittelstand* movement after the German model. In England, small-scale entrepreneurs possess only a rudimentary interest organization. Consumers' cooperatives and department stores have drastically reduced the economic weight of shopkeepers and artisans, particularly in the food business. This had not led, however, to a Poujadist-style protest movement, and it is questionable whether one can speak at all of a political profile in connection with the small shopkeepers and artisans of England. In the United States, too, small business, of which craftsmen and retailers form only a small minority, is characterized by an organization lag. Interest groups for small-scale producers and retailers were not created on the national level until the 1940s; these, however, represent only a minority of small business. Small businessmen tend to identify themselves with independent entrepreneurs as against "anonymous" corporations. Small business distrusts "big business," "big government," and "big labor." It is antiurban and anti-intellectual, it is in favor of all that it takes to be originally "American," and it is against such "foreign ideologies" as socialism. American small business wants security in the face of the "unfair competition" from chain and department stores. It glorifies the virtues of "rugged individualism" and the American Revolution. Many parallels exist to the mentality of small business in continental Europe. In some states, there is strong pressure toward public regulation of interest fights between different professions (e.g., the recent clash between barbers and cosmeticians in Iowa) and a legal demarcation of their respective spheres of activity that looks almost like a *zünftlerisch* (guildlike) restriction of industrial freedom. Nevertheless, it seems that there are still signs of a common business ideology in the United States. At least until the 1930s, the National Association of Manufacturers epitomized a basic consensus among businessmen. Trust-busting belonged, of course, to the credo of the independent entrepreneurs, and the resentment against bigness still has its populist ring. It is important to note, however, that small business in America is basically antistatist. The German *Mittelstand*, by contrast, expected everything from the state and nothing from itself.

A disposition toward moral indignation at different value orientations, an inclination toward collective panic, a readiness to demonize all forces which threaten the traditional social order—these seem to be characteristics of the mentality of the lower middle classes. Such a mentality, however, is obviously not enough to bring about fascism. Fascist movements have come to power only in those societies which have never experienced a successful middle-class revolution, in societies where preindustrial power elites such as landed aristocracy, military, bureaucracy, and church have been able to preserve their privileges beyond the threshold of the Industrial Revolution and to exert decisive influence on the political behavior of other social groups. Not just capitalism alone, as vulgar Marxists assert, produced fascism; equally, if not more important, was a burdensome legacy of feudalism and absolutism.

Precapitalist forces worked together both with leading industrial groups and with the middle classes. In Germany, the Prussian Junkers, a class accustomed to governing, played a decisive role in the destruction of democracy. They were much more skillful than conservative industrialists in the mobilization of mass support for their political objectives, and they had, once Paul von Hindenburg had become president of the Reich, immediate access to the executive—a fact of crucial importance in the last weeks of the Weimar Republic.

The existence of powerful preindustrial groups seems to be a *sine qua non* for authoritarian or Fascist regimes. Wherever the business elite can resort, in times of crisis, to the political support of older social classes it is not forced to compromise with the rest of the middle class or with the workers. Obviously, different national conditions exist for the mobilization of the middle class as a mass basis for a Fascist movement. In Italy, the economically independent parts of the lower middle class prior to Mussolini's seizure of power were hardly organized. Owing to the retardation and defectiveness of the Industrial Revolution in Italy, small business had not yet experienced a real confrontation with big industry. In the early twenties, small shopkeepers supported the Fascists because they regarded them as determined allies in the battle against consumers' cooperatives and other "socialist" enterprises. The political influence of small business under the Fascist regime was as weak as it had been prior to 1922.

According to Rudolf Hilferding, the famous Social Democratic theorist, competitive capitalism was succeeded, at the turn of the century, by "organized capitalism." Hilferding aimed at replacing a competitive economy, operating within the framework of general conditions set by the state, with a highly concentrated and bureaucratized economy based on interest groups and propped up by permanent state intervention. The German bureaucratic tradition of a patriarchal social commitment was the main reason why the shift to "organized capitalism" took place earlier there than in most other countries. If, thus, "organized capitalism" has such obviously deep roots in German society, it is so much the truer for "organized precapitalism," as the regulated small business economy may be called by analogy. Whether with respect to industry or to handicraft and retail business, the state was expected to protect the economy against economic crises and their social consequences, regardless of the costs which consumers had to bear. The protection of small-business as practiced by the Empire became the basis of *Mittelstand* demands in the First German Republic. This was particularly true for the handicrafts, whose very organization had been made possible by Imperial laws. Price regulation through the guilds, already demanded prior to World War I, was a plank with which the parties and the governments of Weimar were confronted time and again. The artisans' argument was simple: if cartels were seen as a legitimate institution for big industry, why should they be unacceptable in the case of small business? The consideration of the vital interests of the consumers, which kept the Weimar governments from meeting such demands, was a permanent source of frustration for craftsmen and shopkeepers.

The experience of massive protection for small-business interests, granted by the patriarchal Empire as part of its quest for social stability, provided *one* condition of the growing *Mittelstand* support for an antiparliamentary movement such as the Nazi party. The social protectionism of the prerevolutionary regime had promoted the segmentation of German society. Ironically, it was the beneficiaries of that policy who assisted in a movement which finally, in the name of the *Volksgemeinschaft* and despite all previous promises to the *Mittelstand*, proceeded to abolish many of the corporate privileges so typical of the traditional social order. To be sure, many objections can be made to the proposition that the Nazi regime brought about a "social revolution." With regard to small business, however, it can hardly be denied that the abolition of protectionism, which was pushed through after the late thirties, has had a modernizing impact on that part of Germany's social fabric.

Modernization was certainly the very last objective of the National Socialists. And it was, in fact, their total collapse and not any positive action of their regime that caused a real break with Germany's social traditionalism. After World War II, the Allied occupation, and its assumption of supreme political responsibility, made the situation decisively different from that in 1918. In short, there was much less political, administrative, military, and social continuity after World War II than after World War I. The disappearance of the landed aristocracy of Prussia is a factor which can hardly be overestimated, and it remains the most striking break in the social as well as political sphere.

Small business, in the Federal Republic, has undergone tremendous structural change. It has used the chances which the economic reconstruction offered. The number of small-scale production enterprises has continuously decreased, whereas the number of employees per entrepreneurial unit has grown. The contribution of crafts to the gross domestic product is rather stable; it amounted to one-tenth in 1968 (one-twelfth in 1936). Small business has altogether a more stable structure today than in Weimar Germany, though parts of it are largely dependent on the decisions of the industrial concerns from which smaller entrepreneurs get their raw materials or for which they work on the basis of delivery contracts. A result of this relative stabilization is a decreasing exposure to political extremism.

The contribution which National Socialism made to the development of postwar Germany is thus predominantly an indirect one. It was its failure which destroyed many of the social, political, and ideological traditions that had helped bring it to power. In this sense, it seems safe to say that the Third Reich constitutes the most cynical and costly example of what Hegel called the cunning of reason.

Modern Politics:
The French Communists

ANNIE KRIEGEL

Politicization is one of the leading features of modernization. Before modernization, the common people had a political system of their own. Peasant assemblies, for example, were often lively gatherings, making decisions on a variety of issues important to the village. Peasants were aware of wider political relationships, notably those that bound them to a manorial lord. But peasant politics were highly personalized. Peasants lacked an ability to grapple with abstract issues, and there is no doubt that the attitude of the common people toward the central government was not politicized in the modern sense. Peasants and city dwellers might have expected the central government to do some things for them—help out in famines, for example. They had a loyalty to the traditional monarch, but they did not see government as something in which they could or should participate. When they rioted they did not do so to challenge a political structure that excluded them. Indeed, they often explicitly declared their allegiance to the king, even as he sent his troops against them, because they believed he was misled by bad advisers.

We have already seen stages of the transition to a modern political outlook. The nature of modern protest, as Charles Tilly sees it emerging in the mid-nineteenth century, was in large measure based on political demands. Socialism served as a vehicle for voicing political as well as economic grievances. Socialist politics became central to the lives of many workers, in Germany and elsewhere. Nazism was politicization of another sort, drawing some types of people into the political process for the first time. These examples alone show how complex politicization has been and how difficult it is to predict the results.

Furthermore, each nation has something of its own political style. In England, where the politicization of the lower classes began early (in the eighteenth century), the ultimate political movement of the workers has been rather moderate. France continues to fascinate because of an addiction to political extremes, and as the following selection suggests, tradition itself is one explanation for the existence of a powerful Communist movement.

Yet even within a single country, the complexity of politics as a phenomenon of modernization remains great. Politics is no neat expression of class. Not all French workers are Communists, nor are all Communists from the working class. If communism is primarily a factory movement, and therefore a rather new one in France, it touches bases also with the skilled elite of workers who have led working-class protest since the glory days of the French Revolution. Correspondingly, the poorest are not the leaders of Communist protest, which was also true in age-old protest tradition. In other words, the "politicization of protest," which has such a modern ring to it, should not conceal serious contact with attributes of nineteenth-century unrest or even preindustrial protest characteristics.

The nature of the protest commitment, along with the social base, requires assessment. Annie Kriegel, one of the leading analysts of the French labor movement, takes pains to discuss not only the different kinds of people but also the different degrees of commitment that go into French communism. The communist movement has been a major force in France for over fifty years. But how seriously is it an expression of worker interests? Is politicization really important to most workers, or is it just an overlay—however important to the political process itself—on traditional views, including a large dose of apathy? Given the number of nonworkers involved and the immensely important bureaucratic apparatus that is required to mobilize and channel any large groups of people, are workers indeed in control of the political movement that claims to express their sentiments? Here, the selection invites comparison with the earlier assessments of working-class attitudes and problems by Price and by Berlanstein. And finally, of course, has politicization made worker protest more effective? The workers whose votes swell the communist totals but whose commitment is lacking may well be wondering if the state can ever be made to serve their ends. The French communist movement, unusually strong in Western Europe from the 1930s until a recent apparent decline, is fascinating in itself. It also poses in a specific form some general questions about the nature of highly organized mass politics and the significance of mass political movements for the masses themselves.

My second observation has to do with the size of another category, that of the nonactive members [of the Communist party]. There is no heading marked "miscellaneous" in the statistics for 1966. We can only deduce from this that retired workers have been tabulated by their original occupations and "housewives" by their husbands' occupations. Since the over-sixty group (comprising a large number of retired people) amounts to 17.3 percent of the total membership, and since housewives represent 46 percent of all female members (25.5 percent of the total membership), we may assume that the sector which consists of those who are not part of the "active population" represents approximately 25 to 30 percent of the total membership. One member out of three or four is not or is no longer "in production."

These two observations correct the excessively flattering impression that the 1966 figures tend to give. But, having made these reservations, I should also point out that the French Communist party is really a party that springs from the *working-class world*—a designation that is perhaps

From Annie Kriegel, *The French Communists: Profile of a People*, trans. by Elaine Halperin (Chicago: The University of Chicago Press, 1972) pp. 72–178.

more precise than "workers' party." This of course does not mean that *all* French workers or even a majority of them are communists. On the other hand, even if one figures, for example, that 981 out of every 1,000 workers are not party members, this does not mean that the communist party is not a workers' party. It merely signifies that in France, as in other countries where social classes are averse to politics, only a small proportion of the working class is organized into a political party. The French Communist party as such is not noteworthy for its large proportion of factory workers—actually, the number of dues-paying communists in the Simca, Citroen, or even Renault [automobile] factories is incredibly small. Moreover, it should also be pointed out that the official party figures for the percentage of "workers" in its ranks are somewhat contrived since there are included under this heading many thousands of party functionaries who are *former* workers. Nevertheless, even if they are no longer "in production," these militants, some of whom have not been workers for at least five years, continue to be steeped in a working-class ambiance through their contacts with relatives, young people, and neighbors. . . .

Although at present the party unquestionably has a socially more diversified membership than it had in the past, it has nonetheless maintained solid ties with its working-clas nucleus. But it would be a mistake to believe that this happens naturally, spontaneously, or that a policy inspired by the interests of the industrial masses is enough to account for the continued existence of such ties. Constant vigilance and a variety of technical approaches are required to insure an adequate flow of new recruits.

Thus constant scrutiny accompanies the selection of candidates for the various communist schools and yields an accurate picture not only of the social composition of administrative bodies at all levels of the apparatus but also of the multiform institutions that enable the party to function in opposition to established society. Whenever necessary, the party does of course seek the help of qualified technicians, but directors or collaborators from the workers' world are assigned to these technicians—a system perfected by the Soviet republic during the early years of its existence.

The organizational measure most effective in preserving the preponderance of working-class people within the party was implemented in 1924–25. It is known as "Bolshevization." At that time the Communist International stipulated that all its sections must radically change the nature of their primary electoral districts upon which the party's structure was henceforward to be based. In the earlier type of socialist parties, the primary electoral district was the *commune*, the traditional scene of electoral battles; in the young "Bolshevized" communist parties, it was replaced by the factory, a privileged terrain "where the two basic classes confront one another."

> It is from the factory, the mine, the shipyard, the office, that the outcry arises which unites in a single struggle all those subject to capitalist rule and to man's exploitation of man. It is in the factory, the mine, the office, the shipyard that thousands and tens of thousands of workers are brought together by the capitalists. The factory is the nerve center of modern society, the very threshold of the class struggle. That is why for you, as communists, the factory should be the center of all your efforts, of all your activities.

This reorganization resulted in an impressive upheaval that constitutes a highly significant episode in the history of French communism. Moreover, this revolution in organizational procedures was remarkable for its durability. Despite winds and storms the principle is still respected and the regulations still observed.

But the winds and storms were violent ones. The structure of a profession (in the building industry, for example, where mobile work-teams are temporarily tied to the existence of a shipyard or some other place of work), the way working time was organized (with day and night shifts, or "brigades" replacing one another), the nature of the labor force (of relevance here was the practice of giving bus service to those who worked in textile mills, mines, and certain steel plants, to say nothing of the presence of large contingents of foreign, non-French-speaking workers)—all these caused endless complications. Only protracted experience could provide solutions to the problem of how to gather communist workers together in companies as complex as the railways or the merchant marine, or how to reach migrant agricultural workers who are employed only seasonally. In every instance there had to be some precise indication of the unit that constituted the "territory" of the cell: workshop, office, shipyard. All things considered, the problem that proved to be the most difficult and also the one that was the most inadequately resolved was invariably that of organizing the unemployed.

Without even taking into account the factors that naturally contribute to instability—restrictive actions by the employers, above all the mergers that forced the less adaptable plants to shut down, labor's growing mobility—one can easily understand why, given the circumstances, the factory cells turned out to be quite fragile. Occasionally the mere departure of a few militant propagandists sufficed to cause the cells' demise.

Subjective factors proved no less powerful. A good many militants in charge of the sale of *l'Humanité-dimanche* arrive at their posts each Sunday with remarkable punctuality. But they are most reluctant to draw attention at their places of work. "The sector," Pierre Sémard conceded, "is at some distance from the employers, from capitalism, but the cell is much closer." Concern for one's career—the humbler it is, the more precious it may seem; a recurring anxiety whenever the labor market shrinks or when advancing age lessens the chances of being reclassified; complications in time schedules wherever collective transportation is available only at the end of the day's work; preoccupation about output—these represent arguments that can be adduced against the pursuit of political activities in the shipyard or the factory. Such activities are not only quite unprotected by law; employers as well as most trade unions regard them with suspicion, sharing as they do a concern that is constant, equivocal, and characteristically French—a profound anxiety to make sure that the company does not become a political battlefield. . . .

Then there is another complication: factory cells, even in the "freest" sector, fail to attract representatives from all categories of workers. Although the party is largely indebted to the cells for its deep roots in the workers' movement generally, it is likewise indebted to them for its initial spread within one specific segment of the working class.

To regard the world of the factory as one that is entirely homogeneous and equal, without structure or hierarchy, is to hold a very superficial and false notion of the actual situation. On the contrary, the existence of hierarchies in the professions and trades, the conflicting ethnic and linguistic loyalties, the length of time people have lived in the city—all these create serious areas of friction. Yet the general image of the worker remains almost immutable: the typical proletarian continues to be thought of as a highly qualified French steelworker, or at least as someone born in France whose rural ancestry is already growing dim.

A Highly Qualified Steelworker: The professional competence of militant workers is well known. Apparently this is due not only to the moral qualities usually associated with skilled workers but also the actual historical circumstances that prevailed in France when trade unionism was at first a defensive reaction on the part of the best-educated journeymen in the old building and steel trades. The priority and predominance of skilled workers represent a fact that has obtained throughout our history. The reasons for this are complex, indeed so much so that the whole subject of the existence of a working-class aristocracy will require considerable investigation. We merely note here that at the Eighteenth Congress of the French Communist party (1967), 349 delegates out of 409 were qualified professionals, compared to sixty unskilled and manual workers.

It would probably be just as profitable to ascertain the extent to which the occupational composition of the party (and of the trade unions) gives rise to the theoretical and practical uncertainties which mark the attitude of communists on the question of wage hierarchies. Curiously enough, the accusations of rigidity in regard to wage scales—including both temporary and regular remuneration—and the proposals for raising the wages of the most poorly paid come from the CFDT (*Confédération française démocratique du travail*, the Catholic trade unions).

This is a far cry from the egalitarian (utopian? of anarchist origin?) preoccupations which in 1939, under the aegis of the international trade-union federation of teachers, the FISE (*Fédération internationale syndicale de l'Enseignement*, an outgrowth of the *Profintern*), pushed the communist minority of the teachers' federation to insist publicly on uniform treatment for all teaching personnel. Besides, the really poor, in the strictly economic sense, who, as we know, do not provide a high proportion of communist electors, also do not furnish many militants, despite periodic appeals to them to do so.

We have said "highly qualified," but why "steelworkers"? The pre-1914 Socialist party was a peoples' party or, to put it better, a plebeian party. The little people felt comfortable in it. The Communist party for its part is made up of factory workers. This does not mean, of course, that you never find in it any village artisans or representatives of the city's little people, those who constituted the nucleus of Jaurès' following. But the worker predominates; and his political development probably coincided with the formation of the French Communist party. Just as the workers' movement during the first decade of the twentieth century was marked by the traditions of building trade employees, so the successful dissemination of communism in working-class circles during the twenties was the particular accomplishment of two groups: railway workers and steelworkers. . . .

The sociology of religion lists indicators that make it possible to measure the degree of loyalty of the faithful. Similarly, political sociology measures loyalty by participation in various kinds of cultic ceremonies. For communists, attendance at cell meetings corresponds, roughly, to attendance at Mass for Catholics. The average number of evenings devoted each week to militant activity probably constitutes a valid criterion that enables us to distinguish between the "active militant" and the ordinary member. The latter, like the "Easter Catholic," can be distinguished by his participation in two major ceremonies: renewal of his membership card in January of each year and attendance at the annual "Fête de *l'Humanité*" in September.

This procedure, however, has one drawback: distinctions between members are made solely on the basis of their outward behavior, which is not the most important issue. The real question is how much change for the better each person undergoes as a result of belonging to the communist movement.

Political Allegiance

There is, to be sure, one initial way of being a communist, a way we might call "Cartesian." This applies to every militant who fulfills his political duties rigorously.

To conceive of one's allegiance to communism as an allegiance to a political party, as the choice of one political policy among many, is in no way proof of intellectual honesty or clarity of vision. It merely signifies that certain communists are to be found at the plebeian levels of society, people who have joined the Communist party because it was the most "radical" of the leftist parties, the most "republican" of groups within the republican camp, the legitimate heir of Jacobin radicalism, of Guesdist socialism. Communists south of the Loire, of the red Midi, and especially those who live in the southwest, often belong to this category. This explains why the communist peasants of Corrèze and the Dordogne never felt guilty because they failed to give fervent support to any program for the collectivization of farms, even in the most modest and modern form of agricultural cooperatives. Communists of this kind would be extremely astonished if one deduced from the mere fact of membership that the party had anything to say or even an opinion about all those things in life that have nothing to do with politics. On the other hand, they like "politics" and they are active in it. But, as we shall see, orthodox communists "do not like politics" and are not active in it—I am using the word *politics* here, not in a strict electoral and parliamentary sense but in a far broader one: public affairs, world affairs.

Speculations at the café; political discussions among friends; the concrete "political dimensions" of local or national life, more rarely those of international affairs: these are some of the things that communists of this stripe like to indulge in. They are the sons of an open-air civilization where attendance at the forum is proof of the dignity of free men. Isn't it to such communists that we owe the widespread idea—one that is well founded—that communists have a feeling for the State? Or, to be more precise, a feeling for the City? To be sure, they have substituted the grimmer, more somber word, "comrade," for the plain one, "citizen," with its consciously intended juridical and "political" resonance. But at the very first appeal from a leftist union, full-bodied republican conceptions of discipline and public welfare spring up in their minds.

Existential Allegiance

There is another, broader, less selective, but no less relaxed way of being a communist: an existential way. This applies to those who equate membership in the Communist party with a state of nature—who belong to the party "from birth." Their attitude is not necessarily attributable to the fact that they were born into communist families. Rather, for them the communist option is of a piece with their national, social, occupational, cultural inclinations. Less a political party than a milieu in which one lives, the Communist party is for them the hospitable structure that is in harmony with and attuned to their initial potentialities; allegiance to it is felt to be something logical, rational, *normal*. This explains why, for such persons, membership in the party rarely takes place in the youthful years. Indeed, unless something exceptional should come along to hasten his evolution—a strike, a period of political agitation, occasionally a political campaign—the young worker is in no hurry. To become a militant is somewhat like becoming a father. It means the assumption of new responsibilities, the kind that are natural enough but that also imply that one is growing older. Unlike the student, who often becomes a party member quite young because membership for him means a break with his family, or at least an attempt to break with it, the worker who joins the party because he is seeking a means of self-expression is usually around twenty-four or twenty-five—when he returns from military service. Often he joins the party after a rather long interval during which he acquires the habits of his trade and a measure of occupational competence. The decision to join the party often stems from an internal debate that centers on whether a person should engage in the political struggle or improve his professional skills. He asks himself: should I become a militant or a technician, maybe an engineer?

One cannot ignore the fact that this pattern, while it indicates choices and implies sacrifices, is nonetheless dominated by the idea of conformity. This explains why such militants—the favorite protagonists of proletarian novelists as well as the leaders of cadres—are solid individuals, entirely mature, having totally internalized their options: serene, convinced, deep-rooted, representative. But they are also men threatened with sclerosis; their consciences tend to wane and they feel too much at home in their environments.

Here we touch upon one of the elements that have caused the party to slip away bit by bit from its revolutionary sphere. Many of its militants are extremely "well adjusted," by which we do not mean that they have become bourgeois, an accusation too readily made, but rather that they have accustomed themselves to a party that has become for them a way of life, part of the air they breathe.

Ideological Allegiance

Finally, there is a third way of being a communist, one that might be called ideological. As a general rule, this is the road traveled by students and intellectuals.

It is quite true that we find many intellectuals who can be classified as belonging to the first of our three categories. These men continue the tradition of the pre-1914 university, of these "flesh and blood socialists": Jacobins, patriots, Freemasons, Cartesians (because they are mechanistic), Kantians (if they had the nerve for it). They scorned a dialectic that a rigorous mind could only condemn; their vision was somewhat narrow; on occasion they were petty, childishly ashamed of human weaknesses whose mysteries offended them, discreetly ambitious but timorous, and ultimately indifferent; not always as naive as they wished to appear, they loved mystification if its object was our Greco-Latin past. All in all, they were scrupulous, erudite, affable; they believed in goodness, progress, justice, work, and truth.

Actually, such intellectuals—professors, physicians, scientists—are quite numerous in the Communist party, and they are highly prized. Care is taken not to trouble them with matters unrelated to their clear conception of the world and to their delicate sensitivity—this last, needless to say, being somewhat arid and devoid of imagination. The party does not bother them, for example, with problems that concern the intelligentsia in the socialist countries. Their penchant for abstraction, their capacity to reduce the complexities of the real and the concrete to notions, essences, blueprints, principles, makes them skeptical and consequently rather easy to handle. In short, never having had to make themselves over in the image of the party, they are quite willing to accept the fact that the party is not necessarily fashioned according to their image. This imperceptible distance between them and the party constitutes that mixture of a little contempt and a good deal of mutual indulgence that makes for good relations. . . .

The communist intellectuals who matter are part of an entirely different heritage; they are motivated by very different dynamics, the dynamics of a *spiritual conversion*. . . .

Tired of the arguments and the excessive logic of our scientists, the French intelligentsia of the 1890s was captivated by anarchism. It was a fire that spread, scorching the edges and cracks of organized society. Having smoldered for a while, it blazed high and clear, with all the suddenness and gratuitousness of cosmic catastrophes. By *intelligentsia* I don't mean intellectuals or professors, those who regard life as a long career in which truth is captured gradually, one point at a time. Nor do I mean the many solid writers and artists who have all the self-assurance that talent bestows. I mean the very young, the marginal people, the lazy, the foolish, the geniuses, the down-and-outers, the dreamers, the restless, those who are incurably ill with an unknown malady, the doctors, the tired heroes, the "outsiders," the "refractory ones," the "black sheep"—these are the sobriquets bestowed upon them by anarchist newspapers—in short, all those who for professional, social, intellectual, or personal reasons are a headache to computer programmers because they are unpredictable, unclassifiable. . . .

But to be an anarchist means something more than breaking with established society. It is a more intimate, more demanding kind of rupture: a break with the established self in an established society. The biography of any anarchist contains evidence of such a split, of such a death and resurrection. This kind of conversion represents an alteration of one's entire person. To change life, one must first change one's own life.

To be a communist, according to a certain interpretation of the phrase, involves this same internal wrench, entails this same process of condemnation, expiation, and rebirth. In accordance with German Social Democracy's orthodox interpretation of Marxism, Bolshevism and its offshoots have assumed the absurd and pathetic task of establishing the theoretical foundations of the party, invoking the socialism of the future, declaring right now what is true and promulgating this truth. Hence the perpetually recurring crises that take place in the relations between the Communist party and its intellectuals. By their very existence, and in any case by the nature of their specific activity, the intellectuals belie the contention that the party—the sole precursor of the world to come—is the source of all science. Herein lies the true originality of the communist intellectuals—and the challenge they address to themselves. A communist intellectual is not only a man who "honors" his party, a militant who contributes to the political life of the organization of which he is a member. He is also a man who dares to initiate within himself a complicated experiment. Or at least he could be such a man; everybody does not move at an identical pace along the path, and sometimes people do not move at all. Membership in the party marks the beginning of a long and hazardous process at the end of which, the individual having "placed himself in the position of the working class," according to the traditional formula, a "new type of intellectual" must appear.

Changes in the Situation
of Modern Woman

HILARY LAND

The following survey of the situation of women in Western Europe raises above all the question of how change is to be measured in this major aspect of modern society. The selection takes a pronounced feminist position. It notes the great changes that have taken place in women's work roles and, to a significant extent, in their family position, as falling birthrates have dramatically reduced the maternal function. But it stresses the continuing "traditional" limitations on women's work, and the efforts of the wider society to tempt women back into more conventional functions as a means, for example, of dealing with what may be dangerously low birth rates. The passage also notes new problems—the growing burdens of caring for older family members, for example—that could reduce the changes in women's work roles from yet another direction. Thus the passage emphasizes the incompleteness of change and suggests potential frustration for women caught between an abandonment of traditional resignation and resultant new expectations on the one hand, and a denial of full equality on the other. This frustration, although it has taken new specific forms in Western Europe during the past three decades—since the revolution in the sheer quantity of women's employment—has been an important aspect of modern life in Western Europe and North America since at least the later nineteenth century.

Consequently, the selection should obviously be compared with Branca's discussion on Victorian women. Branca claims some rather substantial changes for women, in mentality and function, within the home. But women in contemporary society are moving out into a larger world, most notably by taking or maintaining jobs after marriage. Did the previous changes in their outlook prepare them for this? Will they seek occupational levels and behavior comparable to those of men or will they find their own job definition? Did the special nineteenth-century characterization of women's nature and functions prepare society at large for new roles?

Hilary Land, of course, is discussing a variety of social classes, not the middle class alone. It is probable that the transition to more modern values occurred later in worker and peasant households than in the middle class. This created some unsurprising similarities between the nineteenth-century middle class and the twentieth-century working class. Women may be too large a group for precise social analysis. The author's viewpoint must be assessed, as in any study of human society; in this case, the author has rather clear notions of what women's position should be. But with all the qualifications, the special problems of interpreting the impact of modernization on women remain. Although women's lives in all major social classes may have changed more than those of men, their frustrations may be no greater, but simply different. Yet women do seem peculiarly caught between the pull of tradition and new needs and opportunities, victims or beneficiaries of a tension that men faced much earlier in the modernization process. It seems certain, also, that the full implications of the modernization of women have yet to be worked out. Can an understanding of the changes in women's lives over the last century and a half allow prediction of women's future roles?

Trends among women in Western Europe raise one other important issue for analysis. Many of the changes in women's lives, including new job levels and a falling birthrate since the early 1960s, are remarkably similar to those that have occurred in the United States in the same period. Yet on the whole, the feminist movement—such a vital part of the American scene in the past two decades—has been weaker in Europe, particularly outside of Britain, partly because European women seek rights through other political outlets, such as socialist parties or the new Green party in Germany, and partly because the larger civil rights movement in the United States gave particular spur to feminist demands. But are there, beneath the surface of similar trends, some important differences between modern European and modern American women? Are the Europeans more involved in traditionalist expectations? Or is their "advantage" over American women in areas such as birth rate—European families being distinctly smaller than American during the baby boom of the 1950s and the subsequent birth rate decline—such that feminist anxiety is less intense?

Looking back over the past fifteen years in Europe, changes in birthrates, divorce rates, and the rate of participation of women in the labor force all tell a simple story: major change. But how is this story to be interpreted and understood? Are the underlying causes simple? Should we conclude that the ways in which men and women relate to each other at home and in the labor market have significantly altered? At the formal level, at least, it would appear so. In the world of paid employment in most countries not only have women become visible members in greater numbers, although Western Europe has yet to achieve the high participation rates Eastern Europe had reached by the end of the fifties, but there has also been an increased emphasis on equality between the sexes. In the past decade, several Western European countries have implemented equal pay legislation; others have passed sex discrimination laws which aim, among other things, to improve women's opportunities for education and training. The legal framework governing relationships between men and women in the family has become less biased against women, allowing them to be treated as individuals in their own right

From Hilary Land, "The Changing Place of Women in Europe," *Daedalus* Vol. 108 No. 2 (Spring, 1979), pp. 73–7, 78–82, 89–92.

rather than as dependents of their husbands. Laws relating to marriage and divorce, in countries such as Britain and France, are changing to give both partners equal responsibility for providing financial support and care for each other and their families. (Sweden has had such laws since the 1920s and Eastern European countries embodied egalitarian principles in their legislation at least thirty years ago.) In Western Europe abortion became an issue in the sixties and seventies and most countries have relaxed their laws concerning abortion, although the controversy surrounding this measure is by no means over. This, together with the wider availability of reliable contraception, has meant that women have the possibility of exercising greater control over their fertility.

In other words, since the early sixties major inroads have been made into the more explicit forms of discrimination against women. It would be wrong to conclude too readily, however, that these reforms, although necessary, are sufficient in themselves to effect fundamental changes in the relationships betwen women and men. Men still dominate politics, industry, and many fields of employment. Major economic changes are not sufficient either: sex-segregated labor markets with women located predominantly in the least-valued occupations are found in every Western European country; they have persisted in Eastern Europe in spite of more than three decades of formal equality between the sexes.

Moreover, explicit "family policies" in response to falling birthrates, in East and West alike in the 1960s and 1970s, have placed greater, rather than less, emphasis on the need for women to make childbearing and child-rearing their primary, and, for a time, their sole concern. Gender differences within the family are thus being reinforced and, unless the value placed on the experience of motherhood is greatly increased and male work norms challenged, women will be considered to be handicapped in the labor market. Even in Sweden, which is exceptional in the awareness at governmental level of the need to take positive steps to change men's as well as women's attitudes toward marriage and parenthood, it is still women who take the primary responsibility for the care of the young, the sick, and the old. Men's self-esteem still derives from their ability to act as breadwinners. Beliefs about what constitutes masculinity and femininity, and hence the division of labor between the sexes, have not changed as much as some of the rhetoric would lead us to believe.

This essay will first describe the changes that have occurred in the employment patterns of men and women in some of the European countries and will relate them to changes affecting men and women within the family, noting in particular the conflicts and contradictions that arise. We shall see that the tensions between the demands of the workplace and the home are borne disproportionately by women. Increasing numbers of women have questioned their subordinate position, both in the family and in society in general, because these conflicts have grown. In Eastern and

Western European countries alike, more and more women have been required to leave their homes to participate in the labor market while at the same time continuing to be available for and committed to caring for their families. As evidence from Eastern Europe clearly shows, many women have attempted to reduce the heavy and competing claims of paid employment and family by being increasingly reluctant to have more than one or two children. However much a society takes women's work in the home for granted and renders it invisible no society concerned for its future is likely to allow birthrates to persist below replacement level without taking measures to increase them. The second part of this essay will examine the attempts some countries are making to bring the demands of production in the economic sphere and the needs of human reproduction into equilibrium, and will examine how far these policies are likely to hinder, or even reverse, the moves women have been making toward achieving greater equality.

Changes in Employment Patterns

It is important to bear in mind that the data we have on the status of women in the labor markets of various countries are limited in availability and comparability. In 1977, Evelyne Sullerot reminded a United Nations conference on the changing role of men and women:

> That the world of work has been built up, planned and designed for and by men is apparent as soon as one endeavours to describe the situation of working women in statistical terms. Definitions vary from one country to another: in some countries the unpaid wives of farmers, businessmen and skilled craftsmen working in the family enterprise are considered to be unemployed. . . . A particular society will count accurately only what is in its view important, and the statistical haziness surrounding female employment proves that the economic role of women has long been regarded as marginal.

It is therefore difficult to make comparisons within one country over time, and it is even more hazardous to make comparisons over national boundaries. Nevertheless, some of the changes and trends in women's employment can be seen in broad outline. One of the major changes that has occurred in many countries in both Eastern and Western Europe has been the big increase in the number of women who have become part of the formal, paid labor market by joining the secondary and tertiary sectors of the economy. This has taken them out of their homes and the informal labor market and made their economic activity more visible.

In Western Europe, men's and women's employment patterns still differ in many respects. In every country it is still believed that it is the man in the family who has the responsibility to be the breadwinner. Men are therefore expected to be strongly attached to the labor market, joining it after leaving full-time education and remaining until they reach retirement age, unless required for a period of military service. Where different retirement ages exist, it is women who are expected to leave the labor market at a younger age, although they can expect to live longer than men. Male participation rates have remained high and more or less unchanged over the past twenty years, although increases in numbers staying in full-time education, together with reductions in the retirement age, have narrowed the boundaries of the labor market a little, affecting the total numbers in the labor force. In contrast to their effect on women, marriage and parenthood must strengthen men's attachment to the labor market, given their "breadwinner" role. Surveys do show that in Britain, for example, male manual workers do the greatest amount of overtime when they are in the age group most likely to have dependent children, and that fathers of large families work longer hours than fathers of small families. But does marriage per se have the same impact? It is interesting to note that in Britain although female activity rates published by the Department of Employment have been broken down by marital status (but not by number of children) since 1951, comparable figures are not given for men. Men are also most likely to work full-time and, unless they belong to a disadvantaged group on the margins of the labor market because they are disabled or migrant, they are unlikely to be homeworkers. Men without jobs, unless they are migrant workers with no settlement rights, are counted as being unemployed but still members of the labor market. Women may not be, particularly if they are married. Methods of measuring and collecting unemployment figures often underestimate women's unemployment, considering them to be nonemployed and not wishing to participate in the labor market. This is partly because if jobs are scarce women are discouraged from staying in the labor market and partly because of the basis on which statistics are collected. ... In the British House of Lords in June, 1976, the Archbishop of Canterbury, who opened the debate, drew attention to the importance of grandparents. He quoted from an essay by an eight-year-old child who said, "Grandmothers don't have to do anything but be there. . . . Everybody should have one, especially if you don't have television because grandmothers are the only grownups who have time." What will happen when even Grandmother is busy outside the home?

Middle-aged women are more likely than younger women to be involved in the care of elderly relatives. They also provide a very substantial amount of voluntary work among the elderly. Indeed, to a large extent the "young old" look after the very old. The demands on them are likely to increase in the future both because in several countries the numbers of very elderly are growing and because there is greater emphasis in social service policies on community care. This partly reflects a reaction against residential care and the ill effects of institutionalization. Moreover, residential care is expensive. In the past in both Northern and Southern Europe, a large amount of residential care has been provided by the Church. In future this may well diminish: as societies become more secular there are fewer people willing to devote their lives, for religious reasons, to caring for the sick and the old for whom they have no familial obligations. So at a time when in many parts of Western Europe more women are expected to be economically active outside the home, they are increasingly going to be expected to be available to give full-time care to old or infirm relatives and neighbors. It is therefore important that changes in women's family responsibilities over the *whole* of the life cycle should be taken into account both in analyzing their employment patterns and in developing social policies.

STRUCTURAL CHANGES IN THE ECONOMY

The changing picture of women's employment in Italy shows how intricately the level of female employment is bound up not only with the family life cycle but, like men's, with structural changes in the economy, and with attitudes toward what are regarded as women's jobs. In France, in contrast to Italy and the countries of Eastern Europe, it is the women who are leaving the men behind on the farms and taking jobs elsewhere. Between 1960 and 1968 the proportion of the female labor force in France employed in the agricultural sector declined from 25 to 14 percent, while the proportion employed in the service sector increased from 49 to 60 percent. This meant that while three-quarters of a million women left agriculture, nearly a million joined the service sector. In Italy roughly the same number of women disappeared from the agricultural sector during the same period, but the numbers of women in the service sector increased by less than one hundred thousand. Clearly part of the reason for the opposite trend in France is related to the stage in the development of the economy. By and large, jobs in a developing industrial sector are more likely to go to men (or men to move to those jobs), while jobs in an expanding service sector are likely to go to women. Thus the stage in industrialization at which the agricultural sector starts to decline rapidly is one determinant of men's and women's job opportunities. The pattern of economic development of a particular country is not the sole explanatory factor. It is true that in industry women form a majority in branches that represent an extension of their traditional activities; clothing, textiles, and often food; and many jobs in the service sector are similar to those women do in the home. But cultural mores as to what are regarded as traditional female jobs do vary from one country to another. These too have an impact on men's and women's job opportunities. For example, in Italy the whole of the catering industry is largely dominated by men, whereas in other countries in Western Europe men do not have such a monopoly in bars, restaurants, and hotels.

Another important difference between men and women is that it is acceptable for men, both married and single, to migrate to find employment either from one region to another or from one country to another, but it is not legitimate for married women to seek work abroad unless accompanied by their husbands. The number of migrant workers in the north of Western Europe increased during the 1960s, and by 1973 there were over eleven million (excluding Britain). Three-quarters went to France or Germany. In France, in the early seventies, one in five in the industrial labor force were foreigners and in West Germany one out of seven manual workers were immigrants. Many came from Southern Europe but only those from Italy, a member of the EEC, had rights to reside and bring their families. Migration from south to north in Western Europe is an important part of the overall employment scene.

Important internal structural changes have also occurred in the economies of those countries where industrialization and urbanization occurred earlier and where women have formed a substantial and visible proportion of the labor force for several decades. In Britain, for example, women have constituted about a third of the formal labor force for well over a century. During the seventies the proportion has grown slightly to reach nearly 40 percent. However, much of the increase is in part-time employment, primarily in the service sector of the economy. About half of women employed work on average twenty hours a week. While the service sector has been growing, the manufacturing sector has decreased. But since the growth of the service sector has been in part-time employment, labor statistics in terms of numbers of workers as opposed to number of hours exaggerate both the shift out of the productive sectors of the economy and the extent to which, if at all, women can be said to be replacing men.

The Swedish economy, with a high proportion of women in its work force (40 percent in 1977), has also been characterized by a substantial growth in the service sector, much of it accounted for by women. Part-time work (defined in Sweden as working less than 35 hours a week) is as common among Swedish women as among British women. It is interesting to note that in West Germany and France, where there has been a long tradition of female employment and where the proportion of women in the working population is also high for Western Europe (around 40 percent in 1975), only 13 percent of women workers in France and 20 percent in West Germany work part time. Moreover, although the increased availability of part-time employment has enabled women with small children, in countries like Sweden and Britain, to take up paid employment in large numbers, a part-time worker is just as likely to be an older married woman.

Sex-Segregation of the Labor Market

There are other ways in which female patterns of employment differ from male patterns. In every country in Western Europe there is a sex-segregated labor market in which women are found in a far narrower range of occupations than men. Moreover, the status and pay of these occupations are low. In these occupations few men are found. Conversely, most men work in occupations in which there are a small proportion of women. As an OECD report published in 1976 stated: "Women in all countries tend to work principally in white collar and service occupations. They are the secretaries, sales clerks and primary school teachers. Those women who do work in the industrial sector as manual workers constitute substantial majorities in textiles and the garment industry. They are noticeably absent from the steel industry, mining and construction." Within these occupations women are absent from the top positions. Moreover, there is evidence that in countries like Britain where there appears to be an overall decline in employment levels, male employment is falling in all the manual groups. For women, however, employment is falling in the skilled and semi-skilled occupations but growing in the unskilled and personal service sector. In nonmanual employment the growth in male employment between 1961 and 1971 was largely in the professional and managerial occupations. Women made some gains in these areas but moved mainly into junior nonmanual occupations. Similar movements could be detected in France.

With such a degree of segregation of jobs it is not surprising to find disparities in the earnings of men and women. The gaps between men's and women's earnings varied considerably from one country to another. In France, West Germany, and Britain women earn 67 percent as much as men. In West Germany this gap exists despite the fact that since the end of the Second World War, it has been unconstitutional not to give men and women equal pay for equal work; Germans are now considering introducing sex discrimination legislation. It should be remembered that averages obscure wide disparities. For example, in 1976 in Britain, the median gross earnings of full-time women manual workers were *below* the lowest decile for male manual workers. The gap between men's and women's earnings measured in absolute cash as distinct from relative terms has widened, particularly among nonmanual workers in the private sector. Moreover, Britain has an income tax system that gives many more advantages to men than to women, so the disparities in take-home pay are, in practice, greater. The earnings of men and women working full time in

Sweden are much closer together: women earned 86 percent as much as men in 1974. Broadly speaking, in Western Europe in those countries where family allowances are relatively high, the difference between men's and women's wages is smaller. Is this because if women are valued as mothers they are also valued as workers? Or is it because men's wages, implicitly at least, are based on the assumption that they have children to support? This is certainly an argument British male trade unionists have used for decades to justify paying men more than women, and it accounts for some of their opposition to family allowances, which they do not directly determine.

The potential of equal pay legislation, meaning equal pay for equal work, is clearly limited by the fact that most women are crowded into a small number of occupations where they form a majority: they cannot therefore be said to be doing "equal" or "like" work with men. Equal pay for work of equal value could be a tougher version of the law, but in France, which uses this formulation in its legislation, there have been enormous problems in defining "equal value." Other strategies include improving education and training opportunities for girls and women, and deliberate programs to get women into traditional male jobs and vice versa.

Biased and Inferior Education

In most Western European countries there have been improvements in girls' and women's opportunities for education and training. Overtly discriminatory barriers have been removed in many countries. In France vocational schools previously reserved for boys are becoming coeducational, and in Britain since 1975 it is official policy to give boys and girls the same curriculum opportunities. In West Germany in 1978, 57 percent of women aged between thirty and forty years had completed an apprenticeship as well as elementary education, compared with 39 percent of those aged forty and fifty years. As the total number in secondary and postsecondary education has increased, so in many countries has the proportion of female pupils. But women are still likely to be underrepresented in higher education. In West Germany the percentage of men who had completed university or a comparable course was still three times greater than that of women in 1978. In Britain in 1960, one-quarter of under-graduates were women. Ten years later the proportion was nearer one-third. But, although just as many women as men were at this time getting good degrees, only 16 percent of postgraduate students were women. In the early seventies nearly two-fifths of boys leaving school in Britain entered an apprenticeship or the equivalent leading to a skilled occupation, compared with one in twelve girls. Hairdressing accounted for

a large number of these female apprenticeships. In contrast, in the electri-
cal engineering industry, in which women form half the labor force, only
fifty apprentices were girls in 1970, compared with 4,466 boys.

Many of the traditional barriers which prevent girls and women from
utilizing greater opportunities are still very strong and are reinforced in
many ways. Moreover, they operate at a very early age. For example,
schoolbooks reinforce traditional stereotypes of male and female behavior.
Female characters feature in stories less often, and they are less independent and prominent than male characters. They are more likely to be portrayed as mothers, housewives, secretaries, schoolteachers, or nurses,
whereas men appear in a much wider range of occupations. In Sweden
there has been a more conscious effort than in other Western European
countries to break down these stereotypes presented to children, but as an
OECD report comments, although this increased their awareness of sexual
prejudice and sex-role stereotyping due to their teaching, "actual choice of
optional subjects and course lines are still powerfully dominated by conventional attitudes. Thus there is a strong male majority in technical and
industrial fields and an equally pronounced female majority in arts subjects
and nursery education. Change in behaviour as opposed to attitudes
alone, is very slow in coming."

In every Western European country women not only choose
different subjects but after leaving school are more likely, if they continue
to study, to do so in low-status institutions. Patterns of higher education
in Western Europe suggest that whether or not a woman enters higher
education at all seems to depend as much, if not more, on prevailing attitudes toward women's roles as on the level of economic development. It
is not surprising therefore that the socioeconomic status of a girl's parents
affects her chances of higher education far more than a boy's. In Britain,
for example, in 1970 the daughter of a nonmanual worker was ten times
as likely to get to university as was the daughter of a manual worker. The
son of a nonmanual worker was only four times as likely to do so as was
the son of a manual worker. Moreover, although it is generally true that
female graduates have higher rates of employment than those who have
received only the minimum education, where women are not welcome in
higher education or the labor market the rates are lower. For example, in
France in the early seventies 80 percent of female graduates, even when
they had small children, were economically active, compared with Spain,
where only 50 percent were in paid employment.

A legacy of a lower level of formal education makes it harder for
women to take advantage of education and retraining opportunities when
they are older. In addition, many of these courses are full time and the
hours required are difficult to combine with family responsibilities. More
men than women are found in these courses. Four times as many men as
women were enrolled in continuing education courses in France in the

mid-1970s. A similar pattern was found in West Germany. Moreover, most retraining opportunities for women, even in Sweden where both the trade union movement and the government are committed to ending occupational sex-segregation, are in traditional female jobs. As Evelyne Sullerot concluded in her study of women in society in 1971: "Once again it seems clear that the main obstacles to women's careers are not directly related to their work, but to their family life. It is not so much that women lose interest in their studies when they marry, but rather that they find it difficult to be students and housewives at the same time . . . everything conspires to encourage the efforts of male students and to discourage women, whose perseverance is construed as useless or even selfish."

The impact of educational changes on increasing women's actual opportunities in the labor market have been limited, therefore, because in every country in Western Europe, to varying degrees, women's futures are still defined primarily in domestic terms. Nevertheless, the last twenty years in Western Europe have been marked, almost without exception, by the increasing labor force participation of women, particularly married women and women with children of preschool age. Equal pay and equal opportunities for women in the labor market have been a matter not only for debate but for legislation. In the seventies, however, the demographic and economic climate in countries such as Britain, France, and West Germany began to militate against those wanting to challenge the subordinate position of women. Before discussing why and how policy priorities changed as a result, it is worth [noting] the experience of some of the countries of Eastern Europe, where high female activity rates were achieved in the fifties and where for at least a quarter of a century the systems of labor and family law have been based on the kind of egalitarian principles being fought for in Western European countries now.

The Demographic Climate of Western Europe

Western Europe has also been experiencing falling birthrates and rising divorce rates, but these occurred predominantly in the seventies rather than the sixties. Indeed, at the time when many Eastern European countries were getting alarmed by falling birthrates, several Western European countries were experiencing very high birthrates. It was against this background that women acquired easier access to a legal and safe abortion, having first, in contrast to Eastern European women, won the right to have the use of cheap and reliable contraceptives. The abortion laws have remained controversial in those countries that liberalized them, and it is uncertain whether they will become more or less liberal in the next few years. However, it is likely to be much harder to reverse changes which have resulted in women expecting to be able to control their fertility. Part of the debate about contraception was conducted in terms of the individual's right *and* responsibility to choose when and whether to have children.

The more liberal divorce laws were also part of the extension of individual rights. Men, and women, have become freer to choose and reject their marriage partners as divorce laws were liberalized in several Western European countries in the late sixties and early seventies. Women in particular have been exercising this increased freedom. Their greater participation in the labor market and improved social security provision has led to a certain degree of economic independence. However, it would be wrong to interpret the rapid rise in the number of divorces, the majority of petitions being brought by women in Britain, for example, as the rejection of marriage as an institution. The economic and social pressures on women to marry or remarry are still enormous, and the majority do so. In Britain, in 1976, one-third of all marriages were remarriages for one or both partners. If the marriage does not work, most attribute blame to the individuals rather than to the nature of the institution. In this sense easier divorce protects marriage as an institution. Nevertheless, as well over half of divorces involve children, the problem of the welfare of children in one-parent families has attracted growing attention, as it has in Eastern Europe. The rights of fathers not married to the mothers of their children is under increasing discussion in Britain, for example. This results partly from a desire to curb the independence of women, partly from an attempt to increase the responsibilities of men, as well as from a genuine concern for the welfare of the children.

Western European women have clearly not established their right to paid work to the extent to which their Eastern European sisters have. The debate about the problem of combining paid employment with childbearing and childrearing therefore contains more overt moral overtones: a woman's place is in the home. The growing emphasis on family policies placed by politicians in France and Britain in the electioneering during 1978, has meant an emphasis on families in which men are breadwinners and women are first and foremost wives and mothers. Such families are regarded as "normal" or "natural." Any social policy that supports or reinforces this particular pattern of responsibilities is not seen as invading the privacy of the family. It is therefore regarded as a legitimate activity of the state, although of course the relationship between the family and the state and the extent to which the state can explicitly intervene in the family varies betwen one country and another for historical and cultural reasons. Much depends on the strength of the established Church. However, faced with the prospect of a declining population, the legitimacy of pronatalist policies is very strong. One of the important functions of the women's movement as it exists in several countries has been to expose and challenge the legitimacy of state intervention in the family and make personal relationships and conflict between the sexes a matter of public politics.

Women in many Western European countries have achieved a great deal in terms of formal equality. Like women in Eastern Europe they have been drawn into the labor market in spite of the lack of recognition of the huge claims on their time made by their family responsibilities. In some countries this has been eased by the possibility of part-time employment at the price of low pay, poor promotion prospects, and little job security. In others, some expansion of collective child care provisions has occurred. They have moved predominantly into the service sector where, as Rita Liljestrom pointed out in 1976, the values and attitudes appropriate to those jobs do not conflict with those required of women within the family: "As long as the women formed a service proletariat, working at entry level in hospitals, offices and retail stores, they built most of their identity on their role as mother and wife, in the order named. But if they are given tasks that motivate them as well as freedom of action and responsibility can we be sure that the family will receive top priority?" The resistance to allowing women to take not only nontraditional female jobs, but jobs with authority and responsibility, is therefore substantial and likely to grow in the context of growing concern about the stability of the family and falling birthrates.

In the face of major structural changes in the economies of several of the advanced capitalist societies in Western Europe which, among other things, have diminished the demand for labor, how are women going to maintain their position in the labor market in competition with the young and the migrant worker? Or will the substantial excess supply of labor, which leaves even "prime-male" workers unemployed, challenge male work norms? Will it open up the possibility of changing the priorities of the workplace? Will it mean rethinking the basis on which individuals obtain the means of subsistence—which increasingly means receiving a cash income? Probably not: it has always been in the interests of employers to choose those workers who are the cheapest, the most docile, and the least likely to be unionized. Women are more likely than men to belong to this category. Moreover, many men's wages are insufficient to support a wife and children. There are therefore major contradictory tendencies in the present economic systems.

In several countries, including Britain and West Germany, proposals to pay mothers a wage in order to stay at home to look after their children are being seriously discussed. This, as the Eastern European experience shows, does nothing to challenge the division of responsibilities within the family. Indeed, the converse is the case. However, the extended parental leave as introduced in Sweden in 1974, and shorter working hours for the fathers, as well as the mothers, of young children, as has been discussed but not yet implemented in Sweden, open up the possibility of changing relationships with the family. How far this would occur voluntarily is open to question. In Sweden, only a small minority of men choose paternity leave, and there is a move to abandon liberal ways of getting men to take responsibility for their families by making some paternity leave compulsory, for example. In Belgium, where there is discussion about reducing working hours, men want a shorter working week or year; women want a shorter working day.

Relationships between men and women, whether in the home or the workplace, will not change unless men's as well as women's attitudes and priorities change. Equality does not mean women must become like men: if it were to mean that, there would indeed be a population crisis, for men and the economic structures they create give low priority to children and place a low value on child care. The greater involvement of women in the formal labor market outside the home has exposed, in both Eastern and Western Europe, the conflicts between the needs of the family and the demands of employment. As Rita Liljestrom commented in 1976:

> The conflicts between the parents go back in their turn to frictions and tensions in a specialised society, whose different parts or sectors are so much out of phase that they never get co-ordinated into any new whole. To illustrate, the mothers are out on the labour market before facilities for child care have been adequately expanded, before isolation in suburbs has been replaced by concerted action around children and young people, before suitable workplaces have been sited near or in residential areas, before the workplaces have taken the consequences and brought the labour forces' responsibility for children into the work planning calculus, and before legislation has built safeguards to protect the interests of parents, e.g. by shortening the hours of work while the responsibility for childcare is greatest.

The struggle to achieve equality between the sexes involves challenging the societal circumstances that structure women's lives. This means asking fundamental questions about the economic system as well as recognizing that personal relationships come within the realm of public politics. It also means challenging the custom prevalent in every country in Eastern and Western Europe alike, of according less recognition and less value to the work women do than to the work men do. This happened to some extent in Europe in the sixties and seventies. It remains to be seen whether in the face of considerable pressure to push them further back into the home, women can sustain the progress that was made.

Modern Families

FERDYNAND ZWEIG

Most evaluations of modern life require at least passing reference to the family; the more critical ones usually dwell on the subject. The decline of the family has been a constant theme in European history since at least the early nineteenth century. Indeed, its collapse has been suggested so often that it is a wonder there is anything left still to decay. Clearly, many who have found modern life distasteful have exaggerated their laments about the breakup of the family. But this does not mean that they have not correctly identified trends, for no one denies that great changes have taken place in family structure.

There are several key problems in dealing with modern family history, aside from the difficulty of obtaining adequate information. To begin with, any valid judgment requires an evaluation of the quality of family life before the modern age. Most assessments of the modern family reflect, if only implicitly, deeply held beliefs about the premodern family. Those who find family life deteriorating and modern man bereft of the solidarity he needs, point to the strength and diverse functions of the premodern family. Yet we have seen that the premodern family structure may have had serious inadequacies, so that changes in family structure may conceivably have been good, not bad.

There are related disagreements about the facts of change. The modern family may be seen as a total contrast to its predecessors or as a modification only. Take, for example, the extended family. We have long imagined that premodern families united uncles, aunts, cousins, and grandparents with parents and children. This was a unit that could provide for itself and give guidance and support to all members. Recent work, however, suggests that the extended family was not united quite so literally as has been assumed. It did not, in western and central Europe, live under the same roof, and it regularly sent members to work for other families; yet there is little doubt that fairly close relationships existed. What happened, then, with modernization? A common assumption is that the extended family disappeared, and many observers believe this was a great loss. Yet studies of twentieth-century European workers reveal that their social life is centered almost entirely within the extended family circle. Great interest is taken in the doings of distant relatives. It is true that the extended family is sometimes (though not always) spread out geographically, but it has not literally disappeared. The question of the stability of marriage raises another set of factual problems. Without doubt, divorce has increased in Europe over the past hundred years. Yet family breakups may conceivably have declined, for we have no way of knowing the rate of desertions before legal divorce became widespread. Add to this the fact that before 1850 the early death of one marriage partner would frequently dissolve the marriage within a decade or so, and one may wonder how decisive the institution of divorce is in the history of the family. There is broad agreement on many trends in family history, but the facts are by no means entirely clear.

Judgments of the twentieth-century family must be compared to assessments of family change earlier in the modernization process. We have seen that important trends concerning household, affection and sexuality began over two centuries ago. Where have these trends taken the family in recent decades? Have new trends intervened to complicate the process? How much does the twentieth-century working-class family owe to earlier changes in emotional expectations? How many of the heralded problems of contemporary families are due to these same changes?

Finally, after one does the best possible job of getting the facts and making the necessary qualifications, there remains the question of interpretation. We can easily agree that, although its importance as a unit of consumption has increased, the family is no longer a key production unit. What does this mean for the family? For some observers it suggests decay, a loosening of ties, because many family members now work outside the home. For others it suggests a reduction of the tensions and bitterness that family economic relations once involved. No longer, for example, are twenty-five-year-olds normally under their father's economic control, unable to marry before he retires or dies. With this kind of family friction reduced, the family can become a closer emotional unit, with more affectionate ties between husband and wife and between parents and children.

Evaluations of the modern family are usually highly moralistic. They reflect what the analyst thinks a proper life should be—how much independence people should have, what the proper role of women is, what kind of care children deserve and need, and so on. In sum, the family remains at the center of a great deal of analysis of modern society and of the results of a modernization process; the nature of the family engenders more debate than ever before. Today, many students of the family, heirs to a long line of pessimists (and some optimists) who have been proclaiming the decay of the family since the onset of industrialization, find it teetering on the brink of a new communal or individualized existence. Some simply believe that the conditions of modern society have proved progressively less compatible with family life: fathers drawn outside the home to work, children forced into schools, and people encouraged to replace familial with individualistic motivations. Others now see the first reactions to industrialization in the nineteenth century as immensely fruitful. They point particularly to the strength and intensity of the middle-class family, with the strong direction it provided for children. They find the twentieth century far different and far less appealing (thus implicitly rejecting modernization as a schema covering family history, with a distinction between industrial and postindustrial society).

Still others find the family alive and kicking, even healthier than it once was. Ferdynand Zweig, a sociologist, conducted an elaborate poll of English factory workers at the end of the 1950s and found that they had moved to a higher valuation of the family as a center for human contact and recreation than ever before. Indeed, the family and its acquisitions and pastimes provide the basis for a new contentment, an adjustment to the pressures of industrial work. But not all is well. Zweig points to unresolved strains within the family that stem from new expectations and the lowering of the birthrate. One example of this is the new surge of married women into the labor force. He finds a certain blandness in the worker's family ties; the families are comfortable, not venturesome or intense. It would be possible to accept Zweig's judgments and paint a far harsher picture of the human values involved, as the second selection on the contemporary family suggests.

How does Zweig's picture fit any view of modernization? Clearly, this is not a traditional family pattern; it is affluent, leisure- rather than production-centered, possibly more influenced by women, and with more individually defined members, conscious of their freedom. But perhaps, within the structural constraints of modernization—notably the separation of production from the family and the need to seek employment outside the home—the contemporary working class is moving to restore something like a traditional family focus. Family history may not move with the tides of modernization; the family may yet be a partial refuge from a modern world.

Schopenhauer's simile likening human beings to hedgehogs, clustering together for warmth in winter, uncomfortable and pricking each other when too closely packed and miserable when kept apart, struck me during my enquiry as containing a sober truth about human behaviour. Schopenhauer interpreted this as human predicament, as a tragic dilemma. But there is no need to interpret this in a pessimistic way. As hedgehogs try to find the right distance so as not to prick each other and still keep warm, so also we are concerned to keep the right proportion of human warmth and freedom. There is no need to go to extremes to expose ourselves to constant pricking by packing ourselves too close, or to grow cold, deprived of the vivifying experience of human companionship. There is a large range of middle zones where the need for freedom of action and the need for human warmth are met with the intensity required, not being sacrificed to each other. Admittedly, it is not easy to reach this point and the point itself moves all the time, like a most sensitive magnetic needle. The right point depends not only on cultural patterns and social environment, but also on age, temperament, past experience, marital status and social status.

When I submitted for comment the statement: "We can say the least to those we love best," most agreed with me stating that they were afraid of upsetting their wives or being upset by them; obviously those whom we love have the greatest power to upset us. So all through the enquiry whenever the contacts with families of origin, neighbours or workmates were in question one could hear the same *leit-motiv*, "close but not too close," in various versions.

The other outstanding principle in personal contacts is the principle of substitution. When, for instance, contact with family of origin is

From Ferdynand Zweig, *The Worker in an Affluent Society* (New York: The Free Press, 1962), pp. 193–211.

largely lacking, other relationships such as closer contacts with neighbours develop. Where social clubs are very highly developed this may also affect other contacts. Apart from the need for human warmth, the time factor also plays its part, of course.

When a man is very happy at home, this often results in his complete isolation from other contacts; this was often expressed in the phrase "We keep ourselves to ourselves." I rarely heard the term "I keep myself to myself," it was mostly "we." A single man cannot keep himself to himself without the risk of becoming a recluse if not an outcast. In the places I visited between 15 and 20 per cent described themselves in these terms. The majority were older men but there were also young men among them, especially those who had just started their family life and were completely engrossed in it.

The question arises, what is general trend of behaviour in this respect: is the accent more on warmth or more on freedom? I would say that it is more on freedom, while the need for warmth is not so strongly felt as previously. Men suffering poverty and privation, men in a predicament, under strain and stress, need more sympathy and warmth, while men comfortably off, enjoying a good life, are more self-centred, desiring freedom more than anything else, freedom to enjoy life undisturbed. The warmth they need they can find in a small family circle, with their partners in the enjoyment of life. The wider circles of friends are to a large extent replaced by impersonal relationships, such as those developed around T.V. and other media of entertainment. A whole net of relationships which we may call "uncommitted" has grown between the viewer and the T.V. personalities. It is a diluted, mute, and single-track friendship, uncommitted and anonymous, which develops between the viewer and the personality, who is built up by the T.V. into something approaching an idol. A gracious gesture, a smile, open arms, a sweet word, are received by the viewer as addressed to him personally, filling his heart with warmth, without effort or struggle, without commitment and without fear of frustration or upset. It is a counterfeit of the real thing, but the counterfeit is cheap, giving the viewer in essence what he needs and leaving him free. The quest for freedom has assumed an unexpected aspect: the freedom to watch T.V. and the freedom to drive a car. . . .

Closely linked with these traits is his [the worker's] family-mindedness and home-centredness, as security, acquisitiveness and family-mindedness go well together. He seeks his pleasures and comforts at home more than ever. "I am a fairly domesticated animal," was a typical remark which I heard. Family life assumes a romanticized image of happiness and joy. Family life stands, in his mind, for happiness, enjoyment and relaxation. As he sits by his fireside and watches T.V. he feels free and happy. The wife doesn't snap at him as she used to; the children are no longer seen crawling and messing about on the floor, shouting and screaming. The foul air, the vermin, the outside, smelling lavatory, the broken chairs have been removed as if by magic. Instead there is a nicely furnished house of his own, or a council house which is a near equivalent to his own property. His main hobby is decorating his home and he is busy with his brush all the year round: "I never saw my father handling a brush, now it seems I have a use for my brush the whole year round." These contrasts may be slightly over-drawn in relation both to the present and the past, but I believe they have validity in relation to the general trend.

Part of a worker's home and family-centredness is his intense interest in his offspring. If he has no ambition for himself, he has plenty for his children. "In my days a man pushing a pram would have been a laughing-stock; now you see a great many men pushing their pram proudly," said an older man. He not only pushes the pram, he often washes the children and gives them baths, he reads them stories, follows their school records, calls at the school on parents' day, tries to fix them up with a good job or apprenticeship. "It is the finest thing there is to give the children every advantage," or "My boy has everything he wants," or "I scrubbed and scraped to give my children every chance," he may say.

This has an enormous effect on the father-image among the working classes. The bullying father or the father whose authority was used as a bogey has largely disappeared, and instead an older brother relation comes to the fore. The father is there to assist and help, to give guidance; but he is no more the master with a big stick. In my previous enquiries I often found the father-image distorted among the working classes and strongly imbued with the shadow of the Oedipus complex. The working-class child often had only the care and affection of the mother, while the father was an aloof figure. Now the powerful figure of the working-class "Mum" is receding, as in many workers' families the father steps into her place or occupies an equal place beside her, the more so as she often goes out to work. Anyway the balance of affection is nowadays more equitably distributed between the two parents. The changing father-image is an important factor in the changing ethos of the working classes. Whether a child suffers under arbitrary authority at home or enjoys a kindly and reasonable guidance has a great bearing on his character and outlook.

Somehow related to this is the process of softening in the worker, I would venture to call it his feminization. The workers' world was formerly known for its masculinity. The worker had little to do with children or womenfolk. He was a hard-working, hard-swearing and hard-playing man. He manners were often rugged and rough. His voice was often loud, his manner of speaking blunt and harsh. Now he has mellowed considerably. He smiles more frequently, his voice is softer, his manner of approach easier, freer, more obliging. The segregation of sexes, which used to be a marked feature in the worker's life, is on the decline. He marries earlier, he takes his wife or sweetheart out more frequently, he is more of a home-bird. The women around him imbue him with feminine values. He accepts his wife as his companion on more or less equal terms, especially when she goes out to work and earns her own living. The fear of being sponged on by women is not as prevalent as it used to be.

All this means that the worker is moving away from his mates. His home and family-centredness brings in its wake the tendency to keep aloof from his mates. Formerly he used to congregate with his mates, to "knock about" with them, to scheme with them, and there was a great deal of mutual aid. Now he sees his mates outside the works only occasionally, mostly on the sports ground or in a club, or at matches. No help, no scheming is required. There are no campaigns to wage, as little mutual help and assistance are needed. The Unions are taken for granted, and do their work without his help.

Social contacts with neighbours suffer the same fate. "Keeping oneself to oneself," either in the strictest sense or in a larger sense which includes seeing some friends occasionally, is on the ascendant. Is loneliness the outcome? No, the worker has no time for that. He is too busy decorating his house, "doing it himself," or watching T.V. "Nowadays there is no problem what to do with your spare time"—I heard.

In my enquiry I came across some Communist workers, not for the first time. What struck me about even the Communists was their lukewarm interest or lack of interest in the larger issues of the world or social problems at large; this showed a marked difference from the attitudes I had encountered previously. Their interest was primarily in their homes, their wives and children. They were also affected by the general mood and tendency towards domestication.

This moving away from his mates and strong home-centredness, with a romanticized idea of family life, fits well with another new characteristic, the "personalization" of the worker's mind. He is intensely interested in persons, in personal life, personal stories, personal troubles and successes. He is not interested in ideas or general problems or objective situations, but in personal relations. Social relations are soon transfigured and translated into personal terms. Not "what" but "who" is the main question. The press, radio and T.V. have contributed largely to this process. This personalization, as the term suggests, is nothing but a process of identification, a projection of his own personality.

Home-centredness and personalization, together with the decline in gregariousness, involves also the process of greater individualization. The term may be misleading. The colourful or eccentric personalities of a kind once common among the working classes are fewer in number. Workers are more of a pattern, cast in one mould. They are more conformist than ever, but still the tendency is to break away from the mass, to think of oneself not as one of the mass but as an individual, a person. The home-centredness has brought about greater self-centredness as the home is only an extension of the "I."

The worker wants little things instead of big things, he wants them for himself rather than for society at large, he wants better and wider opportunities for getting along. Old slogans, old loyalties tend to leave him cold. The class struggle interests him less and less. The idea of the working class as an oppressed or an exploited class or the romanticized idea of the working class as foremost in the struggle for progress and social justice, is fading from his mind and is more and more replaced by the idea of the working class as a class well established and well-to-do in its own right. "Working class but not poor" is his idea of himself. Class divisions are no longer marked out by hostility and segregation. They are still there, but class feelings are less active and less virulent. Also the ethos of class solidarity, of group movement, seems to be weakened, as a man thinks primarily of himself and his home. . . .

Is he happier than his father was? He is more contented, better pleased with himself, prouder of his achievements. Is he getting bored? Has he too much time on his hands? Has he already joined the leisured class? He is still very busy. The five-day week applies only in theory, as a great deal of overtime is worked at weekends. At home he is again kept very busy. The pressure on his leisure-time comes from many quarters. T.V.-watching for some programmes is almost obligatory. When he has a car or motor cycle, there are family outings to be undertaken. When he has a garden as most working men have, he is kept busy gardening, whether he likes it or not. And when he has a house of his own or a council house, "Do-it-yourself" absorbs a great deal of his time. In spite of this, a considerable number of men take up constructive hobbies such as woodwork, model-making, making and repairing all sorts of things, arts and crafts, not to mention remunerative sidelines. They may not have "money to burn" but they often have enough to venture into new and exciting hobbies which were previously closed to them.

Have the worker's cultural horizons been enlarged, his cultural interests deepened? We can say that stomachs are being filled and bodily needs well taken care of in the affluent society, but whether minds and hearts are being filled is more doubtful. We saw, on the strength of the test paper for cultural horizons, that his cultural interests are still limited. The "two nations" may be a thing of the past in terms of economics but not in terms of education and culture.

The worker is now more prosperous than ever, and if prosperity is a prelude to art and learning we may hope that a rise in his cultural standards will come about in due course, but it is doubtful whether it would be an automatic process, taking place without a determined effort of social action. It is also doubtful whether it can be accomplished without breaking down the resistance of vested interests in mass entertainment. A good case could be made for a movement whose standard programme would be the establishment of common ownership of means of education and culture.

The Family Besieged

CHRISTOPHER LASCH

Writing specifically about American families, Christopher Lasch here sees a basic pattern to modern civilization that robs man of his worth in the outside world, returns him to the family for comfort, and then robs him of a solid family in turn. This picture of the family does not differ entirely from the more optimistic view offered by Ferdynand Zweig; Zweig, too, mentions the family as a source of superficial pleasure rather than emotional intensity. Lasch's view is also compatible in many respects with a pessimistic modernization theory, which would posit great change in the structure of society but immense deterioration in human content. In addition, his views should be juxtaposed to the patterns of women's modernization, for Lasch is particularly unhappy about the decline of male family values in the twentieth century.

Lasch clearly does not believe in a single modern personality type. For him the twentieth century has fostered the elaboration of a shallow narcissistic personality, evolving away from the achievement orientation of nineteenth-century individualism, which was in turn based on intense rather than friendly parent-child ties. Lasch posits then an ongoing structural process, that of industrialization, but two distinct stages in mentality. His judgment should be tested against other views of the contemporary family as well against the implied success of the nineteenth-century family. Were parents so successful in raising children in the past?

By implication, Lasch would reject also the idea that the contemporary family is returning to a pattern rather like that of preindustrial society, with greater husband-wife mutuality; or if it is returning, it is doing so amid such vast social changes, requiring strong individual personalities, that it fails to meet the challenges of contemporary life. Lasch is profoundly pessimistic. He sees no value in modern leisure patterns as a source of individual development or strong family training. If he is accurate in describing a contemporary morass, and the family's decay within it, what can the remedy possibly be?

The rise of bourgeois society enlarged the boundaries of freedom, but it also created new forms of enslavement. Capitalism created unprecedented abundance but simultaneously widened the gap between rich and poor. The conquest of nature liberated mankind from superstition but deprived it of the consolation of religion. The spread of education, designed to make the masses more critical of established authority encouraged a certain cynicism about official protestations but also made the masses avid consumers of advertising and propaganda, which kept them in a chronic state of uncertainty and unsatisfied desire. Private property and the nuclear family, which in the nineteenth century provided new supports for political freedom and personal autonomy, contained within themselves elements fatal to their own existence. When the democratic revolutions freed property from feudal restrictions, they also removed the obstacles to its accumulation and brought about a situation in which the most characteristic form of "private" property would be the multinational corporation. As for the family, its isolation from the marketplace, from the ravages of which it provided a refuge, was precarious from the beginning.

From the moment the conception of the family as a refuge made its historical appearance, the same forces that gave rise to the new privacy began to erode it. The nineteenth-century cult of the home, where the woman ministered to her exhausted husband, repaired the spiritual damage inflicted by the market, and sheltered her children from its corrupting influence, expressed the hope that private satisfactions could make up for the collapse of communal traditions and civic order. But the machinery of organized domination, which had impoverished work and reduced civic life to a competitive free-for-all, soon organized "leisure" itself as an industry. The so-called privatization of experience went hand in hand with an unprecedented assault on privacy. The tension between the family and the economic and political order, which in the early stages of bourgeois society protected the members of the family from the full impact of the market, gradually abated.

The withdrawal into the "emotional fortress" of the family took place not because family life became warmer and more attractive in the nineteenth century, as some historians have argued, but because the outside world came to be seen as more forbidding. Nor did the family's withdrawal take place without a struggle. Older patterns of male conviviality gradually gave way to a life centered on hearth and home, but in the first half of the nineteenth century, the new domesticity still met with resistance, which crystallized in protracted battles over temperance, the rights

From Christopher Lasch, *Haven in a Heartless World: The Family Besieged* (New York: Basic Books, 1977), pp. 167–74, 176–77, 183.

of women, and the attempt to suppress popular amusements and festivities that allegedly distracted the lower orders from familial duties.

Seasonal holidays and festivals, so important to the life of preindustrial societies, disappeared from Western Europe and the United States not because the working class suddenly discovered the delights of polymorphous sexuality but because the champions of temperance and sobriety—the prohibitionists, the feminists, the Society for the Prevention of Vice, the Society for the Prevention of Cruelty to Animals, the Animals' Friend Society—stamped them out as occasions for drunkenness, blood sports, and general debauchery. Bourgeois domesticity did not simply evolve. It was imposed on society by the forces of organized virtue, led by feminists, temperance advocates, educational reformers, liberal ministers, penologists, doctors, and bureaucrats.

In their campaign to establish the family as the seat of civic virtue, the guardians of morality dwelled on the dangers lurking in the streets, the demoralizing effects of "civilization," the growth of crime and violence, and the cutthroat competition that prevailed in the marketplace. They urged right-thinking men and women to seek shelter in the sanctuary of the family. From the beginning, the glorification of domestic life simultaneously condemned the social order of which the family allegedly served as the foundation. In urging a retreat to private satisfactions, the custodians of domestic virtue implicitly acknowledged capitalism's devastation of all forms of collective life, while at the same time they discouraged attempts to repair the damage by depicting it as the price that had to be paid for material and moral improvement.

Nineteenth-century doctors, reformers, and public health officers, like missionaries, regarded themselves as agents of enlightenment, bearers of civilization to the heathen. Like their ecclesiastical counterparts, they believed it their mission to stamp out debauchery and superstition. Neither the disinterested benevolence with which they performed their duties, the dangers they suffered, nor the personal sacrifices they endured gave them an understanding of the customs they were attempting to eradicate. In rural France, doctors reported that peasant husbands unfeelingly exposed their wives to syphilis and that their wives ignored the health of their children. After the domestic revolution engineered by themselves, on the other hand, "unity reigned in the families," in the words of one practitioner, "and this true solicitousness, which means the sharing equally of trouble and joy, fidelity between the spouses, fatherly tenderness, filial respect and domestic intimacy," became the general rule.

The new religion of health, though based on modern science and technology, was no more tolerant of other religions than was Christianity itself. The medical mode of salvation, no less than its predecessors, asserted exclusive rights to virtue and truth. But whereas the missionaries, for all their ignorance of the peoples to whom they ministered, sometimes defended their elementary human rights against the state's attempt to enslave or otherwise exploit them for profit, the medical profession worked hand in hand with the state to modernize the backward sectors of European and American society. This partnership proved to be more effective than Christianity in improving not only the health of the poor but their "morals" as well.

The attack on disease was part of a general attack on preindustrial customs. It went hand in hand with the suppression of public executions, the movement to institutionalize the insane, and the campaign to replace public riot and licentiousness with domestic bliss. Doctors were among the earliest exponents of the new ideology of the family. They extolled domesticity on the grounds that it encouraged regular habits, temperance, and careful attention to the needs of the young. They saw the family as an asylum, analogous in its functions to the hospital, the insane asylum, and the prison. Just as doctors and penologists hoped to cure sickness, madness, and crime by segregating the patient in a professionally supervised environment devoted to his care, they hoped to mold the child's character in the home.

The therapeutic conception of insanity, disease, and crime repudiated theological assumptions of their inevitability and relieved the patient of responsibility for his actions, insisting that he was neither possessed nor willfully sinning, but sick. The new conception of the family as an asylum similarly repudiated fatalism and the assumption of original sin, insisting on the child's innocence and plasticity. The medical profession saw itself as the successor to the church, just as theorists of bourgeois domesticity for a long time upheld marriage as the successor to monasticism. Whereas the church, in attempting to stamp out sex, had merely made it an obsession, these theorists maintained, marriage put sex at the service of procreation and encouraged a healthy acceptance of the body. This affirmation of the physical side of life had demonstrably better effects on the health of the individual and the community, according to bourgeois moralists, than the church's denial of the body.

From the beginning, a medical view of reality thus underlay attempts to remodel private life. The struggle between the new remissions and the old proscriptions, between personal fulfillment and self-sacrifice, between the ideology of work and the ideology of creative leisure, began in the nineteenth century. Liberal clergymen themselves participated in the campaign to transform religion into moral and mental hygiene. They allied themselves with a nascent feminism and with the campaign to feminize society by extending the domesticating influence of women to institutions beyond the home. The religion of health had a special appeal to women because of its concern with personal relations, its attempt to substitute domestic enjoyments for the rough and brutal camaraderie of males, and its glorification of the child and of maternal influence on the child's development. The conflict between the work ethic and the therapeutic point of view, which became sharper as the century wore on, also presented itself as a conflict between masculine and feminine "spheres"—the split between business and "culture," the practical and the aesthetic, so characteristic of bourgeois society and of American society in particular. As late as the 1950s, John R. Seeley and his associates found the same division in the suburbs of Toronto, where women joined with mental experts in combating the competitive, work-oriented values of their husbands. Middle-class Canadian men valued material objects and their production, while their wives concerned themselves with the management of personal relations. Men valued achievement; women, happiness and well-being.

In the United States, relations between the sexes had entered a new stage by this time. When social scientists replaced clergymen as the most prominent purveyors of the new ethic, male resistance, at least among the educated, gradually declined. The once-familiar alignment of domestic forces, in which the father tacitly sides with the children's war against maternally imposed refinement, now survived only in folklore. The ideology of mental health, having routed the residual opposition of American males, effectively ruled the family, thus bringing domestic life under the growing domination of outside experts. The remarkable popularity of Benjamin Spock's *Baby and Child Care*, which went through more than 200 printings between 1946 and the mid-seventies, provided merely the most obvious example of this parental dependence on outside help and advice.

Outside advice, however, weakens parents' already faltering confidence in their own judgment. Thus although Spock urges parents to trust both their own and the child's impulses, he undermines this trust by reminding them of the incalculable consequences of their actions. Words "uttered in a thoughtless or angry moment" can "destroy the child's confidence"; nagging can lead to troubles that "last for years"; and the failure to give the child love and security can cause "irreparable harm." "In the face of this forbidding awareness," Michael Zuckerman writes, "Spock's appeals for confidence fade. He may know that mothers and fathers cannot come to any assurance of their own adequacy if they have to rely on physicians and psychiatrists in every extremity, but he is nonetheless unwilling to leave parents to their own intuitions at such junctures." The proliferation of medical and psychiatric advice undermines parental confidence at the same time that it encourages a vastly inflated idea of the importance of child-rearing techniques and of the parent's responsibility for their failure. Meanwhile, the removal of education and medical care from the household deprives parents of practical experience, during their own childhood, in taking care of children, nursing the sick, and housekeeping. In their ignorance and uncertainty, parents redouble their dependence on experts, who confuse them with a superabundance of conflicting advice, itself subject to constant changes in psychiatric and medical fashion. Because the "immature, narcissistic" American mother "is so barren of spontaneous manifestations of maternal feelings," according to one observer, "she studies vigilantly all the new methods of upbringing and reads treatises about physical and mental hygiene." She acts not on her own feelings or judgment but on the "picture of what a good mother should be."

Thus the family struggles to conform to an ideal of the family imposed from without. The experts agree that parents should neither tyrannize over their children nor burden them with "oversolicitous" attentions. They agree, moreover, that every action is the product of a long causal chain and that moral judgments have no place in child rearing. This proposition, central to the mental health ethic, absolves the child from moral responsibility while leaving that of his parents undiminished. Under these conditions, it is not surprising that many parents seek to escape the exercise of this responsibility by avoiding confrontations with the child and by retreating from the work of discipline and character formation. Permissive ideologies rationalize this retreat. When parents cannot altogether avoid disciplinary decisions, they seek to delegate them to other authorities. The father cites the demands of his work as an excuse for assigning daily discipline to his wife. She in turn avoids the most painful encounters by invoking the ultimate authority of the father, threatening children with a fearful reckoning when he finally returns to the scene. Both parents shift much of the responsibility for the child's development to his peers—against whom, in the absence of firm standards of their own, they also measure the child's academic, athletic, and psychological progress. Seeley and his associates found that upper-middle-class parents in "Crestwood Heights" hesitated to impose their own tastes on the child and left the formation of taste to the child's peers. "Crestwood parents who would deem it morally wrong and psychologically destructive to regulate the expression of their children's tastes, after self-examination realized and stated that they were able to afford these views because . . . in these areas the peer group performed a satisfactory policing function for them." Permissiveness thus rests, in part, on peer-group control.

The peer group not only regulates taste, it puts forward its own version of ideal family life. It circulates information about parental regulations currently in force, about regulations that are violated with impunity, about what the world upholds as the norm of parenthood. The child's mastery of this information gives him an important tactical advantage in negotiations with his parents. If he can show that they have departed from established norms, he further weakens their self-confidence. Having made it clear that their own actions are to be submitted to the same standards of justice to which the child himself is expected to conform, parents find it difficult to specify those standards. In theory, justice derives from reason, but community practice turns out to be the only reliable guide. The child knows more about this ambiguous and constantly shifting practice than his parents do, and he skillfully exploits their uneasiness. Parental training has collapsed not because of the inevitable supersession of parents' technical knowledge but because organized interest groups, such as the health and welfare professions and the adolescent peer group, have a stake in promoting their own conceptions of the world, which compete with those of the family. Like the health industry, the peer group spreads information that parents cannot hope to master in its complexity but on which they nevertheless depend in their unsuccessful struggles to discipline their children and at the same time to retain their devotion.

Relations within the family have come to resemble relations in the rest of society. Parents refrain from arbitrarily imposing their wishes on the child, thereby making it clear that authority deserves to be regarded as valid only insofar as it conforms to reason. Yet in the family as elsewhere, "universalistic" standards prove on examination to be illusory. In American society, most rules exist only to be broken, in the words of a popular axiom. Custom has reestablished itself as in many ways the superior of reason. The administration of justice gives way, in a therapeutic society, to a complicated process of negotiation. Just as prices in the neocapitalist economy, allegedly determined by the impersonal laws of supply and demand, are really fixed by negotiations among corporations, unions, and government (with the corporations taking the leading role), so justice is fixed by means of similar bargains among interested parties. In learning to live by the law, therefore, the child actually learns how to get around the law, in the first place by getting around his parents. . . .

If parents attempt to intervene in their children's lives, family comedies depict them as objects of amusement or contempt. Thus Mother ineffectually attempts to uphold old-fashioned ideas of decorum and refinement, which Father collaborates with the younger generation in subverting. Father's well-meaning attempts to instruct, befriend, or discipline the young lead to situations that expose his incompetence. Having nothing of value to pass on to his sons, he reserves most of his affection, what there is of it, for his daughters. Yet he makes no attempt to keep his daughter to himself. He makes way for her suitors without complaint, even encouraging their courtship. According to Martha Wolfenstein and Nathan Leites, the ease with which fathers welcome sons-in-law as boon companions exposes another important theme in American popular culture: the sharing of a woman by two friends or "buddies." As sex becomes more casual, the jealousy of the male subsides. He not only tolerates promiscuity in his women but finds it titillating, largely because women know how to keep promiscuity within the bounds of what is called sexiness. . . .

The contemporary cult of sensuality implies a repudiation of sensuality in all but its most primitive forms. The fascination with personal relations, which becomes increasingly intense as the hope of political solutions recedes, conceals a thoroughgoing disenchantment with personal relations. Ideologies of impulse gratification and pleasure seeking gain the ascendancy at the very moment that pleasure loses its savor. A narcissistic withdrawal of interest from the external world underlies both the demand for immediate gratification—resoundingly endorsed by advertising, mass promotion, and the health industry—and the intolerable anxiety that continually frustrates this demand. The more the "liberated" man clamors for fulfillment, the more he succumbs to hypochondria, to melancholy, or to a suicidal self-hatred that alternates, not with occasional heights of rapture, but with a chronic mild depression, the dominant mood of the times.

Work and Play

JOHN ARDAGH

European society has changed greatly since 1945. Levels of productivity have soared in comparison with both the European past and the performance of the United States in the same decades. Change has been particularly striking in countries like France, which was not previously known for zealous economic behavior and which suffered from severe dislocation during the years immediately following World War II. Government and corporate officials, often dubbed technocrats because of their devotion to planning, have worked hard to promote economic growth and technological change.

This economic surge has involved other sectors of the French population. The following passage discusses styles of work and leisure in Toulouse, a regional center in southwestern France. The description of work goals and patterns invites comparison with nineteenth-century French middle-class behavior. In some ways, the French are adhering more closely to the classic middle-class ethic now than they did in the nineteenth century when the cultural example of the traditional aristocracy bore more heavily on society. Inevitably, changes in postwar France invite comparison also with the United States. "Americanization," in the form of new drugstores and new eating habits, has been an important phenomenon in contemporary Europe. In the 1950s the term often brought derision, when the Europeans feared American domination. Now, the French seem sufficiently comfortable with aspects of an affluent consumer society that the sense of foreignness has declined.

Inevitably, change in contemporary France brings losses as well as gains. Many observers mark with regret the passing of some eating customs that marked the good old days, at least for the well-to-do. But change is not simply in the direction of American standards. Note that while French eating habits seem to be moving in some American directions, they do not merge entirely. And the French enthusiasm for hard work developed in a period when Americans were developing new worries about their own devotion to labor; yet the French also maintain a devotion to lengthy vacations, in contrast to maintenance of the long working year in the United States. Contemporary Europe, in other words, displays some patterns in work and leisure that differ from their counterparts in other advanced industrial countries. Within Europe, a sense of national and regional lifestyles persists.

In their daily lives, at work and leisure, Toulousains are struggling to reconcile the traditional French ways with a newer, more international style of consumer living. Are the evenings still for long, leisurely talkative meals, or for a quick snack followed by thrillers and quiz-games on television? Does an employee still make his way home every noon for the ritual family lunch, despite commuter problems that make this habit ever less realistic?—or will he opt for the canteen? Does his wife hold out for fresh farm produce, or stock up with tins and frozen packets from the new hypermarket down the road? In these and many other ways, Toulousains are torn between old and new.

Their living standards rose steadily in the 1945–75 period, especially in housing. Twenty or so years ago, the average family ate well and knew how to enjoy itself, but accepted a low level of home comfort. In 1954, only 44 per cent of homes had inside flushing lavatories and a mere 11.4 per cent had bath or shower. This latter figure has now risen to well over 50 per cent, since for some years all new homes have been built with modern plumbing. But most lower-income flats are still equipped with no more than a shower or hip-bath, and their living-rooms are very small: despite the improvement, Toulousains remain noticeably less comfortably housed than [German] Swabians, or even [British] Geordies. Yet they manage to fill up their cramped little dwellings with every kind of modern gadget—levels of ownership of washing-machines and refrigerators are higher than in Britain. Toulousains are finally becoming more house-proud, and their patterns of domestic budgeting are gradually moving closer to those of northern Europe with a relative decline in the high percentage devoted to food and entertainment.

It was claimed to me by Dr. Brouat that the true Toulousain disdains hard work and lives for his pleasures, but I think that today this is only partially true. Much of the city's working life has become infected by the new work mania of the French, imported here by the newcomers, notably the Parisian executives and the energetic *pieds noirs*. *Cadres* and businessmen work with more eagerness and dynamism than in Newcastle, and for longer hours, often staying at their desks till 7 or 8 at night: if they were better at teamwork, the results might reach Swabian levels.

One management consultant told me that he and all his staff work from 8 a.m. to 7 p.m., though this does include the two-hour lunch break that is still the norm in Toulouse despite its growing impracticability. "Many of us," he said, "would like to move over to the Anglo-Saxon short break and go home an hour earlier in the evening. But this would be hard to adopt unless other firms did the same: many of my clients do their busiest work after six and expect me to be here at the end of the

From John Ardagh, *A Tale of Five Cities* (New York: Harper and Row, 1979), pp. 336–41.

'phone." Most shops, banks, offices, hairdressers, still close from 12 till 2—"By staggering my staff, I could easily stay open," said the owner of one big store, "but there's not the public demand for it. My customers are not used to shopping at midday, they expect to be home eating a big lunch." This is still the main meal of the day for most families. School-children as well as their fathers go home for it, even though the growth of the city is making it less convenient: as people move out to new suburbs, they may have to spend half their two-hour lunch break on travel, and rush-hour traffic-jams occur four times a day. In Paris and many northern French cities, there has been a steady move towards the Anglo-Saxon system, which the French call *"la journée continue"*: but Toulouse, conservative in so many things, has been slow to follow this trend, and only in the past few years have some larger stores and banks begun to remain open over lunchtime. On the other hand, supermarkets stay open till 8 p.m., often later, whereas in Newcastle they close at 5:30 or 6. This English practice is also tiresome, though in a town of commuter proportions it seems more logical.

Since they stay at work so late, Toulousains set less stress than Geordies or Swabians on evening leisure activities during the week. They have few hobbies, they are not great club-joiners. But they live for their weekends and their holidays—the French take the longest holidays in Europe. Most families now own a car, and their first aim at the weekend, summer or winter, is to get out of town, for Toulousains adapt little better than Parisians to the new tensions of urban living, and they feel an urgent need to regain contact with nature. Since many are ex-peasants, or the children of peasants, at weekends they go to relatives in the country, or else they retain the old family farmstead for use as a weekend and holiday cottage. People of all classes, including workers, spend money on buying some little rural *résidence secondaire*. Or else they go walking or skiing in the Pyrenees, or for trips to the Mediterranean or Atlantic. And the vast traffic-jams on the roads into Toulouse every Sunday evening bear witness to a weekly migration that is largely responsible for the dearth of social and community life in the city. In the old days, before mass car ownership, most Toulousains were forced to rely on each others' company at weekends: the new mobility has encouraged privacy, hence unsociability. In addition, the average family takes at least four or five weeks' holiday a year, and in the wealthier classes it may be much more. They go to the sea or their country cottage, or they tour abroad, mostly to nearby Spain.

Toulousains spend more time on outdoor sports than most Europeans. All classes go hunting, shooting and fishing on their country weekends; in town, they play tennis or *pelote* (a kind of outdoor fives or squash, Basque in origin) or, above all, *boules*. So popular are sports that the city council has recently built four large new recreation centres in the outskirts, complete with lakes for boating, swimming-pools and playing-fields. The latter are essentially for rugby, which was imported here by the English in the last century and is today more popular than association football throughout the south-west. In Toulouse, rugby is a proud tradition almost on a par with *bel canto* and *cassoulet*: the town has 30 teams, two of them of international class. One of these, the Stade Toulousain, has seven times won the French national championship. When it plays at home to one of its major rivals, such as Bordeaux, the crowd gets almost as excited as Newcastle soccer fans when their team is at home to Liverpool.

An important part of local leisure is good eating. . . . Toulousains may care less for gastronomy than in former days, yet the tradition remains in their bones: they eat well as a matter of course, without thinking twice, and with the innate good taste that a Bolognese, for instance, shows over dress or a Stuttgarter over music. A housewife will spend time and care on choosing just the right cut of meat, or cheeses of perfect ripeness, or the correct fresh vegetable to go with a certain dish, and even an ordinary weekday family lunch is a carefully planned affair. A middle-class family might start with some neat array of *hors d'oeuvres* including *crudités* and *terrine* of duck, then go on to garlicky roast leg of lamb with properly-dressed salad, followed by a cheese tray including the local Roquefort, then a home-made *clafoutis* (a kind of sweet Yorkshire pudding filled with cherries), a regional speciality. Wines are also likely to be local—say, a red from Cahors or Gaillac—for only on special occasions will Toulousains drink a more expensive wine from another region.

Admittedly, the gastronomic tradition is now under pressure, as younger housewives find less time for careful home cooking, as a new generation turns its attention to other things, and as the French food industry begins to adopt the mass-processing habits of other countries. Much later than in Britain or Germany, frozen foods made a cautious appearance in northern France in the 1960s and are now percolating to conservative Toulouse. Some hurried housewives may now accept to buy frozen or tinned vegetables rather than fresh ones, or put some processed ingredients in their soups, casseroles and cakes. Or they may as soon toss a steak under the grill as spend hours preparing some local stew such as *cassoulet* or *boeuf en daube* as their mothers would have done. Gastronomy suffers. Yet there are some bright signs—one, that when the French do go over to processed foods, they often ally them to their own complex classic dishes. Go into a Toulouse hypermarket, and you will find the deep-freeze full of packets of pre-cooked *cassoulet, coq-au-vin, bouillabaisse,* and so on, as well as frozen snails, quail and frogs' legs; and the French are more ready to buy these costly delicacies than staple frozen items such as peas or fish-fingers, so popular in Britain. In fact, many experts believe that the French, after a difficult transition phase, may succeed in preserving their traditional quality within the context of modern techniques. Already one finds instances of how modern mass catering can retain gastronomic flair: in the canteen of the Motorola factory in Toulouse (American-owned!) I had a delicious *cassolette des fruits de mer,* the *plat du jour.* I found no such refinement in the works canteens of Stuttgart or Newcastle.

Toulouse's restaurants are in much the same transitional phase as home cooking, and many have lowered their standards, as they struggle with rising costs, staff shortages, and the temptation to cut corners by using tins and packets. It used to be possible in almost any *bistrot* to find for a modest price an honest *cassoulet,* the famous rich stew of haricot beans, port, mutton, Toulouse sausage and preserved goose. I know a few places in Toulouse where the *cassoulet* is still superb, but in most others the vital ingredient, *confit d'oie,* will have come straight out of a tin and the dish will lack flavour. Another local speciality, as in all the southwest, is truffled *foie gras,* often served hot in a sweet sauce with tiny grapes—delicious, but pricey.

Inevitably, Toulouse has its "Le Grill-Pub", pseudo-smart, with expensive hybrid menu and plush décor hopefully imitating some imagined Victorian pub—one of scores of such places in France today. For a few years recently it also had "Le Drugstore". So-called "drugstores" first appeared in Paris in the early '60s and soon spread to the provinces, Toulouse's being one of the first. They adopted an American name because of the naïf fashion for *franglais* words: but the French "drugstore" is a purely French invention, owing little to American ones. In France, a drugstore is a modernised *brasserie* with a ritzy Paris/New York air and a number of boutiques attached, all open till late: Toulouse's sold books, newspapers, cosmetics, sweets and tobacco, till about midnight, and very useful it was too. Its two restaurants served rather good food. It was a favourite haunt of the younger affluent society, and on a small scale had something of a metropolitan Champs-Elysées air. Unfortunately it lost money, and closed in 1976, to re-open as a simple steak-bar. One or two newer places also call themselves "drugstores", but they have no boutiques, and entirely lack the old ambiance.

The Twentieth-Century Way of Death

PHILIPPE ARIÈS

The way that modern society views death is gaining increasing attention from social historians. All agree that attitudes and practices regarding death have changed greatly with modernization, perhaps more than once. In this selection, an eminent French historian, previously known for his work on the development of modern attitudes toward children, describes what he sees as major weaknesses in the contemporary approach to death. A number of other studies of death, in American as well as European history, roughly coincide with his approach.

Modern values do not neatly harmonize with death, according to this general argument. In the nineteenth century, the clash was not yet clear—death received a great deal of attention. Even then, elaborate new funeral practices suggested a guilt about death. Then in the twentieth century modern hostility to death became clearer, as demonstrated by the reduction of earlier funeral practices and mourning.

Modern people seek pleasure, individual identity, control over their environment, progress in secular terms. Death contradicts these values. Hence, Ariès discusses the various ways that moderns seek to conceal death, which he clearly believes weaken the quality of modern life. In more traditional societies—even in the nineteenth century—death was faced more directly, surrounded by powerful ceremonies; this approach may well have helped the dying and the bereaved to be better reconciled with fate.

The modern approach to death obviously involves our attitudes toward health and medicine. We look to doctors to cure, more than to priests to console. Is this a fault, and should we try to correct it by returning to a more positive acceptance of death? Other explanations for modern attitudes also deserve exploration. Infant deaths were once common. Modern people, shaking off traditional resignation toward infant death, have increasingly confined high death rates to the very old. The nature of death has changed. In the past, lingering respiratory diseases were the major cause of death among adults. Now, quick deaths are somewhat more common, which may affect attitudes quite apart from a general invocation of modern values and a desire to ignore the inevitable. In other words, the Ariès approach, although it is a powerful use of modern history, need not be accepted uncritically; his conclusions can be evaluated and explained in different ways.

In recent years, both in Europe and the United States, new efforts to deal with death have gained ground. A *hospice* movement, designed to help terminally ill people and their families come to terms with death rather than try to fight it through heroic medicine, is a key expression of this new approach. Is this movement likely to produce a radically new stance toward death—and if it does, will this suggest a major change in the overall outlook of modern Western people?

The beginning of the twentieth century saw the completion of the psychological mechanism that removed death from society, eliminated its character of public ceremony, and made it a private act. At first this act was reserved for intimates, but eventually even the family was excluded as the hospitalization of the terminally ill became widespread.

There were still two periods of communication between the dying—or dead—man, and society: the final moments, in which the dying man recovered the initiative that he had lost, and mourning. The second great milestone in the contemporary history of death is the rejection and elimination of mourning. The first complete analysis of this phenomenon was made by Geoffrey Gorer, who was led to the subject by a series of personal experiences.

Gorer lost his father and his grandfather almost at the same time. His father died on the *Lusitania* in 1915, so Gorer was not able to see his body, as was then the custom. Indeed, he did not see his first dead body until 1931. He did observe the conventions of mourning, although he says that these had started to break down during the war because of the high mortality at the front, and also because women were working in men's jobs. The death of a sister-in-law and in 1948 the death of a friend introduced him to the new situation of the bereaved, their behavior, and that of society toward them. He realized that the social function of mourning was changing, and that this change revealed a profound transformation in people's attitude toward death. It was in 1955 that he published in *Encounter* his famous article, "The Pornography of Death," in which he showed that death had become as shameful and unmentionable as sex was in the Victorian era. One taboo had been substituted for another.

In 1961 his brother died of cancer. He was survived by a wife and children. Gorer took charge of the burial and looked after his sister-in-law and nephews, and again he was struck by the rejection of traditional ways of behaving and by the harmful effects of this rejection. He told the whole story in a book. Then he decided to study the phenomenon, no longer as a memorialist but as a sociologist, in a scientific manner. In 1963 he began an investigation of mourning, which resulted in his major work, *Death, Grief, and Mourning in Contemporary Britain.*

His first observation was that death has been removed to a distance. Not only are people no longer present at the deathbed, but burial has ceased to be a familiar sight. Among those interviewed, 70 percent had not attended a funeral in five years. Children do not even attend the funerals of their parents. Of his nephews, Gorer writes, "Their father's death was quite unmarked for them by any ritual of any kind, and was

From Philippe Ariès *The Hour of Our Death,* trans. by Helen Weaver (New York: Random House, 1982), pp. 575–79, 611–14.

even nearly treated as a secret, for it was very many months before Elizabeth could bear to mention him or have him mentioned in her presence." When Gorer went back to his sister-in-law's house after his brother's cremation, she told him very naturally that she had had a good day with the children, that they had gone on a picnic and after that they had watched the grass being cut.

Children have been excluded from death. Either they are not informed or they are told that their father has gone on a trip or that Jesus has taken him. Jesus has become a kind of Santa Claus whom adults use to tell children about death without believing in him themselves.

A questionnaire published in 1971 by the American magazine *Psychology Today* elicited the following letter from a woman of twenty-five: "When I was twelve, my mother died of leukemia. She was there when I went to bed and when I woke up the next morning, my parents were gone. My father came home, took my brother and me on his knee, and burst into screeching sobs and said, 'Jesus took your mother.' Then we never talked about it again. It was too painful for all of us."

In most of the surveys the proportion of those who believe in an afterlife is between 30 and 40 percent. This is only an indication, for it is very difficult to confine in the words of a questionnaire notions that are more sensed than defined. The belief decreases in the young, whereas we have seen that it increases among the very ill.

It is rather remarkable that in 1963, in Gorer's investigation, and only among the old, one encounters the anthropomorphic eschatology of the nineteenth century. The subjects interviewed see their dead again and talk to them. "They are able to watch over us here and give us help and guidance." "Just before my brother died, he saw Mother standing at the foot of the bed." "He was killed in the Air Force, in the war, my youngest boy, and he often comes back and speaks to me." One day when the subject was in bed thinking and worrying about him, a voice said, "It's all right, Mum," and she thought, "Thank God he's all right; but he'd gone. Still, I think I'll see him again someday. In fact it's kept me going." Heaven is "a place where there are no worries, and where we meet all our relatives and friends."

One notes also the complete disappearance of hell. Even those who believe in the devil limit his power to this world and do not believe in eternal damnation. This will not surprise us; we have already noticed the phenomenon since the beginning of the nineteenth century.

The answers to Gorer's survey also show that the clergy have abandoned their traditional role. It is not that they are being dismissed; it is now they who are reticent.

But the most important phenomenon brought out by Gorer's study is the decline in mourning and in the dignity of funerals. From now on,

344 THE TWENTIETH CENTURY

cremation is more popular than burial. Out of sixty-seven cases, there are forty cremations and twenty-seven burials. The most remarkable aspect is the meaning attributed to the choice. To choose cremation is to reject the cult of tombs and cemeteries as it has developed since the beginning of the nineteenth century. "In many cases, it would appear, cremation is chosen because it is felt to get rid of the dead more completely and finally than does burial." Some subjects refuse cremation as being too final. This attitude does not depend on the nature of the act itself (the ancients worshiped the ashes of their dead) but on the comparison with the tomb. For despite the efforts of the directors of crematoria, the families of the cremated generally avoid erecting a monument. Out of the forty cremations in the survey, only one was accompanied by a memorial plaque and fourteen by an inscription in the "Book of Remembrance," which is available for the consultation of visitors. But there are no visitors. Some, and this is even more radical, have their ashes scattered.

But the cemetery remains the place of memory and visits. Of the twenty-seven who were buried, only four have no monuments. The survivor goes to the tomb to lay flowers on it and to remember.

It would be a mistake, however, to interpret the disappearance of the body in cremation as a mark of indifference or neglect. The relative of the cremated person rejects the physical reality of the site, its association with the body, which inspires distaste, and the public character of the cemetery. But he accepts the absolutely personal and private nature of regret. For the cult of the tomb he has substituted a cult of memory in the home: "I'm not one to keep going to the cemetery—I believe in helping the living. On birthdays, I put a bunch of flowers by their photographs" (a woman of forty-four). "I think that's the finish as far as the body goes. I mean, I think you can preserve their memory more at home than where they're actually buried. I'll tell you one thing I always do—perhaps it's silly, but I always buy her a little present at Christmas of some azaleas or flowers of some description; I feel that she's still in the house, you see" (a widower of fifty-five). Sometimes the cult may tend toward mummification: The house, or the room of the deceased, is left exactly as it was during his lifetime. Thus, a profound sense of loss is perfectly compatible with the neglect of the tomb, which is sometimes the hated place of the body.

From now on there are two places to cultivate the memory of the dead: at the tomb, a custom that is disappearing more rapidly in England than on the Continent; and in the home. The Canadian sociologist Fernand Dumont reports the following anecdote, which must have taken place in the early twentieth century: "When I was a child, the whole family used to pray together at home. . . . After the prayer, . . . my father would remain alone for a while, kneeling with his head in his hands. This intrigued me in a man who had never been 'pious' in the usual sense of the word. When I asked him about it, . . . my father admitted that at these times he often spoke to his father, who had been dead for a long time."

After the funeral and burial comes mourning in the true sense of the word. The pain of loss may continue to exist in the secret heart of the survivor, but the rule today, almost throughout the West, is that he must never show it in public. This is exactly the opposite of what used to be required. In France since about 1970 the long line of people offering their condolences to the family after the religious service has been eliminated. And in the country the death notice, which is still sent out, is accompanied by the dry, almost uncivil formula, "The family is not receiving," a way of avoiding the customary visits of neighbors and acquaintances before the funeral.

But generally speaking, the initiative for the refusal to mourn is not taken by the survivors. By withdrawing and avoiding outside contact, the family is affirming the authenticity of its grief, which bears no comparison with the solicitude of well-meaning relatives; it is also adopting the discreet behavior that society requires.

Geoffrey Gorer distinguishes three categories of bereaved: those who succeed in completely mastering their grief, those who hide it from others and keep it to themselves, and those who allow it to appear openly. In the first case the bereaved forces himself to behave as if nothing had happened, to pursue his normal life without interruption: Keep busy, he has been told by the few people he has spoken to, the doctor, the priest, a few friends. In the second case, almost nothing shows on the outside, and mourning goes on in private, "as one undresses or goes to bed in private." Mourning is an extension of modesty. This is probably the attitude most acceptable to common sense, which realizes that one must tolerate some release of emotion, provided it remains private. In the last case, the obstinate bereaved is mercilessly excluded as if he were insane.

Gorer had occasion to experience the judgment of society firsthand after the death of his brother. "A couple of times I refused invitations to cocktail parties, explaining that I was in mourning; the people who invited me responded to this statement with shocked embarrassment, as if I had voiced some appalling obscenity. Indeed, I got the impression that, had I stated that the invitation clashed with some esoteric debauchery I had arranged, I would have had understanding and jocular encouragement; as it was, the people whose invitations I had refused, educated and sophisticated as they were, mumbled and hurried away." They did not know how to behave in a situation that had become unusual. "They clearly no longer had any guidance from ritual as to the way to treat a self-confessed mourner; and I suspect they were frightened lest I give way to my grief, and involve them in a distasteful upsurge of emotion.". . .

If hell is gone, heaven has changed too. . . . We have followed the slow transition from the sleep of the *homo totus* to the glory of the immortal soul. The nineteenth century saw the triumph of another image of the beyond. The next world becomes the scene of the reunion of those whom death has separated but who have never accepted this separation: a recreation of the affections of earth, purged of their dross, assured of eternity. It is the paradise of Christians or the astral world of spiritualists and psychics. But it is also the world of the memories of nonbelievers and freethinkers who deny the reality of a life after death. In the piety of their love, they preserve the memories of their departed with an intensity equal to the realistic afterlife of Christians or psychics. The difference in doctrine between these two groups may be great, but it becomes negligible in the practice of what may be called the cult of the dead. They have all built the same castle, in the image of earthly homes, where they will be reunited—in dream or in reality, who knows?—with those whom they have never ceased to love.

In the nineteenth century the psychological landscape was completely transformed. . . . The situation that resulted did not last more than a century and a half. But the model of death that came next, our model, which I have called the invisible death, does not challenge the underlying tendency or the structural character of the changes of nineteenth century. It continues them, even if it seems to contradict them in its most spectacular effects. It is as if beyond a certain threshold, these tendencies produced the opposite effects.

Our contemporary model of death is still determined by the sense of privacy, but it has become more rigorous, more demanding. It is often said that the sense of privacy is declining. This is because today we demand the perfection of the absolute, we tolerate none of the compromises that romantic society still accepted beneath its rhetoric—or beneath its hypocrisy, as we would say. Intimacy must be either total or nonexistent. There is no middle ground between success and failure. It is possible that our attitude toward life is dominated by the certainty of failure. On the other hand, our attitude toward death is defined by the impossible hypothesis of success. That is why it makes no sense.

The modern attitude toward death is an extension of the affectivity of the nineteenth century. The last inspiration of this inventive affectivity was to protect the dying or the invalid from his own emotions by concealing the seriousness of his condition until the end. When the dying man discovered the pious game, he lent himself to it so as not to disappoint the other's solicitude. The dying man's relations with those around him were now determined by a respect for this loving lie.

In order for the dying man, his entourage, and the society that observed them to consent to this situation, the protection of the patient had to outweigh the joys of a last communion with him. Let us not forget that in the nineteenth century, death, by virtue of its beauty, had become an occasion for the most perfect union between the one leaving and those remaining behind. The last communion with God and/or with others was the great privilege of the dying. For centuries there was no question of depriving them of this privilege. But when the lie was maintained to the end, it eliminated this communion and its joys. Even when it was reciprocal and conspiratorial, the lie destroyed the spontaneity and pathos of the last moments.

Actually, the intimacy of these final exchanges had already been poisoned, first by the ugliness of disease, and later by the transfer to the hospital. Death became dirty, and then it became medicalized. The horror and fascination of death had fixed themselves for a moment on the apparent death and had then been sublimated by the beauty of the Last Communion. But the horror returned, without the fascination, in the repellent form of the serious illness and the care it required.

When the last of the traditional defenses against death and sex gave way, the medical profession could have taken over the role of the community. It did so in the case of sex, as is attested by the medical literature on masturbation. It tried to do so in the case of death by isolating it in the scientific laboratory and the hospital, from which the emotions would be banished. Under these conditions it was better to communicate silently in the complicity of a mutual lie.

It is obvious that the sense of the individual and his identity, what we mean when we speak of "possessing one's own death," has been overcome by the solicitude of the family.

But how are we to explain the abdication of the community? How has the community come to reverse its role and to forbid the mourning which it was responsible for imposing until the twentieth century? The answer is that the community feels less and less involved in the death of one of its members. First, because it no longer thinks it necessary to defend itself against a nature which has been domesticated once and for all by the advance of technology, especially medical technology. Next, because it no longer has a sufficient sense of solidarity; it has actually abandoned responsibility for the organization of collective life. The community in the traditional sense of the word no longer exists. It has been replaced by an enormous mass of atomized individuals.

But if this disappearance explains one abdication, it does not explain the powerful resurgence of other prohibitions. This vast and formless mass that we call society is, as we know, maintained and motivated by a new system of constraints and controls. It is also subject to irresistible movements that put it in a state of crisis and impose a transitory unity of aggression or denial. One of these movements has unified mass society against death. More precisely, it has led society to be ashamed of death, more ashamed than afraid, to behave as if death did not exist. If the sense of the other, which is a form of the sense of the self taken to its logical conclusion, is the first cause of the present state of death, then shame—and the resulting taboo—is the second.

But this shame is a direct consequence of the definitive retreat of evil. As early as the eighteenth century, man had begun to reduce the power of the devil, to question his reality. Hell was abandoned, at least in the case of relatives and dear friends, the only people who counted. Along with hell went sin and all the varieties of spiritual and moral evil. They were no longer regarded as part of human nature but as social problems that could be eliminated by a good system of supervision and punishment. The general advance of science, morality, and organization would lead quite easily to happiness. But in the middle of the nineteenth century, there was still the obstacle of physical illness and death. There was no question of eliminating that. The romantics circumvented or assimilated it. They beautified death, the gateway to an anthropomorphic beyond. They preserved its immemorial association with illness, pain, and agony; these things aroused pity rather than distaste. The trouble began with distaste: Before people thought of abolishing physical illness, they ceased to tolerate its sight, sounds, and smells.

Medicine reduced pain; it even succeeded in eliminating it altogether. The goal glimpsed in the eighteenth century had almost been reached. Evil was no longer part of human nature, as the religions, especially Christianity, believed. It still existed, of course, but outside of man, in certain marginal spaces that morality and politics had not yet colonized, in certain deviant behaviors such as war, crime, and nonconformity, which had not yet been corrected but which would one day be eliminated by society just as illness and pain had been eliminated by medicine.

But if there is no more evil, what do we do about death? To this question modern society offers two answers.

The first is a massive admission of defeat. We ignore the existence of a scandal that we have been unable to prevent; we act as if it did not exist, and thus mercilessly force the bereaved to say nothing. A heavy silence has fallen over the subject of death. When this silence is broken, as it sometimes is in America today, it is to reduce death to the insignificance of an ordinary event that is mentioned with feigned indifference. Either way, the result is the same: Neither the individual nor the community is strong enough to recognize the existence of death.

And yet this attitude has not annihilated death or the fear of death. On the contrary, it has allowed the old savagery to creep back under the mask of medical technology. The death of the patient in the hospital, covered with tubes, is becoming a popular image, more terrifying than the *transi* or skeleton of macabre rhetoric. There seems to be a correlation between the "evacuation" of death, the last refuge of evil, and the return of this same death, no longer tame. This should not surprise us. The belief in evil was necessary to the taming of death; the disappearance of the belief has restored death to its savage state.

A small elite of anthropologists, psychologists, and sociologists has been struck by this contradiction. They propose not so much to "evacuate" death as to humanize it. They acknowledge the necessity of death, but they want it to be accepted and no longer shameful. Although they may consult the ancient wisdom, there is no question of turning back or of rediscovering the evil that has been abolished. They propose to reconcile death with happiness. Death must simply become the discreet but dignified exit of a peaceful person from a helpful society that is not torn, not even overly upset by the idea of a biological transition without significance, without pain or suffering, and ultimately without fear.

PART 5

The Nature of Modern People

Gare St.-Lazare, Paris.

The Nature of Modern People

Most historians are reluctant to define the central characteristics of the modern outlook, perhaps because the modern outlook is too complex and varied to be described clearly. Yet many social scientists believe the modernization process has taken a certain direction; it is important, therefore, after having considered some major features of the process, to discuss its possible end results or at least the results to date.

The first four selections that follow are written by social scientists (though one is more a humanist historian); however, that is almost all the authors have in common. Different professional training and experience lead to different evaluations of the nature of modernization. Different approaches—the attempt to provide a general model, for example, as against a study of a particular class, region, or activity—lead to different evaluations of the extent of the process. Fortunately students of the modernization process in Europe are not forced simply to weigh one contemporary evaluation against another. They can apply their own understanding of key stages in the history of society during recent centuries. They can compare current institutions and values to those that antedate modernization. Perhaps out of this mix will come some sense of the nature of modern man, how new he is, and what his prospects are.

In addition to general comments on modernization, a new issue has recently surfaced: Even if modernization was, for a time, a fairly steady process with at least some good results, are contemporary societies taking a new direction? Some authors have written of a postindustrial society, quite different in key respects from the industrial world we have come to know. A number of observers worry about changes in major characteristics of Americans and Europeans. Commentators on the United States have cited the growth of shallow self-centeredness, quite different from the forceful if sometimes neurotic personalities that dominated the industrial era. Observers of Europe, until recently optimistic about Europe's recovery from World War II and the horrible dislocations that preceded it, worry that Europe has lost momentum, that a major decline lurks beneath the surface of still-respectable economic performance. These views, too, must be included in a final assessment of modern society in the present day.

The following selections all assume that modernization, or some key change at least, has occurred; our present differs from our past. The differences center on the angle from which modernization is viewed (play versus work, for example) and, above all, on the evaluation of the quality of the result. And at this point, instead of pretending to resolve the dichotomy between optimism and pessimism, we must raise three final issues. The optimists, who hold that the modern mentality is becoming increasingly rational and effective, may wear blinders, deliberately shutting themselves off from the pain of modern life, staying close to surface beliefs in progress and science. Can they pretend to describe the modern world when most artistic movements of the twentieth century are busily portraying a deeper, and on the whole more frightening, reality beneath or apart from reason? As to the pessimists, the key issue is the historical quality of their view. Are they blaming modern structures and ideas for sorrows that are inherent in the human condition (which the optimists admittedly ignore)? How much have the incidence, nature, and importance of madness increased? How lacking is the modern family compared to its preindustrial progenitor?

And of course, for optimists and pessimists alike, the final issue involves the future. The more optimistic statements about modernization risk a closed quality: We are close to perfection and, at most, can hope for more of the same in the future, abetted perhaps by further gains in technology and knowledge. But, if this modern world exists, how long can it last, and how adaptable will modern people be to really fundamental change? This is where the newly-worried comments about contemporary Europe take on particular force. On the other hand, if modernization represents humanity gone awry (not just tragic, but newly tragic), how can we escape? Can we really recapture the past, and do we understand our misfortune well enough to wish to do so?

BIBLIOGRAPHY

The twentieth-century French peasant has received considerable attention from scholars, many of whom disagree about the extent of traditional behavior in rural society. See Gordon Wright, *Rural Revolution in France: The Peasantry in the Twentieth Century* (Stanford, 1968), and Robert T. and Barbara G. Anderson, *Bus Stop for Paris* (New York, 1966). Lawrence W. Wylie, ed., *Chanzeaux: A Village in Anjou* (Cambridge, Mass., 1966), studies a particularly conservative region; see also Wylie's *Village in the Vaucluse* (Cambridge, Mass., 1957). A fine study of leisure is Michael Smith, Stanley Parker, and Cyril Smith, eds., *Leisure and Society in Britain* (London, 1973); see also Alisdair Clayre, *Work and Play: Ideas and Experience of Work and Leisure* (New York, 1974).

The modernization model has often been applied to studies of non-Western societies; see Ronald P. Dore, ed., *Aspects of Social Change in Japan* (Princeton, 1967), M. B. Jansen, *Changing Japanese Attitudes Toward Modernization* (Princeton, 1975); Gilbert Rozman, ed., *The Modernization of China* (New York, 1981); Cyril Black and others, *The Modernization of Japan and Russia* (New York, 1975). Cyril Black, *The Dynamics of Modernization: A Study on Comparative History* (New York, 1966), sketches a general history of the subject.

The modern mentality is discussed in Daniel Lerner, *The Passing of Traditional Society* (New York, 1964). For critiques, see Robert Nisbet, *Social Change and History: The Western Theory of Development* (New York, 1969); Dean C. Tipps, "Modernization and the Study of National Societies, A Critical Perspective," *Comparative Studies in Society and History* (1973), pages 199-226; and Reinhard Bendix, "Tradition and Modernity Reconsidered," *Comparative Studies in Society and History* (1967), pages 292-346.

Herbert Marcuse, *One Dimensional Man* (Boston, 1964), is a criticism of modernity somewhat related to Laing's. Fritz R. Stern, *The Politics of Cultural*

Despair: A Study in the Rise of the Germanic Ideology (Berkeley, 1961), traces some earlier manifestations of intellectual hostility to modernity.

On changes in contemporary society, see David Riesman, *The Lonely Crowd* (New Haven, 1968) and Christopher Lasch, *The Culture of Narcissism* (New York, 1978), on dominant attitudes. On technology and social structure, see Daniel Bell, *The Coming of Post-Industrial Society* (New York, 1973) and Alvin Toffler, *Future Shock* (New York, 1971) and *The Third Wave* (New York, 1981). These studies refer to the United States primarily, and have been much debated. Some comparable analysis of Europe can be found in the special issues of *Daedalus*, vol. 108 numbers 1 and 2 (1979), which also discuss the variety of problems that beset contemporary Europe. Older but more optimistic evaluations of Europe's revival include Michel Crozier, *The Renaissance of Contemporary Europe* (New York, 1968) and Stephen R. Graubard, ed., *A New Europe?* (Boston, 1963). On Europe's technocratic elite and social structure, see Michael Young, *The Rise of the Meritocracy* (London, 1958) and Ralf Dahrendorf, *Class and Class Conflict in Industrial Society* (Stanford, 1959).

The Vanishing Peasant

HENRI MENDRAS

Just as the peasantry epitomized the character of traditional society—to the extent that generalizations about the one may too easily be used to describe the other—so modernization seems ultimately to destroy the peasant spirit. Some of the earliest modernizing societies lacked a peasantry in the ordinary sense; the earlier selection by Keith Thomas suggests that key aspects of the peasant mentality were being eroded in Britain as early as the seventeenth century. Elsewhere the peasant spirit was stronger, for example, as it confronted a modern educational system in France as late as the nineteenth century. But structural modernization, through expansion of the cities and industrial production, everywhere reduced the relative numbers and economic importance of the peasantry. Henri Mendras, a noted French sociologist, argues that in recent decades the final vestiges of the peasant mentality have been disappearing as well. Here indeed is one measure of how far modernization has gone and what it means in terms of traditional values: The farming population is converted to a market orientation and manifests the behavior, including the family relationships, that accompanies such orientation. It is important to recall that this process was not sudden, that an identifiable peasantry long held out against complete change. Indeed, against Mendras' argument, we may see remnants of the peasant outlook even in city dwellers who have preserved some of the habits of their ancestors—in reactions to health problems, for example.

Mendras does more than note the disappearance of a basic way of life. He mourns it. The erosion of the peasantry is not an unalloyed triumph of progress over superstition. Mendras reminds us that the peasantry had virtues whose absence may endanger the civilization that uprooted them. Certain kinds of family ties, an attachment to the soil and a willingness to conserve resources to protect future generations, a sense of continuity—these qualities and more may now be irrevocably lost. How much will we suffer as a result? Can we strive to restore some of the solidarity that a peasantry traditionally offered? Should we in fact abandon the basic course of modernization in favor of a return to a more tested social structure, and can we do so even if we wish? The decline of the peasantry may also relate to the new pessimism about Europe's future discussed in the Hoffmann selection later on.

Most historians of agriculture in this country have admired the "French prudence" (*sagesse française*) that kept the nation from pushing the agricultural revolution of the eighteenth century to extreme social consequences and enabled us to conserve a large peasant class, while the British, yielding to the logic of the industrial economy, sacrificed their agriculture to the development of industry. In a way, France stopped in her tracks; she paused for a century and a half while her peasants, though slowly accepting technological innovations, remained peasants.

Today, the second agricultural revolution is upsetting every structure, and the dependable equilibrium has been disturbed. Agriculture, in its turn, is becoming "industrialized," and the French peasantry is being destroyed, one hundred fifty years later, by what we call industrial civilization. Suddenly we feel very close to the eighteenth century. We are rediscovering that nature can be subdued by technology, that agrarian history is marked by constant advances, innovations, and improvements, and that the farmers are living in turmoil.

We live essentially on ideas that were bequeathed us by the nineteenth century, and are today obviously anachronistic. It is important to revise these ideas and to look at the countryside with a new eye; otherwise we will remain blind to the great movement that is carrying the agrarian societies of the entire world toward a complete remodeling of their technology and their social equilibrium. The disappearance of the peasant in countries that have industrialized the most rapidly is due less to the force of economic circumstances than to the misapplication to agriculture of analytical methods, legislative measures, and administrative decisions that were not designed for it.

In countries such as England or the United States, where it was wholly subordinated to the logic of industrial society, agriculture remains an irreducible political and social problem, which seriously concerns leaders in Washington and London. . . .

Peasant society is subdivided into local communities that exist in relative demographic, economic, and cultural autarchy. According to Marx's famous image, the French peasantry of the last century resembled "potatoes in a sack," each community being a social entity, each being unique although all the communities were of the same kind.

Each community is a face-to-face group in which everybody knows everyone else in all his aspects. Its social relations are thus personal and not functional or segmentary. The community unites peasants (independent farmers, stockbreeders, landowners, cultivators, or salaried workers and their families) and nonpeasants (notables, artisans and merchants, and

From Henri Mendras, *The Vanishing Peasant* (Cambridge, Mass.: M.I.T. Press, 1970) pp. 5–61. Published in French by S.É.D.É.I.S., Paris, under the title *La Fin des Paysans, Innovation et Changement dans l'Agriculture Française.*

so on); but the dominant tone of the society is set by the peasants. Power belongs normally to the notables, who are in a marginal position between the local community and the broader society. The principal cleavages are often hierarchical in nature, according to a scale of socioeconomic prestige. If not, they can be of an ideological, ecological, or family nature in the larger sense: there is often no clear distinction between blood relatives and business connections. Finally, categories of age and sex are in general strongly individualized.

In communities as highly structured as this, everything contributes to the stability of the whole, and change can be introduced only by consensus, so slowly as to deny that it is change. These communities are not inflexible, but, except in a grave crisis, they evolve slowly to the rhythm of generations. Every innovation, whether it be technological, economic, or demographic, comes from the outside. In the words of Albert Dauzat, a man hardly to be suspected of prejudice on this subject, "The countryside has created nothing; everything comes to it from the city—dress, customs, songs. . . ." and one could add machines and technology.

In such a social system, the individual does not have to adapt himself to new decisions or make decisions himself; neither does he have to express or reveal himself to others, who know him from every point of view. Hence he has a tendency to remain true to himself and to the image others have of him. Showing or expressing sentiments and personal opinions is not encouraged by the code of values and norms. . . .

The agricultural revolution of the eighteenth century required more than a hundred years to carry its advances into the French countryside. It took place in the rhythm of a traditional society that industry had not yet modified. While it brought social change, supported and sometimes accelerated by political revolution, the essential character of village society remained unaltered. After a century of continual rural exodus, the present revolution in France is reducing the number of farmers at the bewildering rate of 160,000 per year, both through the death of farmers without successors and through the movement of young farmers into other professions. Those who remain become correspondingly richer and can meet the new exigencies of economy and technology, but not without completely upsetting village society. . . .

The ease with which peasants formed in the traditional world can move in a modern world is a source of constant surprise to the observer. Provided that they enter into a coherent and significant economic game, "economic motivations" come to young farmers with disconcerting rapidity. Moreover, when they travel from their farms, these untrained country bumpkins show an amazing aptitude for creating new institutions that are perfectly adapted to modern conditions, such as C.E.T.A. (Center for Technical Farm Studies). . . . Under their constant pressure, modern methods of farm accounting have been introduced in France, and it is in response to their demands that rural economics has come out of its age-old lethargy.

What truth is more self-evident, what fact better substantiated, than the peasant's individualism and love of his land? He gives his life's blood to enlarge his fields, and then fences himself in on his property with fierce independence, like a petty king in his kingdom. Nevertheless for half a century it is in the area of agriculture that cooperation has known its greatest success. Buying and marketing cooperatives, mutual insurance societies, farm credit associations . . .—no other sector of production can offer such a variety of cooperative organizations. Today some farmers are attempting the final step by joining their lands and grouping them into larger units where each product constitutes a workshop under the responsibility of one of the cooperating parties. Such experiments in "group farming" are not proceeding without difficulties, in the absence of legislation and established customs; for these pioneers must invent everything themselves until such time as economists, legislators, and public authorities have codified their experiments.

In devoting themselves enthusiastically to this total remodeling of their social and technical structures, the farmers have the feeling that they are making up for lost time and creating a place for themselves in the era of industrial civilization. Once the crisis of adjustment has passed, they hope in a confused way to rediscover the equilibrium their fathers knew. Having assimilated some new techniques and accepted some economic regulations, they expect to recreate a system of cultivation and independent farming as durable as the previous one. But modern technological civilization lives on continual change and dooms the quietude of immutable habits. Far from rediscovering traditional stability, the peasant will in his turn settle into the perpetual change of technological innovation and economic contingency. Furthermore, he is setting up, more or less consciously, the institutions that will help him to do this. Centers of management and rural economics study the evolution of markets and direct the management of farm workers accordingly. Services for agronomical research and agricultural extension complete the chain that progressively adapts the scientific discoveries of the laboratory so that they can be used by the farmer in his field.

Peasant values, so highly esteemed since the time of Xenophon and Virgil, and heretofore at the very heart of our Western civilization, will not be able to survive the shakeup of their ancient stability. The eternal "peasant soul" is dying before our eyes, just as is the patriarchal family domain founded on subsistence polycultivation. It is the final battle of industrial society against the last stronghold of traditional civilization. What we are undertaking here, then, is not simply a study of a new agricultural revolution but a study of the disappearance of traditional peasant civilization, which is a fundamental element of Western civilization and

Christianity, and its replacement by the new modern technological civilization, which will often take on different forms in the country from those it presently assumes in the city. . . .

In most French regions the farmers are still . . . "real" peasants. The sentiments that tie them to their land have until now been the subject of only one pilot study of a limited region. . . . It is enough to point out here how impossible it is to isolate the land from its entire natural setting, human and social. For the farmer the word "land" evokes simultaneously the soil he works, the farm that has supported his family for generations, and the profession he follows, as well as the peasant condition and the whole body of the nation's farmers. During an interview he jumps from one meaning to another without seeming to realize that these meanings are separate and distinct; and at the same time he says repeatedly that the sentiments evoked by this word are ineffable, that they exist but cannot be expressed. To make them understood, he calls on the interviewer's experience: "If you're from the country, you know what I mean."

On the other hand, a big farmer from the Paris basin can refuse to purchase the fields he works because it is economically more advantageous for him to rent them and invest his capital in livestock and machinery. During an interview, his "economic rationality" is visibly in conflict with his "peasant sentiments," as when he seeks to justify his refusal to buy his land by showing his contempt for it: "It's a poor piece of land where a man wouldn't want to settle his family." Or again, by reducing it to nothing: "This piece of land is like any other . . . nowadays the land doesn't count any more. . . ." To reduce to naught or curse the land one refuses to own betrays sentiments similar to those the "peasant" feels but refuses to express. However, other farmers are able to analyze the origin of these sentiments, if not their content, in astonishingly lucid terms: "To know one's land, to improve it, takes a long time! And the more you know it, the more you become attached to it." Such statements, almost evangelical in tone, are an admission of the fact that sentiment and ownership go together: "What belongs, belongs . . . a peasant is a proprietor of the land. . . . When a man is a proprietor, he has a feeling and a concern for the land." As opposed to the big farmer, and contrary to all economic analysis, a small proprietor can state: "Rented land is expensive and amounts to nothing."

Thus the peasant has a deep conviction that his field is unique because he is the only one to know it, to love it and to own it: knowledge, love, and possession are inseparable. And even when the farmer behaves in a rational economic fashion with respect to land as capital, his feelings for the soil are no less diffuse or deep; he identifies it intimately with his family and his profession, thus with himself. It can be said that these feelings are largely the product of a historical situation that is on the way to extinction, and that they will outlive it by some years. Moreover, they are already disparaged by the ideology that the new generation is fashioning for itself. Young people think that the cultivators should be relieved of land ownership, and that the latter should be considered solely as a factor of production, by farmers as well as by public authorities and capitalists. . . .

As mechanization became general, the concept of technological and urban time invaded agricultural work and introduced into it the new unit of the hour. This concept came first with the threshing contractor, who asked to be paid by the hour; soon the farmer who came with his machine to plow his neighbor's field did the same; and today young farmers, mindful of how profitable their tractors or harvester-threshers can be, keep a notebook in which they carefully record their hours of work and the liters of fuel burned. For the first time abstract time, made up of equal units, has entered into agricultural work. It is tending gradually to modify the time scale of an ever-increasing number of tasks. Thus the process of replacing one concept of time by another can be seen through many easily-measurable indices and hence can be observed by the sociologist with exceptional clarity. . . .

Hourly time already existed in country life. Every farm kitchen displayed proudly a clock with a long pendulum, and most of the farmers had pocket watches. According to the French Institute of Public Opinion, 47 percent of farmers did not carry a watch on their persons in 1953 (compared with 34 percent of the population as a whole). In daily life these instruments served to indicate the progress of the day more than to fix the time exactly or indicate the beginning or end of some activity. Witness to an external civilization, they were employed to "tell time" only when in contact with this civilization, when one must be "on time": to send the children to school, to catch the train or bus, to attend a meeting. And in the latter case, if it was an appointment with neighbors or other country people, everyone knew it was not necessary to be punctual.

Today, on the contrary, as meetings become more frequent all the time, young people particularly want them to start punctually in order not to "lose time"; this is one of the indices which reveal the passage from the peasant to the modern concept of time. In the past, since the means of transportation were slow, people would go to town for the day or half a day if they had a meeting. The meeting began when everyone had arrived at the city hall, the cooperative, or the school. People took advantage of the trip to do other errands or to chat with each other. Now they take the car or the motorbike in order to arrive in time for the meeting and leave immediately afterward if work is pressing. This change in customs was surprising to the rural researcher who went from a French village to an American one in 1950; today it can be observed in every French village.

One must not, however, conclude from our analysis that this concept of "flowing, dreamy" time, vague and slow-moving, was of no value whatever. Just as the Mediterranean peoples, in particular the Greeks, like to "while away the time," so too Mexican peasants are always ready to put off till tomorrow what they can avoid doing today. Most French peasants, on the contrary, do not allow themselves to waste time. Time is so closely connected with the work experience that wasted time is wasted work; it is laziness to put off till tomorrow what one can do today. These two examples suffice to show how dangerous it would be to settle for a simplistic contrast between two extreme types. In each civilization the notion of time is closely linked to the system of values and the organization of daily life. In France we would have to undertake a study, region by region, to try to explain why some have rapidly accepted certain elements of modern time and others have proved more resistant. . . .

But, some will say, how are our traditionalist peasants going to shed the old self so abruptly and take on a new self? The peasant soul will survive the cataclysm that you forecast, if, indeed, it is to come. One has only to open a newspaper to dismiss this objection: there one sees article after article on progressive young farmers, on demonstrations, on conferences where the vocabulary of technical and economic efficiency has replaced the political and moral vocabulary that was in style only a few years ago.

On this point our studies are convincing: if economic structures are changed within a region, they will within a few years change the mentality of the inhabitants. It is striking to see the ease with which peasants formed in a traditional economic and social system can be moved to a modern system, given a few conditions—particularly that the coherence of the new system be rapidly established, visible, and comprehensible. It does not take the young farmers long to acquire "economic motivations," if only these have a meaning and are part of a coherent economic game that permits a glimpse of a successful future.

With astonishingly sure intuition they create entirely new institutions perfectly adapted to modern conditions. . . . But in reconstructing a new society on the dismantled structures of family, farm, and village, they sound the knell of the last vestiges of the peasantry in France, who will not survive their generation.

Thus, with them, the peasantry will itself be extinguished. And what will a world without peasants be like?

Modern Man at Play

JOHAN HUIZINGA

There is little doubt that the values of modern society remain confused in the area of play and leisure. In a period when more and more time is spent not working (due to shorter work days, longer vacations, and earlier retirement), we continue to define work as reality. Our schools, among other things, train students for the job with an often narrow passion. Yet there are observers who hold that leisure, defined as nonwork time in which an individual chooses among diversions, is a phenomenon of modernization.

In this selection, Johan Huizinga, a noted Dutch historian whose interests ranged from the Middle Ages to (rather pessimistic) assessments about modern life, judges that modernity has indeed brought about a distinct and unfortunate trend in the area of play. His views should be compared with the specific assessments of leisure and recreation in premodern societies and during industrialization. Some of the trends that developed when modern leisure was born, in the later nineteenth century, may still constrain leisure today. Insofar as Huizinga focuses on play, which is by nature particularly childlike, his opinions relate also to changes in the treatment and conception of childhood and youth. Quite possibly, in our desire to find purpose in activity (of which education and educational toys are one expression), we have indeed limited the play spirit.

But do we need play? What is it, in contrast to other uses of leisure? Huizinga ironically suggests that we are substituting play for seriousness in work. Yet one could argue that modern life is excitingly recasting the definitions of seriousness and nonseriousness. But, if this is the case, it is largely unwitting. The modern form of life is so new—for example, the amount of time available for nonwork—that we may have difficulty in defining our own mentality, in adjusting our values to our behavior.

Huizinga certainly points to an area far removed from most of the standard valuations of the gains and losses involved in modernization. His own judgment coincides with a pessimistic modernization thesis: We have lost a valued part of our own tradition. It coincides also with many of the criticisms of contemporary leisure that are made without definite historical criteria: Modern people do not know how to relax; we are dominated by remote commercial media rather than really choosing our own leisure; mass taste is degraded, regimented taste. Have we lost a vital capacity to enjoy, to indulge in purposeless expression, and with this a key source of mental balance? Or are we groping to use our undeniably increased material resources to make life itself a form of play?

The question to which we address ourselves is this: To what extent does the civilization we live in still develop in play-forms? How far does the play-spirit dominate the lives of those who share that civilization? The 19th century, we observed, had lost many of the play-elements so characteristic of former ages. Has this leeway been made up or has it increased?

It might seem at first sight that certain phenomena in modern social life have more than compensated for the loss of play-forms. Sport and athletics, as social functions, have steadily increased in scope and conquered ever fresh fields both nationally and internationally.

Contests in skill, strength and perseverance have, as we have shown, always occupied an important place in every culture either in connection with ritual or simply for fun and festivity. Feudal society was only really interested in the tournament; the rest was just popular recreation and nothing more. Now the tournament, with its highly dramatic staging and aristocratic embellishments, can hardly be called a sport. It fulfilled one of the functions of the theatre. Only a numerically small upper class took active part in it. This one-sideness of mediaeval sporting life was due in large measure to the influence of the Church. The Christian ideal left but little room for the organized practice of sport and the cultivation of bodily exercise, except insofar as the latter contributed to gentle education. Similarly, the Renaissance affords fairly numerous examples of body-training cultivated for the sake of perfection, but only on the part of individuals, never groups or classes. If anything, the emphasis laid by the Humanists on learning and erudition tended to perpetuate the old under-estimation of the body, likewise the moral zeal and severe intellectuality of the Reformation and Counter-Reformation. The recognition of games and bodily exercises as important cultural values was withheld right up to the end of the 18th century.

The basic forms of sportive competition are, of course, constant through the ages. In some the trial of strength and speed is the whole essence of the contest, as in running and skating matches, chariot and horse races, weight-lifting, swimming, diving, marksmanship, etc. Though human beings have indulged in such activities since the dawn of time, these only take on the character of organized games to a very slight degree. Yet nobody, bearing in mind the agonistic principle which animates them, would hesitate to call them games in the sense of play—which, as we have seen, can be very serious indeed. There are, however, other forms of contest which develop of their own accord into "sports." These are the ball-games.

From Johan Huizinga, *Homo Ludens: A Study of the Play Element in Culture* (New York: Roy Publishers, 1950), pp. 195–200.

What we are concerned with here is the transition from occasional amusement to the system of organized clubs and matches. Dutch pictures of the 17th century show us burghers and peasants intent upon their game of *kolf*, but, so far as I know, nothing is heard of games being organized in clubs or played as matches. It is obvious that a fixed organization of this kind will most readily occur when two groups play against one another. The great ball-games in particular require the existence of permanent teams, and herein lies the starting-point of modern sport. The process arises quite spontaneously in the meeting of village against village, school against school, one part of a town against the rest, etc. That the process started in 19th-century England is understandable up to a point, though how far the specifically Anglo-Saxon bent of mind can be deemed an efficient cause is less certain. But it cannot be doubted that the structure of English social life had much to do with it. Local self-government encouraged the spirit of association and solidarity. The absence of obligatory military training favoured the occasion for, and the need of, physical exercise. The peculiar form of education tended to work in the same direction, and finally the geography of the country and the nature of the terrain, on the whole flat and, in the ubiquitous commons, offering the most perfect playing-fields that could be desired, were of the greatest importance. Thus England became the cradle and focus of modern sporting life.

Ever since the last quarter of the 19th century games, in the guise of sport, have been taken more and more seriously. The rules have become increasingly strict and elaborate. Records are established at a higher, or faster, or longer level than was ever conceivable before. Everybody knows the delightful prints from the first half of the 19th century, showing the cricketers in top-hats. This speaks for itself.

Now, with the increasing systematization and regimentation of sport, something of the pure play-quality is inevitably lost. We see this very clearly in the official distinction between amateurs and professionals (or "gentlemen and players" as used pointedly to be said). It means that the play-group marks out those for whom playing is no longer play, ranging them inferior to the true players in standing but superior in capacity. The spirit of the professional is no longer the true play-spirit; it is lacking in spontaneity and carelessness. This affects the amateur too, who begins to suffer from an inferiority complex. Between them they push sport further and further away from the play-sphere proper until it becomes a thing *sui generis*: neither play nor earnest. In modern social life sport occupies a place alongside and apart from the cultural process. The great competitions in archaic cultures had always formed part of the sacred festivals and were indispensable as health and happiness-bringing activities. This ritual tie has now been completely severed; sport has become profane, "unholy" in every way and has no organic connection whatever with the structure of society, least of all when prescribed by the government. The ability of modern social techniques to stage mass demonstrations with the maximum of outward show in the field of athletics does not alter the fact that neither the Olympiads nor the organized sports of American Universities nor the loudly trumpeted international contests have, in the smallest degree, raised sport to the level of a culture-creating activity. However important it may be for the players or spectators, it remains sterile. The old play-factor has undergone almost complete atrophy.

This view will probably run counter to the popular feeling of to-day, according to which sport is the apotheosis of the play-element in our civilization. Nevertheless popular feeling is wrong. By way of emphasizing the fatal shift towards over-seriousness we would point out that it has also infected the non-athletic games where calculation is everything, such as chess and some card-games.

A great many board-games have been known since the earliest times, some even in primitive society, which attached great importance to them largely on account of their chanceful character. Whether they are games of chance or skill they all contain an element of seriousness. The merry play-mood has little scope here, particularly where chance is at a minimum as in chess, draughts, backgammon, halma, etc. Even so all these games remain within the definition of play. . . . Only recently has publicity seized on them and annexed them to athletics by means of public championships, world tournaments, registered records and press reportage in a literary style of its own, highly ridiculous to the innocent outsider.

Card-games differ from board-games in that they never succeed in eliminating chance completely. To the extent that chance predominates they fall into the category of gambling and, as such, are little suited to club life and public competition. The more intellectual card-games, on the other hand, leave plenty of room for associative tendencies. It is in this field that the shift towards seriousness and over-seriousness is so striking. From the days of *ombre* and *quadrille* to whist and bridge, card-games have undergone a process of increasing refinement, but only with bridge have the modern social techniques made themselves master of the game. The paraphernalia of handbooks and systems and professional training has made bridge a deadly earnest business. A recent newspaper article estimated that yearly winnings of the Culbertson couple at more than two hundred thousand dollars. An enormous amount of mental energy is expended in this universal craze for bridge with no more tangible result than the exchange of relatively unimportant sums of money. Society as a whole is neither benefited nor damaged by this futile activity. It seems difficult to speak of it as an elevating recreation in the sense of Aristotle's *diagoge*. Proficiency at bridge is a sterile excellence, sharpening the mental faculties very one-sidedly without enriching the soul in any way, fixing and consuming a quantity of intellectual energy that might have been better applied. The most we can say, I think, is that it might have been applied worse. The status of bridge in modern society would indicate, to all appearances, an immense increase in the play-element to-day. But appearances are deceptive. Really to play, a man must play like a child. Can we assert that this is so in the case of such an ingenious game as bridge? If not, the virtue has gone out of the game.

The attempt to assess the play-content in the confusion of modern life is bound to lead us to contradictory conclusions. In the case of sport we have an activity nominally known as play but raised to such a pitch of technical organization and scientific thoroughness that the real play-spirit is threatened with extinction. Over against this tendency to over-seriousness, however, there are other phenomena pointing in the opposite direction. Certain activities whose whole *raison d'être* lies in the field of material interest, and which had nothing of play about them in their initial stages, develop what we can only call play-forms as a secondary charac-teristic. Sport and athletics showed us play stiffening into seriousness but still being felt as play; now we come to serious business degenerating into play but still being called serious. The two phenomena are linked by the strong agonistic habit which still holds universal sway, though in other forms than before.

The impetus given to this agonistic principle which seems to be carrying the world back in the direction of play derives, in the main, from external factors independent of culture proper—in a word, communica-tions, which have made intercourse of every sort so extraordinarily easy for mankind as a whole. Technology, publicity and propaganda every-where promote the competitive spirit and afford means of satisfying it on an unprecedented scale. Commercial competition does not, of course, belong to the immemorial sacred play-forms. It only appears when trade begins to create fields of activity within which each must try to surpass and outwit his neighbour. Commercial rivalry soon makes limiting rules imperative, namely the trading customs. It remained primitive in essence until quite late, only becoming really intensive with the advent of modern communications, propaganda and statistics. Naturally a certain play-element had entered into business competition at an early stage. Statistics stimulated it with an idea that had originally arisen in sporting life, the idea, namely, of trading records. A record, as the word shows, was once simply a memorandum, a note which the innkeeper scrawled on the walls of his inn to say that such and such a rider or traveller had been the first to arrive after covering so and so many miles. The statistics of trade and production could not fail to introduce a sporting element into economic life. In consequence, there is now a sporting side to almost every triumph of commerce or technology: the highest turnover, the biggest tonnage, the fastest crossing, the greatest altitude, etc. Here a purely ludic element has, for once, got the better of utilitarian considerations, since the experts inform us that smaller units—less monstrous steamers and aircraft, etc.—are more efficient in the long run. Business becomes play. This process goes so far that some of the great business concerns deliberately instil the play-spirit into their workers so as to step up production. The trend is now reversed: play becomes business. A captain of industry, on whom the Rotterdam Academy of Commerce had conferred an honorary degree, spoke as follows:

> "Ever since I first entered the business it has been a race between the technicians and the sales department. One tried to produce so much that the sales department would never be able to sell it, while the other tried to sell so much that the technicians would never be able to keep pace. This race has always continued: sometimes one is ahead, sometimes the other. Neither my brother nor myself has regarded the business as a task, but always as a game, the spirit of which it has been our constant endeavour to implant into the younger staff."

These words must, of course, be taken with a grain of salt. Nevertheless there are numerous instances of big concerns forming their own Sports Societies and even engaging workers with a view not so much to their professional capacities as to their fitness for the football eleven. Once more the wheel turns.

Modern Man

ALEX INKELES

In the following description, modern man seems very new and quite a good fellow, well adjusted to a changing environment. Do these virtues—which sound remarkably like those urged by Enlightenment philosophers and middle-class optimists long ago—really describe the evolution toward a modern outlook? Are they consistent, for example, with changes in family relationships through which dignity and even democracy might be concretely expressed? Do they leave sufficient room for national or class differences in values?

Inkeles' approach makes one thing quite clear: For him, rural tradition must not be idealized; it is full of hardship and confusion. Accordingly, movement to the city is actually an opportunity not only for higher earnings, but for a much more constructive human personality.

Inkeles discusses the variety of causes necessary to produce a modern outlook, most of them going back at least a century in European experience. He also leaves room for a gradual evolution toward modern values—an important qualification to what might otherwise seem a simplistic approach. Urban man is not necessarily modern; pockets of tradition remain, and even when they begin to collapse there may be many stages before full modernization is attained.

This basic approach to defining modern values has been used by a number of social scientists studying the modernization process outside the Western world. Inkeles has applied his criteria of modernity to studies of Russia. Others have used similar criteria in assessing the extent of modernization in Japan and elsewhere. They might disagree with Inkeles on some specific points (many definitions stress the secularism of the modern outlook, for example, whereas Inkeles tries to integrate religion), but they would agree that modernity is not only definable but desirable.

But what is the modern man, and what makes him what he is? The answer to this question is inevitably controversial, and almost no one enters on a discussion of it without arousing a good deal of emotion. The reasons are not hard to find. In the first place, the change from more traditional to more modern qualities in man often means someone must

From Alex Inkeles, "The Modernization of Man," in *Modernization: The Dynamics of Growth*, Myron Weiner ed. (New York: Basic Books, 1966), pp. 138–50.

give up ways of thinking and feeling that go back decades, sometimes centuries; and to abandon these ways often seems to be abandoning principle itself. For another thing, the qualities that make a man modern often do not appear to be neutral characteristics that any man might have, but instead represent the distinctive traits of the European, the American, or the Westerner that he is bent on imposing on other people so as to make them over in his own image. In the third place, many of the characteristics that are described as modern, and therefore automatically desirable, in fact are not very useful or suitable to the life and conditions of those on whom they are urged or even imposed. These are most serious issues, and we shall return to them briefly after sketching some details of what we mean by modern man.

The characteristic mark of the modern man has two parts: one internal, the other external; one dealing with his environment, the other with his attitudes, values, and feelings.

The change in the external condition of modern man is well known and widely documented, and it need not detain us long. It may be summarized by reference to a series of key terms: urbanization, education, mass communication, industrialization, politicalization. These terms signify that in contrast to his forebearers living in the traditional order of his society, the modern man is less likely to work the land as a farmer and is more likely to be employed in a large and complex productive enterprise based on the intensive use of power and advanced technologies. The various economies yielded by the concentration of industry in certain sites and the further demands of those industrial concentrations make it likely that the contemporary man will live in a city or some other form of urban conglomeration. Here, he will experience not only crowding but access to all manner of resource and stimulation characteristic of urban life. Inevitably, one of these stimuli will be the media of mass communication: newspapers, radio, movies, and perhaps even television. His experience of new places and ideas will be augmented by the impact of schooling, if not directly for him, then for his children, who may carry the influence of the school into the home. He is much more likely to have some connection with politics, especially on the national scale, as he is more exposed to mass communication, more mobilized in the surge of urban life, more courted by the competing political movements that seek his support as he may enlist their aid to replace that of the chief, the patron, or the family head whose assistance he would ordinarily have sought in his native village. Indeed, another mark of the contemporary man is that he will no longer live enmeshed in a network of primary kin ties, perhaps supplemented by ties to a small number of fellow villagers, but rather will be drawn into a much more impersonal and bureaucratic milieu in which he is dependent for services and aid in times of distress on persons and agencies with which he has a much more formal and perhaps tenuous relationship.

These are all attributes of his life space that may impinge on the modern man, but in themselves they do not constitute modernity. The densest urban centers may still shelter the most traditional network of human relations: the media of mass communication may mainly disseminate folk tales and traditional wisdom, factories may run on principles not far different from those of the estate or the hacienda, and politics may be conducted like an extension of the village council. Although his exposure to the modern setting may certainly contribute to the transformation of traditional man, and although that setting may in turn require new ways of him, it is only when man has undergone a change in spirit—has acquired certain new ways of thinking, feeling, and acting—that we come to consider him truly modern.

Although there is no single standard definition of the modern man that all accept and use, there is quite good agreement among students of the modernization process as to the characteristics that distinguish the more modern man from the more traditional. To convey my impression of his traits, I have chosen to describe him in terms of a series of attitudes and values that we are testing in a study of the modernization process among workers and peasants in six developing countries. This permits me not only to present the characteristic profile we define as modern but also to indicate some of the questions we are using to study its manifestation in concrete cases. The order in which these characteristics are presented here is not meant to suggest that this is the actual sequence in the process of individual modernization. So far, we are not aware that there is a clear-cut sequence, but rather have the impression that the process develops on a broad front with many changes occurring at once. Neither does the order in which the characteristics are given suggest the relative weight or importance of each characteristic in the total syndrome. Here, again, we have yet, through our scientific work, to assess the relative contribution of each characteristic to the larger complex of attitudes, values, and ways of acting that we consider modern. We do, however, assume that this complex of attitudes and values holds together: that in the statistical sense it constitutes a factor, and a relatively coherent factor. In time, our scientific evidence will show whether or not this is a reasonable assumption.

The first element in our definition of the modern man is his readiness for new experience and his openness to innovation and change. We consider the traditional man to be less disposed to accept new ideas, new ways of feeling and acting. We are speaking, therefore, of something that is itself a state of mind, a psychological disposition, an inner readiness, rather than of the specific techniques or skills a man or a group may possess because of the level of technology they have attained. Thus, in our sense, a man may be more modern in spirit, even though he works with a wooden plow, than someone in another part of the world who already drives a tractor. The readiness for new experience and ways of doing things, furthermore, may express itself in a variety of forms and contexts: in the willingness to adopt a new drug or sanitation method, to accept a new seed or try a different fertilizer, to ride on a new means of transportation or turn to a new source of news, to approve a new form of wedding or new type of schooling for young people. Individuals and groups may, of course, show more readiness for the new in one area of life than another, but we can also conceive of the readiness to accept innovation as a more pervasive, general characteristic that makes itself felt across a wide variety of human situations. And we consider those who have this readiness to be more modern.

The second in our complex of themes takes us into the realm of opinion. We define a man as more modern if he has a disposition to form or mold opinions over a large number of the problems and issues that arise not only in his immediate environment but also outside of it. Some pioneering work on this dimension has been done by Daniel Lerner, of the Massachusetts Institute of Technology, who found that the individuals within any country, and the populations of different countries, in the Middle East varied greatly in their ability or readiness to imagine themselves in the position of prime minister or comparable government leader and thus to offer advice as to what should be done to resolve the problems facing the country. The more educated the individual and the more advanced the country, the greater was the readiness to offer opinions in response to this challenge. The more traditional man, we believe, takes an interest in fewer things, mainly those that touch him immediately and intimately; and even when he holds opinions on more distant matters, he is more circumspect in expressing them.

We also consider a man to be more modern if his orientation to the opinion realm is more democratic. We mean by this that he shows more awareness of the diversity of attitude and opinion around him, rather than closing himself off in the belief that everyone thinks alike and, indeed, just like him. The modern man is able to acknowledge differences of opinion without needing rigidly to deny differences out of fear that these will upset his own view of the world. He is also less likely to approach opinion in a strictly autocratic or hierarchical way. He does not automatically accept the ideas of those above him in the power hierarchy and reject the opinions of those whose status is markedly lower than his. We test these values by asking people whether it is proper to think differently from the village headman or other traditional leader and, at the other end, by inquiring as to whether the opinions of a man's wife or young son merit serious consideration when important public issues are being discussed. These questions prove to be a sensitive indicator in helping us to distinguish one man from another and, we believe, will be an important element in the final syndrome of modernity we shall delineate.

A third theme we deal with at some length is that of time. We view a man as more modern if he is oriented to the present or the future, rather than to the past. We consider him as more modern if he accepts fixed hours, that is to say, schedules of time, as something sensible and appropriate, or possibly even desirable, as against the man who thinks these fixed rules are something either bad or perhaps a necessity, but unfortunately also a pity. We also define a man as more modern if he is punctual, regular, and orderly in organizing his affairs. These things can be very complicated, and this is a good opportunity to point out that it is a mistake to assume that our measures of modernity differentiate between traditional and nontraditional people as they would ordinarily be defined. For example, the Maya Indians had a better sense of time than their Spanish conquerors and they preserve it to this day. The qualities we define as modern can, in fact, be manifested in a people who seem to be relatively unmodern when you consider the level of technology or the amount of power they have. We are talking about the properties of the person, which in turn may be a reflection of the properties of a culture that could emerge in any time or place. Indeed, when I described this list to a friend of mine who is doing an extensive study of Greece, he said, "My goodness, you are talking about the ancient Greeks!" He said there were only two respects in which the Greeks did not fit our model of the modern man. And, of course, the Elizabethan Englishman would also fit the model. So, this concept is not limited to our time. "Modern" does not mean merely contemporary in our approach.

A fourth theme that we include in the definition is planning. The more modern man is oriented toward and involved in planning and organizing and believes in it as a way of handling life. ·

A fifth, and important, theme we call efficacy. The modern man is the one who believes that man can learn, in substantial degree, to dominate his environment in order to advance his own purposes and goals, rather than being dominated entirely by that environment. For example, a man who believes in efficacy is more likely to respond positively to the question, "Do you believe that some day men may be able to develop ways of controlling floods or preventing destructive storms?" The more efficacious man, even though in fact he has never seen a dam, would say, "Yes, I think that some day man could do that."

Sixth, an element we consider part of the modern complex and include in our set of themes is calculability. By our definition, the modern man is one who has more confidence that his world is calculable, that other people and institutions around him can be relied on to fulfill or meet their obligations and responsibilities. He does not agree that everything is determined either by fate or by the whims of particular qualities and characters of men. In other words, he believes in a reasonably lawful world under human control.

The seventh theme that we stress is dignity. The more modern man, we feel, is one who has more awareness of the dignity of others and more disposition to show respect for them. We feel this comes through very clearly in attitudes toward women and children.

The modern man has more faith in science and technology, even if in a fairly primitive way. This provides our eighth theme.

Ninth, we hold that modern man is a great believer in what we call, for this purpose, distributive justice. That is to say, he believes that rewards should be according to contribution, and not according to either whim or special properties of the person not related to his contribution.

You could easily extend this list; you could also divide some of these items into still others; but I think this will serve to give an idea of the complex of attitudes and values that we consider important in defining the modern man. We have chosen to emphasize these themes because we see them as intimately related to the individual's successful adjustment as a citizen of a modern industrial nation. They are qualities that we feel will contribute to making a man a more productive worker in his factory, a more effective citizen in his community, a more satisfied and satisfying husband and father in his home.

We must of course, acknowledge that the nine themes just described are not the only way to approach the definition of modernity. Although we have stressed certain themes that cut across numerous concrete realms of behavior, some students of the problem prefer to emphasize attitudes and behavior relating mainly to certain important institutional realms, such as birth control or religion. . . . For each of these realms, one can define a position that can be considered more modern and an attitude one can define as more traditional, although at times the process of definition becomes very complex.

There is, for example, a very widespread notion that people lose their religion merely because they leave the countryside and go to the city. As a matter of fact, exactly the contrary is very often the case. There are two forces that bring this about. In the first place, really to practice your religion well, you must be a reasonably well-composed, well-contained individual. The person who is emotionally disturbed neglects his social obligations and involvements. Despite the idyllic image that many people have of the countryside, the great majority of the world's peasants are in a state of culture shock produced not by modernity but by the hard conditions of rural life. When a man goes to the city, and especially if he secures a job in industry, he comes to have much more respect and becomes much more self-controlled. This makes it more feasible for him to practice his religion. He turns to things that he previously neglected in his effort just to hold himself together. He reintegrates himself, if you like, with the formal things around him, one of which is his religion.

The second factor that may contribute to facilitate religious practice in the city is economic. To practice your religion generally costs something. For example, you may have to buy candles. If there is a religious ceremony, usually the religious specialist who performs the ceremony must be given some kind of payment. Something is required of you. If you are living a sufficiently marginal existence as a peasant, this may be one of the costs you forgo. When you get to the city and earn a more stable and steady income, you may be more willing to underwrite these costs. So, on this issue we are actually taking a rather unorthodox position and predicting that our city workers are going to be more rather than less religious, if not in spirit at least in terms of performing their formal religious obligations.

So much for our conception of the qualities that make a man modern. What can we say about the forces that produce such a man, that most rapidly and effectively inculcate in a population those attitudes, values, needs, and ways of acting that better fit him for life in a modern society? Just as modernity seems to be defined not by any one characteristic, but by a complex of traits, so we find that no one social force, but rather a whole complex of influences, contributes to the transformation from traditional to modern man.

Within this complex of forces, however, one certainly assumes preeminence: namely, education. Almost all serious scientific investigations of the question have shown the individual's degree of modernity to rise with increases in the amount of education he has received. Some reservations must be introduced, of course, to qualify this statement. In many countries, the weakness of the nation's resources permits schooling to be only of very poor quality, and the pressures on the poorer people force the children to be quite irregular in their attendance. In a number of countries, it has been observed that if children can obtain only two or three years of schooling, and especially if they do so under conditions where their environment does not particularly reinforce or support the school, there the effects of education on modernization will be very modest indeed. Similarly, the degree of traditionalism of the school itself plays some role. Little or no change toward modernity is evident in the more traditional schools that devote themselves mainly to passing on religious practices or inculcating and preserving traditional lore and skills. This is a characteristic of schools not only at the primary level; it may apply to those offering nominally advanced education. The "finishing" schools for young ladies from polite society in the United States may be taken as an example. Allowing for reservations of this sort, we may still say that education, especially in schools emphasizing the more modern type of curriculum, seems to be the most powerful factor in developing a population more modern in its attitudes and values. This effect depends in part on the direct instruction provided, but we assume as well that the school as a social organization serves as a model of rationality, of the importance of technical competence, of the rule of objective standards of performance, and of the principle of distributive justice reflected in the grading system. All these models can contribute to shaping young people in the image of the modern man as we have described him.

There is little agreement as to the rank order of influences other than education that we see affecting the degree of modernization of individuals. Many analysts of the problem propose the urban environment as the next most important input. The city is itself a powerful new experience. It encourages, and indeed to some degree obliges, the individual to adopt many new ways of life. By exposing men to a variety of ways of living, a wide range of opinions and ideas, increased mobility, more complex resources of all kinds, it accelerates the process of change. At the same time, in the city the prospect is greater that the individual will be relatively free from the obligations and constraints placed on him in the village by his extended kinship ties, the village elders, and the tight community of his neighbors. These structural differences free the individual to change; but, of course, they do not in themselves guarantee that he will change in ways that make him more modern. In many cities, there are powerful examples of rationality, of the use of technology to master the physical demands of life, of rewards adjusted to technical skill and competence, of the value of education, and of the guarantee of human dignity under law. But many great cities also provide powerful lessons that run counter to these modernizing influences on every score. If they breed a new type of man, they hardly make him in the image we have called modern. In addition, under conditions of very rapid growth, the city is often unable to absorb and integrate all the in-migrants, so that on the outer edges or in the older districts of the city, huge slum communities may develop in which people are in the city but not of it, cut off from many of its benefits and from the modernizing influence of urban life.

One source of modernization which generally accompanies urbanization but is also an independent influence is mass communication. Almost all studies of the growth of individual modernization show that those who are more exposed to the media of mass communication have more modern attitudes. Since such exposure, especially in the case of the newspaper, depends on literacy and education, it is important to stress that the modernization effects of the mass media can be shown to exert their influence within groups at almost any educational level. Of course, there remains the possibility that it is the man with modern attitudes who seeks out the mass media, rather than that the media makes the man modern, but there seems little reason to doubt that influence is at least mutual.

These media greatly enlarge the range of human experience with which the individual can have contact, even if only vicarious. They constantly present and illustrate new tools, items of consumption, means of transportation, and a myriad of new ways of doing things. They show examples of efficacious behavior of the most powerful kind in the building of dams, the taming of floods, the irrigation of deserts, and even the conquest of space. They also provide models of new values and standards of behavior, some of which are far beyond the reach of most men, but many of which can be copied and do influence behavior directly. As in the case of urban influences, we must acknowledge that the media of communication can and often do carry messages that mainly reaffirm traditional values, beliefs, and ways of acting or disseminate a concept of the new that is nevertheless not congruent with the model of the modern man here described.

Another source of modernizing influence is the development of the national state and its associated apparatus of government bureaucracy, political parties and campaigns, military and paramilitary units, and the like. The more mobilized the society, the more dedicated the government to economic development and spreading the ideology of progress, the more rapidly and widely may we expect the attitudes and values of modernity to expand. Some of the agencies of the state—in particular, the army—may play an especially important role in introducing men to the modern world, both in the direct instruction they offer and indirectly in the model of routine, scheduling, technical skill, and efficacy that inheres in many of their operations. Here again, however, we must acknowledge that the power of the state may also be used to reinforce more traditional values: politics may be conducted in a way that hardly sets an example of modern behavior, and armies may be run so as scarcely to induce a man to exert himself, to practice initiative, or to respect the dignity of others.

One last source of modernizing influence that we may cite . . . is the factory or other modern productive and administrative enterprise. Certain features of the modern factory are relatively invariant, and they communicate the same message, no matter what the cultural setting in which they may be installed. In them there is always an intense concentration of physical and mechanical power brought to bear on the transformation of raw materials; orderly and routine procedures to govern the flow of work are essential; time is a powerful influence in guiding the work process; power and authority generally rest on technical competence; and, as a rule, rewards are in rough proportion to performance. In addition, a factory guided by modern management and personnel policies will set its workers an example of rational behavior, emotional balance, open communication, and respect for the opinions, the feelings, and the dignity of the worker which can be a powerful example of the principles and practice of modern living.

In modern times we are experiencing a process of change affecting everything, yet controlled by no one. It is, in a sense, strictly spontaneous; yet it is in some ways the most strictly determined process history has yet known. Since no one can escape it, no one may be unconcerned with it. Man himself is being transformed. Many evils are being erased, but no end of new forms of corruption and wickedness may be loosed in the world. Some people in backward countries are ready to believe that any change is for the good. Others feel that much they now have is superior to what is being offered, and they are deeply convinced that many of the changes the contemporary world is introducing into their lives are no improvement, while others are positively disastrous. I have pointed to a set of qualities of mind that I call modern, which I believe have much to recommend them. They are not compatible in all respects with qualities that are widespread in traditional cultures, but I believe they are qualities men can adopt without coming into conflict, in most cases, with what is best in their cultural tradition and spiritual heritage. I believe they represent some of the best things in the modernization process. But whether we view them as positive or negative, we must recognize these qualities that are fostered by modern institutions, qualities that in many ways are required of the citizens of modern societies. We must, therefore, come to recognize them, to understand them, and to evaluate them as important issues in contemporary life.

The Horror of Modernization

R. D. LAING

Early in the modernization process, important intellectual criticism developed. Conservative intellectuals criticized excessive rationalism and individualism, which they believed endangered public order. By the later nineteenth century, attacks on modern values came even from intellectuals who were not politically conservative, but who thought that society was deteriorating as it moved away from traditional values. It was probably inevitable that many intellectuals would resent a society that placed so much emphasis on material achievement. The intellectuals' uncertainty about their own role in such a society encouraged their frequent hostility.

So intellectual attacks on modernity have a considerable history. They result in part from the impact of the modernization process on an articulate social group, which does not necessarily mean that they are biased or wrong.

R. D. Laing is a British psychoanalyst with a particular interest in schizophrenia. His training therefore differs considerably from that of the sociologist Inkeles. Yet his list of the characteristics of modern man is by no means completely different. He argues that modern man is new, that modern man claims rationality, and so on. But Laing views these attributes from a completely different perspective. It is possible, of course, that he is talking only about *some* modern people, not *all*, or about people only at certain times or in certain moods. But Laing does not think this is so. Like Inkeles, he finds it possible to describe modern man, period.

Laing places the development of modern education and family structure, including childhood, in the forefront of his attack (tangentially he also questions the scientific way of knowing). Above all, he contrasts modern values with those of the past, even though he does not describe the past in detail. Premodern man had faith and dreams. He could accept a creative madness. He was not alienated. Laing's approach invites comparison with earlier selections that traced the rise of modern attitudes toward insanity and toward death.

So in a sense we come full circle—to the question of insanity and the modern mind. Laing invites us to evaluate premodern as well as modern people. If he is right that modern society has deteriorated, is this a cause for hope or despair? Are there values from the past that we should try to recover, and, given the enormous impact of modernization, do we have any hope of success if we do try? Can we, if we are complacently, scientifically modernized, even grasp the world that Laing experiences?

Few books today are forgivable. Black on the canvas, silence on the screen, an empty white sheet of paper, are perhaps feasible. There is little conjunction of truth and social "reality." Around us are pseudo-events, to which we adjust with a false consciousness adapted to see these events as true and real, and even as beautiful. In the society of men the truth resides now less in what things are than in what they are not. Our social realities are so ugly if seen in the light of exiled truth, and beauty is almost no longer possible if it is not a lie.

We live in a moment of history where change is so speeded up that we begin to see the present only when it is already disappearing.

It is difficult for modern man not to see the present in terms of the past. The white European and North American, in particular, commonly has a sense, not of renewal, but of being at an end: of being only half alive in the fibrillating heartland of a senescent civilization. Sometimes it seems that it is not possible to do more than reflect the decay around and within us, than sing sad and bitter songs of disillusion and defeat.

Yet that mood is already dated, at least insofar as it is not a perennial possibility of the human spirit. It entails a sense of time, which is already being dissolved in the instantaneous, stochastic, abrupt, discontinuous electronic cosmos, the dynamic mosaic of the electromagnetic field.

Nevertheless, the requirement of the present, the failure of the past, is the same: to provide a thoroughly self-conscious and self-critical human account of man.

No one can begin to think, feel or act now except from the starting point of his or her own alienation. We shall examine some of its forms in the following pages.

We are all murderers and prostitutes—no matter to what culture, society, class, nation, we belong, no matter how normal, moral, or mature we take ourselves to be.

Humanity is estranged from its authentic possibilities. This basic vision prevents us from taking any unequivocal view of the sanity of common sense, or of the madness of the so-called madman. However, what is required is more than a passionate outcry of outraged humanity.

Our alienation goes to the roots. The realization of this is the essential springboard for any serious reflection on any aspect of present interhuman life. Viewed from different perspectives, construed in different ways and expressed in different idioms, this realization unites men as diverse as Marx, Kierkegaard, Nietzsche, Freud, Heidegger, Tillich and Sartre.

More recent voices in the United States continue to document different facets of our fragmentation and alienation, whether it is the exposure of sham, the spatialization and quantification of experience or the massive economic irrationality of the whole system.

From R. D. Laing, *The Politics of Experience* (London: Penguin Books Ltd., 1967), pp. 11–12, 15–26, 49–51, 53–55.

All such description is forced to describe what is, in the light of different modulations of what is not. What has been, what might have been, what should be or might be. Can we describe the present in terms of its becoming what it is not-yet—a term of Ernest Block's, so frightening, so ominous, so cataclysmic, that it is sometimes easier to see the present already darkened by the shadow of a thermonuclear apocalypse, than either to envisage further declensions from that from which our nostalgia absents us, or to see a redemptive dialectic immanent in the vortex of accelerating change.

At all events, we are bemused and crazed creatures, strangers to our true selves, to one another, and to the spiritual and material world—mad, even, from an ideal standpoint we can glimpse but not adopt.

We are born into a world where alienation awaits us. We are potentially men, but are in an alienated state, and this state is not simply a natural system. Alienation as our present destiny is achieved only by outrageous violence perpetrated by human beings on human beings. . . .

Even facts become fictions without adequate ways of seeing "the facts." We do not need theories so much as the experience that is the source of the theory. We are not satisfied with faith, in the sense of an implausible hypothesis irrationally held: we demand to experience the "evidence." . . .

Natural science is concerned only with the observer's experience of things. Never with the way things *experience* us. That is not to say that things do not react to us, and to each other.

Natural science knows nothing of the relation between behavior and experience. The nature of this relation is mysterious—in Marcel's sense. That is to say, it is not an objective problem. There is no traditional logic to express it. There is no developed method of understanding its nature. But this relation is the copula of our science—if science means a *form of knowledge adequate to its subject.* The relation between experience and behavior is the stone that the builders will reject at their peril. Without it the whole structure of our theory and practice must collapse.

Experience is invisible to the other. But experience is not "subjective" rather than "objective," not "inner" rather than "outer," not process rather than praxis, not input rather than output, not psychic rather than somatic, not some doubtful data dredged up from introspection rather than extrospection. Least of all is experience "intrapsychic process." Such transactions, object relations, interpersonal relations, transference, countertransference, as we suppose to go on between people are not the interplay merely of two objects in space, each equipped with ongoing intrapsychic processes.

This distinction between outer and inner usually refers to the distinction between behavior and experience; but sometimes it refers to some experiences that are supposed to be "inner" in contrast to others that are "outer." More accurately this is a distinction between different modalities of experience, namely, perception (as outer) in contrast to imagination, etc. (as inner). But perception, imagination, fantasy, reverie, dreams, memory, are simply different *modalities of experience*, none more "inner" or "outer" than any other.

Yet this way of talking does reflect a split in our experience. We seem to live in two worlds, and many people are aware only of the "outer" rump. As long as we remember that the "inner" world is not some space "inside" the body or the mind, this way of talking can serve our purpose. (It was good enough for William Blake.) The "inner," then, is our personal idiom of experiencing our bodies, other people, the animate and inanimate world: imagination, dreams, fantasy, and beyond that to ever further reaches of experience.

Bertrand Russell once remarked that the stars are in one's brain.

The stars as I perceive them are no more or less in my brain than the stars as I imagine them. I do not imagine them to be in my head, any more than I see them in my head.

The relation of experience to behavior is not that of inner to outer. My experience is not inside my head. My experience of this room is out there in the room.

To say that my experience is intrapsychic is to presuppose that there is a psyche that my experience is in. My psyche is my experience, my experience is my psyche.

Many people used to believe that angels moved the stars. It now appears that they do not. As a result of this and like revelations, many people do not now believe in angels.

Many people used to believe that the "seat" of the soul was somewhere in the brain. Since brains began to be opened up frequently, no one has seen "the soul." As a result of this and like revelations, many people do not now believe in the soul.

Who could suppose that angels move the stars, or be so superstitious as to suppose that because one cannot see one's soul at the end of a microscope it does not exist? . . .

Can human beings be persons today? Can a man be his actual self with another man or woman? Before we can ask such an optimistic question as, "What is a personal relationship?," we have to ask if a personal relationship is possible, or, *are persons possible* in our present situation? We are concerned with the possibility of man. This question can be asked only through its facets. Is love possible? Is freedom possible?

Whether or not all, or some, or no human beings are persons, I wish to define a person in a twofold way: in terms of experience, as a center of orientation of the objective universe; and in terms of behavior, as the origin of actions. Personal experience transforms a given field into a field of intention and action: only through action can our experience be transformed. It is tempting and facile to regard "persons" as only separate objects in space, who can be studied as any other natural objects can be studied. But just as Kierkegaard remarked that one will never find consciousness by looking down a microscope at brain cells or anything else, so one will never find persons by studying persons as though they were only objects. A person is the me or you, he or she, whereby an object is experienced. Are these centers of experience and origins of actions living in entirely unrelated worlds of their own composition? Everyone must refer here to their own experience. My own experience as a center of experience and origin of action tells me that this is not so. My experience and my action occur in a social field of reciprocal influence and interaction. I experience myself, identifiable as Ronald Laing by myself and others, as experienced by and acted upon by others, who refer to that person I call "me" as "you" or "him," or grouped together as "one of us" or "one of them" or "one of you."

This feature of personal relations does not arise in the correlation of the behavior of nonpersonal objects. Many social scientists deal with their embarrassment by denying its occasion. Nevertheless, the natural scientific world is complicated by the presence of certain identifiable entities, re-identifiable reliably over periods of years, whose behavior is either the manifestation or a concealment of a view of the world equivalent in ontological status to that of the scientist.

People may be observed to sleep, eat, walk, talk, etc. in relatively predictable ways. We must not be content with observation of this kind alone. Observation of behavior must be extended by inference to attributions about experience. Only when we can begin to do this can we really construct the experiential-behavior system that is the human species.

It is quite possible to study the visible, audible, smellable effulgences of human bodies, and much study of human behavior has been in those terms. One can lump together very large numbers of units of behavior and regard them as a statistical population, in no way different from the multiplicity constituting a system of nonhuman objects. But one will not be studying persons. In a science of persons, I shall state as axiomatic that: behavior is a function of experience; and both experience and behavior are always in relation to someone or something other than self.

When two (or more) persons are in relation, the behavior of each towards the other is mediated by the experience by each of the other, and the experience of each is mediated by the behavior of each. There is no contiguity between the behavior of one person and that of the other. Much human behavior can be seen as a unilateral or bilateral *attempt* to eliminate experience. A person may treat another as *though* he were not a person, and he may act himself as *though* he were not a person. There is no contiguity between one person's experience and another's. My experience of you is always mediated through your *behavior*. Behavior that is the direct consequence of impact, as of one billiard ball hitting another, or experience directly transmitted to experience, as in the possible cases of extrasensory perception, is not personal.

Normal Alienation from Experience

The relevance of Freud to our time is largely his insight and, to a very considerable extent, his *demonstration* that the *ordinary* person is a shriveled, desiccated fragment of what a person can be.

As adults, we have forgotten most of our childhood, not only its contents but its flavor; as men of the world, we hardly know of the existence of the inner world: we barely remember our dreams, and make little sense of them when we do; as for our bodies, we retain just sufficient proprioceptive sensations to coordinate our movements and to ensure the minimal requirements for biosocial survival—to register fatigue, signals for food, sex, defecation, sleep; beyond that, little or nothing. Our capacity to think, except in the service of what we are dangerously deluded in supposing is our self-interest and in conformity with common sense, is pitifully limited: our capacity even to see, hear, touch, taste and smell is so shrouded in veils of mystification that an intensive discipline of unlearning is necessary for *anyone* before one can begin to experience the world afresh, with innocence, truth and love.

And immediate experience of, in contrast to belief or faith in, a spiritual realm of demons, spirits, Powers, Dominions, Principalities, Seraphim and Cherubim, the Light, is even more remote. As domains of experience become more alien to us, we need greater and greater open-mindedness even to conceive of their existence.

Many of us do not know, or even believe, that every night we enter zones of reality in which we forget our waking life as regularly as we forget our dreams when we awake. Not all psychologists know of fantasy as a modality of experience, and the, as it were, contrapuntal interweaving of different experiential modes. Many who are aware of fantasy believe that fantasy is the farthest that experience goes under "normal" circumstances. Beyond that are simply "pathological" zones of hallucinations, phantasmagoric mirages, delusions.

This state of affairs represents an almost unbelievable devastation of our experience. Then there is empty chatter about maturity, love, joy, peace.

This is itself a consequence of and further occasion for the divorce of our experience, such as is left of it, from our behavior.

What we call "normal" is a product of repression, denial, splitting, projection, introjection and other forms of destructive action on experience. It is radically estranged from the structure of being.

The more one sees this, the more senseless it is to continue with generalized descriptions of supposedly specifically schizoid, schizophrenic, hysterical "mechanisms."

There are forms of alienation that are relatively strange to statistically "normal" forms of alienation. The "normally" alienated person, by reason of the fact that he acts more or less like everyone else, is taken to be sane. Other forms of alienation that are out of step with the prevailing state of alienation are those that are labeled by the "normal" majority as bad or mad.

The condition of alienation, of being asleep, of being unconscious, of being out of one's mind, is the condition of the normal man.

Society highly values its normal man. It educates children to lose themselves and to become absurd, and thus to be normal.

Normal men have killed perhaps 100,000,000 of their fellow normal men in the last fifty years.

Our behavior is a function of our experience. We act according to the way we see things.

If our experience is destroyed, our behavior will be destructive.

If our experience is destroyed, we have lost our own selves.

How much human *behavior*, whether the interactions between persons themselves or between groups and groups, is intelligible in terms of human *experience*? Either our interhuman behavior is unintelligible, in that we are simply the passive vehicles of inhuman processes whose ends are as obscure as they are at present outside our control, or our own behavior towards each other is a function of our own experience and our own intentions, however alienated we are from them. In the latter case, we must take final responsibility for what we make of what we are made of.

We will find no intelligibility in behavior if we see it as an inessential phase in an essentially inhuman process. We have had accounts of men as animals, men as machines, men as biochemical complexes with certain ways of their own, but there remains the greatest difficulty in achieving a human understanding of man in human terms.

Men at all times have been subject, as they believed or experienced, to forces from the stars, from the gods, or to forces that now blow through society itself, appearing as the stars once did to determine human fate.

Men have, however, always been weighed down not only by their sense of subordination to fate and chance, to ordained external necessities or contingencies, but by a sense that their very own thoughts and feelings, in their most intimate interstices, are the outcome, the resultant, of processes which they undergo.

A man can estrange himself from himself by mystifying himself and others. He can also have what he does stolen from him by the agency of others.

If we are stripped of experience, we are stripped of our deeds; and if our deeds are, so to speak, taken out of our hands like toys from the hands of children, we are bereft of our humanity. We cannot be deceived. Men can and do destroy the humanity of other men, and the condition of this possibility is that we are interdependent. We are not self-contained monads producing no effects on each other except our reflections. We are both acted upon, changed for good or ill, by other men; and we are agents who act upon others to affect them in different ways. Each of us is the other to the others. Man is a patient-agent, agent-patient, interexperiencing and interacting with his fellows.

It is quite certain that unless we can regulate our behavior much more satisfactorily than at present, then we are going to exterminate ourselves. But as we experience the world, so we act, and this principle holds even when action conceals rather than discloses our experience.

We are not able even to *think* adequately about the behavior that is at the annihilating edge. But what we think is less than what we know; what we know is less than what we love; what we love is so much less than what there is. And to that precise extent we are so much less than what we are.

Yet if nothing else, each time a new baby is born there is a possibility of reprieve. Each child is a new being, a potential prophet, a new spiritual prince, a new spark of light precipitated into the outer darkness. Who are we to decide that it is hopeless? . . .

It is not enough to destroy one's own and other people's experience. One must overlay this devastation by a false consciousness inured, as Marcuse puts it, to its own falsity.

Exploitation must not be seen as such. It must be seen as benevolence. Persecution preferably should not need to be invalidated as the figment of a paranoid imagination; it should be experienced as kindness. Marx described mystification and showed its function in his day. Orwell's time is already with us. The colonists not only mystify the natives, in the ways that Fanon so clearly shows, they have to mystify themselves. We in Europe and North America are the colonists, and in order to sustain our amazing images of ourselves as God's gift to the vast majority of the starving human species, we have to interiorize our violence upon ourselves and our children and to employ the rhetoric of morality to describe this process.

In order to rationalize our industrial-military complex, we have to destroy our capacity to see clearly any more what is in front of, and to imagine what is beyond, our noses. Long before a thermonuclear war can come about, we have had to lay waste our own sanity. We begin with the children. It is imperative to catch them in time. Without the most thorough and rapid brainwashing their dirty minds would see through our dirty tricks. Children are not yet fools, but we shall turn them into imbeciles like ourselves, with high I.Q.s if possible.

From the moment of birth, when the Stone Age baby confronts the twentieth-century mother, the baby is subjected to these forces of violence, called love, as its mother and father, and their parents and their parents before them, have been. These forces are mainly concerned with destroying most of its potentialities, and on the whole this enterprise is successful. By the time the new human being is fifteen or so, we are left with a being like ourselves, a half-crazed creature more or less adjusted to a mad world. This is normality in our present age.

Love and violence, properly speaking, are polar opposites. Love lets the other be, but with affection and concern. Violence attempts to constrain the other's freedom, to force him to act in the way we desire, but with ultimate lack of concern, with indifference to the other's own existence or destiny.

We are effectively destroying ourselves by violence masquerading as love.

I am a specialist, God help me, in events in inner space and time, in experiences called thoughts, images, reveries, dreams, visions, hallucinations, dreams of memories, memories of dreams, memories of visions, dreams of hallucinations, refractions of refractions of refractions of that original Alpha and Omega of experience and reality, that Reality on whose repression, denial, splitting, projection, falsification, and general desecration and profanation our civilization as much as on anything is based.

We live equally out of our bodies and out of our minds.

Concerned as I am with this inner world, observing day in and day out its devastation, I ask why this has happened?

One component of an answer . . . is that we can *act* on our *experience* of ourselves, others and the world, as well as take action on the world through behavior itself. Specifically this devastation is largely the work of *violence* that has been perpetrated on each of us, and by each of us on ourselves. The usual name that much of this violence goes under is *love.*

We act on our experience at the behest of the others, just as we learn how to behave in compliance with them. We are taught what to experience and what not to experience, as we are taught what movements to make and what sounds to emit. A child of two is already a moral mover and moral talker and moral experiencer. He already moves the "right" way, makes the "right" noises, and knows what he should feel and what he should not feel. His movements have become stereometric types, enabling the specialist anthropologist to identify, through his rhythm and style, his national, even his regional, characteristics. As he is taught to move in specific ways out of the whole range of possible movements, so he is taught to experience out of the whole range of possible experience. . . .

If human beings are not studied as human beings, then this once more is violence and mystification.

In much contemporary writing on the individual and the family there is assumed some not-too-unhappy confluence, not to say pre-established harmony, between nature and nurture. Some adjustments may have to be made on both sides, but all things work together for good to those who want only security and identity.

Gone is any sense of possible tragedy, of passion. Gone is any language of joy, delight, passion, sex, violence. The language is that of a boardroom. No more primal scenes, but parental coalitions; no more repression of sexual ties to parents, but the child "rescinds" its Oedipal wishes. For instance:

> The mother can properly invest her energies in the care of the young child when economic support, status, and protection of the family are provided by the father. She can also better limit her cathexis of the child to maternal feelings when her wifely needs are satisfied by her husband.

Here is no nasty talk of sexual intercourse or even "primal scene." The economic metaphor is aptly employed. The mother "invests" in her child. What is most revealing is the husband's function. The provision of economic support, status and protection, in that order.

There is frequent reference to security, the esteem of others. What one is supposed to want, to live for, is "gaining pleasure from the esteem and affection of others." If not, one is a psychopath.

Such statements are in a sense true. They describe the frightened, cowed, abject creature that we are admonished to be, if we are to be normal—offering each other mutual protection from our own violence. The family as a "protection racket."

Behind this language lurks the terror that is behind all this mutual backscratching, this esteem-, status-, protection-, security-giving and getting. Through its bland urbanity the cracks still show.

In our world we are "victims burning at the stake, signaling through the flames," but for some, things go blandly on. "Contemporary life requires adaptability." We require also to "utilize intellect," and we require "an emotional equilibrium that permits a person to be malleable, to adjust himself to others without fear of loss of identity with change. It requires a basic trust in others, and a confidence in the integrity of the self."

Sometimes there is a glimpse of more honesty. For instance, when we "consider society rather than the individual, each society has a vital interest in the *indoctrination* of the infants who form its new *recruits.*"

What these authors say may be written ironically, but there is no evidence that it is.

Adaptation to what? To society? To a world gone mad?

The family's function is to repress Eros; to induce a false consciousness of security; to deny death by avoiding life; to cut off transcendence; to believe in God, not to experience the Void; to create, in short, one-dimensional man; to promote respect, conformity, obedience; to con children out of play; to induce a fear of failure; to promote a respect for work; to promote a respect for "respectability."

New Problems for Contemporary Europeans

FRANÇOIS BOURRICAUD

Since at least the early 1970s, some new doubts have arisen about the direction of modern life in Europe. Twenty years ago, even a decade ago, most accounts of postwar Europe were dominated by optimism: Europe had accomplished so much, particularly in comparison with the "bad decades" between the two world wars. Productivity was climbing; political strife and the threat of war, at least intra-European war, receded. Many European countries have indeed outstripped the United States in the modern economic game, and several countries have surpassed the United States in per capita income and in health levels. Clearly, a kind of modern European "renaissance" was underway. A sense of a new European society existed, as was suggested in the earlier selection by Ardagh.

But the pace of economic growth has slowed, particularly since the oil crisis of 1973. Political trends seem more confused, as old parties grope for acceptable platforms and some new movements, including terrorism, have entered the scene. Progress toward a more united Europe has slowed. These changes raise new questions about the direction of modern society.

Some of these questions have arisen in the United States as well. Polls report declining faith in American political institutions, major new doubts about general social progress in the future. But questions in Europe take some distinctive specific forms. Europeans wonder if, after all, they have changed enough. The following passage points to assumptions about the education of a new elite that were not translated fully into actual educational change. A system based on promotion by merit—a system that did indeed change the training and momentum of members of the European elite during the 1950s and 1960s—has not in fact broken down traditional class barriers; most "meritorious" elite members were born into upper- and middle-class families. Accordingly, a general concern that modern Western society has taken on new directions and new problems, during the past decade, translates into some specific questions about Europe itself.

The Crisis of the Universities and Meritocratic Elitism

The educational-professional complex presents itself as a bundle of institutions and roles whose coherence is assured by a set of common cultural orientations. Whatever the importance of national differences, the educational complex presents a certain number of traits emanating from the European cotradition. Up until the Second World War, one can characterize this shared quality—as much in France as in England or Germany—as meritocratic elitism. The elitist principle states that not everyone is fitted for positions of responsibility. It emphasizes competence and intellectual qualifications, but also discipline, assiduity, and moral effort. Thus it has both cognitive and ethical elements. The different educational systems are distinguished by the priority they give to one or the other of these elements—even if neither can be totally neglected. The characteristic institutions of a meritocracy are the exam or the *concours*—in any case, the grading, the evaluation of students by qualified adults, according to universal criteria of respectability and performance.

The educational subsystem trains professionals who must be capable of applying to the solution of individual problems either procedures answerable ultimately to the methods of logic and experimental science, or the general rules of law. Doctors, lawyers, engineers, teachers, to a certain extent bureaucrats—more precisely, the expert who works for the bureaucracy—all belong to this category. Meritocracy is by nature elitist: it *excludes*—more or less brutally, more or less definitively—by the very fact that it *chooses*. But though it excludes, meritocracy seeks not to discriminate. It undertakes to judge in the name of universal criteria. Also, meritocratic elitism is only one regulatory principle among many controlling mobility. One can "climb" the social ladder by winning diplomas and degrees that open access to important and well-paid jobs, but one can also "climb" by acquiring good manners and good contacts. The gentleman remained a model for English education much longer than did the ideal of *l'honnête homme* in the French system. Merit *à la française* became virtually synonymous with intellectual excellence, while English elitism, being more aristocratic, for reasons too complicated to examine here affirmed the excellence of judgment, good manners, and taste.

The explosion in the demand for education inevitably subjected the educational-professional subsystem to a series of extremely powerful tensions, and led to a renewed challenge of the principle of meritocratic

From François Bourricaud, "Individualistic Mobilization and the Crisis of Professional Authority," *Daedalus*, Vol. 108, No. 2 (Spring, 1979), pp. 11–13.

elitism. Universities experienced a crisis from the pressure of mechanical causes (the rapid increase in students and the problems this posed), and from the process of demoralization, of loss of confidence in educational institutions, which, by modalities different but related, affected students, teachers, parents, the public, and politicians. The crisis, then, should be analyzed from the point view of the universities, but should also take into account the judgment of the actors, especially of those who wished to change their style of life—whether it be their own life, that of others, or, more modestly, the rules of certain games.

Mobility preferences, individual and collective, are related to the elasticity of institutions that are supposed to assure the realization of our ambitions and our expectations. Now, in the case of educational institutions, this elasticity was weak. In fact, European universities, right up to the 1960s crisis, had continued to be corporate institutions—that is, managed for the most part by the professors themselves. In the French case, one should not take too seriously the stereotype of the French university in the minds of both the French and foreigners of a "Napoleonic university"—a hierarchy strictly controlled by the central government. It is true that the autonomy of French universities in financial and budgetary matters was weak—much more so than that of English universities, for example. But it would be a mistake to take literally the eternal reproach that French universities are ruled by a *dictature des bureaux*. In fact, until 1968, authority exercised in matters of university policy depended much more on a condominium-style than on an imperium-style hierarchy. The *ministre* appointed the professors, which he continues to do after, as before, 1968, because they are civil servants. But he made these appointments only upon recommendations from the faculty, and only after the candidates had been inscribed on a list of eligibles established by a national commission composed of peer-elected members—a commission to which the minister added (after consultation) a few "sages" of his own choosing. In fact, recruitment and promotion were almost completely in the hands of the professors themselves. That is why even the French university was above all a corporation of professors. What was taught had to conform to national programs, but the latter were defined by the same procedure, combining "sages"—or, if you prefer, mandarins—of each discipline, and the functionaries of the central administration. . . . Despite its high degree of centralization, the French university remained essentially a collegial institution managed by an oligarchy of professors and mandarins (deans of faculties, members of the consultative committee, *patrons* holding prestigious chairs—notably at the Sorbonne, but also in a miniscule number of provincial faculties—who had created for themselves a clientele of young doctoral candidates whose careers they fostered).

It is not hard to understand that a society such as this one, both closed and stratified, was particularly unfit to face the problems presented to it by accelerated social change. In fact, since the 1960s, the expectations of students concerning the university have changed. Up to World War II, students chose their future professions even before entering the university. Their choices were shaped by family urgings and pressures, and by the very nature of their secondary education. Even the relative democratization of secondary education during the 1960s brought to the universities new waves of students, the majority of whom were not destined for the liberal professions or for positions of responsibility in public administration. What has come to prevail is a mass of individuals who enter the university in search of an orientation, which they find all the more difficult to define as the very training they received in secondary school appears to them less clearly relevant to their career plans.

Crisis of Civilization

In what sense, then, can it be said that we are now in the midst of a crisis in European civilization or European culture? . . . Since 1964 there has been a recrudescence of the classic thesis about the decline of the West, the exhaustion of European thought and culture, and the aggravation of the contradictions of capitalism—and this in the very region where capitalism first arose, but which finds itself today increasingly dominated by the center of world imperialism (read: the United States). Let us limit ourselves here to an examination of the relations between the educational-professional complex and meritocratic elitism. Despite its vigor, recent protest has been confined within limits set by the permanence of a technical and scientific current in Western societies. The latter is ebbing. The great positivist hopes of the 1950s are, for now, out of fashion. Ecological criticism has reached a high degree of acrimony, and its effects on the rhythm of capital accumulation and on urban geography, et cetera, could be considerable. Does such criticism have the power to interrupt the movement that for centuries has given its élan to science and technology? The ecology movement underlines the risks from indiscriminate use of science and technology: but does it have much chance of suspending or of proscribing their use? Rousseau himself lost his case against the arts and sciences. (Did he ever really hope to win?) There has yet to be a desertion of scientific and technical careers. It is possible that the income that graduates of institutions of higher learning have expected, and continue to expect, will go down. This change will probably be more the effect of a redistribution within the category of graduates than of a uniform and total reduction of their income. The fact of having spent two years in a university will perhaps be of less importance as universities admit a growing cross section of the population. It does seem that the financial return from long literary studies will fall rapidly and irreversibly. On the other hand, it is highly improbable that the mastery of advanced scientific techniques has ceased to constitute an appreciable and desired advantage. I will leave aside the question of whether among these beneficiaries the relative position of technicians and applied scientists will improve or deteriorate vis-à-vis that of theoreticians and basic researchers (*fondamentalistes*). One can expect short-term fluctuations in the relative status of these two categories, but I would be surprised if, in the long run, the preeminence of the theoreticians and generalists is not confirmed or even enhanced.

Is meritocratic elitism, then, lastingly protected against romantic protest and reaction? Every cultural system is an unstable combination of heterogeneous orientations: of egalitarianism, but also of value given to personal autonomy; of intellectualism and specialization, but also of romanticism and spontaneity. Today the heterogeneity is probably stronger than it has been at any time since the Second World War; it is presumably this development that authorizes us to speak of a "crisis." Just as we dream of an elite to which all would belong, of merit acquired without effort, of excellences which would not confer privileges on others—especially if we are denied them—so too do we dream of a mass culture both exquisite and refined. This trend in aspirations should be linked with a basic social trend: the broadening of the cultivated social strata, a process which is in itself the result of education.

What is pompously called a crisis of civilization is first of all a crisis in professional authority. According to Talcott Parsons, whose classic analyses are worth remembering, professional authority rests on a double proposition—that one partner is in need of a service and that the other can provide it: on the one hand, a need and a dependence; on the other, a theoretical competence and a practical expertise. But professional authority is not founded on competence alone. It is only accepted if the client is convinced that due to institutional guarantees—the doctor's diploma, his scholastic record, his reputation—the constraints to which he must submit are justified by the sincere care the doctor takes to treat and cure him. Now radical criticism has challenged the two guarantees of competence and dedication. Thus a double suspicion hovers over professional authority. First of all, the lag between the advances of science and professional practice is invoked to discredit the practitioner. In the second place, are the independence and the arbitral pretentions of the professional as well-founded as the interested parties affirm? After all, the doctor is paid by either the patient or by social security. The expert is a salaried employee of the organization for which he works.

A Disconnected Europe

STANLEY HOFFMANN

Stanley Hoffmann, a noted analyst of France and of international relations, offers a distinctive and pessimistic assessment of the European version of contemporary society. He finds cause for concern in the very symptoms of Europe's postwar success. Europe has changed too rapidly, has renounced its past too thoroughly, and is left clinging only to material success. Hoffmann's evaluation differs notably from the previous selection, by Bourricaud, in which the theme was insufficient change; but it shares with it a sense that something is going wrong in contemporary Europe.

Hoffmann's analysis takes on added bite in his comparisons between Europe and the United States. Many observers, including Christopher Lasch, have found equal cause for concern about changes in the American personality in recent decades. They point to a shallow materialism, a preoccupation with self, that might seem quite similar to Hoffmann's critiques of Europe. Blasts at American education—its gimmickry and manipulation of curriculum away from substance—are certainly common. But Hoffmann finds the European situation much worse. He therefore applies some general concerns about how contemporary people are moving away from industrial-age values to a specific contemporary setting. It is not the contemporary that is going awry, for the United States still preserves a sense of purpose, but the European. Hoffmann's assessment raises two obvious questions: Is his specific judgment of Europe accurate, in the suggested contrast with another advanced industrial society? And is his general tone of pessimism warranted, concerning developments in contemporary societies? Hoffmann's vision of contemporary Europeans rather desperately clinging to economic progress, and nothing else, might relate to the more sweeping condemnation of modernity offered by Laing. Clearly, during the 1970s both Europe and the United States lost some faith in the post-World War II engine of success. Is the result likely to be a temporary period of uncertainty and readjustment? Or are more profound changes altering the shape of society away from the patterns familiar in earlier modernization? In this connection, Hoffmann's views should be compared with Ardagh's discussion of new French behavior.

Let us take any western European nation in the nineteenth century—say, France, the one I know best. At any given moment, a visitor could have heard vigorous discussions of its past: the nature, flaws, and benefits of the old regime, the causes of its fall, the respective virtues and crimes of the different phases of the Revolution, the reasons for the restless and unsuccessful quest for political stability that followed it, the effect on the nation of the dramatic fracture in its history brought about by the Revolution, the lasting impact of Bonapartism. All of these questions were constantly examined along clear-cut ideological lines and were reassessed by each generation of historians. History played a large part in the school curriculum, and the nation's past was imprinted thereby on the minds of its future citizens, "At age thirteen," says Jean-Marie Domenach—now in his mid-fifties—"my image of France was solidly formed. It linked the recent glory of the fatherland to Greek and Roman antiquity, with the help of classical humanities, which consisted in . . . an aesthetic and moral impregnation." At the same time, intellectuals and politicians were offering various models of the future. Even a society as keen on tight self-protection against economic and social upheavals as that of nineteenth-century France never stopped arguing about what the future might bring and, above all, never stopped believing that it was ultimately up to its citizens to shape that future—whether by the restoration of a beneficial past or by the realization of one or another vision of progress. What struck observers most was the depth and multiplicity of disagreements. But the concern with the past and the future—the conviction that the latter would emerge from acts inspired by a proper reconsideration of the past; the belief that past and future were inextricably linked, less by historical determinism than through one's own consciousness of them; the idea that one was seeking one's future in one's stand toward the past; and that the future ought to be the enactment of the lessons learned from the past—all this seemed perfectly obvious and appropriate.

It may, therefore, appear obvious and equally appropriate to ask whether the same questions are raised in Western Europe today. But when its citizens consult the mirror on the wall to find reflections from the past or intimations of the future, they find a broken mirror and a blurred image. For Europe remains a virtuality, the past is mere spectacle, and the future is a riddle. Why this is so takes us into the story of postwar Europe's political, social, and cultural transformation, as well as of Europe's role in the world. . . .

The most obvious [reason] is the speed of social change, the sweeping away of old customs and rites, the disappearance or transformation of old occupations, the reshaping of class distinctions, the revolutions in

From Stanley Hoffmann, "Fragments Floating in the Here and Now," *Daedalus*, Vol. 108, No. 1 (Winter, 1979), pp. 1–2, 8, 10, 13, 14–16, 20–21, 25–26.

mores and morals, and the collapse of traditional modes of social control, all of which have been catalogued by sociologists (serious and pop). Yesterday, the past was all around us, and the relative stability of the social order preserved the relevance and meaning of old and durable controversies about the past. As long as traditional institutions, practices of social ascent, economic structures, religious dogmas, and personal values persisted, there were people who wanted to preserve them and others who argued for change; both groups had to evaluate the past for their enterprise. Today, so much of the past is dead that there is little left of it to preserve. The old solidarities and communities are gone; often even the old landscapes, along with the rituals, customs, and costumes, have disappeared. The advocates of change argue from the inequalities and perils of the present. Yesterday, there were conservatives and reactionaries; the former were rooted in the past (and tried to prevent rapid change, political or economic); the latter thought there was enough still left of the blessed past to make it possible to bring back what had, unfortunately, been toppled. Today, a conservative is someone who merely wants to slow down the pace of change or (like Pompidou) to make inevitable changes smooth for the individual. The reactionary is the real radical: he argues—as a particular New Right does in France—not for a return to the past, but on behalf of abstract principles—inequality between races and sexes, hierarchy and authority—which he is wise enough not to connect with any particular time or place.

The speed of change is one of the reasons the past seems so little relevant, but there is another related, but slightly different reason: a gradually growing sense of radical discontinuity. After the ordeals of the 1930s and the war years, the loss of the colonies, the seizure of political predominance by the super-powers, Western Europeans feel, more or less confusedly, that their normal historical development has been interrupted, that their past has been devalued, that their highest achievement—nationality—has plunged them into disaster followed by impotence, that they have moved from the age of self-determination to that in which the outside world determines their fate. The more distant past thus seems alien—not a prelude to the present; it is perhaps even a reproach.

Why does the same disconnection not exist to any comparable degree in the United States? Because, I believe, the three destructive forces I have listed have not operated here. In the first place, social changes have been vast and often disruptive, but they have come as organic changes within an established democratic society rather than as the searing agents of democratization—that is, as the gravediggers of values, hierarchies, social patterns, and constellations that were still predemocratic, a mixture of fading aristocratic and narrowly bourgeois societies. Paradoxically, because there has been, ever since the nation's birth, an expectation of quick mutations—the shedding of old skins and the growing of shinier ones that will, in their turn, be discarded when progress next requires it—change looks not like instability but almost like the condition of stability. The past can still be seen as the incubator of the present. This implies, of course, that such change must not be catastrophic. And indeed, in the second place, America has had no reason to experience radical discontinuity: this is the century of its emergence as the most powerful nation on the world stage, a rise for which its whole history has prepared it. In America we are still in the age of romantic history, in the midst of a love affair with the nation. Finally, and most important, we must go back to Tocqueville, or Louis Hartz, and the liberal consensus or common faith. The speed of social change may well be the same as it is in Europe (although one could argue that postwar Europe has been hastily catching up with America's brand of industrial society); but the irrelevance of past beliefs does not appear at all obvious to Americans. Whatever its transformations, their polity still seems in harmony with an unfolding of the "Lockean faith." Tocqueville would probably have some trouble recognizing his preindustrial small-town America; but the basic principles are still there, and the new institutions that have developed since his day are based on them.

The American creed has survived because the United States has been (or appears to the world and to its own people to be) a success story. Both this creed and other powerful bonds—ethnic loyalties, religious communities, class solidarities, or neighborhood associations—have mitigated the effects of social change and crises. In Europe, such ties have, on the contrary, been weakened or destroyed by a combination of factors: the speed and magnitude of change, a disastrous history, the corrosion of religion (and of such a quasireligious force as the early working-class movement) by secular ideological involvements and struggles, and the poverty of associational life in centralized nations. Therefore, contrary to what might have been expected, the democratic society par excellence, the United States, is closer to its past than the historical societies of Europe—a fact that confirms the impossibility of deriving any firm conclusion about politics or culture from a social ideal type such as democracy. The bones tell us nothing about the flesh or about the spirit.

In the educational system the teaching of history regresses. It used to be a major component of mass primary education and of the secondary education that a minority of privileged *and* gifted not-so-privileged youngsters received. Today, this preeminence is challenged by more practical or by more scientific disciplines. In a democracy, the authority of the teacher *qua* teacher is rather low. It rests on his expertise, not on his calling; and the prestige of his expertise depends on the usefulness of the knowledge he imparts. In France, the traditional supremacy of letters and history has ended: glamour glistens on mathematics. High school history is being diluted into social studies—the study of the contemporary. The hold of history in the school thus depends, above all, on the importance of the school as a seminary for teaching a civic faith that is rooted in history. In the United States, schools are often still such seminaries; on the other side of the Atlantic, they no longer are. . . .

For many years, Western Europeans have lived on the moving escalator of economic growth. The social dislocations and political changes it has brought about have, as I have already stated, riveted their minds on the present. At the same time, especially as governments for so long have suggested that (or acted as if) the solution to all tensions would be provided by further growth, the citizens were led to believe that the future could be summed up as a continuing and growing manna—the condition of the fulfillment of individual ambitions and desires, the prerequisite of greater social justice, and the way to equality of opportunity and results. In this sense, the imagined future was no more than a projection of what was most welcome in the present and the hope that what was currently unwelcome would be eliminated or tamed. The British, whose growth was smaller, told pollsters that they felt happy, happier than the continentals. But their own leaders worried about the effects of the lower rate, and the continentals showed a remarkable consensus in rejecting any thought that their tensions and frustrations might be relieved by a slowdown. If we mean by the word *political* a consideration of one's relation to others, to groups, to the community, and to the state in terms of values, beliefs, and power, the prevailing vision was singularly apolitical: its blandishments were bland, its appeal lay in its being so easy.

It was precisely because this vision of quantitative happiness, this somewhat mindless faith in a self-propelled expansion that apparently required no more from each citizen than his labor and a minimum of social integration, this failure to imagine another model of society, another kind of individual fate, another destiny for the nation seemed so tepid or boring to many of the young, that the "events" of May, 1968, occurred. But a rebellion is not a construction: no alternative vision came out of it. May, 1968, showed how the death of *le passé vécu* and the failure to bring a new design to life are linked. The young rebels may have thought they were reliving a revolutionary past, but they were only going through the motions: they acted, they did not reenact. A liquidation of what had become secondhand or bookish memories led nowhere—except to a deluge of books. Most of the young, whether they took part in this "happening" or not, seemed, in fact, to accept the common vision and to think of their own future in terms of individual security amidst general prosperity. There seemed to be nothing between unlimited alienation and limited horizons, a rejection *in toto* of the prevailing values or a somewhat passive acceptance of them.

Then came the experience of the recession. It shattered the expectations of an ever-rising escalator. It revived old critiques of capitalism, old discussions about its final crisis. But no new alternative vision has emerged; it is as if people remained glued to the motionless escalator and waited for it to get well. The Europeans' own "revolution of rising expectations" made its sudden stop that much more jarring. But despite some talk about new models of growth or qualitative rather than quantitative growth, governments and citizens were joined in a desire to put the escalator back in motion; the only disagreements between or within nations have been over rates of recovery, fears of inflation and unemployment, and obligations of mutual solidarity. In other words, little has been learned from the troubles that have blurred the easy vision. No more political action or proposal has appeared. This older and somewhat uninspiring vision—what French rebels had called *métro, boulot, dodo*—has simply been proven unreliable. The recession and its inequities confirmed the rebels in their rejection of the model (and probably helped turn some of them from spontaneous psychodrama to organized terror), while the passive acceptance of this model by the others lost some of its former complacency. And the millions, neither rebels nor conformists, who subscribe to the critique of capitalism offered by the Marxist Left, nevertheless live a double life or practice double-entry bookkeeping. They have seen their reasons for distrusting the model vindicated, yet they see no future other than one of economic growth. (They only wish the authorities in charge to be less distant, unreliable, greedy, or unfair than the profitmakers who have managed it so far.)

As in the intellectual world, we are now witnessing an eclipse of the future in the school system. It has been replaced with "present shock": a proliferation of options and subjects, an often frantic or overstuffed attempt at putting into the hands of the young as many tools as possible to help them understand and navigate in the present (hence a high rate of obsolescence and a breathless, permanent revision of curricula). To be sure, there is much of this kind of scurrying in America as well; but there, the beliefs of the *angewandte Aufklärung* surround and give meaning to the disconnected bits and pieces. This is not the case in Western Europe. The public cult of growth is not a substitute, for it is a cult of means, not ends; and if there is one group that is often sullen, bitter, and hostile toward the cult, it is the teachers. Not only is their prestige falling, as I have pointed out before. But, trained to transmit established knowledge to pupils whose function it is to receive it, they are confronted instead with the need for their own permanent reeducation, with the duty to transmit methods and data that in a short time may prove to be wrong and with young men and women who are increasingly impatient with the old-style pedagogy. Both in reference to what is to be taught and how best to teach it, the very speed of change, already found partly responsible for the receding of the past, also contributes to the blackout of the future. The school is caught between students concerned above all with their own opportunities in nations marked by disruptive changes—as well as by vast surges for collective social ascent—and teachers who do not always comprehend the changes, and who often feel that in growth-obsessed societies they have lost much of the high ground they held in the days when efficiency, consumption, and the production of goods were not the highest values. The only function of the school seems to be running after (or behind) adjustment: its fate parallels that of European societies, which used to see themselves on top of their own fate in a world shaped by them. Yesterday, the school was a force for social integration that taught values drawn from the past and expectations about the future. Today, if it is such a force at all, it is a purely functional agent of preparation for the present.

The disappearance of the past is partly a disappointment with that past—with what history and human action have wrought—thus it is very different from that deliberate historical break that revolutionaries intent on building a new order and creating a new man provoked in 1792, or in 1917, or in 1949 in China. It means exhaustion, not energy; drainage, not arson. In turn, the lack of a sense of the future has further depressed, devalued, and discolored the past; when one does not know where one is going, when there seems to be nowhere to go and nothing new and better to accomplish, what is the point of retracing one's steps? It takes a combination of faith in, ideas about, and will to build one's future to keep an interest in the past from becoming mere scholarship or leisure. There has been enough democratization, in the sense of a liquidation of the residues from the nondemocratic past, enough denationalization—even in France—enough "dis-ideologization" (pardon the word) to disenchant the past. But the result is a vacuum, not a will to build either a common European future, or a new national one. As we have seen, this is a story in which cultural, political, economic, and social factors all mix.

In the nineteenth century, the nations of Western Europe were marked by an original combination of lively, even heated ideological quarrels about different visions of the future, especially the political future; there was broad public consensus about the social order, the general direction, and the nation's role in the world. Those who felt left out had their own vision. Today, the quarrels are more about the present, and the public consensus, almost everywhere, is what I once called, for France, a consensus by default—the present is embraced less for its virtues than for its benefits (when they flow), less for its values than because any alternative is seen as either worse (whether it is the return of a frightening past experience or the imposition of the Soviet model) or more divisive. As a result, the continent that has always prided itself on its sense of roots and innovation appears more uprooted and less creative than the other model that makes Europeans so uncomfortable—the United States. Tocqueville's nightmare of disconnected individuals under a tutelary state is more present in Europe than in America. What he did not foresee was that individuals would also be disconnected from the past and the future, that voluntary associations (in which he saw a corrective to disconnection) would often only add group egoism to individual acquisitiveness, and that the state would be both bloated and trapped.

We are left then with two questions for morose or worried speculation. First, can one live forever in the economic present, comforting oneself with comparative statistics and a half-cozy, half-worried enjoyment of goods, freedom, and rights? Second, to what extent are the poverty of inspiration and imagination, the concentration on the here and now, related to the European nations' fall from international eminence? Are images of the past and visions of the future tied either to struggles for national identity or to the possibility of strutting on the world's stage, to fighting or speaking out for a great cause, national or not? France's intellectuals lost their voice at the moment when France ceased to be a pacesetter for other nations and a leader in world affairs. Britain's inability to have a clearer vision of its future than its partners cannot easily be explained as a result of the cult of growth (although it results in part from the penalties that must be paid for forgetting the criterion of efficiency). It can be explained in part by the "end of ideology"; for even though the scope of ideological battles was not as wide there as on the Continent, Britain was once inspired by deep political and religious creeds. Still, this explanation does not go far enough. Was not Britain's image of its future always associated with a vision of a great role in the world—and was not de Gaulle's intuition about the necessity of such a role as a goad to internal creativity correct after all? If there is such a connection, the plight of Western Europe is not likely to end. For if the fall from the heights has broken that part of the *élan vital* that expresses itself, not in daily work and often-successful responses to the challenges of growth, but in the ability to find stimulation in the past and to will a future, then the very imprisonment in the present, the vital impulse's engulfment in the daily adjustments and crises, make the recovery of a sense of time (backward and forward) and the discovery of a common will unlikely. And so, each nation remains encased in its present self, giving an occasional backward glance at the recent past for remorse or consolation and a worried glance at the near future. Only a uniting Europe that could look at the whole of its fragmented past would be able to will a future. But how can it emerge, if its members have neither the drive nor the necessary incentives to transcend themselves into Europe?

C 5
D 6
E 7
F 8
G 9
H 0
I 1
J 2